THE
Kitchen Master
COOKBOOK

National Library of Australia Card Number and ISBN 0 85835 972 3

This volume first published by Bay Books Pty Ltd 61-69 Anzac Parade Kensington 2033 NSW

©Bay Books, Sydney and London
©Illustrations Bay Books Pty Ltd
©Illustrations "Les Cours de la Cuisine A a Z" — "Femmes d'Aujourd'hui"

Publisher: George Barber

BBCB 86

THE
KitchenMaster
COOKBOOK

Bay Books

Sydney and London

CONTENTS

Weights and Measures

Quantities are given in Metric, Imperial and US cup/avoirdupois measures. Rarely do exact conversions from Imperial/US measures to Metric measures give convenient working quantities, and so Metric measures have been rounded off to a more handy unit: 1 ounce (oz) = 25 grams (g) (28.5g is the exact conversion of 1 oz). The tables below show recommended equivalents:–

As a general rule 1 kilogram (kg) (1000 g) = about 2 pounds (lb) 3 oz (2.2 lb); 1 litre (1000 millilitres (ml) = about 1¾ pints (1.75 pints). However, in some recipes a more exact conversion has been used to maintain the balance between ingredients.

Notes for American Users
In America the American measuring cup is used in conjunction with the American pint – 16 fluid oz (fl oz). Also in this book, remember that the tablespoon measure used in these recipes differs from the American tablespoon, e.g.:
1 British standard tablespoon holds 17.7 ml
1 American tablespoon holds 14.8 ml.

Notes for Australian Users
Ingredients are given in Metric/Imperial/US cup/avoirdupois measures. In Australia the American 8 oz measuring cup is used in conjunction with the Imperial pint – 20 fluid ounces (fl oz). Also in this book, remember that the tablespoon measure used in these recipes differs from the Australian tablespoon, e.g.:
1 British standard tablespoon holds 17.7 ml
1 Australian tablespoon holds 20 ml. However 1 teaspoon holds 5 ml in both systems.

Remember: follow only one set of quantities for any single recipe, as **Metric/Imperial/US measures are not interchangeable.**

WEIGHT		VOLUME			LINEAR MEASURE		Equivalent Oven Temperatures			SPOONS (level unless otherwise stated)	
Metric	*Imperial*	*Metric*	*Imperial*	*US Cup*	*Metric*	*Imperial*	°C	°F	Gas Mark	*Metric*	*Imperial*
15g	½oz	50ml	2fl oz	¼	3mm	⅛in	110	225	¼	1.25ml	¼ teasp.
20g	¾oz	75ml	2½fl oz	⅓	5mm	¼in	130	250	½	2.5ml	½ teasp.
25g	1oz		3fl oz	⅜	1cm	½in	140	275	1	5ml	1 teasp.
40g	1½oz	100ml	4fl oz	½	2.5cm	1in	150	300	2	15ml	1 tablesp.
50g	2oz	150ml	5fl oz *(¼ pint)*	⅝	4cm	1½in	170	325	3	30ml	2 tablesp.
75g	3oz	200ml	6fl oz	¾	5cm	2in	180	350	4		(1fl oz)
100g	4oz *(¼lb)*		7fl oz	⅞	6.5cm	2½in	190	375	5		
150g	5oz	225ml	8fl oz	1	7.5cm	3in	200	400	6		
175g	6oz	275ml	9fl oz	1⅛	10cm	4in	220	425	7		
200g	7oz	300ml	10fl oz *(½ pint)*	1¼	12.5cm	5in	230	450	8		
225g	8oz *(½lb)*		11fl oz	1⅜	15cm	6in	240	475	9		
250g	9oz		12fl oz	1½	18cm	7in				3 teasp.	1 tablesp.
(¼kg)		400ml	14fl oz	1¾	20cm	8in				2 tablesp.	1 fl oz
275g	10oz		16fl oz	2 = *1 pint (US)*	23cm	9in				16 tablesp. (US)	1 cup (US)
300g	11oz	½ litre			25cm	10in					
350g	12oz *(¾lb)*	*(500-600 ml see recipe)*	20fl oz *(1 pint)*	2½	30cm	12in (1ft)					
375g	13oz				35cm	14in					
400g	14oz	750ml	1¼ pints	3	38cm	15in					
425g	15oz	*(¾ litre)*			45cm	18in					
450g	16oz *(1lb)*	900ml	1½ pints	–	60cm	24in					
900-1000g	2lb	1 litre	1¾ pints	–	92cm	36in					
(1kg)											
1½kg	3lb										
2kg	4lb										
2½kg	5lb										
3kg	6lb										
3½kg	7lb										
4kg	8lb										

BAR MEASURES

		Pony/liqueur glass	1fl oz
Dash	4-6 drops	Jigger	1½fl oz
Teaspoon	⅙fl oz	Wineglass	4fl oz
Tablespoon	½fl oz	Cup	8fl oz

Key to Symbols

This symbol indicates the average cost of each recipe (it does not allow for seasonal or regional changes in prices)

Inexpensive 🪙   🪙🪙 **Expensive**

This symbol indicates the degree of difficulty in the preparation and cooking of each recipe

Easy ☆   ☆☆ **More difficult**

This symbol indicates what time is involved in the preparation and cooking of each recipe

⧗   ⧗⧗   ⧗⧗⧗

Less than 1 hour   1-3 hours   Over 3 hours

Hors d'oeuvres

*Cold assortment of vegetables,
salmon, caviar and dips make
an easily prepared and delicious
hors d'oeuvres.*

7

Cocktail Buffets

An ideal cocktail party – or any gathering where alcoholic drinks are being served – should include some food. Although guests will probably not want to eat much, a little food modifies the effect of the alcohol and increases its appreciation. Small, savoury, tempting dishes are ideal. Served in bite-sized portions that can be held in the hand and eaten without mess, they will help to make any party go with a swing. Serve them with pretty canapés such as olives, nuts, and salami slices.

Tarama Tartlets

225 g (½ lb) puff pastry, fresh or
  frozen and thawed
100 g (¼ lb) (½ cup) smoked cod's roe
2 slices white bread
15 ml (1 tablespoon) milk
75 ml (3 fl oz) (⅜ cup) olive oil
30 ml (1 fl oz) (2 tablespoons)
  lemon juice
15 ml (1 tablespoon) grated onion
1 clove garlic, finely chopped
  (optional)
salt and pepper

1 Preheat the oven to 220°C, 425°F, gas 7. On a lightly floured board, roll out the pastry to 3 mm (¼ in) thick. Using a 5 cm (2 in) fluted round pastry cutter, cut out small circles and place them in a grased tartlet tin (pan). Bake for about 15 minutes until risen and golden-brown. Remove from the oven and allow to cool.

2 Meanwhile, if using fresh smoked cod's roe, remove the skin. Then, for fresh or bottled roe, mash it with a fork in a mixing bowl.

3 Remove the crusts from the slices of bread. Soak the slices in the milk and crumble them. Mix the bread with the cod's roe.

4 Gradually beat in the olive oil and the lemon juice, beating constantly to make a smooth mixture. Add the grated onion and the garlic, if wished. Season with a little salt and pepper. Continue beating, adding a little water to make the mixture more fluffy, and adjusting the lemon juice and seasoning to taste.

5 When the mixture is very smooth and creamy, place it in a piping (decorator's) bag and pipe it in swirls into the tartlets. Chill if not to be served immediately.

Makes 10-12

Tip: If you have an electric liquidizer, the mixing can be done much more easily and the result will be smoother. Add more oil or water in small quantities, if necessary.

Cheese Puffs

400 g (14 oz) puff pastry, fresh or
  frozen and thawed
225 g (½ lb) Gruyère cheese, sliced
2 egg yolks
15 ml (1 tablespoon) milk
freshly ground (milled) black
  pepper

1 Preheat the oven to 220°C, 425°F, gas 7. On a floured board, roll out the pastry to 3 mm (¼ in) thick. Cut it into squares of about 4 cm (1½ in). Cut the cheese into squares of the same size.

2 Beat the egg yolks lightly with the milk. Brush the tops of the pastry squares with egg wash. Place a square of cheese on a square of pastry, dust with freshly ground (milled) black pepper, and top with another square of pastry, egg side uppermost. Repeat until all the pastry and cheese is used up.

3 Place the cheese squares on a greased baking (cookie) sheet, and bake for about 15 minutes until golden-brown. Serve warm or cold.

Makes 10-12

Salmon Croissants

225 g (½ lb) puff pastry, fresh or
  frozen and thawed
100 g (¼ lb) canned salmon
25 g (1 oz) (2 tablespoons) butter
25 g (1 oz) (4 tablespoons) flour
300 ml (½ pint) (1¼ cups) milk
salt and pepper
1 egg yolk, beaten

1 Preheat the oven to 220°C, 425°F, gas 7. On a floured board, roll out the puff pastry to 3 mm (¼ in) thick and cut it into triangles with sides about 10 cm (4 in) long.

2 Drain the juice from the canned salmon and reserve it. Remove any skin or bone from the salmon and crush it with a fork.

3 Make a thick white sauce by melting the butter in a saucepan and stirring in the flour. Cook for a minute, then gradually stir in the salmon liquor and enough milk to form a very thick, smooth sauce. Season to taste with salt and pepper. Beat in the salmon meat.

4 Spoon a little of the mixture into the middle of each pastry triangle. Roll up the triangles, starting from a straight side and rolling towards the opposite point, completely enclosing the salmon filling.

5 Twist each piece into a crescent shape and brush the top with beaten egg. Place the croissants on a greased baking (cookie) sheet and bake for 15-20 minutes until golden-brown on top. Serve hot or cold.

Makes 10-12

Tip: For an alternative fish filling: with a fork, mash the drained fish from 1 or 2 large cans of sardines with 15-30 ml (1-2 tablespoons) tomato ketchup (catsup). Season with cayenne pepper. Add a few crushed anchovy fillets if wished.

*Ideas for party snacks include
Cheese Puffs (bottom right),
Salmon Croissants, Tarama Tartlets and sausage rolls
(centre), and toast with liver pâté*

Salmon Boats

shortcrust (pie crust) made with
225 g (½ lb) (2¼ cups) flour
100 g (¼ lb) smoked salmon, thinly
sliced
1 lemon
100 g (¼ lb) canned salmon
50 ml (2 fl oz) (¼ cup) double
(heavy) cream
salt and pepper
pinch paprika

1 Preheat the oven to 190°C, 375°F, gas 5. Roll out the dough thinly. With a fluted barquette (boat-shaped) pastry cutter, cut out the boats, and place the pastry pieces in greased barquette tins (pans). Prick the bottoms of the pastry cases with a fork. Bake for 10-15 minutes until crisp and lightly browned. Allow to cool.

2 Meanwhile, cut the smoked salmon slices into boat shapes, slightly larger than the pastry moulds. Reserve any trimmings. Sprinkle the salmon pieces with the juice of half the lemon.

3 Drain the canned salmon and discard any skin or bones. Flake the flesh with a fork. Cut the reserved smoked salmon trimmings finely and mix them with the canned salmon.

4 Mix the salmon with the double (heavy) cream and season with salt and pepper and a little paprika. Spoon the mixture into the pastry boats. Cover each one with a piece of smoked salmon, and decorate with 'butterflies' of lemon cut from the remaining lemon half. Serve at once.

Makes 8-12

Asparagus Boats

shortcrust (pie crust) made with
225 g (½ lb) (2¼ cups) flour
3 eggs
80 ml (3 fl oz) (⅜ cup) mayonnaise
5 ml (1 teaspoon) made mustard
36 canned asparagus tips

*Salmon Boats are an attractive,
extravagant snack to
hand round to your guests at
an elegant cocktail party*

1 Prepare the pastry boats as described in Salmon Boats.

2 Hard-boil the eggs for 10 minutes. Remove the shells and finely chop the eggs.

3 Mix the chopped egg with the mayonnaise and mustard. Spoon the mixture into the prepared pastry boats.

4 Drain the asparagus tips and arrange them in an attractive pattern on top of the filled pastry boats. Serve cold.

Makes 8-12

Bacon and Banana Kebabs

3 bananas
juice ½ lemon
30 ml (2 tablespoons) tomato
ketchup (catsup)
15 ml (1 tablespoon) malt vinegar
15 ml (1 tablespoon) dark brown
sugar
100 g (¼ lb) thinly sliced streaky
bacon

1 Peel the bananas and cut them into 4 cm (1½ in) lengths. Sprinkle them with lemon juice.

2 Mix the tomato ketchup (catsup) and vinegar over low heat in a saucepan and add the sugar. Heat gently, stirring, until melted and blended.

3 Coat the banana pieces with the sauce. Remove the rind and any cartilage from the bacon slices. Wrap a piece of bacon around each piece of banana to completely enclose it, and fix in place with a cocktail stick, passed through the banana.

4 Place the kebabs under a hot grill (broiler) and cook, turning them occasionally, until the bacon is lightly browned and crisp. Serve hot.

Serves 6

Tip: Similar small kebabs may be made using a variety of fillings. For a cheese 'n bacon kebab, cut pieces of Gruyère cheese about

4 Mix the cooked mushrooms with the cheese sauce. Spoon the mixture into the prepared pastry boats and sprinkle the tops with the rest of the grated cheese. Place the boats under a hot grill (broiler) for a few minutes until the cheese is melted and golden. Serve at once.

Makes 8-12

Cocktail Kebabs

1 pineapple
100 g (¼ lb) thinly sliced streaky
  bacon
100 g (¼ lb) cocktail sausages
25 g (1 oz) (2 tablespoons) butter

For the Sauce:
30 ml (2 tablespoons) tomato
  ketchup (catsup)
30 ml (2 tablespoons) fruit
  chutney
10 ml (2 teaspoons)
  Worcestershire sauce
5 ml (1 teaspoon) vinegar or
  lemon juice
few drops chilli sauce

1 Peel the pineapple and remove the core. Cut the flesh into 2.5 cm (1 in) cubes.

2 Remove the rind and any bits of cartilage from the bacon slices. Cut them into pieces, long enough to be wrapped around a pineapple cube and fixed in place with a cocktail stick.

3 Cut the cocktail sausages into 2.5 cm (1 in) lengths. Spear a piece of sausage together with a piece of pineapple on each cocktail stick.

4 Melt the butter in a frying pan (skillet) and lightly fry the kebabs; or, brush them with melted butter and grill (broil) them until the bacon and sausage pieces are cooked.

5 Meanwhile, make the sauce. Beat together all the ingredients or mix them in a blender. Pour the sauce into a sauceboat or small dish and serve with the hot kebabs.

Serves about 12

2.5 cm (1 in) square and spread with French mustard. Wrap in bacon and grill (broil). Alternatively, wrap the bacon round large pineapple chunks.

Cheese and Mushroom Boats

shortcrust (pie crust) made with
  225 g (½ lb) (2¼ cups) flour
225 g (½ lb) mushrooms
25 g (1 oz) (2 tablespoons) butter
15 ml (1 tablespoon) flour
200 ml (6 fl oz) (¾ cup) milk

Cocktail Kebabs—serve them with celery chunks and succulent dates filled with cream cheese, gherkins and paprika

salt and pepper
100 g (¼ lb) (1 cup) grated cheese

1 Prepare the pastry boats as described in Salmon Boats.

2 Clean the mushrooms and cut them into thin slices. Place them in a saucepan with half of the butter and cook over a low heat for about 3 minutes, until softened and lightly browned.

3 In another pan, melt the rest of the butter and cook the flour for 1 minute. Gradually add the milk, stirring constantly, to make a smooth thick sauce. Season with salt and pepper. Stir in half of the cheese.

Party Pâtés & Dips

Dips and pâtés are ever popular party fare, either as hors d'oeuvres before a quiet dinner party or as a snack to be enjoyed throughout the evening. Easy to prepare, they can be made days before the event and, if covered, will keep indefinitely in the refrigerator. Your guests can help themselves to a slice of French bread and pâté or scoop into a colourful dip with crackers, crudités or even the humble potato crisp. Try serving your favourite cold dip in a hollowed-out red cabbage, grapefruit, aubergine (eggplant), or even a lovely firm pineapple.

Chive Dip

100 g ($\frac{1}{4}$ lb) ($\frac{2}{3}$ cup) cream cheese
30 ml (2 tablespoons) chopped chives
15 ml (1 tablespoon) cream or top of the milk, if necessary

1 Blend the cream cheese and chives to a soft cream, adding the cream or top of the milk, if necessary.

2 Serve in a bowl, surrounded with French bread, chips or crackers.

Makes 150 ml ($\frac{1}{4}$ pint) ($\frac{2}{3}$ cup)

Variations

The cream cheese dip can be endlessly varied. Try mashing 2 small avocados with the cheese or blending in some chopped red and green peppers with a little seasoning. Mix in 50 g (2 oz) of Roquefort or Danish blue cheese with the juice of half a lemon. Try adding 30 ml (2 tablespoons) of tomato purée with a dash of chilli sauce and perhaps a few corn kernels.

Spanish Country Pâté

225 g ($\frac{1}{2}$ lb) chicken livers, minced
450 g (1 lb) pig's liver, minced
225 g ($\frac{1}{2}$ lb) beef, minced
550 g (1$\frac{1}{4}$ lb) belly pork, minced
350 g ($\frac{3}{4}$ lb) bacon fat, minced
15 ml (1 tablespoon) salt
pepper
5 ml (1 teaspoon) ground mace
15 ml (1 tablespoon) chopped fresh herbs or 10 ml (2 teaspoons) dried herbs
30 ml (1 fl oz) (2 tablespoons) sherry
50 ml (2 fl oz) ($\frac{1}{4}$ cup) brandy
3 cloves garlic, crushed
75 g (3 oz) stuffed green olives

1 Preheat the oven to 150°C, 300°F, gas 2. Mix all the ingredients, except the olives, until well blended. Divide the pâté between two well-greased 900 ml (1$\frac{1}{2}$ pint) (3$\frac{1}{4}$ cup) dishes or loaf tins (pans).

2 Disperse the olives throughout the pâté, at different levels.

3 Cover the dishes with aluminium foil and place them in a roasting tin (pan) with 5 cm (2 in) of water and bake for 2 hours. Leave to cool.

4 Refrigerate the pâtés for 1-2 hours before turning them out on to a serving dish.

Serves 8-10

Liver and Olive Pâté

6 rashers (slices) streaky bacon
100 g ($\frac{1}{4}$ lb) chicken livers
225 g ($\frac{1}{2}$ lb) pig's liver
275 g (10 oz) belly pork
175 g (6 oz) bacon fat
100 g ($\frac{1}{4}$ lb) minced beef
2 cloves garlic, crushed
10 ml (2 teaspoons) mixed dried herbs
7.5 ml (1$\frac{1}{2}$ teaspoons) salt
5 ml (1 teaspoon) pepper
1 egg, beaten
6 stuffed green olives

1 Remove the rind from the bacon. Stretch the rashers (slices) with a round-bladed knife. Use the rashers (slices) to line a 450 g (1 lb) loaf tin (pan).

2 Mince the chicken livers, pig's liver, belly pork and bacon fat. Add the beef, garlic, herbs, salt, pepper, egg and olives and beat well.

3 Preheat the oven to 150°C, 300°F, gas 2. Press the mixture into the prepared tin (pan). Stand it in a roasting tin (pan) with 2.5 cm (1 in) of water and bake for 2 hours. Remove the pâté from the roasting tin (pan) and leave to cool thoroughly.

4 Turn it out on to a plate and serve with sliced tomato and crisp lettuce.

Serves 8-10

Mackerel Pâté

4 smoked mackerel fillets
juice 1 lemon
100 g ($\frac{1}{4}$ lb) ($\frac{2}{3}$ cup) cream cheese
225 g ($\frac{1}{2}$ lb) (1 cup) butter, melted
salt and pepper
25 g (1 oz) stuffed green olives, sliced
1 slice lemon

1 Skin and flake the mackerel fillets. Put the fish, lemon juice, cream cheese and melted butter in a blender and blend to a purée. (Alternatively, mash the fillets with a fork and pass them through a sieve before blending them with the lemon juice, cream cheese and butter.) Season to taste.

2 Pour the purée into a 450 g (1 lb) loaf tin (pan) or suitable serving dish. Smooth the top with a knife and decorate with the sliced olives. Chill and serve garnished with a slice of lemon.

Serves 8

Spanish Country Pâté (top left), Mackerel Pâté (top right) and Liver and Olive Pâté all go down well at a buffet party

Look'n Cook Aubergine (Eggplant) Dip

1 The ingredients: aubergine (eggplant), parsley, garlic, onion, cream cheese, lemon and seasoning ·**2** Prick the aubergine (eggplant) with a fork before baking it in the oven **3** Halve it lengthways and scoop out the flesh **4** Blend the flesh with the cream cheese, chopped onion and parsley and the juice of half a lemon **5** Season to taste **6** Spoon the dip into a bowl and serve with crisp crudités

Eastern Dip

100 g (¼ lb) shallots, chopped
2.5 ml (½ teaspoon) fresh
  coriander
60 ml (4 tablespoons) chopped
  parsley
30 ml (2 tablespoons) chopped
  fresh ginger
5 ml (1 teaspoon) soya sauce
30 ml (2 tablespoons) chopped
  canned water chestnuts
225 ml (8 fl oz) (1 cup) sour cream
30 ml (2 tablespoons)
  mayonnaise

1 In a bowl, thoroughly blend all the ingredients.

2 Pile the mixture into a serving bowl and serve with sliced raw button mushrooms and raw cauliflower.

Makes approximately 350 ml (12 fl oz) (1½ cups)

Hot Cheese Dip

350 g (¾ lb) Cheddar cheese
100 g (¼ lb) Roquefort cheese
25 g (1 oz) (2 tablespoons) butter
2.5 ml (½ teaspoon)
  Worcestershire sauce
2.5 ml (½ teaspoon) made
  mustard
pinch salt
½ clove garlic, crushed
225 ml (8 fl oz) (1 cup) flat light
  beer

1 Combine all the dip ingredients in a bowl and melt them over a pan of hot water.

2 Pour the dip immediately into a serving bowl and serve with bite size pieces of celery, cubes of fresh bread or croûtons.

Makes approximately 450 ml (16 fl oz) (2 cups)

Tip: Always have a number of long forks available for your friends to dip the bread or crudités into the cheese. This will save burnt fingers and a messy table.

Aubergine (Eggplant) Dip

1 large aubergine (eggplant)
1 onion, chopped
1 clove garlic, crushed
15 ml (1 tablespoon) chopped
  parsley
juice ½ lemon
225 g (½ lb) (1⅓ cups) cream cheese
salt and pepper

1 Preheat the oven to 190°C, 375°F, gas 5. Prick the aubergine (eggplant) all over with a fork and bake it in the oven for 45 minutes or until very soft. Cool it under

Aubergine (Eggplant) Dip — your guests can use the crisp crudités to help themselves to this chunky-textured dip

cold water and halve it lengthways. Use a tablespoon to scoop out the flesh.

2 In a bowl, blend the aubergine (eggplant) flesh with the onion, garlic, chopped parsley, lemon juice and cream cheese. Season to taste.

3 Pile the dip into a serving dish on a plate. Garnish it with a sprig of parsley and serve surrounded by sliced carrots, cauliflower florets, celery, cucumber and mushrooms.

Serves 4

Tip: Instead of baking the aubergine (eggplant), you can grill (broil) it for 20 minutes, or until the outside is black and the flesh has collapsed.

Party Buffets

The following beautifully presented buffet dishes have been designed as composite meals but they can be interchanged and, of course, how many dishes you prepare will depend on the number of people you invite. Serve the buffets with bowls of colourful fresh fruit and your favourite punch.

Celery, Walnut and Orange Salad

rind 1 orange
15 ml (1 tablespoon) butter
30 ml (2 tablespoons) plain flour
juice 1 orange
salt and pepper
15 ml (1 tablespoon) castor (fine granulated) sugar
10 ml (2 teaspoons) vinegar
1 head celery
50 g (2 oz) (½ cup) walnuts, chopped

1 Place the orange rind with 300 ml (½ pint) (1¼ cups) of water in a saucepan. Simmer for 10 minutes. Strain and reserve the liquid.

2 Melt the butter in a saucepan and stir in the flour. Gradually stir in the orange juice and reserved orange water. Bring to the boil, stirring continuously. Season and stir in the sugar and vinegar. Cool.

3 Slice the celery, mix it with the walnuts in a bowl and pour over the orange dressing. Toss and chill.

Serves 10-12

Tip: For a fruitier flavour, try including 6 canned apricot halves, drained and finely sliced. Add the apricots to the celery and walnuts before pouring over the orange dressing.

Green Bean Salad

25 g (1 oz) (2 tablespoons) margarine
25 g (1 oz) (4 tablespoons) flour
300 ml (½ pint) (1¼ cups) milk
salt and pepper
15 ml (1 tablespoon) vinegar
450 g (1 lb) fresh beans
350 g (12 oz) canned asparagus, drained
4 large tomatoes, sliced
½ large cucumber, peeled and diced
15 ml (1 tablespoon) chopped parsley

1 Melt the margarine in a saucepan. Stir in the flour and cook for 1-2 minutes. Gradually stir in the milk and bring it to the boil. Season, stir in the vinegar, cover and leave to cool.

2 Cut the beans into 5 cm (2 in) lengths and cook them for 5 minutes in boiling salted water. Cut the asparagus into 2.5 cm (1 in) lengths. Drain the beans and leave them to cool.

3 Arrange the tomatoes around the rim of a serving bowl and place the beans, asparagus, cucumber and parsley in the centre. Pour over the sauce and toss lightly.

Serves 10-12

Orange Meringue Gâteau

350 g (¾ lb) (1½ cups) margarine
650 g (1 lb 7 oz) (3 cups) castor (fine granulated) sugar
10 large eggs
350 g (¾ lb) (3¼ cups) self-raising flour
75 g (3 oz) (¾ cup) plain flour
grated rind 2 oranges
550 ml (1 pint) (2½ cups) milk
juice 1 orange
45 ml (3 tablespoons) orange liqueur
450 g (1 lb) (1⅜ cups) pineapple jam
4 slices orange

1 Preheat the oven to 190°C, 375°F, gas 5. Place the margarine, 350 g (¾ lb) (1½ cups) of the sugar, 6 eggs and the self-raising flour in a mixing bowl. Beat well until smooth and spoon the mixture into a greased and lined 27.5 cm (11 in) cake tin (pan). Bake in the centre of the oven for 1 hour, or until well-risen and firm to the touch. Cool on a rack.

2 Put 75 g (3 oz) (⅜ cup) castor (fine granulated) sugar, the plain flour, 4 egg yolks and the finely grated orange rind in a mixing bowl. Whisk well, together with a little of the milk.

3 Bring the rest of the milk to the boil and, whisking continuously, gradually pour it on to the orange mixture. Return to the saucepan and bring the sauce to the boil, still whisking. Cool slightly, whisk in the orange juice, cover and chill.

4 Cut the cake into 3 layers and pour the liqueur over each one. Place the bottom layer on a large baking (cookie) sheet. Spread with half of the jam and half of the orange cream. Put the centre layer on top and spread it with the remaining jam and cream. Top with the remaining layer.

5 Preheat the oven to 220°C, 425°F, gas 7. Whisk 4 egg whites until very stiff and mix in the remaining castor (fine granulated) sugar, one tablespoon at a time and whisking well between each addition.

6 Spread a smooth layer of the meringue over the top of the cake. Place the rest in a piping (decorator's) bag fitted with a large star nozzle and pipe lines of meringue around the side. Bake in the oven for 2-3 minutes until the meringue is lightly brown. Cool, decorate with the orange slices and serve.

Serves 10-12

Front, left to right: Green Bean Salad; Celery, Walnut and Orange Salad; and Curried Pasta Salad. Behind: Chicken Vol-au-Vent; Orange Meringue Gâteau; and Cauliflower Salad

Chicken Vol-au-Vent

one 2½ kg (5 lb) chicken
2 bay leaves
salt and pepper
1 small onion, skinned
1 carrot, peeled
950 g (2 lb 2 oz) puff pastry, fresh
  or frozen and thawed
1 egg, beaten
50 g (2 oz) (¼ cup) butter
50 g (2 oz) (½ cup) flour
300 ml (½ pint) (1¼ cups) milk
1 chicken stock cube
225 g (½ lb) mushrooms, washed
  and sliced
150 ml (¼ pint) (⅝ cup) single
  (light) cream

1 Wash the chicken and giblets and place them in a large saucepan. Add the bay leaves, salt, pepper, onion and carrot. Just cover the chicken with water and cook gently for 1½ – 2 hours.

2 Preheat the oven to 230°C, 450°F, gas 8. Roll out the pastry to a thickness of 15 mm (¾ in) and cut out a 27.5 cm (11 in) round, using a flan ring or saucepan lid as a guide.

3 Cutting almost through the pastry, cut a smaller round in the centre about 23 cm (9 in) diameter. Brush the pastry with beaten egg and bake it in the centre of the oven for 40-45 minutes until well-risen and crisp. Cool.

4 Cut out the 'lid' and scoop out any uncooked pastry.

5 Drain the stock from the chicken, reserving 300 ml (½ pint) (1¼ cups). Remove the chicken meat from the bones and cut into chunks.

6 Melt the butter in a saucepan. Stir in the flour and cook for 1-2 minutes. Gradually stir in the chicken stock and milk. Add the stock cube and, stirring continuously, bring to the boil. Add the mushrooms and simmer for 10 minutes before stirring in the chicken and cream.

7 Fill the vol-au-vent with the chicken mixture and replace the lid. Serve hot or cold.

Serves 10-12

Cauliflower Salad

25 g (1 oz) (2 tablespoons) butter
25 g (1 oz) (4 tablespoons) flour
300 ml (½ pint) (1¼ cups) milk
salt and pepper
1 bunch watercress, chopped
15 ml (1 tablespoon) chopped
  chives
15 ml (1 tablespoon) mayonnaise
1 large cauliflower
10 radishes, sliced

1 Melt the butter in a saucepan. Stir in the flour and cook gently for 1-2 minutes. Gradually stir in the milk and bring to the boil. Season, cover and cool. Beat the watercress, chives and mayonnaise into the sauce.

2 Divide the cauliflower into florets and cook them in salted water for 5 minutes. Drain and cool. Place the cauliflower and radishes on a bed of lettuce leaves in a salad bowl. Pour over the sauce and toss lightly. Chill and serve.

Serves 10-12

Curried Pasta Salad

1 onion, chopped
15 ml (1 tablespoon) corn oil
25 g (1 oz) (4 tablespoons) flour
300 ml (½ pint) (1¼ cups) beef stock
15 ml (1 tablespoon) curry
  powder
15 ml (1 tablespoon) tomato
  ketchup (catsup)
200 g (7 oz) peeled tomatoes
salt and pepper
1 onion, sliced
½ large cucumber, diced
225 g (½ lb) bow pasta, cooked
lemon wedges

1 Fry the chopped onion in the oil until soft. Stir in the flour and cook for 1 minute. Gradually stir in the stock and add the curry powder, ketchup (catsup) and tomatoes. Season and simmer for 20 minutes. Cool.

2 Place the sliced onion,

cucumber and pasta in a large bowl. Pour over the cooled curry sauce and toss gently. Serve with lemon wedges.

Serves 10-12

Salmon and Avocado Flan

175 g (6 oz) (1⅝ cups) flour
salt and pepper
75 g (3 oz) (6 tablespoons)
  margarine
4 large eggs
15 ml (1 tablespoon) corn oil
1 small onion, chopped
3 spring onions (scallions), finely
  chopped
350 g (¾ lb) canned red salmon
milk
40 g (1½ oz) (⅜ cup) grated Cheddar
1 ripe avocado
1 lemon, sliced

1 Preheat the oven to 220°C, 425°F, gas 7. Sieve the flour and a pinch of salt into a bowl and rub in the margarine. Mix to a stiff dough with one of the eggs and a little water. Roll out the dough and use it to line a 20 cm (8 in) flan tin (pan). Trim the edges.

2 Heat the oil in a pan and fry the onion and spring onion (scallion) until soft. Drain.

3 Drain the salmon, reserving the liquid. Flake the salmon and make the liquid up to 400 ml (¾ pint) (1¾ cups) with milk.

4 Whisk the remaining eggs and salmon liquid. Add the fish, onions and cheese. Season and spoon into the tin (pan).

5 Cook the flan in the centre of the oven for 45 minutes until golden-brown and set. Cool.

6 Peel, halve and stone (deseed) the avocado, and cut it lengthways into slices. Decorate the flan with avocado and lemon slices and garnish with parsley.

Serves 8-10

Salmon and Avocado Flan has an economical filling of canned salmon, milk and cheese, with an avocado covering

Pork and Veal Loaf

45 ml (3 tablespoons) oil
50 g (2 oz) (¼ cup) butter
1 onion, chopped
4 sticks celery, chopped
2 cloves garlic, crushed
300 ml (½ pint) (1¼ cups) red wine
5 slices white bread with crusts removed
550 g (1¼ lb) (2½ cups) minced pork
550 g (1¼ lb) (2½ cups) minced veal
225 g (½ lb) (1 cup) sausagemeat
salt and pepper
pinch allspice
pinch thyme
2 bay leaves, crushed
3 eggs, beaten
1 tomato, thinly sliced
few sprigs parsley

1 Preheat the oven to 170°C, 325°F, gas. 3. Heat the oil and butter and fry the onion, celery and garlic until soft. Add the wine and simmer for 5 minutes.

2 Crumble the bread and add to the pan with the meats, seasonings, herbs and egg. Mix well.

3 Spoon the mixture into a well-buttered loaf tin (pan) and bake for 1½-2 hours. You can baste the loaf with a little warm wine.

4 Turn out the Pork and Veal Loaf and allow to cool. Decorate the top with overlapping tomato slices and sprigs of parsley.

Serves 10-12

Curried Chicken Salad

25 g (1 oz) (2 tablespoons) butter
25 g (1 oz) (4 tablespoons) flour
300 ml (½ pint) (1¼ cups) milk
150 ml (¼ pint) (⅝ cup) chicken stock
5 ml (1 teaspoon) curry powder
salt and pepper
pinch paprika
grated rind 1 lemon
150 ml (¼ pint) (⅝ cup) single (light) cream
50 g (2 oz) (⅓ cup) raisins

350 g (¾ lb) (2 cups) cooked chicken meat, diced or cut in strips
30 ml (2 tablespoons) chopped parsley

1 Make a roux with the butter and flour and cook gently for 2 minutes without browning. Gradually add the milk and chicken stock, stirring all the time, until the sauce boils and becomes thick and smooth.

2 Add the curry powder, seasoning and lemon rind. Reduce the heat and simmer gently.

3 Remove from the heat and beat in the cream. Then mix in the raisins and chicken meat.

4 Arrange the chicken curry on a serving plate and surround by a border of saffron rice. Sprinkle the top with parsley and serve either hot or cold.

Serves 8-10

Celery à la Grecque

4 celery hearts
juice 2 lemons
550 ml (1 pint) (2½ cups) water
150 ml (¼ pint) (⅝ cup) olive oil
1 bay leaf
12 peppercorns
12 coriander seeds
pinch salt
300 ml (½ pint) (1¼ cups) mayonnaise
30 ml (1 fl oz) (2 tablespoons) tarragon vinegar
16 anchovy fillets
8 black olives

1 Cut each celery heart in half and wash thoroughly.

2 Place the lemon juice, water, oil, bay leaf and seasonings in a pan and bring to the boil. Add the celery hearts, cover, and simmer until tender. Drain and cool.

3 Arrange the celery on a dish. Mix the mayonnaise and vinegar and coat each celery heart. Decorate with the anchovy fillets and olives.

Serves 8

Grape Flan

350 g (¾ lb) (2 cups) cream cheese
juice 2 oranges
grated rind 1 orange
one 22.5 cm (9 in) cooked pie shell
100 g (¼ lb) green grapes, halved and deseeded
100 g (¼ lb) black grapes, halved and deseeded
15 ml (1 tablespoon) castor (fine granulated) sugar
30 ml (1 fl oz) (2 tablespoons) water

1 Mix together the cream cheese, orange juice and rind. Spread this mixture across the base of the pie shell.

2 Arrange 2 triangles of green grapes and 2 of black grapes on top of the filling, facing inwards.

3 Boil the sugar and water until syrupy and brush over the grapes. Serve with whipped cream.

Serves 8

Guacamole Dip

2 ripe avocados, peeled
juice 1 lemon
1 clove garlic, crushed
4 tomatoes, skinned, deseeded and chopped
½ onion, chopped
2 sticks celery, chopped
15 ml (1 tablespoon) chopped parsley
30 ml (1 fl oz) (2 tablespoons) olive oil
salt and pepper

1 Mash the avocados and blend with the other ingredients.

2 Chill and serve with crudités – celery and carrot sticks, and chunks of pepper.

Serves 8-10

A delicious buffet spread to suit everybody's taste: Grape Flan, a Mandarin Cheesecake, Pork and Veal Loaf, a crunchy salad, Guacamole Dip, Celery à la Grecque and a Curried Chicken Salad

Grapefruit Cocktail

8 grapefruit
2 red dessert apples, cored and
  sliced
50 g (2 oz) (½ cup) walnuts,
  quartered
100 g (¼ lb) blue cheese, cubed
100 g (¼ lb) green grapes,
  deseeded and halved
60 ml (4 tablespoons) oil
30 ml (2 tablespoons) lemon juice

1 Cut the top off each grapefruit by cutting round the sides in a zig-zag pattern. Scoop out the flesh and pith and remove the membrane or skin between each section.

2 Mix with the apple, walnuts, cheese and grapes and blend in the oil and lemon juice.

3 Fill each grapefruit shell with this mixture. Chill and serve.

Serves 8

Tip: The best blue cheese to use in this recipe is Roquefort.

Mandarin Cheesecake

275 g (10 oz) sweetmeal biscuits
  (cookies), crushed
150 g (5 oz) (⅔ cup) butter, melted
50 g (2 oz) (¼ cup) sugar
pinch cinnamon
450 g (1 lb) (2⅔ cups) cream cheese
225 g (½ lb) (1⅔ cups) icing
  (confectioners') sugar
300 ml (½ pint) (1¼ cups) double
  (heavy) cream
450 g (1 lb) (1¾ cups) canned
  mandarin oranges, drained
30 ml (2 tablespoons) powdered
  gelatine
grated rind 1 lemon
50 g (2 oz) chocolate, grated

1 Mix together the crushed biscuits (cookies), butter, sugar and cinnamon. Press firmly into a 22.5 cm (9 in) loose-bottomed cake tin (pan) and chill.

2 Blend the cream cheese, sugar

Grapefruit Cocktail, with its tasty sweet and savoury stuffing of blue cheese, fruits and walnuts, tastes tremendous

and cream. Chop half of the mandarins and mix into the cheese mixture.

3 Soften the gelatine in a little warm water and add with the lemon rind to the mixture.

4 Line the sides of the tin (pan) with greaseproof (parchment) paper and pour in the mixture. Level the top and chill until set.

5 Remove from the tin (pan) and decorate with the reserved mandarins and grated chocolate.

Serves 8-10

Stuffed Melon Salad

1 ripe avocado, peeled, halved
  and deseeded
juice 1 lemon
one 1½ kg (3 lb) chicken, roasted
1 ogen melon
1 green pepper, deseeded and cut
  in strips
1 small onion, chopped
50 g (2 oz) (⅓ cup) raisins
salt and pepper
250 g (9 oz) (1 cup) cooked rice

1 Cut the avocado flesh into chunks, cover with lemon juice and put aside.

2 Cut the chicken meat into strips. Cut around the top of the melon in a zig-zag motion and remove the lid. With a parisian cutter, hollow out the flesh to form balls.

3 Mix the avocado, chicken, melon balls, pepper, onion, raisins, seasoning and rice. Fill the melon shell with this mixture and serve the rest separately or use it to stuff another melon. Surround the melon(s) with a coleslaw salad and serve with mayonnaise.

Serves 8

Stuffed Melon Salad is served with crunchy coleslaw. Your guests can help themselves to the delicious rice filling

Cold Appetizers

Tomatoes Stuffed with Cream and Herbs

4 large, round firm tomatoes
bunch mixed fresh herbs
 (chervil, tarragon, chives, etc.)
2 shallots
1 clove garlic
90 ml (6 tablespoons) double
 (heavy) cream
salt and pepper
few lettuce leaves

1 Scoop out the tomatoes (see opposite page). Wash, dry and chop the herbs finely. Peel and chop the shallots and garlic.

2 Rinse and dry the tomato shells. Whip the cream until fairly stiff, then fold in the herbs, shallots, garlic, salt and pepper. Fill the tomatoes with this mixture and put a lid on each one. Chill until ready to serve.

3 Wash and dry the lettuce leaves, then arrange on a serving dish. Arrange the stuffed tomatoes on the dish and serve.

Serves 4

Swedish Herring Rissoles

3 medium potatoes
2 onions
25 g (1 oz) (2 tablespoons) butter
3 fresh herrings (ask the fishmonger to skin and fillet them)
salt and pepper
nutmeg
225 g (½ lb) (1 cup)
 redcurrant jelly
150 ml (4 fl oz) (½ cup) oil

1 Wash the potatoes without peeling them, and cook them in salted boiling water. Peel and finely chop the onions.

2 Melt the butter in a pan, and cook the onions, without letting them colour too much, for 7 or 8 minutes. Put them on one side and leave to cool.

Stuffed Tomatoes with Cream and Herbs are simple to prepare and make a light, refreshing start to any meal

3 When the potatoes are cooked, cool them in cold water, then peel them and mash them to a purée.

4 Put the herring fillets through the mincer (grinder). Add the onions, potatoes, a little salt, pepper and a little grated nut meg. Mix well together, then shape into round flat rissoles.

5 Put the redcurrant jelly and 150 ml (¼ pint) (⅔ cup) water in a saucepan and heat slowly.

6 Heat the oil in a frying pan (skillet). When it is hot, cook the rissoles for about 10 minutes, turning them over once or twice.

7 Heat a serving dish and a sauce-boat.

8 Arrange the rissoles on the dish. Pour the hot redcurrant jelly sauce into the sauce-boat and serve very hot.

Serves 4

Tip: The mixture of sweet and savoury is typical of Scandinavian cookery. Ascertain the tastes of guests before serving this recipe or miss out the sauce.

Herring in Sherry Pickle

2 salted herrings, filleted and
 skinned
90 ml (6 tablespoons) (⅓ cup)
 sherry
60 ml (4 tablespoons) (¼ cup)
 water
45 ml (3 tablespoons) wine
 vinegar
1.25 ml (¼ teaspoon) allspice
2 onions, thinly sliced into rings
chopped fresh dill

1 Cover the herrings with cold water and leave to soak for 24 hours. Drain, rinse and dry. Place in a non-metallic bowl.

2 Combine the sherry, water, vinegar and allspice. Pour over the herrings. Cover with plastic film and refrigerate for 24 hours.

3 Serve garnished with the onion rings and dill.

Serves 4

Seafood Hors d'oeuvre

1 litre (1¾ pints) (approx 5 cups)
  cockles
pinch sea salt
1 onion
bay leaf
bouquet garni
1 litre (1¾ pints) (approx 5 cups)
  mussels
1 can crab
1 small can tomato concentrate
  (paste)
15 ml (1 tablespoon) brandy
200 ml (7 fl oz) (scant 1 cup) double (whipping or heavy) cream
salt and pepper
¼ kg (1 lb), fresh or frozen prawns
small bunch parsley

1 Put the cockles into a basin with water and a pinch of sea salt.

2 Peel the onion and cut in slices.

3 Prepare the cooking liquid (court bouillon): in a large saucepan put 300 ml (½ pint) (1¼ cups) water, the onion, the bay leaf and the bouquet garni; simmer for 20 minutes.

4 Scrape the mussels and wash them in several changes of water. Clean and rinse the cockles. Put the shellfish in the court bouillon and cook gently, stirring now and then, until they open. Discard any which do not open.

5 When the mussels and cockles are fully open, lift them out of the saucepan with a skimming ladle. Shell them and put in a dish.

6 Put the liquid through a strainer lined with a fine cloth and set it aside.

7 Open the can of crab, drain it, remove any cartilage and quickly flake the flesh.

8 Open the can of tomato concentrate (paste). Pour the contents into a bowl. Stir in the brandy, then pour in the cream, stirring constantly, as though thickening mayonnaise. Then add 75 ml (5 tablespoons) of the reserved seafood liquid and mix. Add a little salt and a generous sprinkling of pepper. The sauce should now be well seasoned and very smooth.

9 Divide the mussels, cockles, flaked crab and peeled prawns among 8 individual serving dishes and pour sauce over each.

10 Wash, dry and chop the parsley. Sprinkle some on top of each dish.

11 Refrigerate and serve chilled.

Serves 8

Crunchy Salad Starter

1 small tight white cabbage
coarse salt
salt and pepper
100 g (¼ lb) (⅔ packed cup)
  sultanas (seedless white
  raisins)
½ head celery
2 apples
juice ½ lemon
¼ lb walnuts
5 ml (1 teaspoon) made mustard
15 ml (1 tablespoon) vinegar
45 ml (3 tablespoons) oil
100 g (¼ lb) (1 generous cup)
  shelled chopped walnuts

1 Trim the cabbage, pulling off any withered leaves, the hard stalk and side leaves. Wash the remainder. Dry and shred them finely with a large kitchen knife. Sprinkle with coarse salt and leave for about 30 minutes to draw out excess moisture.

2 Soak the sultanas (seedless white raisins) in warm water for 10 minutes.

3 Clean the celery. Wash, dry and shred it. Peel and core the apples, then dice, sprinkle with lemon juice.

4 Drain the shredded cabbage, dry it on absorbent paper and put into a salad bowl with the celery. Mix well.

5 Make a dressing by blending together the mustard, vinegar and oil, season with salt and pepper and stir well. Pour this over the cabbage and celery and mix well but do not crush the ingredients.

6 Drain and dry the sultanas (seedless white raisins) and add them to the bowl, together with the nuts and diced apple. Stir again and serve immediately.

Serves 6

Ham Logs

6 thick slices very lean ham
1½ small celery heart
2 shallots
handful parsley
small bunch chives
juice ½ lemon
3 portions Demi-sel cheese
5 ml (1 teaspoon) strong mustard
salt
5 ml (1 teaspoon) paprika
pinch cayenne pepper
100 g (¼ lb) chopped walnuts

1 Cut 2 of the slices of ham into fine strips.

2 Clean the celery and chop it as finely as possible. Peel and finely chop the shallots. Wash, dry and chop the parsley and chives.

3 Mash the cheese and beat in the parsley, chives, shallots 15 ml (1 tablespoon) lemon juice, the mustard, salt, paprika and cayenne pepper.

4 Stir in the chopped ham, celery and nuts. Beat well until the mixture is very smooth and creamy. Spread this mixture on the four remaining ham slices and roll these up to form 'logs'. Serve chilled, on a bed of lettuce and decorated with sliced tomatoes and a few sprigs of parsley.

Serves 4

Seafood Hors d'oeuvre is a delicious medley of shellfish, brandy and cream

Artichoke Hearts with Cottage Cheese

300 g (11 oz) (2 cups) cottage
  cheese
4 large globe artichokes
large bunch chives, chervil and
  parsley, mixed
salt and pepper
pinch cayenne pepper
few lettuce leaves

For the Blanching Mixture:
juice 3 lemons
15 g (1 tablespoon) flour
1½ litres (2¾ pints) (7 cups) water

1 Put the cottage cheese in a cloth-lined sieve (strainer) and leave to drain completely.

2 Prepare the artichoke hearts and blanch (see pages 58-59). Cook them for 40 minutes in the blanching mixture, or till tender, then drain and cool.

3 Wash the herbs; dry them well and chop finely. Tip them into a bowl. Add the cottage cheese, salt and pepper, and cayenne, and mix well with a fork; then whisk (beat) vigorously.

4 Wash and dry the lettuce leaves. Arrange them on a serving dish. Lay the artichoke hearts on the lettuce and pile a pyramid of the cheese mixture on each one. Serve chilled.

Serves 4

Apple Hors d'oeuvre

1 lemon
1 small celery heart
1 small cucumber
few lettuce leaves
3 tomatoes
few sprigs chives and chervil
150 ml (6 fl oz) (¾ cup) double
  (whipping or heavy) cream
2.5 ml (½ teaspoon) paprika
salt and pepper
3 eating apples
12 radishes

1 Squeeze the lemon and reserve the juice. Wash the celery and chop it into fine strips.

2 Peel the cucumber, split it in half lengthways and remove the seeds. Sprinkle both halves with salt, to remove the excess moisture.

3 Wash and dry the lettuce leaves. Wash and dry the tomatoes and then quarter them. Wash the chives and the chervil; dry and chop them.

4 In a bowl beat together the cream, lemon juice and paprika, and season with salt and pepper.

5 Rinse and dry the cucumber and cut it into small cubes. Peel and core the apples and dice them.

6 Put the cucumber, apples, celery and tomatoes into a dish. Pour the cream sauce over and stir it in

7 Wash and scrape the radishes. Cut them into flower shapes.

8 Line the sides and bottom of a salad bowl with the lettuce leaves. Arrange the salad in the centre. Sprinkle with the chopped chives and chervil, and decorate with the radishes. Serve chilled.

Serves 6

Apple Hors d'oeuvre is a refreshing starter which sharpens the taste buds

over the cocktails together with some paprika. Chill the glasses or bowls in the refrigerator for 1 hour and serve very cold.

Serves 4

Anchovy and Garlic Stuffed Eggs

4 eggs
4 large cloves garlic
40 g (1½ oz) (3 tablespoons) butter
salt and pepper
8 olives
8 anchovy fillets
few lettuce leaves
chopped parsley
4 small tomatoes

1 Put the eggs in a pan of cold water and bring to the boil. Peel the garlic cloves and add to the boiling water. Remove them after 7 minutes, drain and then pound in a mortar.

2 When the water has been boiling for 10 minutes, take out the eggs, cool them in cold water and shell. Cut the shelled hard-boiled eggs in half lengthways. Leave them to cool.

3 Put the butter in a bowl and work it to a very soft paste with a wooden spoon.

4 Carefully remove the yolks from the eggs, without damaging the whites. Mash and sieve the yolks, and add them to the softened butter. Then add the garlic purée and stir well until smooth. Season.

5 Pile this paste back into the half egg whites. Decorate each with an olive with an anchovy fillet wrapped around it.

6 Arrange the lettuce leaves on a serving platter, place the stuffed eggs on top and sprinkle with the finely-chopped parsley. Slice the tomatoes in half horizontally and use the halves to garnish the platter. Refrigerate and serve cold.

Serves 4

Anchovy and Garlic Stuffed Eggs make an attractive egg starter

Oyster Cocktails

2 dozen fresh oysters
2 small sticks celery, taken from the heart
60 ml (4 tablespoons) tomato ketchup (catsup)
75 ml (2½ fl oz) (⅓ cup) gin
15 ml (1 tablespoon) cream
5 ml (1 teaspoon) lemon juice
salt and pepper
pinch cayenne pepper
bunch chervil
5 ml (1 teaspoon) paprika

1 Open the oysters with an oyster knife and scrape them from the shells. Drain them, keeping the juice. Strain the juice through muslin (cheesecloth) and put the oysters in a bowl.

2 Wash and dry the celery sticks. Chop them finely and add to the oysters.

3 Stir into the oyster liquor the tomato ketchup (catsup), gin cream and lemon juice and beat for a moment. Taste and adjust the seasoning. Then add a pinch of cayenne pepper.

4 Pour this sauce over the oysters and celery and mix gently. Spoon the oyster cocktail into 4 glasses or small bowls.

5 Wash, dry and chop the chervil. Sprinkle the chopped chervil

Mussels in Spicy Sauce

100 g (4 oz) (1 cup) canned or
  bottled mussels, drained
30 ml (2 tablespoons)
  mayonnaise
10 ml (2 teaspoons) mustard
5 ml (1 teaspoon) sherry
2.5 ml (½ teaspoon) lemon juice
70 g (2 oz) bottled or
  canned pimientoes

1 Put the mussels in the serving dish.

2 To the mayonnaise add the mustard, sherry and lemon juice and stir carefully until blended. Cut the pimientoes into strips and stir into the sauce.

3 Spoon this sauce over the mussels.

Serves 2

Tip: This is a tasty way of serving mussels when fresh ones are not in season.
  If using fresh, reserve a few shells for decoration.

Cauliflower in Vinegar

1 medium cauliflower
salt
225 ml (8 fl oz) (1 cup) vinegar
225 ml (8 fl oz) (1 cup) water
1 clove garlic, cut in half
4 g (2 teaspoons) dried basil
45 ml (3 tablespoons) oil
15 ml (1 tablespoon) lime or
  lemon juice
2 g (1 teaspoon) chopped
  parsley
2 g (1 teaspoon) chopped chives
freshly ground black pepper

1 Wash and trim the cauliflower and divide into florets or sprigs. Add to boiling salted water and cook for 10-15 minutes. Drain.

2 Bring the vinegar, water, garlic and basil to the boil and pour over the cauliflower. Leave until cold, then chill.

3 Mix the oil, lime or lemon juice, parsley, chives, salt and black pepper to make a smooth dressing. Drain the cauliflower, pour on the dressing and serve at once.

Serves 6

Red Peppers and Mushrooms

200 g (¼ lb) button mushrooms
salt and pepper
2 lemons
75 ml (5 tablespoons) olive oil
6 large red peppers
small bunch chervil

1 Clean the mushrooms. Cut the ends off the stalks. Wash the mushrooms quickly but do not leave them under water longer than necessary. Slice them thinly and season with salt and pepper.

2 Squeeze 1 of the lemons and sprinkle 30 ml (2 tablespoons) of the juice and 30 ml (2 table-spoons) olive oil over the mushrooms. Leave them to marinate.

3 Wash and dry the peppers. Grill (broil) them under a high heat (the skin should swell and darken) or hold over a flame on a skewer. Then rinse them under cold water and peel them. The darkened outer skin should come off very easily, exposing the soft red flesh underneath.

4 Cut the peppers in half and remove the seeds. Cut the flesh in strips. Season with salt and pepper, and sprinkle over the rest of the lemon juice and oil.

5 Wash the other lemon and quarter it. Wash, dry and chop the chervil.

6 Mix the peppers and mush-

rooms together in a deep dish. Garnish with the lemon quarters and sprinkle chervil over the top. Chill 1 hour before serving.

Serves 6

Red Herrings with Sauerkraut

6 herring fillets (smoked and
  salted)
45 ml (3 tablespoons) oil
2 dessert apples
450 g (1 lb) (6 cups packed) raw
  sauerkraut
2 mild onions
1 lemon
30 ml (2 tablespoons) double
  (heavy) cream
1 carton plain yogurt
pepper
bunch parsley

1 Cut the herring fillets into small pieces. Put them on a deep plate and pour the oil over them.

2 Peel, core and dice the apples.

3 Wash the sauerkraut in fresh water. Drain it thoroughly, squeezing with the hands to extract all the water. Put it into a cloth, dry it well then separate the shreds.

4 Peel the onions. Cut them into rounds, then separate into rings. Squeeze the juice from the lemon.

5 Mix the lemon juice with the cream and yogurt. Add pepper to taste and blend all these ingredients together.

6 Mix the sauerkraut and the diced apple, pour on the lemon-flavoured yogurt and stir gently.

7 Wash, dry and chop the parsley.

8 Arrange the sauerkraut and apple salad round the edge of a serving dish.

9 Drain the herring fillets and place them in the centre of the dish. Cover them with the onion rings. Sprinkle with chopped parsley and serve very cold.

Serves 6

Tuna Fish with Aubergines (Eggplant) in Sweet-sour Sauce

In Sicily this dish is a speciality and is called Caponata; some versions omit the tuna fish.

3 aubergines (eggplants)
1 head young celery
1 litre (1¾ pints) (4½ cups) water
6 canned anchovies, drained
5 large ripe firm tomatoes
1 large onion
1 bunch parsley
100 ml (4 fl oz) (½ cup) oil
salt and pepper
few sprigs thyme
1 bay leaf, imported
40 g (1½ oz) (1½ tablespoons) sugar
10 ml (2 teaspoons) vinegar
100 g (¼ lb) (1 cup) small black
  olives, stoned (pitted) if large
50 g (2 oz) capers
350 g (¾ lb) (1½ cups) canned
  tuna fish

1 Peel the aubergines (egg plants). Cut them into cubes, sprinkle with salt to draw out the excess moisture and any bitterness and leave for about 30 minutes. Wash and trim the celery, and slice thinly.

2 Bring the water to the boil, add salt and put in the celery; simmer for about 8 minutes, then drain and plunge into a pan of cold water; drain again and set aside.

3 Wash the anchovies to remove the excess salt. Separate the fillets and rinse again thoroughly in water. Cut them into small pieces.

4 Skin the tomatoes; quarter them, remove the seeds and chop the flesh. Peel and thinly slice the onion. Wash, dry and chop the parsley.

5 Heat 30 ml (2 tablespoons) oil in a saucepan. When hot, add the onion and cook gently until soft but not browned. Add the tomatoes, season with salt and pepper, add the thyme and bay leaf and cook over a very low heat until the mixture is a soft pulp. Remove the thyme and bay leaf and rub the mixture through a conical sieve (strainer).

6 Put the tomato purée in a pan, add the sugar and cook until thickened and lightly browned. Then add the vinegar and cook for a further 3-4 minutes.

7 Meanwhile, drain and dry the aubergine (eggplant) pieces. Heat the rest of the oil in a saucepan, put in the aubergine (eggplant) and cook briskly until lightly browned. Drain off the oil.

8 Remove the pan of tomato sauce from the heat and stir into the aubergines (eggplants), together with the celery, anchovies, black olives and capers. Correct the seasoning – this dish should be fairly spicy – and mix together.

9 Set the mixture aside to cool, then chill in the refrigerator overnight. Turn the mixture into a salad bowl. Break the tuna fish into regular bite-sized pieces and arrange over the top. Chill and serve.
Serves 6

Tuna fish and aubergines (eggplant) in a piquant sauce, a deliciously refreshing dish for a hot summer's day

Smoked Fish Starter

1 tight white cabbage heart
  (small)
2 marinated herrings
2.5 ml (½ teaspoon) cumin seed
90 ml (6 tablespoons) double
  (heavy) cream
3 smoked sprats (sardines)
2 lemons
2 apples
12 thin slices wholemeal bread
50 g (2 oz) (4 tablespoons) butter
75 g (scant ½ lb) thin slices
  smoked salmon
6 thin slices smoked eel
coarse salt and pepper

1 Trim, wash and dry the cabbage and shred it finely with a large sharp kitchen knife. Put the shredded cabbage into a bowl, sprinkle lightly with salt and leave to stand while continuing with the preparation.

2 Drain the marinated herrings and fillet them. Put the fillets in a blender or through a mincer (grinder) to make a purée. Add to this half the cumin and 30 ml (2 tablespoons) cream.

3 Wash the smoked sprats.

4 Squeeze 1 lemon and reserve juice. Wash and dry the second lemon and cut it in thin rounds, then each round in half.

5 Peel the apples and cut them in quarters, remove the cores and pips and dice the flesh.

6 Butter 9 slices of wholemeal bread and cut them diagonally to make 18 triangles. Arrange the slices of smoked eel on 6 of these triangles, and the slices of smoked salmon on the others. Pipe round a border of mayonnaise if liked.

7 Butter the remainder of the slices of bread with the herring purée, and cut them into triangles. Place 1 sprat fillet on each of the triangles, and a semi-circle of lemon on each slice.

8 Drain and dry the cabbage. Add to it the diced apple and the rest of the cumin. Sprinkle with lemon juice and pepper and mix gently.

9 Arrange the cabbage in a heap in the centre of a serving dish, and pour over the rest of the cream. Arrange the various fish-covered triangles of bread round the edge of the dish and serve cold.
Serves 6

An eye-catching appetizer, choose several kinds of smoked fish for colour and flavour contrast

Vegetables à la Grecque

3 globe artichoke hearts
1 small cauliflower
1 lemon
225 g (½ lb) mushrooms
3 carrots
2 bulbs fennel
3 turnips
2 leeks
3 cloves garlic
225 g (½ lb) green olives
¼ litre (8 fl oz) (1 cup) oil
15 ml (1 tablespoon) tomato
  concentrate (paste)
5 ml (1 teaspoon) coriander seeds
100 ml (4 fl oz) (½ cup) wine
  vinegar
salt and pepper

1 Peel and wash all the vegetables. Break the cauliflower into florets. Squeeze the juice of the lemon.

2 Put the artichoke hearts, the cauliflower florets, the mushrooms (whole small ones, cut in half if large) into water. Add the lemon juice to prevent the vegetables discolouring.

3 Slice the carrots, fennel, turnips and leeks. Peel and crush the garlic. Stone (pit) the olives and wash in cold water.

4 Heat the oil in a pan. When it is hot, add the leeks, then all the other vegetables, stirring all the time to prevent them sticking.

5 Add the crushed garlic, the tomato concentrate (paste), the coriander, the vinegar, the water, salt and pepper.

6 Leave to cook for 30 minutes, stirring from time to time. The vegetables should stay firm. When cooked, leave to cool.

Serves 8-10

Artichokes à la Grecque

4 globe artichokes
2 lemons
225 g (½ lb) canned tomatoes,
  drained

6 shallots
100 ml (4 fl oz) (½ cup) oil
6 coriander seeds
1 bouquet garni
100 ml (4 fl oz) (½ cup) dry white
  wine
salt and pepper

1 Prepare the artichoke hearts (see page 58). Cut 1 lemon in half. Rub the artichoke hearts with one half. Squeeze the other half, pouring the juice into a bowl. Fill the bowl with water.

2 Cut the hearts into 4 or 6 pieces. Remove all the hairs with a serrated-edge knife. Dip the artichokes into the lemon water.

3 Put the artichokes into a saucepan. Add the lemon water. Bring to the boil and boil for 1 minute. Chop the tomatoes

roughly. Peel the baby onions and squeeze the last lemon.

4 Warm the oil in a sauté pan. Drain the artichokes and put them into the pan. Add the tomatoes, the onions, the coriander seeds, the bouquet garni, the lemon juice and the white wine. Add seasoning, cover and cook on a low heat for 30 minutes.

5 When the cooking is finished, remove the bouquet garni, tip the artichoke pieces into an hors d'oeuvre dish. Leave to cool, then put the dish in the refrigerator.

Serves 4

Vegetables à la Grecque — mixed vegetables served cold in this way make a delicious starter

Crayfish with Avocados

1kg (2lb) crayfish
sea salt
1 bouquet garni
1 small cucumber
2 avocados
30ml (2 tablespoons) gin
2.5ml (½ teaspoon) Tabasco sauce
salt and pepper
300ml (½ pint) (1¼ cups)
  mayonnaise,
  home-made or bottled
pinch cayenne pepper
2.5ml (½ teaspoon) paprika

1 Wash and drain the crayfish.

2 Boil water in a large saucepan with a handful or sea salt and the bouquet garni. Drop the crayfish into the boiling water and cook for about 10 minutes.

3 Drain the crayfish and leave to cool.

4 Peel the cucumber and split in two lengthwise. Take out the seeds with a small spoon. Grate the flesh of the cucumber, put it into a bowl and leave to drain without salting it.

5 Cut the avocados into halves, remove the stone (pit), and, with a melon baller, scoop the flesh into balls.

6 When the crayfish are cold, remove the meat from the tails.

7 Put the avocado balls and the crayfish tails into a glass serving bowl. Pour over the gin and Tabasco sauce. Season with a little salt and pepper and mix well. Leave to marinate for about 20 minutes.

8 Lay a piece of muslin (cheesecloth) over a colander. Pour in the cucumber pulp, and press down well to extract as much water as possible. Blend this pulp into the mayonnaise, folding it in gently. Then season with cayenne.

9 Pour the cucumber mayonnaise over the crayfish and avocado, mixing well. Sprinkle with paprika and serve very cold.

Serves 4

Crab and Avocado Cocktail

4 eggs
225g (½lb) (1 cup) crabmeat
1 tablespoon (15ml) tomato
  concentrate (paste)
300ml (½ pint) (1¼ cups)
  mayonnaise, home-made or
  bottled
salt and pepper
3 avocados
paprika

1 Put 6 small glass dishes into the refrigerator.

2 Cook the eggs in boiling water for 10 minutes. Cool them in cold water and then shell them.

3 Flake the crabmeat, removing the cartilage. Add the tomato concentrate (paste) to the mayonnaise. Pass the hard-boiled eggs through a food mill or chop them.

4 Mix together the crabmeat, chopped eggs and the mayonnaise in a bowl. Season.

5 Cut the avocados in half, take out the stones (pits), cut the flesh into large cubes and place them in the chilled dishes. Cover with the crab mixture and sprinkle with paprika. Chill until ready to serve.

Serves 6

Peaches Filled with Crab — a mixture of fruit and fish gives an interesting light first course

Tomatoes Stuffed with Anchovies and Rice

6 firm tomatoes
salt
125g (¼lb) (¾ cup) long-grain rice
24 canned anchovy fillets
24 black olives
1 small head fennel
2 shallots
chopped parsley
1 green pepper
2.5ml (½ teaspoon) Pernod
  (optional)
juice of ½ lemon
300ml (½ pint) (1¼ cups) mayonnaise, home-made or bottled

1 Scoop out the tomatoes. Wash the rice under running cold water until the water is clear.

2 Bring to the boil a pan of salted water, twice the volume of the rice (i.e. 300ml (½ pint) (1¼ cups). Add the rice, simmer for about 12 minutes or until tender, then drain and leave until cold.

3 Put aside 6 anchovy fillets and 6 olives. Chop the rest of the anchovies. Stone (pit) the olives and cut into quarters.

4 Trim the fennel, wash, dry and chop. Peel and chop the shallots. Wash, dry and chop the parsley.

Wash and dry the pepper; cut it in half, remove the seeds and white membrane and chop finely.

5 Add the pastis, if used, and the lemon juice to the mayonaise. Add the cooked rice, chopped anchovies, olives, shallots, fennel, pepper and the parsley to the mayonnaise. Fold carefully together.

6 Rince and dry the tomatoes. Fill with the rice salad and make a dome on top. Top with an olive and a rolled anchovy fillet. Arrange the stuffed tomatoes on a serving dish and refrigerate for 1 hour before serving.

Serves 6

Peaches Filled with Crab

5 large peaches
100 g (¼ lb) canned crabmeat
100 ml (4 fl oz) (½ cup) double
 (heavy) cream
1.25 ml (¼ teaspoon) lemon juice
10 ml (2 teaspoons) brandy
8 lettuce leaves
large pinch paprika
salt and pepper

1 Peel the peaches: halve them and remove the stones (pits).

2 Drain the crab, and mash the crabmeat together with 1 of the peaches in a basin.

3 Add the cream, lemon juice, brandy, paprika, salt and pepper, and blend all the ingredients together well.

4 Wash the lettuce leaves, and dry them on absorbent paper. Make a bed of the leaves on a flat serving dish, and place a peach half on each of the leaves. Fill each peach half with the crab mixture.

5 Chill the dish for at least 1 hour before serving.

Serves 4

Tomatoes Stuffed with Anchovies and Rice — this simple dish goes down well at buffet parties

All about Salads

An exotic salad with cheese and fruit

All about Salads

In the next three issues we give you lots of new ideas for salads. Salads need not only be a mixture of lettuce and tomatoes which are served as an accompaniment to cold meat; they can also be served as hors d'oeuvres or as main meals in themselves. The term 'salad' is now used to encompass a wide range of dishes and foods. Salads can be made with herbs, plants, raw or cooked vegetables, eggs, cheese, meat, fish, fruits, nuts, pasta or rice. The list is seemingly endless.

With the emphasis on healthy, raw and wholefoods and the present trend towards a more natural way of eating, salads are becoming ever more popular and original. They are also ideal if you are slimming or diet-conscious, as usually they contain very little carbohydrate or fat and are rich in vitamins and roughage.

Salad Dressings

A perfect salad should be crisp, cool and served in a delicious dressing. Never toss a salad in an acid dressing too long before serving it—it will go soggy. Always toss it at the last moment. The French are masters of the salad dressing. They use only the best olive oil and wine vinegars. A few useful tips to remember when making a French dressing are:

1 Use the best oil if possible – *eg* olive, walnut or ground-nut oil
2 Never use malt vinegar – it will give your salad a bitter flavour.
3 If you want to use mustard in your dressing, add a wine-flavoured type.

There are four types of dressings: the classical French dressing; mayonnaise; creamy white sauce; and blue cheese dressing. Of course, there are many variations on these. Try adding tomato concentrate (paste), lemon juice, chutneys, herbs and spices, curry powder or Tabasco to mayonnaise for an unusual flavour. French dressings can be more tasty and tangy if you mix in some chopped onions or capers.

Salad Hors d'Oeuvres

Salads are delicious for hors d'oeuvres or appetizers before a main course. They make a light and refreshing start to a meal. Opposite are some ideas for salad starters which will whet your appetite for what is to come. Try them as appetizers or serve them as canapés at a buffet or party. They are all quickly and easily prepared, and can be made in advance and refrigerated until you wish to serve them. The key below will help you to identify them.

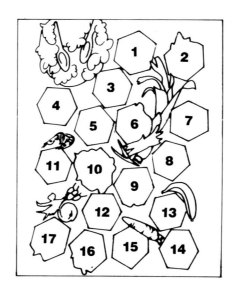

1 Black olives, sliced tomato, halved green grapes and nuts surrounded by orange segments (sections) and thinly sliced cucumber, then topped with onion rings.

2 Alternate slices of tomato and hard-boiled egg on a bed of chicory leaves garnished with black and green olives.

3 Chopped beetroot (beet) with spring onions (scallions) on deseeded tomato slices arranged like the petals of a flower.

4 Tomato slices and onion rings in a classic French dressing, sprinkled with chopped chives.

5 Sliced tomato, cucumber, hard-boiled eggs and black olives, with onion rings and anchovy strips on a bed of lettuce leaves.

6 Sliced blanched courgettes (zucchini) and sliced tomatoes on a bed of lettuce leaves, generously sprinkled with chopped chives.

7 Deseeded segments of tomato with pineapple chunks in an oily dressing to which pineapple juice is added.

8 Lobster chunks in a spicy mayonnaise with sliced bananas and tiny onions, garnished with a sprig of fresh watercress.

9 Hard-boiled eggs, split and filled with chopped red pepper and prawns in sour cream. Then sprinkled with finely grated cheese on a bed of cress.

10 Prawns, tomato wedges and black olives heaped on a bed of crisp lettuce leaves.

11 A hollowed-out tomato stuffed with cream cheese, celery seeds and chives surrounded by an attractive border of cress.

12 Chunks of canned meat with cooked rice, mixed with chopped red and green peppers, onion and hard-boiled eggs.

13 Overlapping thinly sliced tomatoes, dressed with natural yogurt and chopped chives with a cucumber border, and a slice of cucumber in the centre.

14 Sliced tomatoes, prawns and bean sprouts surrounded by sliced apples which have been sprinkled with lemon juice.

15 Sliced tomatoes and raw mushrooms on a bed of lettuce leaves, sprinkled with chopped chives in a French dressing.

16 Half an avocado pear on a plain lettuce leaf, filled with chopped ham, onions and red pepper in a vinaigrette dressing.

17 Sliced tomatoes, garnished with Cheddar cheese cubes on a bed of flower-shaped chicory leaves.

Ham and Egg Salad

1 apple
100 g (¼ lb) ham cut into 5 mm
  (¼ in) cubes
100 g (¼ lb) boiled new potatoes,
  cut into 5 mm (¼ in) cubes
15 ml (1 tablespoon) chopped
  chives or shallots
150 ml (¼ pint) (⅝ cup) mayonnaise
4 lettuce leaves
4 hard-boiled eggs
5 ml (1 teaspoon) chopped
  parsley

1 Peel and core the apple. Dice it finely. Combine with the ham, potatoes and chives or shallots. Pour over the mayonnaise, reserving a little for later, and toss.

2 Wash, dry and shred the lettuce. Place a quarter of the lettuce in the bottom of each of 4 glasses. Top with the ham and potato mixture.

3 Cut each egg into 8 wedges and arrange them like the spokes of a wheel on each serving. Dot the yolks with a little mayonnaise and sprinkle with the chopped parsley.

Serves 4

Avocado Starter

2 avocados
1 grapefruit
8 lettuce leaves

For the Dressing:
150 ml (¼ pint) (⅝ cup) mayonnaise
15 ml (1 tablespoon) tomato
  ketchup (catsup)
2-3 drops Worcestershire sauce
dash Tabasco (optional)
juice half lemon

1 Prepare the dressing by combining the mayonnaise, tomato ketchup (catsup), Worcestershire sauce, and Tabasco if desired. Add the lemon juice.

2 Peel and stone (seed) the

avocados and cut them into small pieces.

3 Peel the grapefruit, remove the white skin, and divide into segments (sections). Cut each segment (section) into 4 and combine with the avocado.

4 Wash and dry the lettuce. Place one leaf at the bottom of each of 4 glasses. Shred the remaining leaves and place equal amounts in the glasses. Pour in the avocado mixture.

5 Chill for 1 hour before serving.

Serves 4

Ham and Egg Salad is easy to make and attractively served in glasses, garnished with parsley and eggs

Prawn Starter

2 oranges
8 walnuts, shelled
2 apples, cored
1 stick celery
100 g (¼ lb) (¾ cup) cooked, peeled
  prawns
½ lettuce
4 slices lemon

Prawn Starter combines juicy apples and oranges with nuts, prawns and vegetables in a glass, garnished with lemon

1 Peel the oranges, remove the white skin and divide into segments (sections). Roughly chop the walnuts and apples and dice the celery. Combine these ingredients in a bowl with the prawns.

2 Wash and drain the lettuce. Shred it finely and place equal portions in 4 glasses. Pour in the mixture. Chill for 1 hour and garnish with a slice of lemon.

Serves 4

Prawn Salad

450 g (1 lb) (3 cups) cooked, peeled prawns
225 g (½ lb) (2½ cups) sliced mushrooms
2 medium tomatoes, each cut into 8
225 g (½ lb) canned asparagus tips, drained
100 g (¼ lb) (1 cup) cooked peas
30 ml (2 tablespoons) oil
5 ml (1 teaspoon) white wine vinegar
2.5 ml (½ teaspoon) salt

Avocado Starter makes a fruity and refreshing start to any meal, and it can easily be prepared the previous day

1.25 ml (¼ teaspoon) pickled dill weed
2 hard-boiled eggs

1 Put the prawns, mushrooms, tomatoes, asparagus and peas into a salad bowl.

2 Mix the oil, wine vinegar, salt and dill together and pour over the salad. Cut each egg into 8 pieces and use as garnish.

Serves 4

Ratatouille Salads

Ratatouille means a mixture of vegetables in French. The basic ingredients, aubergines (eggplants) and courgettes (zucchini) are members of the marrow family, but tomatoes, onions and peppers are also traditionally included. For a variation you may add celery, fennel or sliced mushrooms.

It may be served as a hot dish or a cold salad, either on its own or with an assortment of cold meats or fish. Below, we provide a recipe for basic ratatouille. It can be garnished in any number of tasty ways. Try sprinkling it with sliced black olives or gherkins. For a complete meal, blend in cooked green noodles and serve with a crisp green salad. Ratatouille also makes a delicious appetizer when served cold on a hot summer's day.

Ratatouille

2 courgettes (zucchini)
2 aubergines (eggplants)
salt and pepper
2 green peppers
1 red pepper
100 ml (4 fl oz) (½ cup) oil
2 medium onions, chopped
2 cloves garlic, chopped
4 tomatoes, skinned, deseeded
  and chopped
pinch thyme
1 bay leaf
2.5 ml (½ teaspoon) sugar
  (optional)
25 g (1 oz) (4 tablespoons) flour
15 ml (1 tablespoon) vinegar
juice ½ lemon
2.5 ml (½ teaspoon) basil

Ratatouille is a sautéed dish of vegetables from Provence which can be served hot or cold as a starter or salad

1 Cut the courgettes (zucchini) and aubergines (eggplants) into slices, 1.5 cm (¾ in) thick. Sprinkle with salt and leave for 30 minutes. Wash, drain and dry.

2 Split the peppers lengthways. Remove the seeds and cut in thin slices.

3 Heat ½ of the oil in a large pan and sauté the onions for 3 minutes or until tender. Do not allow them to brown.

4 Add the peppers, courgettes (zucchini) and garlic to the pan. Cook for 2 minutes, then add the tomatoes, thyme, bay leaf and sugar (optional). Season and cook for a further 6 minutes.

5 In a separate pan, heat the remaining oil. Coat the aubergine (eggplant) slices in flour. Shake off any excess. If the slices are large, halve or quarter them so that they are equivalent to the courgettes (zucchini) in diameter. Fry for ½ minute on each side or until golden. Remove and drain well.

6 Combine all the vegetables in a casserole dish. Add the vinegar and lemon juice, and mix well. Chill and serve sprinkled with chopped basil.

Serves 6

Ratatouille with Tuna

225 g (½ lb) (1 cup) canned tuna
juice ½ lemon
950 g (2 lb) ratatouille

1 Place the tuna fish in the centre of a shallow serving dish.

2 Pour over the lemon juice and surround the tuna with the ratatouille. Alternatively, you can flake the fish and blend it with the ratatouille.

Serves 6

Ratatouille with Tuna brings a taste of the Mediterranean to your dinner table – try it as a main meal with green salad

Exotic Salads

As exotic vegetables and fruits become more widely available, there is a growing tendency to use them in salads. Citrus fruits such as oranges, lemons and limes, and the more unusual avocados, papaws, pineapples and mangoes are now often mixed with salad vegetables and nuts or cheese in a delicious dressing or flavoured mayonnaise.

Hawaiian Salad

1 lettuce
8 radishes
100 g (¼ lb) (⅔ cup) diced ham
100 g (¼ lb) (¾ cup) diced fresh
  pineapple
1 stick celery, chopped
½ small cucumber, thinly sliced
few sprigs parsley

For the Dressing:
50 ml (2 fl oz) (¼ cup) pineapple
  juice
30 ml (1 fl oz) (2 tablespoons)
  lemon juice
15 ml (1 tablespoon) sugar
50 ml (2 fl oz) (¼ cup) oil
pinch salt
pinch paprika

1 Wash the lettuce and radishes. Separate the lettuce leaves and arrange on a serving dish. Slice downwards through each radish to make a star-shape on top. Place them in iced water until they open out into flowers.

2 Mix together the dressing ingredients and toss the ham, pineapple and celery in the dressing. Pile on top of the lettuce leaves and decorate with cucumber slices, radishes and parsley.

Serves 4

Hawaiian Salad combines the fresh, sharp taste of pineapple with ham and celery in a tangy lemon dressing

Avocado and Cervelas Salad

1 avocado pear, stoned (pitted),
  peeled and thinly sliced
100 g (¼ lb) (⅔ cup) diced cervelas
  or ham sausage
100 g (¼ lb) (1 cup) diced Gruyère
  cheese
2 sticks celery, thinly sliced
100 g (¼ lb) (1 cup) chopped
  walnuts
225 ml (8 fl oz) (1 cup) mayonnaise
15 ml (1 tablespoon) lemon juice
30 ml (1 fl oz) (2 tablespoons)
  apple purée
salt and pepper
15 ml (tablespoon) chopped
  chives
pinch paprika

1 In a bowl, mix together the sliced avocado, cervelas, Gruyère cheese, celery and walnuts. Mix in the mayonnaise, lemon juice and apple purée. Make sure that all the ingredients are coated with the mayonnaise mixture.

2 Season with the salt and pepper.

3 Transfer the salad to a serving

dish and sprinkle with the chopped chives and paprika. Or, alternatively, you can serve it in individual bowls as an appetizer.

Serves 4

Ham and Pineapple Salad

100 g (¼ lb) (⅔ cup) **diced ham**
100 g (¼ lb) (1 cup) **diced cooked potatoes**
100 g (¼ lb) (1 cup) **diced Gruyère cheese**

Ham and Pineapple Salad, mixed with grapes and Gruyere in a fruity mayonnaise, tastes as delicious as it looks

---

100 g (¼ lb) **seedless green grapes, skinned**
100 g (¼ lb) (½ cup) **canned pineapple chunks**
200 ml (6 fl oz) (¾ cup) **mayonnaise**
30 ml (1 fl oz) (2 tablespoons) **pineapple juice**
salt and pepper
30 ml (1 fl oz) (2 tablespoons) **sour cream**
15 g (½ oz) (3 tablespoons) **chopped parsley**

1 Combine together the ham,

cooked potatoes, Gruyère, grapes and pineapple chunks in a bowl.

2 Mix in the mayonnaise and pineapple juice so that all the ingredients are well coated. Season with the salt and pepper and stir in the sour cream.

3 Serve in an attractive dish, sprinkled with the chopped parsley.

Serves 4

Tip: As a delicious variation on this salad, why not try adding some sliced bananas or cashew nuts? You can give it a more spicy flavour by mixing in a pinch of curry powder.

Cheese Salads

Cheese has always been a favourite accompaniment for salads. Its mild but tangy flavour and smooth texture is an excellent complement to crisp, juicy salad vegetables. Mellow, firm English, Dutch and Swiss cheeses can be diced, or cut in strips, to hold their own with crunchy salads. Blue cheeses bring extra flavour to salads and salad dressings. Cream cheese forms an ideal base for mixed salads, or mild dressings that go as well with fruit as with vegetables.

Blue Cheese Salad

1 large lettuce
3 large tomatoes
45 ml (2 fl oz) (3 tablespoons)
  olive oil
15 ml (1 tablespoon) white wine
  vinegar
salt and pepper
100 g (¼ lb) firm blue cheese –
  Danish Blue, Auvergne Blue, or
  Stilton

1 Wash the lettuce thoroughly, separating the leaves and discarding any damaged ones.

2 Wash the tomatoes and cut them into 1 cm (⅜ in) slices.

3 In a bowl or jug, blend the olive oil, vinegar, and a pinch of salt and freshly ground black pepper to taste.

4 Cut the cheese into 2 cm (¾ in) cubes, and mix them into the salad dressing.

5 Arrange the lettuce and tomato in a salad bowl and pour the cheese dressing over them, tossing the salad lightly so that all the pieces are covered in dressing. Serve with crisp French bread.

Serves 4

*Blue Cheese Salad – vinegar,
oil and firm blue cheese
mixed together and poured over a
lettuce and tomato salad*

Blue Cheese Salad Dressing

50 g (2 oz) blue cheese – Danish
  Blue, Roquefort, or Stilton
300 ml (½ pint) (1¼ cups)
  mayonnaise
50 ml (2 fl oz) (¼ cup) double
  (heavy) cream
5 g (1 tablespoon) chopped fresh
  parsley and sage
1 clove garlic, crushed
salt and pepper

1 Crumble the blue cheese into small pieces, and stir them into the mayonnaise and the cream.

2 Add the chopped herbs, garlic and salt and pepper to taste. Place all ingredients in an electric blender and beat until smooth.

3 Serve the Blue Cheese Salad Dressing with a crisp green salad or a potato salad. It may also be poured over hot baked potatoes.

Makes 450 ml (¾ pint) (1⅞ cups)

Tagliatelle Salad

100 g (¼ lb) (1 cup) green
  tagliatelle noodles
1 bunch radishes
4 large tomatoes
12 spring onions (scallions)
50 g (2 oz) Gruyere cheese
½ red pepper, deseeded and diced
30 ml (2 tablespoons) olive oil
15 ml (1 tablespoon) lemon juice
5 ml (1 teaspoon) each chopped
  fresh parsley, chives and basil
pinch garlic salt
salt and pepper

1 Boil the tagliatelle noodles in
salted water until just tender.
Rinse them in cold water, drain
and leave to cool.

2 Clean the radishes and remove
the leaves from all but 6 (for decoration). Clean and quarter the
tomatoes. Wash the spring onions
(scallions) and discard the green
leaves.

3 Cut the Gruyère cheese into
2 cm (¾ in) cubes. Mix the cold
noodles, radishes, spring onions
(scallions) and red pepper.

4 Blend the oil, lemon juice,
herbs, garlic salt, and salt and
pepper to taste. Pour the dressing
over the salad, tossing to ensure
that all the ingredients are evenly
coated.

5 Arrange the tomato quarters
around the salad, decorate with
the leafy radishes, and serve.

Serves 4

Dutch Salad

100 g (¼ lb) Edam or Gouda
  cheese
6 crisp white cabbage leaves
6 crisp red cabbage leaves
2 large carrots
½ green pepper, deseeded
30 ml (2 tablespoons) oil
15 ml (1 tablespoon) vinegar
15 ml (1 tablespoon) chopped
  celery leaves
5 ml (1 teaspoon) cumin seeds
salt and pepper

1 Remove any rind from the
cheese and cut it into matchstick
strips about ½ cm (¼ in) thick and
4 cm (1½ in) long.

2 Cut the white and red cabbage
leaves, carrots and green pepper
into strips of a similar size

3 Blend together the oil, vinegar,
chopped celery leaves, cumin
seeds, and salt and pepper to
taste. Mix all the ingredients
together in a wooden salad bowl
and serve with boiled ham or cold
meats.

Serves 4

*Tagliatelle Salad contains
pasta, cheese and lots
of salad vegetables and so makes
a colourful and filling meal*

Chicken Salads

The use of chicken as an ingredient in a mixed salad is often overlooked. The following recipes show just how tasty this delicate meat can be, blended with various dressings and combined with different salad vegetables.

Chicken Salad New York

1 avocado
100 g (¼ lb) white grapes
1 cos lettuce
1 Webb's or iceberg lettuce
2 sticks celery, diced
175 g (6 oz) (1 cup) thin strips ham, 4 cm (1½ in) long
175 g (6 oz) (1 cup) thin strips cooked chicken, 4 cm (1½ in) long
40 g (1½ oz) Swiss cheese, cut into thin strips

For the Dressing:
75 ml (2½ fl oz) (⅓ cup) oil
30 ml (1 fl oz) (2 tablespoons) vinegar
30 ml (1 fl oz) (2 tablespoons) tomato ketchup (catsup)
10 ml (2 teaspoons) grated onion
5 ml (1 teaspoon) prepared mustard
2.5 ml (½ teaspoon) salt
1.25 ml (¼ teaspoon) sugar
dash Tabasco (chilli) sauce

1 Prepare the dressing. Place all the ingredients in a screw top jar or any watertight container. Cover and shake well. Chill.

2 Peel and halve the avocado. Remove the stone (seed), quarter and slice. Halve the grapes and remove the pips.

3 Wash the lettuce leaves and dry. Tear them into bite-size pieces. Place them in a salad bowl and toss.

4 Arrange the celery, ham, chicken, cheese, avocado and grapes on top of the lettuce.

5 Just before serving toss the salad with the chilled dressing.

Serves 8

Chicken and Cranberry Salad

225 g (½ lb) (1 cup) cranberry jelly
100 ml (4 fl oz) (½ cup) sour cream
100 g (¼ lb) (⅔ cup) cream cheese, softened
2 sticks celery, diced
50 g (2 oz) (½ cup) chopped walnuts
1 green pepper, deseeded and finely chopped
225 g (½ lb) (1⅓ cups) diced cooked chicken
350 g (¾ lb) (1½ cups) canned pineapple pieces, drained

1 Spread the cranberry jelly 1 cm (½ in) thick over the base of a freezing tray. Freeze the jelly for 1 hour or until it has set solid.

2 Blend the sour cream with the cheese. Stir in the celery, walnuts and pepper. Finally fold in the chicken and pineapple pieces, and season to taste. Chill.

3 Cut the frozen cranberry jelly into small cubes and sprinkle them over the salad before serving.

Serves 4

Chicken Tapenade

225 g (½ lb) (1⅓ cups) diced cooked chicken
1 lettuce
100 g (¼ lb) anchovy fillets
8 stuffed green olives

For the Dressing:
2 egg yolks
5 ml (1 teaspoon) made mustard
salt and pepper
150 ml (¼ pint) (⅔ cup) olive oil
juice ½ lemon
30 ml (1 fl oz) (2 tablespoons) double (heavy) cream

1 small onion, chopped
5 ml (1 teaspoon) capers, chopped

1 First, prepare the dressing. Whisk together the egg yolks (make sure there is no white remaining on the yolk), mustard, salt and pepper in a bowl. Slowly blend in the oil a little at a time until you have a thick creamy mixture of even consistency. Stir in the lemon juice and cream and finally the chopped onion and capers.

2 Toss the diced chicken in the dressing and chill for 30 minutes.

3 Break up the lettuce and wash and dry the leaves. Use as many leaves as necessary to line the base and sides of a salad bowl.

4 Spoon in the chicken and mayonnaise mixture. Decorate with the anchovy fillets by lining them criss-cross over the top of the salad and garnish with the olives. Serve.

Serves 4

Peppers Stuffed with Chicken

2 red peppers, deseeded
salt and pepper
30 ml (1 fl oz) (2 tablespoons) plain yogurt
30 ml (1 fl oz) (2 tablespoons) canned corn kernels
225 g (½ lb) (1⅓ cups) diced cooked chicken
few sprigs parsley

1 Halve the peppers and boil them for 5 minutes in salted water. Refresh, dry and allow them to cool.

2 Blend the yogurt with the corn and chicken. Season and spoon into the pepper halves. Garnish with the parsley and serve.

Serves 4

Chicken Tapenade – the chicken is mixed with a creamy dressing and garnished with anchovies and stuffed olives

Mayonnaise Chicken Salad

150 ml (¼ pint) (⅝ cup) chicken
  stock
30 ml (2 tablespoons) powdered
  gelatine
300 ml (½ pint) (1¼ cups)
  mayonnaise
500 g (1 lb) (2⅔ cups) diced cooked
  chicken meat
few lettuce leaves
75 g (3 oz) cooked ox tongue, cut
  in strips
75 g (3 oz) cooked ham, cut in
  strips
50 g (2 oz) canned anchovy fillets,
  drained
4 olives, sliced
1 avocado
juice 1 lemon

1 Place the chicken stock in a
pan and bring just to the boil.
Remove from the heat, add the
gelatine and stir until dissolved.
Leave to cool.

2 When the gelatine mixture is
cool, blend in the mayonnaise. In
a bowl, mix the chicken meat
with ¾ of the mayonnaise.

3 Arrange the lettuce leaves in a
glass salad bowl and place the
chicken and mayonnaise mixture on top. Pour the rest of the
mayonnaise over the top and
smooth the surface with the blade
of a knife.

4 Make a lattice pattern on the
mayonnaise with the strips of
tongue and ham and with the
anchovy fillets. Place olive slices
in the spaces of the lattice. Chill.

5 Just before serving, peel and
slice the avocado and sprinkle
the slices with the lemon juice.
Arrange the avocado around the
edge of the salad and serve
immediately.

Serves 8

Tip: The mayonnaise can be varied by adding a fruit purée, which
will taste delicious with cooked
meat. Apple would be ideal – for
each 225 ml (8 fl oz) (1 cup) of mayonnaise, add 60 ml (4 tablespoons)
of the fruit purée. You could also
use crushed pineapple, or a purée
of blackcurrants or cooked

plums. For a lower-calorie meal,
the mayonnaise could be
replaced by low-fat yogurt, to
which you could again add a fruit
purée.

Chicken and Orange Salad

100 g (¼ lb) (½ cup) long grain rice
1 small onion, chopped
salt and pepper
225 g (½ lb) (1⅓ cups) diced cooked
  chicken
2 sticks celery, diced
½ green pepper, chopped
4 stuffed olives, chopped
100 ml (4 fl oz) (½ cup) mayonnaise
2 oranges
few lettuce leaves

1 Cook the rice in boiling salted
water until tender. Drain and,
while still hot, mix with the onion
and seasoning. Leave to cool.

2 Add the chicken, celery,
pepper, olives and mayonnaise
and toss lightly. Peel the oranges,
split them into segments (sections) and cut half into small
pieces.

3 Add the orange pieces to the
salad and mix well. Chill
thoroughly.

4 To serve, place the salad on a
bed of lettuce and garnish with
the rest of the orange segments
(sections).

Serves 4

Chicken Noodle Salad

225 g (½ lb) cooked chicken meat,
  cut in 1 cm (½ in) cubes
1 small onion, finely chopped
15 ml (1 tablespoon) chopped
  pimento
3 olives, chopped
75 g (3 oz) (¾ cup) walnuts,
  chopped
15 ml (1 tablespoon) chopped
  parsley

juice half lemon
5 ml (1 teaspoon) Worcestershire
  sauce
salt and pepper
100 g (¼ lb) noodles
100 ml (4 fl oz) (½ cup) mayonnaise

1 Combine the chicken, onion,
pimento, olives, walnuts, parsley,
lemon juice, Worcestershire
sauce and seasoning.

2 Cook the noodles in boiling
salted water, drain and rinse in
cold water.

3 Combine the chicken mixture
and the cooked noodles, add the
mayonnaise and toss lightly until
all the ingredients are well mixed.
Chill and serve.

Serves 4

Chicken and Peach Salad

8 fresh or canned peach halves,
  sliced
4 cold roast chicken breasts,
  skinned and diced
few lettuce leaves
5 ml (1 teaspoon) chopped
  parsley

For the Mustard Dressing:
150 ml (¼ pint) (⅝ cup) mayonnaise
2 peach halves, chopped
juice 1 lemon
5 ml (1 teaspoon) made mustard

1 Mix the sliced peaches and
diced chicken in a bowl.

2 Make the dressing: blend the
mayonnaise with the chopped
peaches, lemon juice and mustard. Toss the chicken mixture in
the dressing.

3 Chill the salad for 30 minutes.

4 When ready to serve, arrange
the salad in the centre of a serving
dish on a bed of lettuce leaves.
Decorate the top of the salad with
the chopped parsley.

Serves 4

---

*Chicken and Peach Salad is
a delicious combination
of flavours which is topped with
a tangy mustard dressing*

All about
Garden Vegetables

50

Vegetables have been an integral part of our diets since the beginning of time. In early days, poor people relied on root vegetables to eke out a starvation diet. Every labourer who had access to a plot of land grew what he could: carrots, onions, radishes, parsnips, and other root vegetables in addition to herbs grown for medicinal purposes.

Plants brought back from the 'new world' to Europe enriched the scope for creating more imaginative dishes. It is difficult to think of a time when there were no potatoes, tomatoes, corn cobs or sweet peppers. Even the rich, who ate more meat and fish in a month than any peasant saw in a lifetime, were not immune to the lure of vegetables.

Varieties of vegetables have been bred and brought to near perfection – not least because market gardening has been a profitable industry in Europe since the seventeenth century, and in America and Australasia as soon as trade was established. French cooks have always had a reputation for cooking vegetables well, and often serve them as a separate course. The English, however, are infamous for boiling vegetables until no hint of flavour is left, then demanding that they be eaten up 'because they are good for you'. The reputation is largely undeserved; cooks like Mrs Hannah Glasse, whose book was published in 1747, had excellent recipes for asparagus, broad beans, cucumbers and a 'fricassey of mushrooms'.

We now have access to fresh vegetables all the year round – and good frozen or canned brands. We have become aware of their importance in creating a balanced, healthy diet. Through their alkalis, they help neutralize acids produced by proteins.

A diet rich in animal fats is currently thought to contribute to the high rate of heart disease endemic in the western world, and thus the substitution of vegetables and vegetable oils is recommended by many doctors. Vegetables, in addition to their dietary value, lend complementary flavours to other foods and, with their different colours and textures, can make a meal look as good as it tastes.

Vegetables can be defined according to the way they grow:
Roots and tubers are cultivated in the earth. Potatoes, carrots, turnips, celeriac, beetroot, Jerusalem artichokes and swedes are all in this family. They all have a high carbohydrate value and contain vitamin C.
Fruits include tomatoes, aubergines (eggplants) and peppers, all high in vitamins A, B, C and E and abundant in minerals.
Leaves Lettuce, cabbage, spinach and chicory are just a few. They are rich in vitamin C, iron and calcium.
Legumes Peas, beans and lentils are full of protein and carbohydrates, plus vitamin B complex and iron. Soya beans are now widely accepted as a protein-substitute for meat.
Bulbs include onions and garlic.
Shoots Chives, leeks, celery, asparagus are all shoots.
Flowers Cauliflower and broccoli are in this category.
Fungi Mushrooms and truffles are edible fungi.

As a general rule, buy vegetables of medium size, when they will have developed their flavour and still be tender.

To cook vegetables, clean them well, scrubbing if appropriate. If they can be eaten in their skins, do not peel them because much of their nutrient value lies close to the skin. If you must peel them, do so thinly.

Avoid overcooking vegetables – if possible, steam them. If they are to be boiled or simmered, use very little water, and after cooking add the water to your stock pot. (Try cooking green vegetables in a stock made with ½ a chicken or vegetable stock cube, water and a little butter.)

To keep the colour of green vegetables, before cooking them blanch for 1 minute in a pan of boiling salted water, then plunge them immediately into cold water. *Never* use bicarbonate of soda (baking soda).

Root Vegetables

Carrot Casserole with Mushrooms in Sherry

450 g (1 lb) (8 cups) button mushrooms
50 g (2 oz) (4 tablespoons) butter
1 small onion, chopped
1 kg (2 lb) (8 cups) small carrots, sliced
15 g (½ oz) (1 tablespoon) tomato concentrate (paste)
350 ml (12 fl oz) (1½ cups) water
1 chicken stock cube
150 ml (¼ pint) (⅝ cup) sherry
salt and pepper
pinch each mace and oregano
5 g (1 tablespoon) chives and parsley, chopped

1 Wash the mushrooms and trim the ends of the stalks.

2 Heat the butter and gently sauté the onion for 4 minutes without browning it.

3 Add to the onion, the carrots, tomato concentrate (paste) and water. Bring to the boil and boil for 30 minutes.

4 Crumble the stock cube into the mixture and add the sherry, seasoning, spices and mushrooms. Simmer for 10 minutes.

5 Place in a serving dish and sprinkle with the chopped chives and parsley.

Serves 4

Tips: The mushroom stalks can be trimmed from the raw mushrooms and used for making stuffing (chop them and blend with meat or breadcrumbs), or puréed for mushroom soup.

Carrot Casserole with Mushrooms in Sherry is a delicious accompaniment for roast pork or lamb

The Marrow Family

Stuffed Cucumber Alphonso

1 whole cucumber
salt and pepper
25 g (1 oz) (2 tablespoons) butter
75 g (3 oz) (¾ cup) grated Cheddar
  cheese

For the Rice Stuffing:
50 ml (2 fl oz) (¼ cup) oil
1 onion, chopped
4 mushrooms, chopped
50 g (2 oz) (½ cup) pecan nuts,
  chopped
125 g (5 oz) (⅝ cup) long grain rice
1 clove garlic, peeled and
  crushed
300 ml (½ pint) (1¼ cups) water
1 chicken stock cube
pinch ground (powdered) mace
25 g (1 oz) (2 tablespoons) butter

1 Peel the cucumber and cut into two, lengthways. Scoop out the seeds and cut each side into 2 pieces. Season.

2 Butter a shallow, ovenproof dish and place the cucumber pieces on the dish.

3 Preheat the oven to 200°C, 400°F, gas 6.

4 Prepare the rice stuffing. Heat the oil in a pan and sauté the onions, without colouring, for 4 minutes. Add the mushrooms and pecan nuts, then stir in the rice. Simmer for 2 minutes.

5 Add the garlic and water, then crumble in the stock cube. Cover the pan and boil gently for 15 minutes. Season with salt and pepper and mace, then add the butter. The rice should have absorbed all the liquid.

6 Pile the rice stuffing into the cucumber pieces and sprinkle with the grated cheese. Bake in the oven for 20 minutes.
Serves 4

Aubergines (Eggplants) au Gratin

1 kg (2 lb) aubergines (eggplants)
50 g (2 oz) (¼ cup) salt
2 kg (4 lb) tomatoes
75 ml (5 tablespoons) oil
salt and pepper
2 cloves garlic
1 bunch parsley
oil for deep frying
50 g (2 oz) (½ cup) grated Gruyère
  cheese

1 Peel the aubergines (eggplants). Cut into slices about 1 cm. (½ in) thick. Sprinkle with salt and leave for 20 minutes, wash and dry.

2 Meanwhile, skin the tomatoes and cut into halves. Remove the seeds and chop up the pulp.

3 Heat 60 ml (4 tablespoons) of the oil in a frying pan (skillet). Add the tomatoes. Cook gently for 15 minutes, mashing from time to time with a fork. Season with salt and pepper to taste.

4 Peel and chop the garlic. Wash and chop the parsley. Add the garlic and parsley to the tomato sauce.

5 Heat the deep fat fryer to 185°C, 360°F.

6 Lower the aubergine (eggplant) slices into the hot oil and fry until they are golden-brown. Remove from the oil and drain

7 Preheat the oven to 220°C, 425°F, gas 7.

8 Arrange the slices of aubergine (eggplant) and the tomato sauce in alternate layers in an attractive ovenproof dish, finishing with a layer of tomato sauce. Sprinkle with the Gruyère cheese and trickle the remaining 15 ml (1 tablespoon) of oil on to the top. Brown in the oven for about 10 minutes.
Serves 6

Stuffed Courgettes (Zucchini) with Sausagemeat

4 large firm courgettes
  (zucchini)
sprig parsley
100 g (¼ lb) (½ cup) butter
15 ml (1 tablespoon) milk
75 g (3 oz) (1½ cups) fresh
  breadcrumbs
5 g (1 teaspoon) chopped chives
pinch dried thyme
150 g (5 oz) (½ cup +
  2 tablespoons) sausagemeat

1 Wash and dry the courgettes (zucchini). Cut them in half lengthways and scoop out the insides. Chop the parsley.

2 Using 20 g (¾ oz) (1½ tablespoons) of the butter, grease an ovenproof dish. Arrange the halved courgettes (zucchini) in the dish.

3 Put the milk, 25 g (1 oz) (½ cup) breadcrumbs and 50 g (2 oz) (¼ cup) of the butter in a small pan. Add the parsley, chives and thyme and cook for a few minutes, stirring.

4 Preheat the oven to 220°C, 425°F, gas 7.

5 Remove the pan from the heat and thoroughly mix in the sausagemeat. Fill the courgette (zucchini) shells with stuffing.

6 Sprinkle the remaining fresh breadcrumbs over the courgette (zucchini) halves. Cut the remaining butter into small pieces and dot over the top.

7 Put the dish towards the top of the oven and bake for 25 minutes or until the topping is golden and the courgettes (zucchini) are tender.
Serves 4

Stuffed Cucumber Alphonso – hollowed out cucumbers stuffed with rice and mushrooms, and topped with melted cheese

Beef Casserole with Aubergines (Eggplants) and Chick Peas

¼ kg (½ lb) (1 cup) canned chick
  peas, or half that quantity of
  dried chick peas
1 kg (2 lb) braising or stewing
  beef, eg chuck steak
50 ml (2 fl oz) (¼ cup) oil
5 g (1 teaspoon) paprika
4 cloves garlic, peeled and
  crushed
2 chopped onions
25 g (1 oz) (2 tablespoons) tomato
  concentrate (paste)
1½ litres (2½ pints) (6 cups) water
4 medium aubergines
  (eggplants)
salt and pepper
oil for deep frying

1 If using dried chick peas, soak them overnight in water.

2 Cut the steak into 4 cm (1½ in) chunks. Heat a little oil in a large pan, and brown the meat and the paprika for 5-10 minutes, stirring occasionally.

3 Strain off excess oil. Add the strained chick peas, garlic, onions, tomato concentrate (paste) and water. Bring to the boil, cover and simmer gently for 2-2½ hours.

4 Meanwhile slice the aubergines (eggplants), place on a dish or wooden board and sprinkle liberally with salt. Leave for 30 minutes, then rinse and dry the slices.

5 Heat the oil in a deep fat fryer to 185°C, 360°F . Deep fry the aubergine (eggplant) slices until golden-brown. Drain on absorbent paper.

6 Add the aubergine (eggplant) slices to the beef casserole, and season to taste with salt and pepper. Simmer for another 30 minutes. Serve immediately in a heated serving dish.

Serves 6

Tip: Like many other dishes originating in North Africa and the Middle East, this casserole should contain plenty of richly-flavoured liquid which may be eaten with a spoon, like a soup.

Ratatouille

2 large aubergines (eggplants),
  about 350 g (12 oz)
4 medium courgettes (zucchini)
50 g (2 oz) (good ½ cup) flour
  seasoned with salt
oil for deep frying
50 ml (2 fl oz) (¼ cup) cooking oil
1 onion, chopped
1 clove garlic, chopped
2 green peppers, split, deseeded,
  and cut in strips
4 tomatoes, skinned, deseeded
  and chopped
25 g (1 oz) (2 tablespoons) tomato
  concentrate (paste)
1 sprig mint leaves
pinch oregano or basil
salt and pepper

1 Peel the aubergines (eggplants) and cut slantwise in 1 cm (½ in) slices. Slice the courgettes (zucchini) slantwise. Put the aubergine (eggplant) and courgette (zucchini) slices on a dish or board, sprinkle with salt and let them stand for 30 minutes.

2 Rinse, drain and dry the slices. Dredge in the seasoned flour. Heat the deep fryer to 190°C, 375°F and fry the aubergine (eggplant) and courgette (zucchini) slices for 1 minute.

3 Drain and dry the fried slices and place in a casserole dish.

4 In a sauté pan, heat the oil. Fry the onion gently for 2 minutes. Add the garlic and green pepper, and fry for 2 minutes, stirring frequently.

5 Preheat the oven to 180°C, 350°F, gas 4.

6 Add the chopped tomatoes, tomato concentrate (paste), mint, oregano or basil, and a pinch of salt and pepper to taste. Cover and simmer gently for 10 minutes.

7 Pour this mixture over the aubergines (eggplants) and courgettes (zucchini) in the casserole dish. Mix them together lightly and bake in the oven for 20-30 minutes. Serve hot or cold.

Serves 6

Aubergine (Eggplant) and Mushroom Quiche

1 large aubergine (eggplant),
  about 275 g (10 oz)
175 g (6 oz) frozen shortcrust
  pastry, thawed
2 eggs
300 ml (½ pint) (1¼ cups) milk
75 g (3 oz) (¾ cup) grated cheese
salt and pepper
100 g (¼ lb) small mushrooms
  (or 2 tomatoes, sliced)

1 Preheat the oven to 200°C, 400°F, gas 6.

2 Bake the aubergine (eggplant) in its skin for 20 minutes.

3 Meanwhile roll out the pastry and use it to line an 18 cm (7 in) flan case. Cover pastry with foil or greaseproof (waxed) paper, scatter in dried beans or bread crusts to weight the pastry down, and bake in the same oven for 15 minutes. Remove the paper and beans or crusts. Reduce the oven temperature to 180°C, 350°F, gas 4.

4 Scoop the pulp out of the baked aubergine (eggplant) skin, crush or liquidize to a purée, and spoon into the pastry shell.

5 Beat the eggs lightly and mix in the milk. Add the grated cheese, salt and pepper. Pour the mixture into the pastry shell. Arrange the mushrooms (or tomatoes) on top.

6 Bake for 30 minutes, until the top is golden-brown. Serve hot or cold.

Serves 4

---

*Aubergine (Eggplant) and
Mushroom Quiche is easy
to prepare and makes a
tasty supper snack or
buffet dish*

Peppers & Tomatoes

Vegetable Casserole with Caraway Scones

50 ml (2 fl oz) (¼ cup) oil
1 onion, chopped
1 green pepper, deseeded and cut in strips
1 red pepper, deseeded and cut in strips
1 carrot, sliced
salt and pepper
150 ml (¼ pint) (⅝ cup) dry white wine
150 ml (¼ pint) (⅝ cup) water
15 ml (1 tablespoon) soya sauce

For the Caraway Scones:
225 g (½ lb) (2¼ cups) plain flour
5 g (1 teaspoon) baking powder
50 g (2 oz) (4 tablespoons) margarine
7 g (¼ oz) (1½ teaspoons) caraway seeds
150 ml (¼ pint) (⅝ cup) milk

1 Heat the oil in a pan, add the onion and cook for 5 minutes until soft. Add the peppers and carrots, stir well and season.

2 Add the wine, water and soya sauce, mix and cook, covered, for 20 minutes or until the carrots are tender. Check the seasoning.

3 Place the mixture in a shallow dish and keep warm.

4 Make the caraway scones: preheat the oven to 200°C, 400°F, gas 6.

5 Sift the flour and baking powder into a bowl, add a pinch of salt and rub in the margarine. Add the caraway seeds and enough milk to make a stiff dough. Roll out the dough to 5 mm (¼ in) thickness and cut into rounds.

6 Place the rounds on a greased baking (cookie) sheet and brush the tops with a little cold milk. Bake in the preheated oven for 15 minutes.

7 Arrange the cooked scones around the vegetable casserole and serve.

Serves 4

Vegetable Casserole with Caraway Scones – an economical casserole with a delicious scone topping

Vegetable Curry

450 g (1 lb) new potatoes, peeled
500 ml (1 pint) (2½ cups) water
50 g (2 oz) (4 tablespoons)
  margarine
50 ml (2 fl oz) (¼ cup) oil
2 onions, chopped
25 g (1 oz) (2 tablespoons) curry
  powder
pinch paprika
1 red pepper, deseeded and
  diced
1 green pepper, deseeded and
  diced
4 courgettes (zuccini), sliced
4 tomatoes, quartered
1 clove garlic, crushed
5 g (1 tablespoon) desiccated
  coconut
15 g (½ oz) (2 tablespoons) flour
1 chicken stock cube
15 g (½ oz) (1 tablespoon) tomato
  concentrate (paste)
50 g (2 oz) (⅓ cup) sultanas
salt and pepper

1 Put the potatoes and water in a pan, add a little salt, and boil for 20 minutes. Strain the liquid into a bowl and reserve.

2 Heat the margarine and oil together in a pan, add the onion and cook for 5 minutes until brown.

3 Add the curry powder and paprika and cook for 2 minutes. Add the peppers, courgettes (zucchini), tomatoes, garlic coconut, flour, stock cube, tomato concentrate(paste) and sultanas and cook gently for 10 minutes. Add the potatoes and cook for a further 10 minutes to heat the potatoes through. Check the seasoning and serve the curry with boiled rice and salted peanuts.

Serves 6

Stuffed Peppers with Pine Kernels

75 ml (5 tablespoons) oil
2 onions, chopped

Vegetable Curry is a delicious mixture of tomatoes, peppers, potatoes and courgettes (zucchini) in a curry sauce

2 tomatoes, skinned, deseeded
  and chopped
150 g (5 oz) (⅝ cup) long grain rice
5 g (1 tablespoon) chopped
  parsley
15 g (½ oz) (1 tablespoon) raisins
15 g (½ oz) (1 tablespoon) pine
  kernels
¾ litre (1¼ pints) (3 cups) boiling
  water
salt and pepper
4 large green or red peppers
15 g (½ oz) (3 tablespoons) dried
  white breadcrumbs

1 Heat 45 ml (3 tablespoons) of the oil in a saucepan. Fry the onions until softened. Add the tomato pulp and leave to cook over a low heat.

2 Add the rice, parsley, raisins

and pine kernels to the tomato mixture and stir well. Cook, stirring, for 2 minutes. Pour in the boiling water and add salt and pepper to taste. Cover the saucepan and simmer for 15 minutes over a low heat. All the water should be absorbed.

3 Preheat the oven to 220°C, 425°F, gas 7.

4 Wash and dry the peppers. Cut out a little lid at the stalk end. Remove the white pith and seeds through the hole. Salt and pepper the insides.

5 Fill the peppers with the rice mixture. Place them in a baking dish. Replace the lids. Sprinkle the peppers with breadcrumbs and then with the rest of the oil. Put the dish in the oven and cook for 15 minutes. Serve hot or cold.

Serves 4

French Beans Old Style

50 g (2 oz) (4 tablespoons) butter
100 g (¼ lb) unsmoked rashers
  (slices) bacon, cut into strips
12 button (pearl) onions, peeled
12 young carrots, peeled
1 kg (2 lb) French beans, washed
600 ml (1 pint) (2½ cups) water
1 bouquet garni
salt and pepper
pinch sugar
1 chicken stock cube
50 ml (2 fl oz) (¼ cup) single (light)
  cream

1 Heat the butter in a pan and sauté the bacon for 2 minutes. Add the onions and lightly brown them. Add the carrots and simmer for 3 minutes.

2 Add the French beans and cover with the water. Bring to the boil and crumble in a stock cube. Add the bouquet garni, salt, pepper and sugar. Cook for 20 minutes until the vegetables are tender and the liquid has almost evaporated. Remove the bouquet garni.

3 Stir in the cream, check the seasoning and serve.

Serves 4

Tip: If you boil the French beans separately in salted water and add them to the other ingredients at the last minute, they will retain their green colouring. However, although this method improves the appearance of the dish there may be a loss of flavour in the beans.

French Bean Fritters

1 kg (2 lb) French beans
50 g (2 oz) (good ½ cup) seasoned
  flour
2 eggs, beaten
oil for deep frying
pinch salt

1 Top, tail and wash the beans. Boil in salted water for 12 minutes and drain.

2 Dredge the beans in seasoned flour and then dip in beaten egg.

3 Heat the deep fat fryer to 190°C, 375°F. Fry the beans until golden-brown.

4 Drain on absorbent paper, sprinkle with salt and serve.

Serves 6

French Beans with Ham, Mushrooms and Tomatoes

1 kg (2 lb) French beans
50 g (2 oz) (4 tablespoons) butter
100 g (¼ lb) ham, cut into strips
100 g (¼ lb) (1¼ cups) mushrooms,
  sliced
4 tomatoes, skinned, deseeded
  and chopped
salt and pepper
pinch garlic salt

1 Top and tail and wash the beans. Boil them in salted water for 20 minutes and drain.

2 Heat the butter in a sauté pan. Sauté the ham and mushrooms for 5 minutes. Add the beans and tomatoes, salt, pepper and garlic salt.

3 Simmer for 6 minutes, stirring occasionally and then serve.

Serves 6

Peas Westminster

2 mint leaves
25 g (1 oz) (2 tablespoons) brown
  sugar
450 g (1 lb) (4 cups) peas
50 g (2 oz) (4 tablespoons) butter
salt and pepper

1 Chop the mint leaves and mix

them with the brown sugar.

2 Add the peas to boiling salted water and parboil for 5 minutes. Refresh in cold water. Drain.

3 Heat the butter in a pan, add the peas, chopped mint and seasoning and toss for a few minutes until heated through. Serve.

Serves 4

Petits Pois à la Sevigné

50 g (2 oz) (4 tablespoons) butter
150 g (5 oz) (1¼ cups) button (pearl)
  onions
150 g (5 oz) (2½ cups) button
  mushrooms
450 g (1 lb) (4 cups) small peas
salt and pepper
pinch caraway seeds
15 g (½ oz) (1½ teaspoons) sugar
100 ml (4 fl oz) (½ cup) dry white
  wine
50 ml (2 fl oz) (¼ cup) single (light)
  cream

1 Heat the butter in a pan, add the onions and cook, covered, for 5 minutes without browning. Add the mushrooms and cook for 1 minute more.

2 Add the peas to boiling salted water and parboil for 5 minutes. Drain and add to the onions. Season and add the caraway seeds, sugar and wine. Boil gently for 8 minutes, then stir in the cream. Boil for 4 minutes. Serve, decorated with fried croutons.

Serves 4

Peas Bonne Femme

100 g (¼ lb) (½ cup) button (pearl)
  onions
450 g (1 lb) (4 cups) peas
100 g (¼ lb) lean rashers (slices)

bacon, cut into thin strips
300 ml (½ pint) (1¼ cups) water
1 chicken stock cube
1 bouquet garni
salt and pepper
25 g (1 oz) (2 tablespoons) butter
25 g (1 oz) (4 tablespoons) flour

1 Parboil the button (pearl) onions for 5 minutes and drain.

2 Place the peas, onions and bacon in a pan, cover with water and sprinkle in the stock cube. Add the bouquet garni, season with salt and pepper and cook for 20 minutes with the lid on.

3 Cream together the butter and flour and add to the peas, a little at a time. Stir over a low heat until the sauce thickens.

Remove the bouquet garni and serve.

Serves 6

Petits Pois à la Française

450 g (1 lb) (4 cups) small peas
225 g (½ lb) (2 cups) button (pearl) onions, peeled
50 g (2 oz) (½ cup) shredded lettuce leaves
salt and pepper
15 g (½ oz) (1½ teaspoons) sugar
300 ml (½ pint) (1¼ cups) water or stock

French Beans Old Style – beans, French onions, baby carrots and bacon served in a creamy sauce

15 g (½ oz) (2 tablespoons) flour
25 g (1 oz) (2 tablespoons) butter

1 Place the peas in a pan, add the onions, lettuce, salt, pepper and sugar. Add the water or stock and cook gently for 10-15 minutes. Strain, reserving the liquid. Keep the peas warm.

2 Pour the liquid into a pan. Blend the flour and butter together and add this mixture to the liquid. Cook until thickened and add to the peas. Mix well and serve.

Serves 4

Cabbage & Spinach

Bubble and Squeak (Colcannon)

½ medium cabbage
40 g (1½ oz) (3 tablespoons) butter
  or bacon fat
1 small onion, finely chopped
leftover mashed potato
  equal to the amount of
  cabbage

1 Bring a saucepan of water to the boil.

2 Remove the core and any damaged leaves from the cabbage. Shred the cabbage.

3 Put the cabbage into the water and cook for 6-7 minutes. Drain well.

4 Heat the butter or bacon fat in a large frying pan (skillet). Fry the onion gently until softened. Add the cabbage and stir over a low heat for 2 minutes.

5 Fold in the mashed potato until it is completely mixed with the cabbage. Press the mixture lightly into the frying pan (skillet) to form a large pancake (crêpe).

6 Cook for 5 minutes or until the underside is lightly browned. Turn and brown on the other side for 5 minutes. Serve very hot.

Serves 4

Tip: The easiest way to turn Bubble and Squeak is to put a plate over it and invert the pan and the plate together so it falls out onto the plate with the browned side uppermost. Then slide it back into the pan.

This is an excellent way of using up leftover cooked cabbage and mashed potatoes.

Spring Green Cabbage and Celery Royal

900 g (2 lb) spring green cabbage
50 g (2 oz) (4 tablespoons) butter
4 celery sticks, sliced
salt and pepper
pinch nutmeg
100 g (¼ lb) (¾ cup) salted peanuts

1 Discard the core of the cabbage and slice the leaves. Boil the cabbage in salted water for 10 minutes. Drain.

2 Heat the butter in a pan, add the cabbage and celery and cook for 5 minutes. Season with salt, pepper and nutmeg. Serve sprinkled with the salted peanuts.

Serves 4

Tip: To make this into a main dish, add 100 g (¼ lb) (⅔ cup) ham, cut in strips, to the cooked cabbage and cook for a few minutes until the ham is heated through.

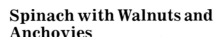

Spinach with Walnuts and Anchovies

900 g (2 lb) frozen leaf spinach,
  thawed
4 canned anchovy fillets,
  drained
100 g (¼ lb) (½ cup) butter
100 g (¼ lb) (1 cup) shelled walnuts
salt and pepper
pinch mace
50 g (2 oz) (⅓ cup) grated
  Parmesan cheese

1 Squeeze any moisture from the spinach and chop. Chop the anchovy fillets.

2 Heat the butter in a pan, add the spinach and cook, covered, for 10 minutes. Add the walnuts. Season with salt, pepper and mace and simmer for a further 5 minutes.

3 Transfer the mixture to a shallow dish, sprinkle with the cheese

and brown under the grill (broiler) for 3-4 minutes.

Serves 4

Tip: Adding nuts to vegetables increases the protein content of the dish. Any nuts can be used such as pecan nuts, peanuts, almonds and hazel nuts.

Sprouts and Swede with Chestnuts

450 g (1 lb) swede, peeled and cut
  in cubes
450 g (1 lb) (6 cups) brussels
  sprouts, trimmed
350 g (¾ lb) (3 cups) chestnuts,
  canned or fresh and skinned
100 g (¼ lb) (½ cup) butter
1 onion, chopped
1 small red pepper, deseeded and
  chopped
2 sticks celery, diced
salt and pepper
pinch grated nutmeg

1 Boil the swede, sprouts, and chestnuts separately in salted water for 5 minutes, 8 minutes and 10 minutes respectively. Drain.

2 Heat the butter in a pan, add the onion and cook for 4 minutes without browning. Add the swede, sprouts, chestnuts, pepper and celery, cover and simmer gently for 8 minutes. Season with salt, pepper and nutmeg and serve.

Serves 6

Tip: To give the sprouts a good colour, refresh them in iced water after they have been boiled and drained.

Stem Vegetables

Hungarian Asparagus with Yogurt

1 kg (2 lb) (about 28 spears)
  asparagus
100 g ($\frac{1}{4}$ lb) (1 cup) very dry bread
75 g (3 oz) (6 tablespoons) butter
2 cartons plain yogurt
100 ml (4 fl oz) ($\frac{1}{2}$ cup) single
  (light) cream
5 g (1 teaspoon) paprika
salt and pepper

1 Bring a pan of salted water to
the boil.

2 Peel the asparagus and tie in
bundles. Plunge them in the boiling water, tips uppermost, and
simmer for 20 minutes.

3 In the meantime, cut off and
discard the crust of the dry bread
and make into very fine crumbs
in a blender or with a rolling pin.

4 Melt the butter in a sauté pan.
When it begins to brown, add the
breadcrumbs and cook till gold-
en brown, stirring with a wooden
spoon.

5 Preheat the oven to 220°C,
425°F, gas 7.

6 Sprinkle about half the breadcrumbs in the bottom of an
ovenproof dish.

7 Drain the bundles of asparagus, untie the strings and arrange
in the dish. Beat the yogurt, the
cream and the paprika together
and salt lightly but season liberally with pepper. Pour over the
asparagus and cover with the
rest of the breadcrumbs.

8 Brown in the oven for 10-12
minutes.

9 Remove from the oven and
serve very hot in the same dish.

Serves 4

Asparagus with Cheese and Ham Sauce

1$\frac{1}{2}$ kg (3 lb) very tender asparagus
  spears
6 eggs
50 g (2 oz) ($\frac{1}{2}$ cup) Gruyère cheese,
  grated
20 g ($\frac{3}{4}$ oz) (1$\frac{1}{2}$ tablespoons) butter

*Hungarian Asparagus with
Yogurt – the asparagus spears
are baked in yogurt, topped with
breadcrumbs and seasoned with
paprika*

For the Sauce:
3 slices cooked ham
50 g (2 oz) ($\frac{1}{4}$ cup) butter
50 g (2 oz) ($\frac{1}{2}$ cup) flour
$\frac{1}{4}$ litre (8 fl oz) (1 cup) milk
60 ml (2 fl oz) (4 tablespoons)
  single (light) cream
salt and pepper
pinch grated nutmeg

1 Bring a saucepan of salted
water to the boil.

2 Scrape the asparagus spears,
or peel them if necessary. Trim
them all to the same length and
tie into several bundles to make
it easier to remove them from
the water. Put them into the

boiling water, keeping the tips above the water level, cook for 10-15 minutes or until tender.

3 Meanwhile, hard-boil (hardcook) the eggs. Drain the eggs and cool in cold water. Remove the shells and slice the eggs.

4 Chop the ham for the sauce roughly.

5 Make a white sauce with the butter, flour, milk and ¼ litre (8 fl oz) (1 cup) of the cooking liquid from the asparagus.

6 Stir in the cream and season with salt, pepper and a pinch of grated nutmeg.

7 Mix in the chopped ham.

8 Spread a few spoonfuls of the sauce on the bottom of a rectangular or oval ovenproof dish.

9 Preheat the oven to 220°C, 425°F, gas 7.

10 Drain the asparagus and untie the strings. Arrange a layer of asparagus in the ovenproof dish. Cover with slices of egg and then with a few spoonfuls of sauce. Repeat until all the ingredients are used up.

11 Sprinkle the top of the dish with the grated Gruyère cheese.

12 Melt the 20 g (¾ oz) (1½ tablespoons) butter and pour over the cheese. Cook in the oven until the cheese is beginning to brown (about 10 minutes).

13 Serve very hot in the same dish.

Serves 6

Asparagus au Gratin

1 kg (2 lb) thick asparagus spears
4 tomatoes
50 g (2 oz) (½ cup) grated cheese
5 g (1 tablespoon) chopped
 parsley
salt and pepper
50 g (2 oz) (4 tablespoons) butter

1 Wash the asparagus. Trim any tough parts from the thick end of the stalks, and scrape the stems lightly with a potato peeler. Tie in bundles of about 8 stalks, and boil for 15 minutes in salted water.

2 Preheat the oven to 200°C, 400°F, gas 6.

3 Drain the asparagus and arrange the spears in rows in a lightly greased, ovenproof dish.

4 Slice the tomatoes, and lay the slices in overlapping rows between the asparagus heads. Sprinkle with the grated cheese and chopped parsley. Season with the salt and pepper, and bake in the oven for 10 minutes. Melt the butter and pour over the dish before serving.

Serves 4

Tip: The inedible, tough ends of asparagus stalks, together with the cooking water, can be used to make a delicious soup. Just blend with an equal quantity of white sauce and a little chopped ham. Liquidize the mixture to a purée and season to taste.

Asparagus au Gratin – the asparagus is baked in the oven with sliced tomatoes and grated cheese

Braised Onions with Sultanas (Raisins)

½ kg (1 lb) small onions,
  all about the same size
300 ml (½ pint) (1¼ cups) water
225 ml (8 fl oz) (1 cup) white
  wine vinegar
45 ml (3 tablespoons) olive oil
4 tomatoes, skinned
salt and freshly ground (milled)
  pepper

50 g (2 oz) (⅓ cup) sultanas
  (raisins)
1 bouquet garni
2 pinches sugar

1 Peel the onions, without cutting off the root ends. Put the onions into a pan with the water and vinegar. Stir in the olive oil. Bring to the boil and simmer gently.

Braised Onions with Sultanas (Raisins) – the onions are braised in a tangy tomato and vinegar sauce

2 Slice the tomatoes thinly. Add to the onions with a pinch of salt and pepper.

3 Add the sultanas (raisins), bouquet garni and sugar.

4 Return to the boil. Reduce the heat. Cover and cook slowly for about 30 minutes, stirring occasionally.

5 Remove from the heat and leave to cool. Chill for at least 2 hours.

6 Before serving, remove the bouquet garni.

Serves 4

Braised Onions in Vermouth

60 very small onions
juice 4 lemons
50 ml (2 fl oz) (¼ cup) dry
  vermouth
30 ml (2 tablespoons) olive oil
25 g (1 oz) (2 tablespoons) tomato
  concentrate (paste)
30 coriander seeds
1 g (½ teaspoon) fennel seeds
1 g (½ teaspoon) dried (powdered)
  rosemary
pinch sugar
salt and pepper

1 Peel the onions, without cutting off the root ends.

2 Put the lemon juice into a saucepan with the vermouth, olive oil and tomato concentrate (paste). Stir well.

3 Bring the vermouth mixture to the boil. Add the coriander seeds, fennel, rosemary, sugar and season with salt and pepper.

4 Reduce the heat and cook for a further 3 minutes. Add the onions, cover and simmer for about 25 minutes or until very tender.

5 Arrange the onions in a serving dish. Pour over a little of the liquid in which they were cooked.

6 Leave to cool completely, then chill in the refrigerator. Serve very cold.

Serves 6

Stuffed Onions

  ☆ ⌛

6 large Spanish onions
225 g (½ lb) (1 cup) pork
  sausagemeat
1 egg
50 ml (2 fl oz) (¼ cup) milk
5 g (1 tablespoon) chopped
  parsley
salt and pepper
50 g (2 oz) (1 cup) breadcrumbs
100 ml (4 fl oz) (½ cup) oil

1 Peel the onions. Cut off one third at their tips ends, leaving the two thirds of the stem end. Boil them in salted water for 15 minutes, then drain.

2 Preheat the oven to 180°C, 350°F, gas 4.

3 Squeeze out the centre of each onion, leaving the outer layers to form a case. Chop the squeezed-out onion, put it in a bowl and blend well with the sausagemeat, egg, milk and parsley.

4 Fill each onion case with the sausagemeat mixture. Place the onions in a shallow dish, sprinkle with breadcrumbs and pour a little oil over each.

5 Bake in the oven for 45 minutes. Serve with a tomato sauce.

Serves 6

Tip: Sweet and Sour Onions make an excellent accompaniment to boiled beef or gammon. Cook peeled button (pearl) onions in a mixture of water, vinegar and sugar in the proportions of 2:1:1,

Onions in Cream Sauce

sea salt
18 medium onions
75 g (3 oz) (6 tablespoons) butter
25 g (1 oz) (1 tablespoon) sugar
100 ml (4 fl oz) (½ cup) dry white
  wine
200 ml (7 fl oz) (⅞ cup) double
  (heavy) cream

salt and freshly ground (milled)
  pepper
pinch ground (powdered) ginger
few sprigs chervil, chopped

1 Bring a large pan of water to the boil. Add a handful of sea salt.

2 Peel the onions, without cutting off the root end. Drop them into the boiling water and simmer until they begin to soften. Drain.

3 Melt the butter in a heavy-based saucepan. Add the onions. Sprinkle them with the sugar and let them caramelize, turning gently with a wooden spoon without breaking them.

4 When the onions are well and evenly browned, pour them into a heated serving dish and keep hot.

Stuffed Onions are filled with sausagemeat and parsley, topped with breadcrumbs and baked until crispy

5 Pour the wine into the saucepan. Stir quickly to mix with the caramelized juices. Stir in the cream and let the sauce thicken over a low heat, stirring constantly.

6 Season to taste with salt and pepper and the ground (powdered) ginger. Pour this sauce over the onions.

7 Sprinkle the onions with the chopped chervil and serve very hot.

Serves 6

Braised Sliced Carrots

450 g (1 lb) (4 cups) old carrots,
  peeled and sliced
50 g (2 oz) (4 tablespoons) butter
1 onion, chopped
500 ml (1 pint) (2½ cups) water
salt and pepper
pinch sugar
pinch bicarbonate of soda

1 Place the carrots in a pan with the butter and onion and sauté gently for 5 minutes with the lid on.

2 Pour in the water and add the seasoning, sugar and bicarbonate of soda. Bring to the boil and simmer gently, uncovered, for about 35 minutes or until the carrots are tender and the liquid has almost evaporated.

Serves 4

Tip: A rasher (slice) of bacon cooked with the carrots gives them a delicious meaty flavour.

In France, this dish is cooked in Vichy water because it contains the natural minerals which enrich and tenderize the carrots.

The bicarbonate of soda can be omitted if the carrots are young and fresh.

Baked Turnip au Gratin

50 g (2 oz) (4 tablespoons) butter
450 g (1 lb) (3 cups) peeled and
  sliced small white turnips
1 onion, chopped
225 g (½ lb) (2 cups) chopped
  mushrooms
1 clove garlic, chopped
150 ml (¼ pint) (⅝ cup) natural
  yogurt
salt and pepper
25 g (1 oz) (½ cup) fresh white
  breadcrumbs

1 Preheat the oven to 200°C, 400°F, gas 6.

2 Heat the butter in a frying pan (skillet), add the turnips, onion, mushrooms and garlic and fry gently for 4 minutes.

3 Stir in the yogurt and seasoning. Transfer the mixture to a small shallow ovenproof dish and sprinkle over the breadcrumbs. Bake in the preheated oven for 15 minutes.

Serves 4

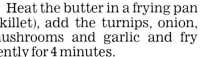

Baked Parsnips with Radishes in Cream Sauce

6 large parsnips, peeled and cut
  in strips
50 g (2 oz) (4 tablespoons) butter
  or margarine
25 g (1 oz) (4 tablespoons) flour
500 ml (1 pint) (2½ cups) milk
salt and pepper
60 ml (2¼ fl oz) (4 tablespoons)
  single (light) cream
2 egg yolks
juice 1 lemon

For the Garnish:
6 radishes, diced
5 g (1 tablespoon) chopped
  parsley and chervil
5 g (1 tablespoon) chopped
  chives

1 Preheat the oven to 180°C, 350°F, gas 4. Boil the parsnips in salted water for 15 minutes. Drain.

2 Heat the fat in a pan and sauté the parsnips for 5 minutes then transfer them to a shallow ovenproof dish.

3 Add the flour to the fat left in the pan and cook for 1 minute. Blend in the milk to produce a smooth white sauce. Simmer the sauce for 10 minutes and season with salt and pepper.

4 Remove the pan from the heat and beat in the cream and egg yolks. Pour the sauce over the parsnips and bake in the preheated oven for 15 minutes.

5 Remove the dish from the oven and sprinkle the lemon juice over the parsnips. Garnish with the radishes and herbs and serve.

Serves 6

Tip: Enrich the flavour of this dish by including a little garlic, and for a touch of colour, add 2 tomatoes, skinned, deseeded and chopped.

Braised Parsnips with Chopped Eggs and Tomatoes

450 g (1 lb) (4 cups) peeled and
  sliced parsnips
50 g (2 oz) (4 tablespoons) butter
1 medium onion, chopped
1 clove garlic, chopped
2 tomatoes, skinned, deseeded
  and chopped
salt and pepper
2 hard-boiled (hard-cooked)
  eggs, chopped
5 g (1 tablespoon) chopped
  parsley

1 Preheat the oven to 200°C, 400°F, gas 6. Boil the parsnips in salted water for 15 minutes only. Drain.

2 In a sauté pan, heat the butter and fry the onion and garlic for 4 minutes until tender but not coloured. Add the tomatoes, parsnips and seasoning.

3 Transfer the mixture to a shallow ovenproof dish and bake in the preheated oven for 20 minutes. Serve sprinkled with the chopped egg and parsley.

Serves 4

Tip: For a more nutritious dish, add 125 g (5 oz) (1 cup) to the chopped eggs, and sprinkle with a little grated cheese.

*Baked Parsnips with Radishes
in Cream Sauce – an attractive
and easy dish to prepare*

Stuffed Cabbage Provençale

1 kg (2 lb) cabbage
25 g (1 oz) (½ cup) fresh
  breadcrumbs
¼ litre (8 fl oz) (1 cup) milk
225 g (½ lb) salt pork, blanched
  and finely chopped
100 g (¼ lb) lean belly pork, finely
  chopped
100 g (¼ lb) lean veal, finely
  chopped
2 medium onions, chopped
2 cloves garlic, peeled and
  crushed
2 sprigs parsley, chopped
30 ml (2 tablespoons) oil
1 egg yolk
25 g (1 oz) (2 tablespoons) tomato
  concentrate (paste)
25 g (1 oz) (2 tablespoons) butter

For the Tomato Sauce:
30 ml (2 tablespoons) oil
675 g (1½ lb) tomatoes, skinned,
  deseeded and chopped
1 onion, chopped
2 cloves garlic, peeled and
  crushed
1 carrot, sliced
pinch dried thyme
1 bay leaf, imported
5 g (1 tablespoon) chopped
  parsley
salt and pepper

1 Remove the outer cabbage leaves and cut into wide strips. Keep the heart intact.

2 Add the cabbage strips to a pan of boiling water and simmer for 10 minutes. Drain and dry.

3 Prepare the sauce. Heat the oil and add the tomatoes, onion, garlic, carrot, thyme, bay leaf and parsley. Season and cook gently, stirring occasionally, for 5 minutes. Increase the heat and cook until the liquid has evaporated.

4 Strain and set aside.

5 Soak the breadcrumbs in the milk. Finely chop the cabbage heart and mix with the salt pork, belly pork, veal, onions, garlic and parsley and season to taste.

6 Heat the oil in a frying pan. Fry the mixture for a few minutes, remove from the heat.

7 Add the egg yolk and the tomato concentrate (paste) and mix well.

8 Divide the stuffing between the cabbage strips and roll up to make small parcels. Tie with string.

9 Heat the butter in a pan and fry the cabbage parcels until golden-brown.

10 Coat with the tomato sauce, cover and simmer for 20 minutes.

Stuffed Cabbage Provençale – cabbage parcels with a meaty stuffing served in a piquant, tomato sauce

11 Arrange on a serving dish.

Serves 4

Cabbage and Bacon Hotpot

1 kg (2 lb) unsmoked gammon
  joint
450 g (1 lb) lean, salted belly pork
1½ litres (2½ pints) (6 cups) water
1 kg (2 lb) cabbage, washed and
  quartered
4 celery sticks, halved
4 leeks, cleaned and halved
3 onions, peeled and studded
  with cloves
4 carrots, peeled and quartered
4 small turnips, quartered
1 bouquet garni
3 cloves garlic, peeled and
  crushed
salt and pepper
2 beef stock cubes
450 g (½ lb) beef sausages

1 Soak the gammon and belly pork in water overnight and drain.

2 Cover the meat with the water and bring to the boil, then simmer for 1½ hours, removing the surface scum.

3 Add the cabbage, celery, leeks, onions, carrots, turnips, bouquet garni and garlic. Season and crumble in the stock cubes. Bring to the boil, then simmer for 20 minutes until tender.

4 Meanwhile, grill (broil) the beef sausages for 20 minutes, slice thickly and keep warm.

5 Add the cabbage to the hotpot and cook for a further 15 minutes. Strain off the liquid and place the vegetables on a serving dish.

6 Remove the cooked meat and cut into thick slices. Arrange the meat and sausages on top of the vegetables and serve.

Serves 8

Cabbage and Bacon Hotpot is a hearty meal of vegetables, gammon and sausages for all the family

Cauliflower & Broccoli

Broccoli with Red Pepper

1 kg (2 lb) broccoli
2 sticks celery
50 g (2 oz) (¼ cup) butter
1 small red pepper, deseeded and
  chopped
30 ml (2 tablespoons) lemon juice
salt and black pepper

1 Wash and trim the broccoli, discarding any slightly wilted leaves. Drain. Bring a pan of salted water to the boil. Put in the broccoli and simmer for 10-15 minutes or until tender.

2 Meanwhile, wash, drain and chop the celery. Melt the butter in a small pan. Cook for 1 minute.

3 Add the chopped pepper to the celery with the lemon juice, salt and pepper.

4 Drain the broccoli very well. Put into a heated serving dish. Pour the contents of the small pan over the broccoli and serve.

Serves 4

Broccoli Siciliana

450 g (1 lb) broccoli
1 onion, chopped
50 ml (2 fl oz) (¼ cup) oil
2 anchovy fillets, diced
150 ml (¼ pint) (⅔ cup) white wine
salt and pepper
4 black olives, stoned (pitted)

1 Preheat the oven to 180°C, 350°F, gas 4. Wash the broccoli and trim surplus stalks.

2 Boil the broccoli in salted

water for 10 minutes, then drain. Place in a casserole.

3 Gently fry the onion in the oil without browning and when it is tender, add the anchovies and cook for a further 2 minutes.

4 Pour the onion mixture over the broccoli. Cover with white wine and season to taste.

5 Bake, with the lid on, for 20 minutes.

6 Garnish with the olives.

Serves 4

Cauliflower Cheese with Potatoes

1 small cauliflower
4 large potatoes, peeled and
  sliced
75 g (3 oz) (6 tablespoons) butter
40 g (1½ oz) (6 tablespoons) flour
350 ml (12 fl oz) (1½ cups) milk
pinch grated nutmeg
salt and pepper
100 g (¼ lb) (1 cup) grated cheese

1 Bring a pan of salted water to the boil.

2 Clean the cauliflower, break it into small florets and wash them. Put the potatoes into the boiling water. Cook for 10 minutes, then add the cauliflower. Continue to cook until the cauliflower is just tender but still firm.

3 Meanwhile, make a white sauce with 40g (1½oz) (3 tablespoons) of the butter, the flour, milk, a pinch of nutmeg and salt and pepper to taste. Add half the cheese and stir well until it is melted. Keep hot.

4 Drain the potatoes and cauliflower. Keep hot.

5 Use half of the remaining butter to grease a flameproof dish. Heat the grill (broiler).

6 Spread the drained potatoes and cauliflower evenly over the buttered dish and cover with the cheese sauce.

7 Sprinkle the remaining grated

cheese over the top. Cut the rest of the butter into small pieces and dot over the top. Put the dish under the grill (broiler) and brown.

Serves 4-5

Hungarian Style Cauliflower

1 medium cauliflower

For the Sauce:
50 ml (2 fl oz) (¼ cup) oil
1 medium onion, sliced
10 g (1 tablespoon) paprika
450 g (1 lb) boiled salted beef, cut
  into strips
25 g (1 oz) (2 tablespoons) tomato
  concentrate (paste)
4 tomatoes, skinned, deseeded
  and chopped
1 red pepper, deseeded and cut
  into strips
15 g (½ oz) (1½ tablespoons)
  cornflour (cornstarch)
100 ml (4 fl oz) (½ cup) sour cream
salt and pepper
5 g (1 tablespoon) chopped
  parsley

1 Remove the leaves, wash the cauliflower and boil for 20 minutes in just enough salted water to cover. Reserve ½ pint of the cauliflower water. Keep the cauliflower hot.

2 Meanwhile, heat the oil and fry the onion gently without browning. Add the paprika, the boiled salted beef, the tomato concentrate (paste), the tomatoes and red pepper strips and cook for 4 minutes. Stir in the reserved cauliflower stock and boil for 8 minutes. Mix the cornflour (cornstarch) with the cream and stir into the sauce and boil for 3 minutes until it thickens. Season.

3 Sprinkle the cauliflower with chopped parsley and serve the sauce separately.

Serves 4

Hungarian Style Cauliflower – Cauliflower served with strips of red pepper and beef in a paprika flavoured sauce

Leeks in Tomato Sauce

900 g (2 lb) small leeks, washed
  and trimmed
225 g (½ lb) sliced carrots
300 ml (½ pint) (1¼ cups) water
salt

For the Sauce:
50 ml (2 fl oz) (¼ cup) oil
225 g (½ lb) (1 cup) chopped onions
50 g (2 oz) (4 tablespoons) tomato
  concentrate (paste)
15 g (½ oz) (1½ tablespoons)
  arrowroot
150 ml (¼ pint) (⅔ cup) water
salt and pepper
pinch sugar
pinch grated nutmeg
pinch dried basil or oregano

1 Boil the leeks and carrots in
the water, adding salt to taste, for
15 minutes. Drain, keep warm and
reserve cooking liquor.

2 To make the sauce: heat the
oil in a frying pan (skillet) and
sauté the chopped onions until
they are soft but not brown (about
10 minutes).

3 Add the tomato concentrate
(paste) and the liquor in which the
leeks were cooked. Bring to the
boil and simmer for 10 minutes.

4 Blend the arrowroot with the
water and stir into the sauce.
Cook for a further 5 minutes, then
add seasonings to taste. Pour
over the leeks and carrots and
serve.

Serves 4

Braised Fennel

1 bulb fennel, about 450 g (1 lb),
  trimmed and quartered
1 carrot, chopped
1 onion, chopped
75 g (3 oz) (⅜ cup) bacon fat or
  75 ml (3 fl oz) (⅜ cup) oil
1 chicken stock cube dissolved
  in 450 ml (16 fl oz) (2 cups) water
salt and pepper

For the Sauce:
25 g (1 oz) (2 tablespoons) butter
25 g (1 oz) (4 tablespoons) flour
25 g (1 oz) (2 tablespoons) tomato
  concentrate (paste)

1 Preheat the oven to 180°C,
350°F, gas 4.

2 Parboil the fennel in salted
water for 5 minutes. Refresh.

3 Lightly fry the carrot and
onion in the bacon fat or oil in a
frying pan (skillet). Add the
drained fennel, pour over the
chicken stock and transfer to an
ovenproof dish. Braise, covered,
for 1 hour in the oven.

4 To make the sauce, prepare a
roux with the butter and flour and
stir in the tomato concentrate
(paste). Pour over the braising
liquor (strained). Bring to the boil
and season to taste. Simmer for 15
minutes and pour over the fennel.

Serves 4

---

*Celery and Onion Casserole –
onions, bacon and celery in a
tomato sauce make a delicious
snack or accompaniment for
meat*

Celery and Onion Casserole

50 ml (2 fl oz) (¼ cup) oil
225 g (½ lb) (1⅓ cups) diced bacon
225 g (½ lb) button (pearl) onions,
  peeled
1 head of celery, about 900 g (2 lb),
  trimmed into 10 cm (4 in) pieces
15 g (½ oz) (1 tablespoon) tomato
  concentrate (paste)
2 chicken stock cubes dissolved
  in 450 ml (¾ pint) (2 cups) water
bouquet garni
salt and pepper

1 Preheat the oven to 180°C,
350°F, gas 4.

2 Heat the oil in a frying pan
(skillet), add the bacon and sauté
for 4 minutes. Remove and add
the peeled onions, then the celery.
Cook for 5 minutes.

3 Stir in the tomato concentrate
(paste) and pour over the chicken
stock; add bouquet garni. Season,
replace the bacon, and transfer to
an ovenproof dish. Cover and
cook in the oven for 35 minutes.

Serves 4

Spanish Artichokes

6 large artichokes
100 g (¼ lb) (¾ cup) long grain rice
2 peppers
1 onion
3 tomatoes
275 g (10 oz) smoked streaky
  bacon
2 cloves garlic
bunch parsley
75 ml (5 tablespoons) olive oil
pinch saffron
salt and pepper
½ lemon

1 Trim the artichokes by cutting the stalk and leaves 3 cm (1¼ in) from the base. (Use a serrated knife or scissors for the leaves.) Wash and drain them.

2 Boil salted water in a large saucepan. Put in the artichokes and boil for 15 minutes.

3 Meanwhile, wash the rice until the water is quite clear.

4 Put the rice in twice its volume of boiling salted water, and simmer for 12 minutes.

5 Drain the rice, rinse it under cold running water, then drain once more.

6 Wash and dry the peppers. Split them in two and remove the seeds and white fibre. Dice the flesh. Peel and chop the onion. Peel the tomatoes, cut them in quarters, remove the seeds, then dice them also. Dice the bacon finely. Peel and chop the garlic cloves. Wash, dry and chop the parsley.

7 Heat 30 ml (2 tablespoons) olive oil in a sauté pan. Put in the diced bacon, onion and peppers, and fry.

8 When they are golden-brown, add the diced tomatoes, garlic, parsley, saffron and rice. Season with salt and pepper. Stir for 3 or 4 minutes over a moderate heat.

9 Drain the artichokes, and put them in cold water, then drain and dry. Pull the outside leaves apart and, with a small spoon, remove the hairy centres (chokes) and little leaves. Fill the

artichokes with the rice mixture.

10 Heat the rest of the oil in a sauté pan. Put in the artichokes, cover and leave to finish cooking on a low heat for 40 minutes.

11 Squeeze the half lemon. Heat a serving dish.

12 Half-way through the cooking, add the lemon juice and 45 ml (3 tablespoons) hot water to the artichokes.

13 Arrange the artichokes on a serving dish and serve very hot.

Serves 6

Artichoke Hearts with Herbs

4 globe artichokes
½ lemon
large bunch chives, parsley and
  tarragon, mixed
40 g (1½ oz) (3 tablespoons) butter
salt and pepper

Trimmed and prepared artichoke in boiling water

For the blanching mixture:
2½ lemons
1½ litres (2¾ pints) (3⅜ pints) water
15 g (1 tablespoon) flour

1 Prepare the artichokes to give you 4 hearts, then rub each heart all over with a ½ lemon. Prepare the blanching mixture with the lemons, water and flour and cook the hearts in the boiling liquid for 40 minutes or until tender. Drain them, rinse under cold water and cool.

2 Wash the bunch of herbs, dry and chop finely.

3 Melt the butter in a frying pan (skillet). Cut the hearts into pieces and sauté them until they are golden-brown, then add the chopped herbs. Add a little pepper, mixing with the wooden spoon.

4 Warm a vegetable dish. Put in the artichoke hearts and serve hot.

Serves 4

Duchesse Potatoes

900 g (2 lb) floury, old potatoes,
 peeled
2 egg yolks, beaten
50 g (2 oz) ($\frac{1}{4}$ cup) butter
salt and pepper
pinch grated nutmeg
1 egg, beaten

1 Preheat the oven to 200°C, 400°F, gas 6.

2 Boil the potatoes in salted water. When soft but not mushy, drain. Return to the pan, and shake gently over medium heat to dry thoroughly.

Duchesse Potatoes with Almonds
—duchesse potato nests filled
with chicken in a sherry sauce
and topped with flaked almonds

2 Mash, and blend in the egg yolks and butter. Season and add a pinch of nutmeg.

3 Pass the potatoes through a sieve (strainer).

4 Lightly oil a baking tray (cookie sheet). Fill a piping (decorator's) bag with the potato mixture and fit a star-shaped nozzle. Pipe the mixture onto the tray (sheet), forming small cones. Bake in the oven for 15 minutes.

5 Take out and brush the cones with the beaten egg. Return to the oven for 4-5 minutes to brown. Serve immediately.

Serves 6

Tip: Pipe duchesse potatoes in a variety of different shapes and sizes. Tiny rosettes, topped with grated cheese or chopped nuts, are delicious with cocktails.

Use your favourite vol-au-vent filling with duchesse potato nests. Any kind of creamy, savoury mixture of meat, fish or vegetables is suitable.

Duchesse Potatoes with Almonds

450 g (1 lb) duchesse potato
 mixture
1 beaten egg
25 g (1 oz) (2 tablespoons) melted
 butter

For the Filling:
75 ml (2$\frac{1}{2}$ fl oz) ($\frac{1}{3}$ cup) medium
 sherry
225 g ($\frac{1}{2}$ lb) (1$\frac{1}{3}$ cups) diced, cooked
 turkey or chicken

300 ml ($\frac{1}{2}$ pint) (1$\frac{1}{4}$ cups) white
  sauce
1 egg yolk
50 ml (2 fl oz) ($\frac{1}{4}$ cup) double
  (heavy) cream
salt and pepper
pinch grated nutmeg
50 g (2 oz) ($\frac{2}{3}$ cup) flaked almonds,
  toasted

1 Preheat the oven at 180°C,
350°F, gas 4.

2 Fill a piping (decorator's) bag
with the duchesse potato mixture
and fit it with a star-shaped
nozzle. Pipe the mixture neatly
onto a greased baking tray
(cookie sheet) to make six nest
shapes.

3 Dry in the oven for 10 minutes,
then brush the potato nests with
the beaten egg. Return to the
oven for 4-5 minutes. Take out
and keep warm.

4 Next make the filling. Pour the
sherry into a saucepan, add the
turkey or chicken and bring to the
boil. Stir in the white sauce and
reduce heat to simmering. Take
off the heat, blend in the egg yolk
and cream and season with salt
and pepper and grated nutmeg.
Return to the heat, stirring all the
time.

5 Fill each potato nest with the
sauce and sprinkle over the
flaked almonds. Brush the potato
with the melted butter and return
to the oven for 4-5 minutes. Serve
immediately.

Serves 6

*Duchesse Potato and Prawn
Scallops — the scallop shells are
filled with prawn and tomato
sauce and surrounded with
piped duchesse potato*

Duchesse Potato and Prawn Scallops

4 scallop shells
225 g ($\frac{1}{2}$ lb) duchesse potato
  mixture
1 beaten egg
25 g (1 oz) (2 tablespoons) melted
  butter

For the Filling:
25 ml (1 fl oz) ($\frac{1}{8}$ cup) oil
25 g (1 oz) (2 tablespoons) butter
1 onion, finely chopped
15 g ($\frac{1}{2}$ oz) (1 tablespoon) flour
4 tomatoes, peeled, deseeded and
  chopped
15 g ($\frac{1}{2}$ oz) (1 tablespoon) tomato
  concentrate (paste)
150 ml ($\frac{1}{4}$ pint) ($\frac{5}{8}$ cup) water
$\frac{1}{2}$ chicken stock cube
15 ml (1 tablespoon) anchovy
  essence
juice $\frac{1}{2}$ lemon
salt and pepper
225 g ($\frac{1}{2}$ lb) (1$\frac{1}{2}$ cups) peeled
  prawns

1 Preheat the oven to 180°C,
350°F, gas 4.

2 Using a piping (decorator's)
bag with a star-shaped nozzle,
pipe the edges of the scallop shells
with the duchesse potato mix-

*Duchesse Potatoes can be piped
into decorative pyramids, glazed
with beaten egg and browned in
a hot oven*

ture. Place them on a baking tray
(cookie sheet) and dry in the oven
for 10 minutes. Remove and brush
the potato with the beaten egg.

3 Now make the filling. Heat the
oil and the butter in a frying pan
(skillet), and gently fry the
chopped onion until it is soft
but not brown – about 5 minutes.
Stir in the flour and cook for
2 minutes more.

4 Add the chopped tomatoes
and the tomato concentrate
(paste). Pour over the water and
add the crumbled $\frac{1}{2}$ stock cube.
Bring to the boil, then simmer for
5 minutes.

5 Flavour the sauce with the
anchovy essence, lemon juice and
salt and pepper to taste. Add the
peeled prawns, bring to the boil
again, then cook gently for a
further 5-6 minutes.

6 Increase the heat of the oven to
200°C, 400°F, gas 6.

7 Fill each scallop shell with the
prawn and tomato sauce inside
the border of piped potato. Place
them on the baking tray (cookie
sheet) and bake for 8 minutes,
until the potato is golden-brown.
Take out, brush the potato with
melted butter and serve immediately.

Serves 4

Entertaining: Memorable Meals
Hawaiian Chicken

Italian Spread

Cozzi Anacapri
★
Vitello Venezia
★
Duchess Potatoes
★
Broccoli
★
Strawberry Meringue

Cozzi Anacapri

32 mussels, washed and
  scrubbed
2 cloves garlic, crushed
2 onions, chopped
300 ml (½ pint) (1¼ cups) dry white
  wine
sprig thyme
salt and pepper
30 ml (2 tablespoons) chopped
  parsley
25 g (1 oz) (2 tablespoons) butter
30 ml (2 tablespoons) flour
3 egg yolks, beaten
juice ½ lemon

1 Place the mussels, garlic, onion, wine, thyme, seasoning and parsley in a large pan and bring to the boil. Boil for 5-6 minutes until the mussels open – discard any mussels which remain closed.

2 Strain off the liquid into another pan. Break off and throw away one side of each hinged mussel shell. Arrange the mussels in an ovenproof dish and keep warm.

3 Melt the butter in another pan and stir in the flour. Cook for 1 minute, without colouring, then add the reserved mussel liquid. Bring to the boil, stirring all the time.

4 Gradually mix the sauce into the beaten egg yolks. When well blended, return to the pan and bring back to the boil. Add the

Cozzi Anacapri are served in a delicious wine flavoured sauce and are a typically Italian way to start a formal meal

lemon juice and check the seasoning. Pour the sauce over the mussels and serve.

Serves 4

Vitello Venezia

four 100 g (¼ lb) veal escalopes
30 ml (2 tablespoons) flour
100 g (¼ lb) (½ cup) butter
2 cloves garlic, crushed
1 small shallot, chopped
150 ml (¼ pint) (⅝ cup) red
  vermouth
30 ml (2 tablespoons) tomato
  paste
2 tomatoes, skinned, deseeded
  and chopped
salt and pepper
pinch oregano
100 g (¼ lb) (1½ cups) button
  mushrooms, sliced

1 Beat the escalopes until flat. Sprinkle them with flour.

2 Heat 50 g (2 oz) (¼ cup) butter in a frying pan (skillet) and gently fry the veal until golden-brown. Remove and keep warm.

3 Fry the garlic and shallot for 2-3 minutes, than add the vermouth, tomato paste and chopped tomato. Season with salt and pepper and sprinkle in the oregano. Bring to the boil, stirring well, then simmer for about 10 minutes.

4 Heat the remaining butter in another pan and sauté the mushrooms until golden.

5 Arrange the escalopes in a serving dish and pour over the sauce. Garnish with the mushrooms. Serve with fresh broccoli and duchess potatoes.

Serves 4

Tip: You can also make this dish with red wine or that well-known Italian fortified wine – Marsala. Marsala will make the sauce sweeter in flavour and darker in colour. For a more attractive appearance, sprinkle the finished dish with chopped fresh parsley.

Vitello Venezia has a garnish of duchess potatoes and fried mushrooms, and evokes the flavours of Italian cuisine

For the Caramel:
20 sugar lumps
15 ml (1 tablespoon) water

1 Preheat the oven to 130°C, 250°F, gas ½. Place the egg whites in a mixing bowl and beat well until stiff and glossy. It will save time and energy if you use an electric whisk.

2 Gradually add the sugar, 15 ml (1 tablespoon) at a time, whisking well after each addition. When all the sugar has been added, the meringue should be very stiff.

3 Whisk in the vanilla essence and fill a piping (decorator's) bag with the meringue mixture.

4 Pipe a circle of meringue, 18 cm (7 in) in diameter on to a sheet of non-stick baking paper. Pipe the remaining meringue into seven individual blocks, each 8 cm (3 in) long and 4 cm (1½ in) wide.

5 Place the meringue on a baking (cookie) sheet and bake in the oven for about 2 hours. Remove when dried out but not coloured. If the meringue starts to colour, open the oven door for a while.

6 Make the caramel: place the sugar and water in a saucepan and boil until you have a toffee-like sticky consistency.

7 Place the cooled meringue base on a serving plate. Arrange the meringue blocks around the sides to form a border, lying them on their sides. Stick them together with the caramel and place them in position.

8 Wash and hull the strawberries. Whip the cream until thick and stiff and flavour it with the Marsala. Fill a piping (decorator's) bag with the cream and pipe some across the base. Pile the strawberries up on top and pipe a large swirl of cream in the centre, surrounded by smaller rosettes. Pipe a small swirl of cream between each of the meringue blocks on the edge of the plate. Decorate with the crystallized violets and serve.

Serves 4

Strawberry Meringue

 ☆

Strawberry Meringue, decorated generously with swirls of whipped cream and violets, is a perfect dessert for summer

4 egg whites
225 g (½ lb) (1 cup) castor (fine granulated) sugar
2-3 drops vanilla essence
450 g (1 lb) strawberries

300 ml (½ pint) (1¼ cups) double (heavy) cream
30 ml (1 fl oz) (2 tablespoons) Marsala
7 crystallized violets

Provençale Dîner

Filets de Sole aux Raisins

★

Brochettes de Porc au Romarin

★

Buttered Courgettes

★

Green Salad

★

Apricot Compôte

Filets de Sole aux Raisins

8 fillets of sole
65 g (2½ oz) (5 tablespoons) butter
1 onion, chopped
bouquet garni
400 ml (14 fl oz) (1¾ cups) court
  bouillon
salt and pepper
225 g (½ lb) grapes
30 ml (1 fl oz) (2 tablespoons)
  apple brandy

2 shallots, chopped
15 ml (1 tablespoon) flour
100 ml (4 fl oz) (½ cup) white wine
150 ml (¼ pint) (⅝ cup) single
  (light) cream

1 Roll up the fillets and secure them with cocktail sticks. Melt 15 ml (1 tablespoon) of the butter in a large frying pan (skillet). Sauté the onion until soft and add the bouquet garni, court bouillon and finally the fish. Season, cover and simmer for 15-20 minutes.

2 Mix the grapes and apple brandy and leave to macerate for 15 minutes. Transfer the fish to a warmed serving dish and keep warm. Reserve 225 ml (8 fl oz) (1 cup) of the court bouillon.

3 In a clean pan, melt the remaining butter and gently sauté the shallots. Stir in the flour and white wine and gradually add the reserved court bouillon. Season. Simmer gently for 5 minutes. Stir in the cream and grapes, pour over the fish and serve.

Serves 6-8

Filets de Sole aux Raisins are served in a rich, cream sauce, and garnished with prawns (shrimps) and grapes

Brochettes de Porc au Romarin

675 g (1½ lb) lean pork from the
  shoulder or loin
15 ml (1 tablespoon) fresh
  rosemary, chopped
salt and pepper
50 ml (2 fl oz) (¼ cup) olive oil
few sprigs fresh rosemary

1 Cut the pork into 2.5 cm (1 in) cubes and thread on 4 skewers. Blend the rosemary, seasoning and oil. Marinate the brochettes in the oil overnight.

2 Remove them from the marinade and grill (broil), turning occasionally, for 10-15 minutes or until tender. Baste occasionally with a little oil from the marinade.

3 Arrange on a dish and decorate with a few rosemary sprigs.

Serves 4

Apricot Compôte

1 kg (2 lb) apricots
100 g (¼ lb) (½ cup) sugar
15 ml (1 tablespoon) flaked
  almonds

1 Halve the apricots and remove their stones (seeds). Place them in a large saucepan with just enough water to half-cover them and sprinkle with the sugar. Cook gently for 5-10 minutes, watching to make sure that they do not dissolve into a purée. Transfer the apricots to a serving dish.

2 Boil the remaining syrup until it is thick and pour it over the apricots. Sprinkle with the flaked almonds and chill in the refrigerator. Serve with a bowl of whipped cream.

Serves 4-6

Brochettes de Porc au Romarin are large meaty chunks of pork flavoured with aromatic fresh sprigs of rosemary

Caribbean Calypso

Caribbean Avocado
★
Turkey Barbados
★
Green Pepper Salad
★
Anguilla Peach Tart

Caribbean Avocado

2 ripe avocados
45 ml (3 tablespoons) oil
22 ml (1½ tablespoons) lemon
 juice
salt and pepper
5 ml (1 teaspoon) soft brown
 sugar
22 ml (1½ tablespoons) rum

1 Split the avocados lengthways and remove the stones (seeds). Blend the oil, lemon juice, seasoning and sugar together and pour a little over each avocado.

2 Chill in the refrigerator and, just before serving, arrange each avocado half on a lettuce leaf, sprinkle over a little rum and garnish with a twist of lemon.

Serves 4

Turkey Barbados

25 g (1 oz) (4 tablespoons) flour
5 ml (1 teaspoon) powdered
 ginger
5 ml (1 teaspoon) curry powder
four 100 g (¼ lb) turkey escalopes
75 g (3 oz) (6 tablespoons) butter
50 ml (2 fl oz) (¼ cup) rum
50 g (2 oz) (⅝ cup) desiccated
 coconut
45 ml (3 tablespoons) pineapple
 juice
70 ml (2½ fl oz) (⅓ cup) stock
50 ml (2 fl oz) (¼ cup) double
 (heavy) cream
salt and pepper
few sprigs parsley

*Anguilla Peach Tart is the
perfect summer dessert
with overlapping juicy peaches
in a sticky apricot glaze*

6-8 slices canned or fresh
 pineapple

1 Mix together the flour, ginger and curry powder and use to coat the turkey. Heat the butter and fry the escalopes until golden. Add the rum and set it alight. When the flames die down, remove the escalopes.

2 Add the coconut to the pan and brown quickly. Then stir in the pineapple juice and stock. Boil for 5 minutes, reduce the heat and stir in the cream and seasoning.

3 Arrange the escalopes in a serving dish and cover with the sauce. Garnish with the parsley and pineapple and surround with small piles of boiled rice.

Serves 4

Anguilla Peach Tart

shortcrust (pie crust) made with
 225 g (½ lb) (2¼ cups) flour
5-6 peaches
25 g (1 oz) (2 tablespoons) sugar
75 g (3 oz) (¼ cup) apricot jam
15 ml (1 tablespoon) water
5 ml (1 teaspoon) lemon juice

1 Preheat the oven to 180°C, 350°F, gas 4. Line a 20 cm (8 in) flan ring with the pastry, and prick the base.

2 Scald the peaches in boiling water for a few seconds only. Skin the peaches and remove the stones (seeds). Slice them thinly and arrange them, overlapping, in the pastry case. Sprinkle with sugar and bake for 25 minutes.

3 Heat the apricot jam, water and lemon juice in a small pan. Bring to the boil, simmer for 5 minutes, then strain and boil again. Brush over the peaches and serve cold with cream.

Serves 4

*Turkey Barbados has a spicy
and exotic flavour —
serve just with plain, boiled rice
and a sliced pepper salad*

Chinese Banquet

Pork Spare Ribs
★
Oriental Fish Kebabs
★
Sweet and Sour Duck
★
Asparagus Salad
★
Fried Egg Noodles
★
Peking Apple Fritters

Pork Spare Ribs

3 kg (6 lb) pork spare ribs, cut
  into separate ribs
salt
85 ml (3 fl oz) (⅜ cup) clear honey
45 ml (3 tablespoons) soya sauce
15 ml (1 tablespoon) lemon juice
2.5 ml (½ teaspoon) ground ginger
few canned pineapple chunks

1 Preheat the oven to 190°C, 375°F, gas 5. Place the ribs in a roasting dish. Sprinkle with salt and bake for 45 minutes, pouring off the fat as it collects.

2 Meanwhile, gently heat the honey in a small saucepan. Stir in the soya sauce, lemon juice and ginger. Remove from the heat.

3 After 45 minutes, lower the oven temperature to 170°C, 325°F, gas 3. Pour the honey sauce over the ribs and cook for 30 minutes more, turning the ribs occasionally. Decorate with the pineapple chunks and serve.

Serves 6

Oriental Fish Kebabs

225 g (½ lb) fillets of plaice or any
  white fish

6 pieces stem ginger
100 g (¼ lb) cooked prawns
  (shrimps), peeled
15 ml (1 tablespoon) melted
  butter

For the Marinade:
30 ml (2 tablespoons) clear honey
30 ml (1 fl oz) (2 tablespoons) oil

1 Mix the honey and oil. Place the fish in a non-metallic container, pour over the honey and oil and leave to marinate for 1 hour.

2 Drain and dry the fish and cut it into strips. Cut the stem ginger into small pieces. Thread the prawns (shrimps), fish and ginger alternately on to 6 skewers. Brush them with the melted butter and cook them under a moderately hot grill (broiler) for 6-10 minutes or until the fish is cooked but not brown. Turn the kebabs occasionally while they cook.

Serves 6

Sweet and Sour Duck

one 2½ kg (5 lb) duck
275 g (10 oz) (1 cup) clear honey
15 ml (1 tablespoon) soya sauce
15 ml (1 tablespoon) sherry

1 Preheat the oven to 220°C, 425°F, gas 7.

2 Prick the duck all over with a carving fork and rub well with salt. Place the duck on the middle shelf in the oven with a roasting pan on the shelf, directly underneath, and roast it for 30 minutes.

3 Reduce the heat to 190°C, 375°F, gas 5 and turn the duck over. Mix the honey, soya sauce and sherry, and spread some over the top of the duck. Continue roasting for 2½ hours, turning the duck frequently and basting with the rest of the sauce.

4 Transfer the duck to a serving dish. Surround it with deep-fried chinese egg noodles, pineapple rings and a few sprigs of parsley. Garnish with a few pineapple pieces and serve.

Serves 6

Asparagus Salad

675 g (1½ lb) asparagus
45 ml (3 tablespoons) soya sauce
7.5 ml (1½ teaspoons) sugar
2.5 ml (½ teaspoon) sesame oil

1 Trim the asparagus and cut it in 7.5 cm (3 in) pieces. Parboil the tender tops for 30 seconds and the stems for 2 minutes. Drain.

2 Mix the soya sauce, sugar and oil and pour it over the asparagus. Chill in the refrigerator and serve.

Serves 6

Peking Apple Fritters

4 firm apples
1 egg
1 egg white
30 ml (2 tablespoons) flour
30 ml (2 tablespoons) cornflour
  (cornstarch)
oil for deep frying
50 ml (2 fl oz) (¼ cup) oil
175 g (6 oz) (¾ cup) sugar
20 ml (4 teaspoons) white sesame
  seeds

1 Peel, core and cut each apple into quarters. Beat the egg and egg white until well blended and mix in the flour and cornflour (cornstarch).

2 Heat the oil for deep frying to 190°C, 375°F. Dip the apple wedges in the egg batter and fry them in the oil until golden-brown. Remove and drain.

3 Place the oil and sugar in a saucepan. Heat gently, stirring constantly, until the sugar dissolves. Increase the heat and cook until the sugar begins to caramelize. Place the fritters on a serving dish and pour over the caramel. Sprinkle with the sesame seeds and serve immediately.

Serves 6

*Peking Apple Fritters
are encased in a crisp batter
and served in a delicious
caramel sauce with sesame seeds*

Mediterranean Fare

Mint and Cucumber Fish Salad

★

Veal Marsala

★

Sautéed Potatoes

★

Zabaglione *or*
Apricot Gelato

Mint and Cucumber Fish Salad

15 ml (1 tablespoon) butter
1 small onion, chopped
150 ml (¼ pint) (⅝ cup) dry white wine
salt and pepper
225 g (½ lb) white fish fillets
½ small cucumber
10 ml (2 teaspoons) chopped mint
juice 1 lemon
12 cooked, peeled prawns (shrimps)

1 Melt the butter in a frying pan (skillet) and sauté the chopped onion until soft. Add the white wine and seasoning and bring to the boil. Add the fish fillets, and reduce the heat to a gentle simmer. Cover and cook for 10 minutes. Remove from the heat and leave the fish to cool in the pan.

2 Scoop the seeds out of the cucumber and cut it into small 5 mm (¼ in) cubes.

3 When the fish has cooled, remove it from the pan and drain on absorbent paper. Flake it into small pieces and place them in a bowl with the cucumber and chopped mint. Sprinkle with the lemon juice, toss and chill for 30 minutes.

4 Just before serving, spoon the fish salad into 4 large scallop shells. Garnish each one with

Mint and Cucumber Fish Salad is a tasty and refreshing start to a summer dinner party which is always appreciated

3 prawns (shrimps) and serve with lemon wedges and a bowl of mayonnaise.

Serves 4

Veal Marsala

625 g (1½ lb) cushion of veal (fillet part of the thick portion of leg)
25 g (1 oz) (4 tablespoons) flour
piece of blade mace
pinch paprika
pinch basil
pinch oregano
salt and black pepper
30 ml (1 fl oz) (2 tablespoons) oil
50 g (2 oz) (¼ cup) butter
150 ml (¼ pint) (⅝ cup) Marsala
150 ml (¼ pint) (⅝ cup) double (heavy) cream
juice ½ lemon
100 g (¼ lb) (1½ cups) button mushrooms
10 ml (2 teaspoons) chopped parsley

1 Cut the veal into 4 slices, 5 mm (¼ in) thick, and beat each one with a meat mallet, flattening it to the largest possible size. Cut each slice in half.

2 Sieve the flour on to a plate. Powder the mace, and add it to the flour with the remaining

Veal Marsala is served with an attractive garnish of vegetables and makes a tasty dish for a formal dinner

1 Place the egg yolks and sugar in a bowl and beat until light and fluffy.

2 Place the bowl over a saucepan of gently boiling water. Gradually add the brandy and Marsala, beating continuously, until the mixture thickens and becomes frothy.

3 Pour the Zabaglione into 4 glasses and serve immediately with sponge fingers.

Serves 4

Apricot Gelato

50 g (2 oz) dried apricots
15 ml (1 tablespoon) brandy
150 ml (¼ pint) (⅝ cup) double (heavy) cream
2.5 ml (½ teaspoon) grated lemon rind
2 egg yolks, beaten
45 ml (3 tablespoons) icing (confectioners') sugar

1 Place the apricots in a bowl and just cover them with boiling water. Leave for 1 hour. Drain and place them in a saucepan with fresh water. Simmer for 40-50 minutes or until they are soft. Pour off the water and force the apricots through a coarse sieve, or purée them in an electric blender.

2 Place the puréed apricots in a bowl and stir in the brandy.

3 Place the cream, lemon rind and beaten egg yolks in a bowl over a saucepan of hot water and stir until a thick soft custard is formed. Remove from the heat and stir frequently to prevent a skin forming until the custard begins to cool.

4 Stir in the icing (confectioners') sugar and leave the custard to get thoroughly cold before straining it on to the apricot purée. Blend well and transfer the mixture to a refrigerator tray. Freeze, stirring the mixture lightly 2 or 3 times. Serve in tall glasses.

Serves 4

---

spices, herbs and seasoning.

3 Pass each escalope in the seasoned flour and shake off any excess. Heat the oil and butter in a large frying pan (skillet) over a table spirit burner. When it is sizzling hot, add the escalopes and fry for 1½ minutes on each side, or until golden. Drain off the excess butter and oil.

4 Stir the Marsala into the pan and boil for 2 minutes. Stir in the cream and lemon juice and boil for 1 minute, shaking.

5 Transfer the escalopes to serving plates. Add the mushrooms to the sauce in the pan. Simmer, stirring continually, for 2 more minutes and pour the sauce over the escalopes. Garnish the escalopes with a little chopped parsley and serve with fried new potatoes, and buttered asparagus and celery.

Serves 4

Zabaglione

6 egg yolks
100 g (¼ lb) (½ cup) sugar
50 ml (2 fl oz) (¼ cup) brandy
50 ml (2 fl oz) (¼ cup) Marsala

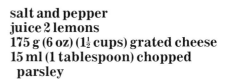

Seafood Special

Seafood Appetizer

★

Langouste Gratinée

★

Tomato and Basil Salad

★

Toledo Figs

Seafood Appetizer

½ litre (1 pint) (2½ cups) cockles, cooked and shelled
½ litre (1 pint) (2½ cups) mussels, cooked and shelled
100 g (¼ lb) (¾ cup) cooked, peeled prawns (shrimps)
100 ml (4 fl oz) (½ cup) mayonnaise
10 ml (2 teaspoons) lemon juice
salt and pepper
1 lettuce, washed and shredded
18 whole prawns (shrimps)

1 Mix the shellfish, mayonnaise,

lemon juice and seasoning.

2 Arrange in 6 individual glasses on the shredded lettuce.

3 Decorate each glass with 3 whole prawns (shrimps), a twist of lemon and a sprig of parsley.

Serves 6

Langouste Gratinée

three 675 g (1½ lb) crawfish (crayfish), cooked
50 ml (2 fl oz) (¼ cup) oil
1 small onion, chopped
100 g (¼ lb) (1 cup) diced mushrooms
50 g (2 oz) fennel, chopped
50 g (2 oz) celery, chopped
100 g (¼ lb) (2 cups) breadcrumbs
225 ml (8 fl oz) (1 cup) white wine
400 ml (14 fl oz) (1¾ cups) white sauce
1 hard-boiled egg, chopped
5 ml (1 teaspoon) mustard
150 ml (¼ pint) (⅝ cup) Pernod

Seafood Appetizer, with its attractive garnish of prawns (shrimps), parsley sprigs and lemon, tastes delicious

salt and pepper
juice 2 lemons
175 g (6 oz) (1½ cups) grated cheese
15 ml (1 tablespoon) chopped parsley

1 Run the point of a sharp knife along the groove which runs across the crayfish (crawfish) between the base of the head and the top of the tail. Then draw the knife through the groove running along the tail piece. Separate the two tail pieces as illustrated opposite. Remove and slice the meat and clean the shells.

2 Heat the oil and sauté the chopped vegetables until soft. Add the breadcrumbs and wine and bring to the boil. Stir in the white sauce and the chopped egg, mustard and Pernod. Cook gently for 5 minutes, season and add the crayfish (crawfish) meat. Heat through before dividing the mixture between the shells.

3 Sprinkle with lemon juice and grated cheese. Flash under a hot grill (broiler) until golden-brown. Sprinkle with chopped parsley, and garnish with parsley sprigs and lemon slices.

Serves 6

Toledo Figs

18 fresh or canned figs
100 ml (4 fl oz) (½ cup) brandy
100 ml (4 fl oz) (½ cup) sherry
2.5 ml (½ teaspoon) cinnamon
grated rind 1 orange
a little icing (confectioners') sugar

1 Place the figs in a bowl and cover with the brandy, sherry, cinnamon and orange rind. Sweeten to taste with the sugar. Leave to marinate for 1-2 hours.

2 Serve with whipped cream and chopped nuts.

Serves 6

Langouste Gratinée tastes as good as its flamboyant appearance suggests — its tasty sauce is topped with cheese

Menu

Broccoli au Gratin

★

Chicken Juliet

★

Raspberry Sorbet Surprise

★

Almond Tuile Biscuits

Broccoli au Gratin

225 g (½ lb) broccoli florets
4 large slices cooked ham
25 g (1 oz) (2 tablespoons) butter
45 ml (3 tablespoons) flour
450 ml (¾ pint) (2¼ cups) milk
75 g (3 oz) (¾ cup) grated cheese
salt and pepper

1 Preheat the oven to 200°C, 400°F, gas 6.

2 Cook the broccoli in boiling salted water for 5 minutes, drain and divide between the slices of ham. Roll them up and arrange in a shallow ovenproof dish.

3 Melt the butter, stir in the flour and cook for 1 or 2 minutes. Gradually add the milk, bring to the boil and simmer for 2 or 3 minutes, stirring continuously. Add 50 g (2 oz) (½ cup) of the cheese, season to taste and pour over the ham rolls.

4 Sprinkle the remaining cheese over the top and bake for 25-35 minutes. Serve immediately.

Serves 4

Chicken Juliet

1 orange
25 g (1 oz) (2 tablespoons) butter
15 ml (1 tablespoon) oil

1 onion, peeled and sliced
4 chicken pieces
50 g (2 oz) (½ cup) seasoned flour
550 ml (1 pint) (2½ cups) chicken stock
150 ml (¼ pint) (⅝ cup) white wine
15 ml (1 tablespoon) Worcestershire sauce
50 g (2 oz) (⅓ cup) sultanas or raisins
sprigs of watercress

1 Preheat the oven to 180°C, 350°F, gas 4. Thinly pare the orange rind and cut it into thin strips. Squeeze the juice.

2 Heat the butter and oil and fry the onion gently until soft but not browned. Remove with a draining spoon and place in an ovenproof casserole.

3 Toss the chicken in the seasoned flour, and fry until evenly browned. Add to the casserole with the stock, wine, Worcestershire sauce, orange strips and juice and sultanas or raisins.

4 Cover the casserole and cook in the preheated oven for 1 hour.

5 Transfer to a heated serving dish and garnish with sprigs of watercress. Serve with cauliflower.

Serves 4

Raspberry Sorbet Surprise

50 g (2 oz) (¼ cup) sugar
300 ml (½ pint) (1¼ cups) water
350 g (¾ lb) frozen raspberries, thawed
juice ½ lemon
2 egg whites
frozen and thawed raspberries to decorate

1 Dissolve the sugar in the water in a pan. Bring to the boil, simmer for 10 minutes, then cool.

2 Sieve the raspberries and add half of the purée to the cooled sugar syrup with the lemon juice. Pour into a 900 ml (1½ pint) (3¾ cup) pudding basin and place in the freezer until it begins to thicken.

3 Whisk the egg whites until stiff and peaking and fold lightly into the thickened mixture. Place an empty cream or yogurt carton in the centre and hold it in place with a weight, so that the sorbet freezes evenly around the sides of the bowl. Freeze until firm.

4 Remove the carton from the centre of the sorbet and fill the hole with the remaining raspberry purée. Refreeze until firm.

5 Thirty minutes before serving, place the sorbet in the refrigerator to soften. Turn out on to a chilled serving plate and decorate with the whole raspberries. Serve with Almond Tuile Biscuits.

Serves 6

Almond Tuile Biscuits

75 g (3 oz) (⅜ cup) butter
75 g (3 oz) (⅜ cup) castor (fine granulated) sugar
50 g (2 oz) (good ½ cup) flour
pinch salt
75 g (3 oz) (½ cup) almonds, finely shredded

1 Preheat the oven to 200°C, 400°F, gas 6.

2 Cream the butter and sugar until light and fluffy. Sieve the flour and salt and stir into the creamed mixture with the almonds.

3 Place a teaspoonful of the mixture on a well-greased baking (cookie) sheet and flatten with a wet fork. Repeat with 3 more teaspoonfuls and bake for 6-8 minutes until lightly coloured. Allow to stand for a second or two, then remove with a sharp knife and curl on a rolling pin until set.

4 Repeat the process until all of the mixture is used up.

Makes about 12

Broccoli au Gratin, Chicken Juliet, Raspberry Sorbet Surprise and Almond Tuile Biscuits make a fine meal

Menu

Chilled Celery
Starter *or*
Pumpkin Soup
★
Roast Beef
★
Brandy Mince Tart
★
Cinnamon Cherries
in Wine

Chilled Celery Starter

8 sticks celery
175 g (6 oz) button mushrooms
10 ml (2 teaspoons) paprika
10 ml (2 teaspoons) curry powder
70 ml (2½ fl oz) (⅓ cup) olive oil
45 ml (3 tablespoons) lemon juice
salt and pepper
225 g (½ lb) peeled prawns
 (shrimps)
30 ml (2 tablespoons) chopped
 parsley

1 Cut the celery into 2.5 cm (1 in) lengths. Slice the mushrooms and mix them in a bowl with the celery. Mix the paprika and curry powder with the olive oil. Add the lemon juice, seasoning, prawns (shrimps), and chopped parsley.

2 Pour the oil sauce over the celery and mushrooms. Toss well and chill before serving.

Serves 8

Pumpkin Soup

50 g (2 oz) (¼ cup) butter
1 large white onion, finely
 chopped
550 ml (1 pint) (2½ cups) chicken
 stock

450 g (1 lb) pumpkin
550 ml (1 pint) (2½ cups) hot milk
pinch grated nutmeg
salt and pepper
croûtons for garnish

1 Melt the butter in a large saucepan and gently fry the onion for 10 minutes, or until soft. Add the chicken stock and bring it to the boil.

2 Peel the pumpkin and cut it into 5 cm (2 in) chunks. Add it to the stock and simmer for about 30 minutes or until tender. Cool. Rub the pumpkin and stock through a sieve, or purée it in an electric blender.

3 Return to the pan, add the hot milk, nutmeg and seasoning and heat gently. Serve in a tureen garnished with croûtons.

Serves 8

Tip: This soup is quite delicious served with a little sour cream and chopped chives. You can make pumpkin and turnip soup by substituting 225 g (½ lb) of turnips for half of the pumpkin and preparing it in the same way.

Roast Rib of Beef with Potatoes and Celery

2 kg (4 lb) rib of beef
50 g (2 oz) (¼ cup) softened butter
salt and pepper
1½ kg (3 lb) potatoes, peeled
50 g (2 oz) (good ½ cup) flour
lard or dripping
2 heads celery
30 ml (2 tablespoons) butter
300 ml (½ pint) (1¼ cups) stock
watercress to garnish

1 Preheat the oven to 180°C, 350°F, gas 4.

2 Rub the meat all over with the softened butter. Season to taste and place it in a large roasting bag. Tie the bag, according to the instructions, and bake the meat in a roasting tin (pan) for 1½ hours or until tender.

3 When the meat has been in the oven for ½ hour, prepare the

potatoes. Cut them into equal-sized pieces and parboil them in salted water for 5 minutes. Drain and dry them before sprinkling with a little of the flour. Place them in a clean roasting dish with the lard or dripping and bake them for the last hour of the meat's cooking time.

4 Wash and peel the celery heads and cut off the tops, leaving 15-20 cm (6-8 in) of heart. Remove the outer leaves, then cut the hearts in half, or into three if they are large. Sprinkle them with seasoning and place them in a roasting bag with the butter, cut into knobs. Tie the bag according to instructions and place it in the roasting tin (pan) with the meat for the last 45 minutes of the meat's cooking time.

5 When the meat and vegetables are ready, reduce the heat and leave the potatoes in the oven to keep warm. Remove the meat and celery from the roasting bags, reserving the juices. Place the meat on a serving dish and the celery in a vegetable dish. Keep them warm. Make the gravy: place the reserved juices in the meat's roasting tray. Blend them with the remaining flour and cook over a gentle heat until it bubbles. Add the stock and bring to the boil, stirring constantly. If it is too pale, add a little gravy browning. Serve the meat garnished with watercress and surrounded by the roast potatoes and celery hearts. Serve the gravy separately.

Serves 8-9

Brandy Mince Tart

shortcrust (pie crust) made with
 225 g (½ lb) (2¼ cups) flour
225 g (½ lb) (¾ cup) mincemeat
1 large cooking (green) apple,
 peeled and cored
juice 1 lemon
60 ml (4 tablespoons) apricot jam
15 ml (1 tablespoon) brandy
10 ml (2 teaspoons) water

1 Preheat the oven to 190°C, 375°F, gas 5. Roll out the pastry to a thickness of 5 mm (¼ in) and use it to line a 23 cm (9 in) fluted flan ring set on a baking (cookie) sheet. Trim the edges and spread the pastry with the mincemeat. Bake for 20 minutes, or until crisp and golden. Remove from the oven.

2 Cut the apple into even-sized slices and sprinkle them with the lemon juice. Arrange the slices in an overlapping ring around the edge of the mincemeat.

3 In a pan, stir the jam, brandy and water over a gentle heat until well combined. Strain and brush over the tart. Bake for a further 15-20 minutes, and serve hot or cold, with whipped cream and brandy butter.

Serves 8

Tip: To make brandy butter, cream 100 g (¼ lb) (½ cup) each of

Pumpkin Soup, Chilled Celery Starter and juicy Roast Rib of Beef are followed by a delicious Brandy Mince Tart

unsalted butter and castor (fine granulated) sugar until white. Beat in 30-45 ml (2-3 tablespoons) brandy, 5 ml (1 teaspoon) at a time. Chill until firm.

Cinnamon Cherries in Wine

1 kg (2 lb) fresh cherries
300 ml (½ pint) (1¼ cups) water
175 g (6 oz) (¾ cup) sugar
300 ml (½ pint) (1¼ cups) red wine

30 ml (2 tablespoons) redcurrant jelly
small piece cinnamon stick

1 Discard the cherry stalks and, if you prefer, remove the stones (pits) with a cherry stoner.

2 Place the water, sugar, wine, redcurrant jelly and cinnamon stick in a saucepan and bring it to the boil.

3 Add the cherries and return to the boil. Reduce the heat and simmer uncovered for about 10 minutes.

4 Use a draining spoon to transfer the cherries to a serving dish.

5 Bring the syrup to the boil and boil rapidly for a few minutes to reduce (evaporate) it a little. Strain the syrup over the cherries and leave to cool slightly. Serve warm, not hot or cold, with a bowl of thick cream.

Serves 8

Menu

Fresh Melon

★

Spicy Turkey with Beans

★

Green Salad

★

Baklava

Spicy Turkey with Beans

 ★

2 turkey breasts
25 g (1 oz) (4 tablespoons) flour
30 ml (2 tablespoons) oil
300 ml (½ pint) (1¼ cups) yogurt
10 ml (2 teaspoons) tomato paste
5 ml (1 teaspoon) mixed spice
2.5 ml (½ teaspoon) ground
   nutmeg
5 ml (1 teaspoon) paprika pepper
salt and black pepper
5 ml (1 teaspoon) Worcestershire
   sauce
450 g (1 lb) canned red kidney
   beans, drained

1 Preheat the oven to 170°C, 325°F, gas 3.

2 Coat the turkey in the flour. Heat the oil and fry the turkey quickly until golden-brown on both sides. Transfer to a casserole dish.

3 Combine the yogurt with the tomato paste, spices, seasoning and Worcestershire sauce and pour over the turkey. Bake for 1 hour.

4 Heat the beans and place them in a heated serving dish. Place the turkey on top and pour the sauce over. Garnish with chopped parsley and lemon. Serve with hot garlic bread and salad.

Serves 4

Baklava

 ★

shortcrust pastry (pie crust)
   made with 225 g (½ lb) (2¼ cups)
   flour

Baklava, an eastern Mediterranean speciality, is rich with nuts and honey which make it an irresistible dessert

100 g (¼ lb) (½ cup) butter
melted butter for brushing

For the Filling:
75 g (3 oz) (⅜ cup) unsalted butter,
   softened
50 g (2 oz) (⅔ cup) each finely
   chopped walnuts, almonds and
   pistachio nuts
25 g (1 oz) (2 tablespoons) castor
   (fine granulated) sugar
5 ml (1 teaspoon) cinnamon
pinch ground cloves
5 ml (1 teaspoon) lemon juice
5 ml (1 teaspoon) orange flower
   water

For the Syrup:
175 g (6 oz) (½ cup) honey
225 ml (8 fl oz) (1 cup) water
2 whole cloves
1 stick cinnamon
10 ml (2 teaspoons) lemon juice
1 strip thinly pared lemon rind
5 ml (1 teaspoon) orange flower
   water

1 Roll out the prepared dough to a large oblong. Dot the butter over the dough, fold in three and seal the edges. Leave to rest for 10 minutes. Repeat the rolling, folding and resting 7 more times, starting each time with the fold on the right.

2 Preheat the oven to 220°C, 425°F, gas 7. Beat together the filling ingredients to form a thick paste. Roll out the pastry very thinly to a large square, brush with melted butter and cut it in half. Sandwich with the filling. Brush with more melted butter, cut into 15 triangles and place on a baking (cookie) sheet lined with non-stick baking paper.

3 Bake for 15-20 minutes, reduce the oven temperature to 170°C, 325°F, gas 3 and bake for a further 20 minutes, until well-risen and golden-brown.

4 Meanwhile, heat all the syrup ingredients in a pan and simmer for 10 minutes. Strain and cool, then pour over the cooked baklava and leave for a few hours to soak in. Serve cold.

Makes 15 pieces

Spicy Turkey with Beans, an unusual but effective mixture of flavours and colours, is sure to please all the family

Menu

Figs in Parma Ham *or*
Vegetable Fondue
★
Duck Italian-style
★
Green Salad
★
Pineapple Cream

Figs in Parma Ham

8 lettuce leaves
8 figs, quartered lengthways
8 slices Parma ham
watercress for garnishing

1 Arrange the lettuce leaves on 8 serving plates.

2 Wrap 4 fig quarters in each slice of ham and place each one on a lettuce leaf. Garnish each dish with a little watercress and serve immediately.

Serves 8

Vegetable Fondue

This fondue is a famous speciality of the Piedmont region of Italy. In the country of its origin it is called Bagno Caldo which means 'hot bath'. It is a traditional Christmas Eve delicacy but we think it makes an exciting and novel appetizer.

300 ml (½ pint) (1¼ cups) olive oil
3 cloves garlic, sliced
2.5 ml (½ teaspoon) freshly
  ground (milled) black pepper
100 g (¼ lb) canned anchovy fillets

For the Dipping Vegetables:
sliced carrots
radishes
celery sticks
spring onions (scallions)
chicory leaves

1 Heat the oil in a fondue pot with the garlic and pepper. Drain the anchovy fillets, reserving the oil. Chop the fillets and add them to the oil with the reserved anchovy oil. Heat until the oil is bubbling.

2 Arrange the fresh vegetables in

Pineapple Cream is a rich and creamy dessert with a velvet smooth texture, decorated with cherries and angelica

a serving bowl, remembering to put toothpicks in the radishes. Allow each guest to dip his own vegetables in the oil.

Serves 8

Duck Italian-style

2 small ducks
50 g (2 oz) (¼ cup) butter
50 ml (2 fl oz) (¼ cup) oil
2 large onions, chopped
2 carrots, sliced
2 sticks celery, chopped
100 g (¼ lb) bacon, sliced
1 kg (2 lb) tomatoes, peeled
  deseeded and chopped
300 ml (½ pint) (1¼ cups) chicken
  stock
150 ml (¼ pint) (⅝ cup) dry white
  wine
pinch basil
pinch sage
5 ml (1 teaspoon) parsley
salt and pepper
350 g (¾ lb) ribbon pasta
50 g (2 oz) (⅓ cup) grated
  parmesan cheese
10 ml (2 teaspoons) cornflour
  (cornstarch)

1 Cut each duck into 4 pieces. Heat half of the butter and the oil in a large frying pan (skillet). Add the duck pieces, cover and brown on both sides for 10 minutes. Transfer the browned duck to a large flameproof casserole.

2 Add the onions to the pan and fry them gently until transparent. Add the carrots and celery and stir-fry for a further 5 minutes until lightly browned. Transfer all the vegetables to the casserole and discard the fats in the pan.

3 Add the bacon to the casserole with the chopped tomatoes, chicken stock and wine. Stir in the herbs and season to taste. Cover and cook the casserole slowly over a gentle heat for 45-60 minutes or until the duck is tender. Remove the pieces of duck and strain the casserole liquids into a clean pan. Keep the duck warm in the oven.

4 Boil the ribbon pasta in salted

water for 10 minutes. Strain and arrange it on a large ovenproof serving dish. Toss the pasta in the remaining butter and the cheese and arrange the duck on top. Keep warm.

5 Skim off any fat that may have formed from the top of the casserole juices. Mix the cornflour (cornstarch) and 50 ml (2 fl oz) ($\frac{1}{4}$ cup) of warm water to a paste.

6 Heat the juices gently and stir in the cornflour (cornstarch) paste. Continue to stir over a gentle heat until you have a smooth, thick gravy. Pour some of the gravy over the duck and pasta and serve the rest in a gravy boat. Return the duck and pasta to the oven for 5 minutes to allow the gravy to soak through the pasta.

7 Serve with a crisp green salad and a green vegetable of your choice.

Serves 8

Duck Italian-style is cooked in wine with fresh celery, and then served on a bed of ribbon macaroni for a tasty meal

Pineapple Cream

225 ml (8 fl oz) (1 cup) milk
5 ml (1 teaspoon) vanilla essence
25 g (1 oz) ($\frac{1}{4}$ cup) plain flour
50 g (2 oz) ($\frac{1}{2}$ cup) icing (confectioners') sugar
3 egg yolks
30 ml (2 tablespoons) powdered gelatine
30 ml (2 tablespoons) kirsch
75 g (3 oz) canned chopped pineapple
225 ml (8 fl oz) (1 cup) double (heavy) cream, whipped

For the Decoration:
pineapple pieces
glacé cherries
angelica

1 In a small saucepan, gently heat the milk and vanilla essence to just below boiling point. In a bowl, mix the flour and sugar and beat in the egg yolks until throughly blended. Pour the milk gradually into the flour mixture, stirring constantly until smooth.

2 Soften the gelatine in 50 ml (2 fl oz) ($\frac{1}{4}$ cup) of warm water and stir it into the custard cream. Leave to become lukewarm. Add the kirsch and mix well. Chill until partially set and then fold in the pineapple.

3 Whip the cream until it forms stiff peaks and fold it into the pineapple mixture. Turn the pineapple mixture into a 1.5 litre (2$\frac{1}{2}$ pint) (6 cup) mould and chill in the refrigerator until well set.

4 Unmould the cream and decorate with the pineapple, cherries and angelica. Serve at once.

Serves 8

Glazed Loin of Pork with Stuffed Pears

1½ kg (3 lb) boned and rolled loin
   of pork
45 ml (3 tablespoons) cream
   cheese
30 ml (2 tablespoons) sweet
   pickle
40 g (1½ oz) (½ cup) chopped
   walnuts
6 canned pear halves, drained

6 gherkins, cut into fans

For the Marinade:
30 ml (2 tablespoons) each clear
   honey, vinegar and oil
60 ml (4 tablespoons) orange
   juice
15 ml (1 tablespoon) soya sauce
5 ml (1 teaspoon) paprika
salt and pepper

1 Weigh the meat and calculate the cooking time, allowing 20 minutes per 450 g (1 lb) and 20 minutes over.

2 Combine the marinade ingredients and place in a shallow dish with the pork. Marinate for several hours, turning frequently.

3 Preheat the oven to 200°C, 400°F, gas 6. Remove the pork from the marinade and place it in a roasting pan. Bake for the calculated cooking time, reducing the oven temperature after 15 minutes to 190°C, 375°F, gas 5, and basting with the marinade for the last 30 minutes. Cool the meat on a rack. Remove the string.

4 Blend the cream cheese, pickle

Bananas Créole are a tropical speciality from the sunny Caribbean, and are flamed in rum with pineapple syrup

and walnuts and divide between the pear halves. Garnish the cold meat with the stuffed pears and the gherkins.

Serves 6

Tivoli Salad

450 g (1 lb) red cabbage, shredded
1 cooked beetroot, cut into strips
4 sticks celery, cut into strips
2 apples, cored and sliced
½ small onion, grated
100 ml (4 fl oz) (½ cup) wine
   vinegar
30 ml (2 tablespoons) oil
salt and pepper

1 Combine the vegetables.

2 Mix the remaining ingredients and toss with the salad.

Serves 6

Bananas Créole

50 g (2 oz) (¼ cup) butter
6 bananas, peeled
3 canned pineapple rings, diced
50 g (2 oz) (bare ½ cup) icing
   (confectioners') sugar
45 ml (3 tablespoons) syrup from
   canned pineapple
50 g (2 oz) (⅓ cup) raisins, soaked
   in 50 ml (2 fl oz) (¼ cup) rum

1 Melt the butter in a frying pan (skillet). Add the bananas and turn them in the butter, over a medium heat, until golden.

2 Add the pineapple and sugar, and cook until the sugar has caramelized.

3 Stir in the pineapple syrup, raisins and rum, heat through and ignite. Serve immediately.

Serves 6

Glazed Loin of Pork with Stuffed Pears is served with a colourful, crisp Tivoli Salad of red cabbage and apple

21st Birthday Buffets

Lotus Blossom Chicken
Sea Bass Melbourne
Spiced Sirloin
Sandringham
Muscovite Salad
Buffet Bouchées
Orange Surprises
Exotic Fruit Salad
Petit Fours

This 21st birthday buffet spread looks impressive and difficult to prepare but appearances can be deceptive and it is relatively easy when you know how. Although our buffet is for a 21st birthday celebration, you can, of course, prepare this spread for any special occasion or party. The beauty of this menu is that many of the dishes can be prepared and cooked in advance and frozen until the big day. So if you have a deep freezer, you can save yourself a lot of time and trouble. For example, the brioches, bread rolls and bouchée cases can be made beforehand and frozen until needed, then thawed and topped with fresh fillings and spreads or frozen and thawed sauces. The cake, of course, will benefit from

being stored in an airtight tin for several weeks before icing.

The most important thing to remember when you are planning a buffet is that all the food should be capable of being eaten with forks, spoons or fingers – there should be no necessity for knives. Most probably, it will be eaten standing up and each guest will need a free hand to hold the plate. Be sensible about including chicken and other meats on your buffet spread. If possible, carve them in advance, preferably with an electric carving knife, if you have one. It not only takes the hard work out of carving, you can also slice thinner portions and so there is ultimately less waste and more portions to go round. If you are serving whole legs or wings of poultry, it is perfectly good and acceptable etiquette to pick them up and eat them in your fingers.

Laying the table and its decoration are also important points. It is a good idea to make sure that the table is approachable from all

sides – this will cut down on long queues for food. Cover it with a pretty table cloth and provide plenty of serviettes. Paper ones are best – they are cheap and easily disposed of. If you can, arrange the forks and spoons down both sides so that they are easily accessible. Lay the table carefully with shallower dishes at the front, deeper ones at the back so that when people lean over they do not dangle their sleeves in the food. There should be plenty of serving spoons for people to help themselves. You can stand the serving plates on liner plates so that spilt and dribbled food is neatly caught and does not mark the cloth. Do not use your best plates for guests, however tempted to impress – they may break.

1 *Petit Fours*
2 *Birthday Cake*
3 *Muscovite Salad*
4 *Fish Mayonnaise*
5 *Sea Bass Melbourne*
6 *Orange Surprises*
7 *Lotus Blossom Chicken*
8 *Party Rolls and Brioches*
9 *Exotic Fruit Salad*
10 *Buffet Bouchées*

Instead, use attractive china serving dishes and provide your guests with the disposable paper sort. It will also save you washing up afterwards.

Cut a slice out of flans and gâteaux to encourage guests to go ahead and help themselves – they are sometimes inhibited about digging in or may even take gluttonously large portions so that there is not enough to go round. Cover the table loosely with a cloth or wrap the food in foil until it is time to eat – some food dries out very quickly (it also stops guests from picking).

Last, but not least, choose the dishes you make with care. Provide something to suit everybody's taste, whether vegetarian, carnivorous or committed slimmer. Individual dishes should be light, not too rich or heavy. The accent should be on attractive colours and presentation. Garnish savoury dishes prettily with sprigs of parsley and watercress and lemon wedges

and slices. Cream, whipped and piped, will always improve the appearance of desserts and gâteaux. Also, remember that most people will not try every dish and that they eat smaller portions than at a normal dinner. Therefore, for a party of 20 guests, you need not provide 20 portions of absolutely everything. You can cheat and, at the same time, appear the perfect, thoughtful hostess, by strategically placing bowls of nuts, olives, crisps and small savouries around the room so that they can nibble at will before the food is served.

Party Rolls and Brioches

Small bridge rolls and brioches are ideal party fare. They can be filled with an enormous variety of tempting foods; they are easy to prepare and easy to eat. To fill brioches, first lift off the topknots, then remove some of the soft bread centre to make space for a filling. The fillings shown here are only a few of the possibilities; those shown in the bouchées, opposite, could equally well be used in soft rolls, and vice versa. The presentation of rolls and bouchées is important – arrange them on a large serving dish, and garnish with lettuce leaves, or sprigs of watercress or parsley for a fresh effect.

Egg Cream

Place 4 eggs in a pan and cover with cold water. Add 5 ml (1 teaspoon) salt and bring to the boil. Reduce the heat and simmer for 8 minutes. Cool the hard-boiled eggs under running cold water and then remove the shells. Finely chop the eggs and mix them with 150 ml ($\frac{1}{4}$ pint) ($\frac{5}{8}$ cup) mayonnaise, 10 ml (2 teaspoons) made mustard, one finely chopped small onion, and seasoning to taste. Spread the mixture over halved bridge rolls and garnish each roll with an anchovy fillet and a halved black olive, or three capers arranged in a row and a sprig of cress.

Ham Salad

Finely chop: 100 g ($\frac{1}{4}$ lb) lean ham, half a dill pickle, 1 small onion, and 1 cooked potato. Mix these ingredients into 150 ml ($\frac{1}{4}$ pint) ($\frac{5}{8}$ cup) mayonnaise. Stir in a pinch of paprika, salt and pepper to taste, and 15 ml (1 tablespoon) finely chopped parsley or chives. Spoon on to rolls.

Spring Salmon

Drain 100 g ($\frac{1}{4}$ lb) canned salmon. Remove any skin or pieces of bone and mash the meat with a fork. Stir in the juice of half a lemon, 15 ml (1 tablespoon) cream, and a dash of paprika. For extra piquancy, add a few drops of anchovy essence and some chopped spring onion (scallion). Spread on rolls.

Party Rolls and Brioches can be topped and filled with a wide variety of savoury, creamy mixtures and sauces

Tongue and Asparagus

Drain a large can of asparagus tips. Curl half a slice of finely sliced tongue round three or four asparagus tips, and arrange on a roll.

Cottage Cheese

Cream 100 g ($\frac{1}{4}$ lb) ($\frac{2}{3}$ cup) cottage cheese with a fork. Finely chop three pickled cocktail onions and mix them into the cheese. Spread on rolls and garnish with a lettuce leaf or a slice of fresh orange.

Piquant Pâté

Cream together 100 g ($\frac{1}{4}$ lb) soft liver pâté with 50 ml (2 fl oz) ($\frac{1}{4}$ cup) double (heavy) cream. Mix in a finely chopped dill pickle, some chopped capers and a few drops of chilli sauce. Place in a piping (decorator's) bag with a star nozzle and pipe into the hollowed brioches. Replace the topknots of the brioches.

Avocado Surprise

Remove the flesh of an avocado and cream it with the juice of half a lemon. Spoon the mixture into hollowed brioches. Beat 100 g ($\frac{1}{4}$ lb) ($\frac{2}{3}$ cup) cream cheese with 50 ml (2 fl oz) ($\frac{1}{4}$ cup) double (heavy) cream. Place in a piping (decorator's) bag with a star nozzle and pipe swirls of cheese on top of the avocado filling. Top with the topknots of the brioches.

Shrimp and Cucumber

Butter some bridge rolls and arrange slices of cucumber on them. In the middle, place an overlapping row of peeled shrimps or prawns. Alternatively, mix 100 g ($\frac{1}{4}$ lb) shrimps or prawns with 150 ml ($\frac{1}{4}$ pint) ($\frac{5}{8}$ cup) mayonnaise and 10 ml (2 teaspoons)

tomato ketchup (catsup), and place this mixture on the cucumber slices.

Sardine and Watercress

Drain the oil from a large can of sardines. Arrange one or two sardines on each bridge roll and top with a sprig of washed watercress and a half slice of lemon. If wished, the sardines can be mashed with 30 ml (2 tablespoons) mayonnaise and 10 ml (2 teaspoons) tomato paste.

Mustard Spread

Mix together 15 ml (1 tablespoon) made French mustard with 30 ml (2 tablespoons) mayonnaise. Add 15 ml (1 tablespoon) each of: finely chopped red pepper, green pepper, onion, dill pickle, and corn kernels. Spread on rolls; top, if wished, with a slice of tongue or thinly sliced cheese, garnished with tomato.

Buffet Bouchées are bite-sized puff pastry cases filled with different coloured lumpfish roe and savoury mixtures

Buffet Bouchées

Bouchées – small vol-au-vents – are easy to make, but when catering for a large party you may prefer to buy ready-made frozen ones. Fill them with some of these delicious ideas.

As with party rolls and brioches, presentation of these bouchées is important – they should look as delicious as they taste. Pretty paper napkins will serve as well as plates for this finger-food – and save on washing-up too!

Duxelles

Finely chop: 175 g (6 oz) button mushrooms, 50 g (2 oz) lean ham, and half an onion. Fry the onion for 1 minute in 40 g ($1\frac{1}{2}$ oz) (3 table-spoons) butter, then stir in the mushrooms and ham and cook for 3 more minutes, stirring, over low heat. Add 15 ml (1 tablespoon) finely chopped parsley, 5 ml (1 teaspoon) tomato paste, and seasoning to taste. Allow to cool and spoon into the bouchée cases.

Salmon Cream

Drain 225 g ($\frac{1}{2}$ lb) canned salmon, remove any skin or bone, and flake the meat. Mix it with 50 ml (2 fl oz) ($\frac{1}{4}$ cup) double (heavy) cream and 30 ml (2 tablespoons) mayonnaise. Add 5 ml (1 teaspoon) paprika, 15 ml (1 tablespoon) sherry, and a little salt and pepper. Place in the bouchée cases and garnish with small parsley sprigs.

Fruity Chicken

Finely dice 100 g ($\frac{1}{4}$ lb) cooked chicken meat. Mix it with 30 ml (2 tablespoons) fruit chutney, such as mango or apricot. Add 15 ml (1 tablespoon) chopped canned red pepper (pimento) and 15 ml (1 tablespoon) mayonnaise; mix well. Stir in a few drops of chilli sauce, and spoon the mixture into bouchée cases.

Ham and Egg Salad

Hard-boil three eggs; cool and remove the shells. Finely chop the egg and mix it with 50 ml (2 fl oz) ($\frac{1}{4}$ cup) mayonnaise. Chop 50 g (2 oz) lean ham and three spring onions (scallions) and mix into the egg; season to taste. Spoon into the bouchée cases.

Caviar-Avocado

Cream the flesh of a large avocado with 50 ml (2 fl oz) ($\frac{1}{4}$ cup) sour cream and a few drops of chilli sauce. Spoon or pipe the mixture into the bouchée cases and top with a teaspoonful of red or black caviar-style lumpfish roe. Sprinkle a little lemon juice on top.

Anchovy Cream Cheese

Beat 100 g ($\frac{1}{4}$ lb) ($\frac{5}{8}$ cup) cream cheese with 50 ml (2 fl oz) ($\frac{1}{4}$ cup) double (heavy) cream. Stir in 15 ml (1 tablespoon) grated onion, a little salt and pepper, 2.5 ml ($\frac{1}{2}$ teaspoon) paprika, and six finely chopped anchovy fillets. Spoon or pipe the mixture into the bouchée cases and sprinkle a dusting of paprika on top.

Sea Bass Melbourne

one 1 kg (2 lb) sea bass or grey
  mullet
25 g (1 oz) (4 tablespoons)
  powdered gelatine
50 g (2 oz) (¼ cup) butter
225 g (½ lb) prawns (shrimps),
  cooked
1 lemon, sliced
1 cucumber, sliced
¼ red pepper, deseeded and
  chopped

For the Stock:
1 litre (1¾ pints) (4½ cups) water
550 ml (1 pint) (2½ cups) dry cider
150 ml (¼ pint) (⅝ cup) tomato
  juice
15 ml (1 tablespoon) honey
1 large onion, cut in rings
1 carrot, sliced
1 clove garlic, crushed
1 stick celery, sliced
bouquet garni
salt and pepper

For the Sauce:
15 ml (1 tablespoon) butter
30 ml (2 tablespoons) flour
5 ml (1 teaspoon) mustard
4 egg yolks
300 ml (½ pint) (1¼ cups) oil
pulp 1 avocado, mashed
½ small onion, chopped
15 ml (1 tablespoon) mixture of
  chopped parsley and coriander
  leaves

1 Place the ingredients for the
stock in a large saucepan and
boil for 10 minutes, stirring
occasionally.

2 Tie up the fish to hold it in a
figure 'S' shape and place it in a
fish kettle. Cover with the stock
and simmer for 20-25 minutes.
Cool the fish in the stock. Remove
the fish and peel off its body skin.
Strain and reserve 550 ml (1 pint)
(2½ cups) of the stock. Reheat half
of this stock and dissolve the
gelatine in it.

3 Brush the fish twice with a
little of this aspic and pour the
rest into the centre of a large, shallow serving dish. Place the fish on
top and leave in a cool place until
set.

4 Beat the butter until light and
fluffy and place it in a piping

(decorator's) bag fitted with a
plain nozzle. Pipe a rim of butter
along the spine of the fish and
decorate the head.

5 Peel the prawns (shrimps) and
reserve 8 heads. Flute the edges of
the sliced lemon and halve each
slice. Do the same with the
cucumber slices.

6 Place the prawn (shrimp)
heads along the spine of the fish
on top of the butter and arrange
the prawns (shrimps) on the aspic
along either side of the fish.
Decorate the side of the dish with
lemon slices dotted with red
pepper and the cucumber slices.
Chill.

7 Prepare the sauce. Melt the
butter in a pan and stir in the flour.
Cook for 1 minute and gradually
stir in the remaining fish stock.
Allow to cool.

8 Place the mustard, egg yolks,
salt and pepper in a bowl. Add the
oil in a thin trickle, whisking continually until the sauce is emulsi-
fied and thick. Stir in the fish
stock sauce, mashed avocado
pulp, chopped onion, parsley and
coriander. Check the seasoning
and serve the Melbourne sauce
separately.

Serves 6-8

Spiced Sirloin
Sandringham

1 kg (2 lb) boned sirloin
salt and pepper
50 ml (2 fl oz) (¼ cup) oil
4 chicory (Belgian endive)
  leaves
24 asparagus spears, cooked
2 slices red pepper

For the Glaze:
100 g (¼ lb) (⅜ cup) redcurrant jelly
15 ml (1 tablespoon) vinegar
juice 1 orange
5 ml (1 teaspoon) ground ginger
garlic salt
5 ml (1 teaspoon) mixed spices

1 Preheat the oven to 200°C,
400°F, gas 6. Season the meat and

rub it with oil. Roast it for 45
minutes. Cool.

2 Slice the beef and arrange the
slices in overlapping layers on a
large shallow dish.

3 Boil the ingredients for the
glaze for 4 minutes, stirring continuously. Brush the cooled slices
of meat 3 times with the glaze and
leave to set.

4 Cut each chicory leaf in two
and place 3 asparagus spears in
the hollow of each half. Cut the red
pepper into 8 equal strips and
place them over each asparagus
basket. Chill and serve garnished
with watercress.

Serves 6-8

Muscovite Salad

50 g (2 oz) ham, cubed
50 g (2 oz) tongue, cooked and
  cubed
100 g (¼ lb) cooked carrots, diced
100 g (¼ lb) canned corn kernels,
  drained
100 g (¼ lb) cooked peas
100 g (¼ lb) cooked beans, diced
225 g (½ lb) potatoes, boiled and
  cubed
1 red pepper, deseeded and
  chopped
salt and pepper
300 ml (½ pint) (1¼ cups)
  mayonnaise
50 g (2 oz) anchovy fillets
drained capers for decoration

1 Place the ham, tongue, carrots,
corn, peas, beans, potatoes and
red pepper in a large salad bowl.
Season and add the mayonnaise.
Toss gently but thoroughly.

2 Arrange the anchovy fillets
over the top in a lattice pattern
and place a caper in the centre of
each diamond. Chill and serve.

Serves 8-10

---

*Spiced Sirloin Sandringham, is
garnished with chicory
and asparagus, and served with
a tasty Muscovite Salad*

Orange Surprises

9 oranges
100 g (¼ lb) sponge cake, cubed
50 ml (2 fl oz) (¼ cup) Cointreau
300 ml (½ pint) (1¼ cups) whipping
  cream
25 g (1 oz) (2 tablespoons) castor
  (fine granulated) sugar
25 cm (10 in) candied angelica,
  chopped

1 Cut the tops off the oranges and scoop out the flesh; squeeze the juice and reserve. Place the sponge cake cubes inside the oranges. Sprinkle with Cointreau and orange juice.

2 Whip the cream and sugar until stiff and pipe on to the oranges. Garnish with the orange tops and chopped angelica.

Serves 9

Lotus Blossom Chicken

one 1.5 kg (3 lb) roasting chicken
salt and pepper
25 g (1 oz) (2 tablespoons) butter
30 ml (1 fl oz) (2 tablespoons) oil

For the Glaze:
100 g (¼ lb) (⅜ cup) clear honey
15 ml (1 tablespoon) vinegar
15 ml (1 tablespoon) soya sauce
3 drops yellow food colouring
1 drop red food colouring

For the Aspic:
150 ml (¼ pint) (⅝ cup) water
75 ml (2½ fl oz) (⅓ cup) orange juice
15 g (½ oz) aspic jelly crystals

Orange Surprises, topped with swirls of fresh cream and angelica 'leaves', will make a juicy refreshing dessert

1 orange
3 black olives

For the Accompaniments:
6 canned pineapple slices
50 g (2 oz) (¼ cup) cream cheese
50 ml (2 fl oz) (¼ cup) double
  (heavy) cream
6 black olives
1 cucumber
150 ml (¼ pint) (⅝ cup) fruit
  chutney

1 Preheat the oven to 200°C, 400°F, gas 6. Sprinkle the chicken with salt and pepper and place in a roasting pan with the butter and oil. Roast for 45-60 minutes, basting from time to time.

2 To make the glaze: melt the honey, vinegar, soya sauce and food colouring in a pan. Cook for 5 minutes. Spread the glaze all over the chicken. Replace the chicken in the oven and cook for 5-10 minutes. Allow to cool.

3 To make the aspic: warm the water and orange juice and dissolve the aspic crystals in it. Brush the liquid over the cold chicken. Peel the orange and cut three slices. Dip them in the aspic liquid and fasten them on the breast of the chicken with toothpicks; top the ends of the toothpicks with black olives. Brush the remaining aspic liquid over the chicken. Leave in the refrigerator until set.

4 To make the accompaniments: lay the pineapple slices on the serving dish round the chicken. Beat the cream cheese and cream together and spoon or pipe the mixture into the middle of the pineapple slices. Top each one with a black olive. Cut grooves along the cucumber with a canelling knife and cut the cucumber into 4 cm (1½ in) chunks. Fill each one with fruit chutney. Arrange the cucumber pieces between the pineapple slices. Garnish with coriander leaves or parsley.

Serves 10-12

Lotus Blossom Chicken with its delicate Chinese flavour and a colourful garnish will delight your guests

Cucumber, Celery and Apple Salad

4 apples
1 cucumber
5 sticks celery
150 ml ($\frac{1}{4}$ pint) ($\frac{5}{8}$ cup) natural
  yogurt
50 ml (2 fl oz) ($\frac{1}{4}$ cup) mayonnaise
juice 1 lemon
coriander leaves for decoration

1 Peel, core and chop the apples. Make grooves lengthways along the cucumber using a canelling knife, and slice it thinly. Slice the celery.

2 Combine the yogurt, mayonnaise and lemon juice.

3 Mix the apples, cucumber and celery with the prepared dressing, then transfer to a serving dish and decorate with the coriander leaves.

Serves 8

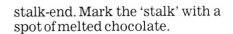

Petit Fours

Oranges
Colour the marzipan with a few drops of orange food colouring and shape into small balls. Roll them on a grater, and use a cocktail stick to mark lines at the

---

An assortment of Petit Fours, marzipan fruits, frosted grapes and chocolate lychees, are a tempting finish to a buffet

stalk-end. Mark the 'stalk' with a spot of melted chocolate.

Bananas
Roll the marzipan into small sausages, taper the ends and bend slightly to form banana shapes. Mark the bananas with melted chocolate, using a cocktail stick.

Pears
Colour some marzipan with green food colouring and form into pear shapes. Indent the stalk-ends and insert a clove to represent a stalk. Using a fingertip, rub a little red food colouring on to each 'pear'.

Dates
Slit some fresh or dried dates along one side and remove the stone (pit). Fill each with a sausage-shaped piece of marzipan.

Chocolate Lychees
Dip some peeled lychees into melted plain chocolate and leave on waxed or greaseproof (parchment) paper to set. When they are set, pipe a decoration of melted milk chocolate on to each. The stone can be removed from the lychee before dipping, if preferred, although this makes the process more difficult.

Grapes
Melt some sugar in a pan, then boil until it is a rich golden colour. Remove from the heat and immediately dip small clusters of green grapes into it. Stand on greaseproof (parchment) paper to set.

All about Fish

Fish can add variety to your daily menu. There is a wide range of fish (and shellfish) to choose from, with many different tastes and textures, from the kings of fish, salmon and trout, through flat fish, halibut and sole, and oily fish, mackerel and herring, to the tiny whitebait and sardines. Whether planning an everyday meal or a dinner party, there is always a fish to suit the occasion.

Your choice of fish will probably depend on the occasion and how much money you wish to spend but all fish, no matter what the cost, contain many vital nutrients. Fish muscle is made up of protein, fat and water and also contains vitamins and minerals. For example, 225 g (8 oz) herring contains: $23\frac{1}{2}$ g protein; $14\frac{1}{2}$ mg calcium; 200 i.u. vitamin A; 1300 i.u. vitamin D; 2 mg iron; 0.05 mg vitamin B.

Protein Cod is very rich in protein, particularly the liver and the roes. The protein content in salmon and trout is higher still, but a little lower in white fish. A rich egg sauce will increase the protein content in a white fish dish.

Poached Fish

Poached Cod Andalouse

25 g (1 oz) (2 tablespoons) butter
25 g (1 oz) (2 tablespoons)
  margarine
8 boneless cod steaks
pinch garlic salt, pepper, paprika
1 large onion, cut into rings
25 g (1 oz) (¼ cup) red pepper, cut
  into strips
2 large white mushrooms, sliced
grated rind and juice 1 lemon
15 ml (1 tablespoon) white wine
  vinegar
75 ml (2½ fl oz) (⅓ cup) dry white
  wine
150 ml (¼ pint) (½ cup) water
1 chicken stock cube
1 celery stalk, chopped
25 g (1 oz) (2 tablespoons) tomato
  concentrate (paste)
1 bouquet garni
150 ml (¼ pint) (⅝ cup) single
  (light) cream or milk
15 g (½ oz) (1 tablespoon) cornflour
  (cornstarch)

1 Preheat the oven to 200°C, 400°F, gas 6. Grease a shallow baking dish with half of the butter and margarine. Arrange the fish steaks in the dish and dot with small pieces of butter. Season with salt, pepper and paprika.

2 Place the onion rings, strips of red pepper and sliced mushrooms over the fish steaks. Sprinkle with grated lemon, lemon juice and vinegar.

3 Place the wine, water, stock cube, chopped celery and tomato concentrate (paste) in a saucepan and boil for 2 minutes. Pour over the fish steaks.

4 Place a bouquet garni on the side and bake in the preheated oven for 18 minutes.

5 Pour the fish liquid into a small saucepan and bring to the boil. Boil for 5 minutes.

6 Blend together the cream and cornflour (cornstarch). Pour into the boiling fish stock, stirring all the time until it thickens. Cook for 5 minutes. Coat the fish evenly with the sauce and serve.

Serves 4

Red Mullets Breton-style

6 fillets medium-sized red
  mullet
1 chicken stock cube
400 ml (14 fl oz) (1¾ cups) water
100 ml (4 fl oz) (6 tablespoons) dry
  white wine
50 g (2 oz) (4 tablespoons) butter
white parts 2 leeks, sliced
2 onions, chopped
30 g (2 oz) (good ½ cup) flour
200 ml (7 fl oz) (⅞ cup) single
  (light) cream
3 sprigs parsley, chopped

1 Preheat the oven to 190°C,

Poached Cod Andalouse — a delicious way of serving cod in a wine sauce flavoured with red pepper, mushrooms and onions

375°F, gas 5. Prepare the stock from the cube and hot water. Butter a flameproof dish and place the fillets of fish on it. Add the stock and white wine and cover with a sheet of aluminium foil.

2 Bring to the boil over a high heat, then cook for 8 minutes in the oven. Adjust the seasoning. Remove the fish to a deep serving dish and keep hot.

3 Heat the butter in a pan and cook the leeks and onions until lightly browned. Add the flour and stir well, with a wooden spoon, for 5 minutes over a low heat.

4 Pour 400 ml (¾ pint) (1¾ cups) of the stock into the pan. Stir until blended and cook a further 5 minutes. Then incorporate the cream and cook carefully for 3 minutes.

5 Pour the sauce over the fish and sprinkle with the chopped parsley.

Serves 6

Fillet of Sole Melone

1 medium onion, chopped
50 g (2 oz) (4 tablespoons) butter
four 75 g (3 oz) soles or plaice,
 filleted
pinch salt and pepper
pinch ground (powdered) ginger
grated rind and juice 1 lemon
150 ml (¼ pint) (⅝ cup) water
1 chicken stock cube
150 ml (¼ pint) (⅝ cup) single
 (light) cream
½ honeydew melon, peeled and
 deseeded
10 g (⅓ oz) cornflour (cornstarch)
480 g (1 lb) mashed potatoes
1 egg yolk
25 g (1 oz) (2 tablespoons) butter
salt and pepper
1 egg, beaten
chopped parsley

1 Preheat the oven to 200°C, 400°F, gas 6. Butter a shallow dish and sprinkle the bottom with the chopped onion.

2 Pound the fish fillets lightly with a rolling pin – to break down the fibres – then season with salt, pepper and ground (powdered) ginger. Fold the fillets in two and lay in the shallow dish. Add the grated lemon rind and lemon juice, the water and crumbled chicken stock cube. Cover with a piece of greaseproof (waxed) paper.

3 Bake on the top shelf of the preheated oven for 15 minutes. When cooked, pour the fish liquor (reduced stock) into a small saucepan. Leave the oven at the same temperature.

4 Boil the fish liquor for 3 minutes and thicken it with the cream and cornflour (cornstarch) which have been blended together. Season.

Fillet of Sole Melone, served with a salad of lettuce, hard-boiled (hard-cooked) eggs, red pepper, celery, carrot and raisins

5 Cut the melon into small cubes.

6 Blend the mashed potatoes with the egg yolk and butter and season. Place in a piping bag and pipe an attractive border around a clean, shallow dish. Dry it in the oven for 6 minutes. Then brush it with beaten egg. Arrange the cooked fish and raw melon cubes in the centre and pour over the cream sauce. Brown in the oven for 8 minutes. Decorate with melon balls and parsley.

Serves 4

Cod Dugleré

25 g (1 oz) (⅛ cup) chopped onions
four 225 g (½ lb) cod steaks
salt and pepper
450 g (1 lb) chopped, peeled
 tomatoes
50 g (2 oz) (4 tablespoons) soft
 butter
150 ml (5 fl oz) (⅝ cup) dry white
 wine
75 ml (3 fl oz) (⅜ cup) fish stock
1 bay leaf, imported
pinch tarragon
juice ½ lemon
pinch cayenne pepper
5 g (1 tablespoon) chopped
 parsley

1 Preheat the oven to 200°C, 400°F, gas 6. Butter a shallow dish and sprinkle with the chopped onions. Place the cod steaks on top and season with salt and pepper.

2 Cover with the coarsely chopped tomatoes and dot with half of the butter.

3 Pour over the wine and fish stock. Add the bay leaf and tarragon.

4 Bake in the preheated oven for 15-20 minutes.

5 Pour the sauce into a saucepan and boil to reduce by half. Season well and add the lemon juice and cayenne pepper.

6 Remove from the heat and stir in the remaining soft butter to cream it.

7 Pour the sauce over the fish and garnish with chopped parsley.

Serves 4

Plaice Belomar

 ★

450 g (1 lb) plaice fillets
juice ½ lemon
pinch salt
25 g (1 oz) (2 tablespoons) butter
2 onions, chopped

100 g (¼ lb) (1¼ cups) sliced, white
  mushrooms
100 g (¼ lb) (1 cup) chopped
  gherkins (dill pickles)
50 ml (2 fl oz) (¼ cup) brandy
  (optional)
40 g (1½ oz) (3 tablespoons) tomato
  concentrate (paste)
150 ml (¼ pint) (⅝ cup) single
  (light) cream
freshly ground (milled) black
  pepper

1 Rub the plaice fillets with the lemon juice and lightly sprinkle them with salt.

2 Heat the butter and add the onions and mushrooms. Fry over a low heat.

*Plaice Belomar —
fillets of fish served in a rich
creamy sauce, flavoured with
brandy*

3 Add the gherkins (dill pickles) and pour in the brandy. Set alight and let the flames die down.

4 Stir in the tomato concentrate (paste) and cream. Season with salt and pepper.

5 Fold over the plaice fillets and put them in the sauce. Cover and simmer for 10 minutes.

6 Pour into a serving dish and serve with boiled rice or potatoes.

Serves 4

Fish Stocks & Sauces

Fish Stocks and Sauces

When making fish stock, do not use the bones of oily fish which are not suitable for white sauces. A fish stock must be neutral with a sweetish taste. Sweating bones and onions in margarine or clarified butter produces a good flavour but tends to colour the sauce.

Fish sauces must always be more acidic than those served with meat and poultry. This can be done by adding the juice of 1 lemon per litre (1¾ pints) (4½ cups) of sauce and also some dry white wine – sweet wine tends to make the sauce grey in colour. Wine vinegar is always preferable to dark vinegar when used with fish stock.

Basic Fish Stock

450 g (1 lb) fish heads, bones and trimmings
25 g (1 oz) (2 tablespoons) butter
25 ml (1 fl oz) (⅛ cup) oil
1 carrot, sliced
1 onion, sliced
900 ml (1½ pints) (3⅝ cups) water
300 ml (½ pint) (1¼ cups) dry white wine
1 bouquet garni
pinch salt and pepper
1 chicken stock cube

1 Wash the fish heads and trimmings well.

2 Heat the butter and oil in a large pan and add the sliced carrot and onion. Cover and cook gently for 5 minutes.

3 Add the fish trimmings to the vegetables in the pan. Cook for 5 minutes.

4 Pour in the water and wine and add the bouquet garni. Season. Cook for 15 minutes.

5 Crumble in the stock cube and simmer for 5 minutes.

6 Strain through clean muslin (cheesecloth) or a fine sieve (strainer), cover and cool. Refrigerate until required.

Makes 900 ml (1½ pints) (3⅝ cups)

Tip: Fish stock should always be used the same day.

Basic White Wine Sauce

25 g (1 oz) (2 tablespoons) butter or margarine
25 g (1 oz) (4 tablespoons) flour
600 ml (1 pint) (2½ cups) fish stock
50 g (2 oz) (½ cup) chopped shallots
150 ml (¼ pint) (⅝ cup) dry white wine
4 egg yolks
150 ml (¼ pint) (⅝ cup) single (light) cream
pinch salt and pepper
pinch cayenne pepper
juice ½ lemon

1 Melt the fat in a saucepan and stir in the flour. Cook the roux for 3 minutes.

2 Add the fish stock gradually, stirring all the time, until the velouté sauce is smooth. Simmer for 20 minutes.

3 Boil the shallots in the wine until soft and add to the velouté sauce. Simmer for 15 minutes.

4 Blend the egg yolks with the cream and some of the sauce until well mixed. Pour into the velouté sauce and reheat, but do not allow the sauce to boil.

5 Season with salt and pepper and stir in the cayenne pepper and lemon juice.

Makes about 900 ml (1½ pints) (3⅝ cups)

Fillet of Cod Véronique

four 175 g (6 oz) fillets of cod
pinch salt and pepper
50 g (2 oz) (4 tablespoons) butter
150 ml (¼ pint) (⅝ cup) dry white wine
300 ml (½ pint) (1¼ cups) velouté sauce
50 ml (2 fl oz) (¼ cup) single (light) cream
pinch cayenne
juice ½ lemon
150 g (5 oz) skinned, seeded and split white Muscat grapes

1 Preheat the oven to 200°C, 400°F, gas 6.

2 Wash and dry the cod fillets. Season with salt and pepper.

3 Butter a shallow baking dish and arrange the fish fillets in it, side by side.

4 Pour in the dry white wine and velouté sauce, and cover with damp greaseproof (waxed) paper.

5 Bake in the oven for 15 minutes. Remove the paper and pour off the liquor into a saucepan. Keep the fish warm.

6 Boil the liquor to reduce (evaporate) by half and stir in the cream, whisking all the time. Season with salt, pepper and cayenne and stir in the lemon juice.

7 Arrange the fish in a clean, shallow dish. Pour over the sauce, and decorate with a border of grapes.

Serves 4

Tips: A fish sauce should always be made with ingredients which will enhance the flavour of the fish used. Aromatic herb sauces are best with oily fish such as sardines, trout or mackerel. The best stock you can make for a fish sauce is usually derived from the liquid in which the fish is poached. A fish liquor of wine and onions, infused with a bouquet garni, can constitute the base for a delicious sauce. Thicken with a liaison of egg yolks and cream, or simply blend with a basic white sauce.

Braised fish

Haddock with Anchovies

1½ kg (3 lb) haddock
salt and pepper
6 canned anchovy fillets,
  drained
25 g (1 oz) (½ cup) fine
  breadcrumbs
75 g (3 oz)) (6 tablespoons) soft
  butter or margarine
5 g (1 tablespoon) chopped
  parsley
grated rind 1 lemon

1 Preheat the oven to 200°C, 400°F, gas 6.

2 Clean and wash the fish. Season with salt. Make several small incisions across the backbone of the fish with a sharp knife. Cut the anchovy fillets into thin strips and place in the slits.

3 Place the fish in a greased baking dish and sprinkle with the breadcrumbs. Melt 25 g (1 oz) (2 tablespoons) fat and baste the fish.

4 Bake the fish for 20 minutes, basting it occasionally.

5 Cream the chopped parsley with the remaining butter and the grated lemon rind. Season with salt and pepper. Place in the refrigerator until firm but still malleable. Turn onto a sheet of aluminium foil and roll into a cylindrical shape. Refrigerate again. When really cold, cut into thin, round slices.

6 Serve the fish with the rounds of parsley butter and coleslaw tossed in a vinaigrette dressing.

Serves 4

*Haddock with Anchovies —
served with a salad of finely
grated carrot, white cabbage and
beetroot (beets) tossed in French
dressing*

Fillet of Sole Bonne Femme

75 g (3 oz) (6 tablespoons) butter
25 g (1 oz) (¼ cup) chopped shallots
5 g (1 tablespoon) chopped
  parsley
100 g (¼ lb) (1¼ cups) sliced, white
  mushrooms
four 100 g (¼ lb) fillets of sole
salt and pepper
150 ml (¼ pint) (⅝ cup) dry white
  wine
75 ml (3 fl oz) (⅜ cup) fish stock
150 ml (¼ pint) (⅝ cup) veloute
  sauce
juice ½ lemon
pinch cayenne pepper

1 Preheat oven to 200°C, 400°F, gas 6.

2 Butter a shallow baking dish with 15 g (½ oz) butter. Sprinkle with the chopped shallots, parsley and sliced mushrooms.

3 Season the fillets of sole with salt and pepper and arrange them in the baking dish.

4 Add the wine, fish stock and

velouté sauce and heat the dish on top of the stove until the liquor is boiling.

5 Cover the dish and place in the oven for 8 minutes.

6 Keeping the fillets warm, pour the liquor into a pan and boil to reduce (evaporate) by one-third.

7 Cut the butter into small pieces and whisk it in, one piece at a time, until it is all blended and the liquor is creamy.

8 Check the seasoning and add the lemon juice.

9 Place the fish on a flat serving dish and cover with the sauce. Sprinkle with cayenne pepper and place under a grill (broiler) for a few seconds to brown it. Decorate with sautéd button mushrooms.

Serves 4

Tip: To make Sole Bercy, a delicious alternative to Sole Bonne Femme, just follow the recipe as indicated but omit the mushrooms.

Fillet of Lemon Sole Stockholm

50 g (2 oz) (4 tablespoons) butter
25 g (1 oz) (⅛ cup) chopped onions
four 175 g (6 oz) fillets of lemon sole
salt and pepper
pinch paprika
150 ml (¼ pint) (⅝ cup) dry white wine
300 ml (½ pint) (1¼ cups) velouté sauce
75 ml (3 fl oz) (⅜ cup) single (light) cream
pinch dill
8 peeled, cooked prawns

1 Preheat the oven to 200°C, 400°F, gas 6.

2 Grease a shallow baking dish with butter and sprinkle with chopped onions.

Fillets of Lemon Sole Stockholm, cooked in white wine and cream, and served with whole prawns and buttered rice

3 Arrange the fish fillets in the dish and season with salt, pepper and paprika.

4 Add the wine and cover with a sheet of greaseproof (waxed) paper and bake for 15 minutes.

5 Pour off the fish liquor into a pan and stir in the velouté sauce and cream. Boil for 10 minutes.

6 Check the seasoning and pour over the fish. Sprinkle with dill and garnish with the peeled prawns. Serve with buttered, boiled rice.

Serves 4

Tip: Baking with dry heat is impossible for fish, thus no fish can be 'baked' without a certain amount of moisture. Always remember to add sufficient moisture to make up the loss from evaporation during the cooking process. To ensure that the moisture is retained either baste occasionally or cover the fish with a lid or greaseproof (waxed) paper.

Cod Manuella

eight 100 g (¼ lb) cod fillets
25 g (1 oz) (4 tablespoons) flour
salt and pepper
50 ml (2 fl oz) (¼ cup) oil
1 onion, chopped
1 courgette (zucchini), peeled
  and sliced
3 tomatoes, peeled and chopped
1 red pepper, deseeded and
  chopped
15 g (½ oz) (1 tablespoon) tomato
  concentrate (paste)
15 ml (1 tablespoon) wine
  vinegar
150 ml (¼ pint) (⅝ cup) dry sherry
150 ml (¼ pint) (⅝ cup) water
1 chicken stock cube
pinch garlic salt
5 g (1 tablespoon) chopped
  parsley

1 Clean and wash the cod fillets and cut into small pieces. Season the flour and sprinkle it over the cod.

2 Heat the oil and sauté the onion, sliced courgette (zucchini), chopped tomatoes and red pepper until soft (about 8 minutes).

3 Stir in the tomato concentrate (paste), vinegar, sherry and water. Crumble in the stock cube and boil for 12 minutes, stirring from time to time.

4 Place the fish fillets on top. Season with salt and pepper and cover with a lid. Simmer gently on top of the stove for 12 minutes.

5 Pour into a serving dish and sprinkle with chopped parsley.

Serves 4

Cod Manuella — a Spanish dish in which cod is poached with courgettes (zucchini), tomatoes and red peppers in a delicious sherry sauce

Fish Stuffings

Both stuffings are enough for 4 whole small fish or 4 – 6 fillets.

Mousseline Stuffing

225 g (½ lb) (1 cup) raw finely
  minced (ground) whiting or
  haddock
1 egg white
75 ml (⅛ pint) (⅜ cup) double
  (heavy) cream
salt and pepper

1 Mix the fish paste with the egg white in a bowl. Place inside a larger bowl containing crushed ice and chill for at least 1 hour.

2 Add the double (heavy) cream gradually, stirring all the time and season with salt and pepper.

Herb and Breadcrumbs Stuffing

225 g (½ lb) (1 cup) coarsely
  minced (ground) whiting or
  haddock
5 g (1 tablespoon) chopped
  parsley
1 grated small onion
150 g (5 oz) (1 cup) fresh white
  breadcrumbs
1 whole egg
salt and pepper
pinch of garlic salt

1 Mix the minced (ground) fish, chopped parsley, grated onion and breadcrumbs together.

2 Blend with the beaten egg and season with salt and pepper and the garlic salt. Use as a stuffing for any fish – whole round or flat fish and fillets.

Stuffed Fillets of Sole with White Wine Sauce (Paupiettes de Sole)

For the Stuffing:
1 slice bread
225 g (½ lb) whiting fillets
75 g (3 oz) (6 tablespoons) butter
pinch grated nutmeg
1 egg, beaten
salt and pepper

For the Sauce:
eight 75 g (3 oz) fillets of sole
25 g (1 oz) (2 tablespoons) chopped shallots
225 ml (8 fl oz) (1 cup) dry white wine
225 ml (8 fl oz) (1 cup) fish stock
15 g (½ oz) (1 tablespoon) butter
15 g (½ oz) (1 tablespoon) flour
2 egg yolks
juice of 1 lemon
salt and pepper

1 Soak the bread in a little water and mash it with a fork. Put the whiting fillets through the mincer (grinder) or in a blender. (If using a blender, add 15 ml (1-2 tablespoons) water or milk.)

2 Heat 25 g (1 oz) butter in a small saucepan and add the soaked, crumbled bread. Stir with a wooden spoon until blended but do not brown.

3 Melt the remainder of the butter in a small saucepan over a low heat.

4 Mix in a bowl the minced (ground) whiting and breadcrumb mixture. Add the melted butter, grated nutmeg, beaten egg, and season with salt and pepper. Blend well together.

5 Preheat the oven to 200°C, 400°F, gas 6.

6 Flatten the fillets of sole on both sides with a wooden mallet or a rolling pin. (First place the fish between two pieces of greaseproof (waxed) paper or foil, so that it does not stick to the board or the mallet.) Then season them with salt and pepper.

7 Spread the stuffing over the fillets and roll them up from the tail end. Be careful not to squeeze them, or the stuffing will ooze out.

Tie them round with thread or fine string.

8 Butter a small, round oven-proof dish (about 18 cm (6 in) in diameter) and sprinkle with the chopped shallots. Arrange the stuffed fillets on top, standing upright and packed in tightly, very close to each other.

9 Pour over the wine and fish stock. Cover with a lid or aluminium foil and cook in the oven for about 30 minutes.

10 Blend the butter and flour together to make a firm paste.

11 Remove the string from the stuffed fillets. Arrange them on a serving dish and keep warm.

12 Pour off the fish liquor into a saucepan and boil to reduce by one third. Add the butter paste (*beurre manié*), a little at a time, stirring constantly to make a thick, smooth sauce.

13 Beat the egg yolks with the lemon juice and add to the sauce. Adjust the seasoning. Heat gently over a low heat, stirring constantly until the sauce coats the back of the spoon. Do not allow it to boil.

14 Pour the sauce over the stuffed fillets. Serve with crescents of puff pastry (fleurons) and baked potatoes or plain rice.

Serves 4

Tip: Lemon sole or flounder could both be substituted for sole in this dish. Also, a mousseline stuffing could be used, as shown in the step-by-step picture sequence, instead of the coarser breadcrumb-based stuffing.

Fillets of Sole, paupiette – style, may be stuffed with a mixture of either breadcrumbs and fish or minced (ground) whiting and cream

Grilled Fish

Grilling (broiling) is one of the best methods of cooking fish. It is especially suited to oily (fat) fish: herring, mackerel, sardine, trout, salmon, shad and others. When grilling a whole, round fish, first clean it, if necessary (the fishmonger will usually do this for you), then descale, wash and dry. If liked, the head and tail can be removed, though it is usual to leave them on both grilled and fried fish. The practice of cutting the tail into a deep V-shape is known as 'Vandyking'. Score the fish on both sides by making 2-3 diagonal cuts with a knife: this helps it to cook evenly, without burning the outside and leaving the inside half-raw. Brush it with oil or clarified butter, sprinkle with salt, a little made mustard or lemon juice – or top with a delicious savoury butter. Line the grill (broiler) with foil so that the fishy smell doesn't linger in your kitchen after cooking. Grill (broil) at a high temperature, turning the fish once, carefully, and brushing the second side with oil. Allow 8 minutes to cook a fish 2.5 cm (1 in) thick. For a special decorative touch, heat a skewer in an open flame till red-hot, then mark the fish with a criss-cross pattern just before serving. Serve grilled fish with a piquant sauce – the sharpness takes the edge off the richness of the fish – or one with a garlic or herb base, or topped with pats of savoury butter, and accompany with plain boiled potatoes or rice.

White fish is also excellent grilled, especially if it has been lightly marinated first to bring out its flavour. Steep it in a mixture of oil, lemon juice or wine vinegar, seasoned with salt and pepper. Add crushed garlic, a little sugar, soya sauce, sliced onion, a pinch of cayenne and fresh herbs such as tarragon, fennel or thyme: the combinations are endless.

Grilled fish is rich in protein and vitamins, and is a vital part of a calory-controlled, low fat diet. Serving fish as kebabs or with an oriental sauce is an original variation on plain grilled fish, and both make excellent party dishes.

Baltic Cod Kebabs

400 g (14 oz) cod fingers or fillets
4 button (pearl) onions
4 firm tomatoes, skinned and halved
4 button mushrooms, washed
2 g (1 teaspoon) chopped dill
1 sprig parsley
1 lemon, cut in wedges

For the Marinade:
75 ml (8 fl oz) (⅜ cup) oil
juice 1 lemon
10 ml (2 teaspoons) Worcestershire sauce
salt and pepper

1 Cut the fish into 2.5 cm (1 in) cubes and place in a bowl.

2 Mix the marinade ingredients together and pour over the cubes of cod. Leave to soak in the marinade for 30 minutes.

3 Parboil the button (pearl) onions for 5 minutes.

4 Impale the cod cubes, tomatoes, mushrooms and onions on four long, metal skewers. Brush with the remaining marinade and season.

5 Place under a grill (broiler) for 8-10 minutes. Brush with oil or melted butter from time to time.

6 Sprinkle the cooked kebabs with chopped dill and garnish with parsley and lemon wedges. Serve with tartare sauce and plain boiled rice.

Serves 4

Baltic Cod Kebabs – marinated pieces of cod threaded on skewers with mushrooms, onions and tomatoes

Shallow-fried Fish

Fish, shallow-fried, should be tasty, crisp and fresh. All kinds of fish lend themselves to this method of cooking, from herring or trout to fillets of plaice or sole; and cod or haddock steaks. First clean and dry the fish, scaling and gutting if necessary. Then coat it in seasoned flour, or matzo or corn meal. (This seals in its flavour, and prevents it from sticking to the pan.) Make sure the fish is evenly coated – shake off excess flour. Heat a heavy frying pan (skillet) and pour in enough oil to reach a depth of about $\frac{1}{2}$ cm ($\frac{1}{4}$ in). When the oil is very hot, place the fish in it and fry it quickly, turning it once, for 2 minutes. Lower the heat, and let it cook thoroughly. Drain and dry on absorbent paper. Serve immediately, with a tangy sauce, French fries or creamed potatoes, seasonal vegetables, and a generous wedge of lemon.

You may fry in cooking fats (shortening) or use a mixture of oil and clarified butter. Fish dipped in beaten egg, then rolled in fine breadcrumbs or oatmeal (after being floured) is especially delicious fried. Fried fish is a perennial family favourite – but when it is cooked a là Meunière, it becomes a classic of French cuisine. Coat the fish evenly with seasoned flour, then cook it gently in clarified butter which is seething hot, but not browning. (Add a little oil.) When it is ready, keep the fish hot, squeeze the juice of $\frac{1}{2}$ a lemon over it, and sprinkle with chopped parsley. Melt a little butter until it is frothy and lightly coloured and pour it, hot, over the fish. Fish Meunière can be adapted to a whole range of recipes, and each different garnish – like tomatoes, capers, or shrimps and mushrooms – has its own title in classic French cookery.

Trout with Almonds. Coat the fish with seasoned flour and shallow-fry. Then sprinkle with lightly-toasted, flaked almonds and serve garnished with lemon slices

118

Deep-fried Fish

Deep-fried fish, coated with crisp batter or egg-and-breadcrumbs and served piping hot, is an irresistible family dish. Deep-frying is a good way of cooking white and oily fish, either whole, if small, or as fillets, strips, fish-balls and made-up mixtures like croquettes, patties and fish cakes.

You need a deep-fat fryer with a basket inside to hold the fish. You can use any vegetable oil or solid cooking fat, but do not mix the two. Never fill the pan more than half-full of oil or fat, as it can very easily froth up and make sure the cooking fat is completely clean.

To prepare fish for frying

1 Egg and crumb method: (see pages 330-331) wash and dry the fish completely – hot fat and water do not mix and spitting will occur. Dust the fish evenly with flour (shake off the excess) and dip it first in beaten egg, then in fine breadcrumbs (they can be white or brown).

2 Batter method: coat the floured fish in a savoury batter (see page 342) seasoned to your taste.

Heat the oil or fat to 190°C, 375°F – check with a frying thermometer or by putting in a cube of bread which should turn brown within 1 minute and the oil or fat bubble round it as soon as it is submerged. Dip the basket into the hot fat or oil (this prevents food sticking to it), then lower the fish into the fryer. Fillets take 3-4 minutes to cook; thicker fish 5-6 minutes. When the fish is crisp and golden, take it out carefully, drain and dry thoroughly on absorbent paper. Serve immediately.

Never overfill the frying basket, as too much food causes a reduction in temperature, resulting in soggy or under-cooked food. And *never* leave the fryer over heat unattended. Make sure the handle is turned inwards and away from you, so there is no danger of knocking it over.

Deep-frying is a particularly tasty way of cooking white fish such as sole or flounder

Fried Perch

oil for deep frying
four 225 g (½ lb) fillets perch
225 ml (8 fl oz) (1 cup) beer (lager)
20 g (¾ oz) (3 tablespoons) flour
bunch parsley
2 lemons
salt

1 Heat the oil to 190°C, 375°F.

2 Clean the fish fillets. Wash and dry them. Put them into a dish and cover with beer (lager).

3 Pour the flour onto a plate, dip the drained fish into it and shake to remove excess flour.

4 Dip the basket into the hot oil and then lower the fish into the basket. Leave until the fish are cooked through and browned (about 4-5 minutes).

5 Wash and dry the parsley and untie the bunch.

6 Wash and dry the lemons. Cut into halves, serrating the edges. Heat a serving dish.

7 When the fish are cooked, drain them and place on a serving dish. Salt them, then arrange the half lemons around the dish.

8 Lower the parsley into the oil. Leave for about 2 seconds, then drain it. Decorate the plate with the parsley.

9 Serve very hot.

Serves 4

Tip: The oil should be very hot, but not boiling. Serve with a fluffy purée of potatoes.

Fried Sardines

16 large fresh sardines
handful rough sea salt
8 g (1 tablespoon) dry breadcrumbs
15 ml (1 tablespoon) single (light) cream
1 egg, separated
1 clove garlic, chopped
2 shallots, chopped
5 g (1 tablespoon) chopped chives
5 g (1 tablespoon) chopped

chervil
salt and pepper
150 g (5 oz) (1¼ cups) flour
oil for deep frying
300 ml (½ pint) (1¼ cups) milk
bunch parsley

1 Wash and dry the sardines. Place them in an earthenware dish. Sprinkle with the sea salt. Leave them for 4 hours in a cool place.

2 Mix the breadcrumbs and cream in a bowl. Add the egg yolk and mix again.

3 Add the garlic, shallots, chives and chervil to the cream and breadcrumbs. Add salt and pepper. Mix thoroughly with a wooden spoon.

4 Pour the flour onto a plate. Heat the oil to 190°C, 375°F.

5 Clean the sardines. Gut them, cut out the backbone and fill with the cream stuffing. Reshape and secure the sardines with a wooden cocktail stick.

6 Put the stuffed sardines back into the earthenware dish, cover with the milk. Then dry them and dip into the flour one by one. Put them into the frying basket. Gently shake the basket to remove excess flour.

7 Lower the basket into the hot oil and fry until brown.

8 Heat a serving dish. Wash the parsley, dry well.

9 When the fish have browned, drain them and arrange on the serving dish.

10 Lower the parsley into the oil. Fry for 2 minutes, then drain it and arrange with the fish.

11 Serve very hot.

Serves 4

Tip: Sprats can be used as an alternative to sardines.

Deep-Fried Sole or Flounder with Courgette (Zucchini) Fritters

115 g (4½ oz) (1 cup + 4 tablespoons) flour

2 eggs
400 ml (¾ pint) (1¾ cups) milk
5 g (1 tablespoon) chopped parsley
1 garlic clove, peeled and crushed
salt and pepper
oil for deep frying
2 large courgettes (zucchini), thinly sliced
four 225 g (½ lb) sole or flounder fillets
2 lemons

1 Preheat the oven to 140°C, 275°F, gas 1.

2 Prepare the batter for the courgettes (zucchini). Sift 75 g (3 oz) (good ¾ cup) of the flour into a bowl. Add the eggs and mix well together. Gradually stir in 200 ml (7 fl oz) (⅞ cup) of the milk. Add the chopped parsley, garlic and salt and pepper to taste. Mix well.

3 Half fill a deep fat fryer with oil and heat to 190°C, 375°F.

4 Dip courgette (zucchini) slices in flour, then coat with batter and lower into the oil. Cook for 3-4 minutes.

5 When the fritters are well browned, take them out of the oil, drain them on absorbent paper, put them into a heated vegetable dish, and keep them warm in the oven.

6 Rinse and dry the fish fillets. Pour the rest of the milk into a bowl. Spread the rest of the flour on a plate.

7 Dip the fillets into the milk, then coat them in the flour. Shake to remove excess flour. Dip the basket in the hot oil and then lower the fish into the basket and cook until brown on both sides.

8 Cut the lemons into halves (with a zig-zag edge, if liked).

9 Drain the fillets and arrange them on a white napkin on a heated serving dish. Place a lemon half on each fillet. Serve very hot with the courgette (zucchini) fritters.

Serves 4

Tip: The fritter batter should be a lot thicker than pancake (crêpe) batter, so add a little extra flour if necessary.

Baked Fish

Baking Fish

Baking is one of the most versatile methods of cooking. Fish may be baked simply, with a little butter, lemon juice and parsley; in a variety of different liquids such as stock, wine, apple cider, or cream; or stuffed, in a rich sauce. Baking retains the flavour of the fish supremely well, and cooking smells are kept to a minimum.

Arrange the fish attractively in a casserole – which can also be used as a serving dish. Always preheat the oven. Set it at 180°C, 350°F, gas 4 for dishes to be cooked in a covered casserole; 200°C, 400°F, gas 6 if you want a golden brown or gratinéed surface.

The possibilities for experimenting with different ingredients, herbs and seasonings are almost limitless. Sousing is a form of baking: cook at 180°C, 350°F, gas 4 and allow the fish to cool in its spiced vinegar.

Cooked 'en papillote', the fish is placed on a sheet of aluminium foil or greaseproof (waxed) paper, covered with a garnish, rich or simple. The sheet is folded to make an airtight parcel and the fish cooks in its own juices in the oven. Serve the fish in its wrapping on each plate. This method of cooking is excellent as part of a calorie-controlled diet.

A popular American method of cooking fish is 'planking'. The fish is partially grilled (broiled), then transferred to an oiled oak plank, and baked. The planks imparts a delicious, barbecue-like flavour and aroma – and makes an impressive dish to present to guests, especially if the platter is decorated with a piped border of duchesse potatoes before it is placed in the oven.

Serve boiled or creamed potatoes with baked fish – or make a rice pilaff. A crisp green salad is an excellent accompaniment.

Baked Fish Fillets in Soured Cream

four 150 g (5 oz) fish fillets
salt and pepper
50 ml (2 fl oz) (¼ cup) oil
25 g (1 oz) (4 tablespoons) chopped chives
150 ml (¼ pint) (⅝ cup) soured cream
1 bay leaf, imported
pinch caraway seeds, optional
pinch paprika
sprig parsley
4 lemon wedges

1 Set the oven at 200°C, 400°F, gas 6.

2 Place the fish fillets on a greased, shallow dish. Season with salt and pepper and brush with oil. Bake for 5 minutes in the pre heated oven.

3 Add the chopped chives, soured cream, bay leaf and caraway seeds, cover with a lid, return to the oven and bake for 15 minutes at the same temperature.

4 Serve the fish in the same dish, with boiled new potatoes and turnips. Sprinkle with paprika just before serving and decorate with parsley and lemon wedges.

Serves 4

Baked Mackerel Stuffed with Apple

four 225 g (½ lb) mackerel
100 g (¼ lb) (½ cup) butter
100 g (¼ lb) (1 cup) celery, finely chopped
1 apple, peeled and finely chopped
small onion, chopped
50 g (2 oz) (1 cup) fresh breadcrumbs
5 g (1 tablespoon) chopped parsley
salt and pepper
pinch ground (powdered) ginger
juice and grated rind 1 lemon

1 Preheat the oven to 180°C, 350°F, gas 4.

2 Using a sharp knife, remove the backbones from the fish without damaging the belly. Open out the fish to form a pocket for the stuffing, and clean it thoroughly.

3 Make the stuffing. Melt 50 g (2 oz) (¼ cup) butter in a saucepan and sauté the celery, apple and onion for 4 minutes. Stir in the breadcrumbs and chopped parsley. Season with salt and pepper and add the ginger, grated lemon rind and juice.

4 Spread the filling evenly on each mackerel, and fold over. Melt the remaining butter in a pan and use to brush the mackerel. Wrap them in foil and bake in the oven for 20 minutes.

Serves 4

Baking en Papillote

A papillote is a heart-shaped piece of greaseproof (waxed) paper or aluminium foil, well-oiled or buttered, and folded around the ingredients to be cooked. This method of cooking is advantageous because it ensures that the fish simmers in its own juices and thus does not lose its own distinctive flavour.

Many fish can be cooked in this way – trout, red mullet, sole or herrings to name but a few. Really, the term only implies half-cooking because the fish used is often pre-cooked before it is placed in the paper bag or foil.

Always serve papillotes in their puffed-up paper shells and let your guests cut them open themselves at the table with a knife. If you use aluminium foil, remove the fish from the foil to serve.

Scampi

Scampi are hard-shelled crustaceans measuring about 10 cm (4 in) in length, also known as Dublin Bay prawns, Norway lobsters, Langoustine in France and Cigala in Spain. They are sold alive or cooked, with shells or without, or frozen. Scampi are available in England all year round, the best season being May to November, but king prawns (large shrimps) can be substituted in the following recipes if scampi are not available.

Scampi Pernod

175 g (6 oz) (¾ cup) butter
15 ml (1 tablespoon) very finely chopped shallot
4 anchovy fillets, chopped
15 ml (1 tablespoon) finely chopped parsley
15 ml (1 tablespoon) Pernod
salt and pepper
20 scampi, peeled
25 g (1 oz) (4 tablespoons) seasoned flour
2 eggs, beaten
30 ml (2 tablespoons) oil

1 Soften the butter and mix in the chopped shallot, anchovies and parsley. Gradually blend in the Pernod and season to taste.

2 Roll the scampi in half of the flour and spread them on all sides with the Pernod butter. Put them into the freezer for 10 minutes to harden the butter.

3 Roll the scampi in the remaining flour and dip in beaten egg.

4 Quickly fry the scampi in the hot oil until golden (about 2 minutes).

5 Serve immediately, garnished with parsley and lemon wedges.

Serves 4

Scampi Fritters with Mayonnaise Dressings

100 g (¼ lb) (1 cup + 2 tablespoons) flour
salt and pepper
2 eggs, separated
200 ml (6 fl oz) (¾ cup) beer
20 scampi, peeled
juice ½ lemon
oil for deep frying

For the Dressings:
1 onion, finely chopped
2 cloves garlic, crushed
15 ml (1 tablespoon) oil
4 tomatoes, skinned, deseeded and chopped
15 ml (1 tablespoon) tomato paste
salt and paprika pepper
450 ml (¾ pint) (2 cups) mayonnaise
30 ml (2 tablespoons) each finely chopped fresh chives, parsley, tarragon and watercress
15 ml (1 tablespoon) lemon juice

1 Sieve the flour into a bowl and season. Add the egg yolks and beer and beat until smooth. Leave to stand for 2 hours. Sprinkle the scampi with the lemon juice.

2 Prepare the Provençale Mayonnaise: fry the onion and garlic in the oil until soft but not brown. Add the tomatoes to the pan with the tomato paste and salt and paprika pepper to taste. Simmer for 5 minutes, then cool and mix with half the mayonnaise.

3 Prepare the Green Mayonnaise: mix the remaining mayonnaise with the chopped herbs, watercress and lemon juice.

4 When the batter has stood for 2 hours, stiffly whisk the egg whites and fold them into the batter with a metal spoon.

5 Heat the oil to 190°C, 375°F. Dip the scampi in the batter and fry a few at a time, for 5 or 6 minutes until golden. Drain on absorbent paper and keep warm while frying the remainder.

6 Serve the scampi very hot with the prepared dressings and lemon wedges.

Serves 4

Stir-fried Scampi and Vegetables

16 scampi, peeled
100 g (¼ lb) (1 cup) frozen peas
1 onion, peeled
1 carrot, peeled
2 tomatoes, peeled and deseeded
30 ml (1 fl oz) (2 tablespoons) oil
1 clove garlic, crushed
1 cm (½ in) piece fresh root ginger, grated
½ green pepper, deseeded and thinly sliced
½ chicken stock cube, dissolved in 225 ml (8 fl oz) (1 cup) boiling water
15 ml (1 tablespoon) soya sauce
15 ml (1 tablespoon) sherry
5 ml (1 teaspoon) honey
pepper
15 ml (1 tablespoon) cornflour (cornstarch)

1 Cut the scampi in half lengthwise. Cook the frozen peas. Quarter the onion, cut each piece in half lengthwise and separate into leaves. Slice the carrot lengthwise and cut into matchstick-sized strips. Cut the tomato into wedges.

2 Heat the oil in a large frying pan (skillet) and stir-fry the garlic and ginger for ½ minute. Add the onion, pepper and carrot and stir-fry for 1 minute. Add the scampi, peas and tomatoes to the pan and stir-fry for a further minute.

3 Pour in the stock, soya sauce and sherry, add the honey, season with pepper and bring quickly to the boil.

4 Mix the cornflour (cornstarch) with 45 ml (2 fl oz) (3 tablespoons) water and stir into the boiling liquid. Simmer for 2 minutes stirring continuously and serve immediately with freshly boiled rice or noodles.

Serves 4

Tip: Add some fruit juice to enhance the sweet 'n sour flavour.

Scampi Fritters with Mayonnaise Dressings — there's a choice of creamy piquant dips to go with the fritters

Scampi Provençal

450 g (1 lb) peeled scampi
25 g (1 oz) (¼ cup) seasoned flour
25 g (1 oz) (2 tablespoons) butter
50 ml (2 fl oz) (¼ cup) oil
50 g (2 oz) (¼ cup) chopped onion
3 cloves garlic, chopped
450 g (1 lb) tomatoes, skinned, deseeded and chopped
25 g (1 oz) (2 tablespoons) tomato paste
150 ml (¼ pint) (⅝ cup) dry white wine
bouquet garni
juice ½ lemon
pinch paprika
2.5 ml (½ teaspoon) cornflour (cornstarch)
45 ml (1½ fl oz) (3 tablespoons) water
5 cooked scampi, unpeeled, for decoration
15 ml (1 tablespoon) chopped parsley and tarragon

For the Rice Mould:
40 g (1½ oz) (3 tablespoons) butter
15 ml (1 tablespoon) oil
25 g (1 oz) (2 tablespoons) chopped onion
225 g (½ lb) (1 cup) long grain rice
½ chicken stock cube dissolved in 550 ml (1 pint) (2½ cups) boiling water
bouquet garni
pinch turmeric
salt and pepper

1 Prepare the rice: preheat the oven to 200°C, 400°F, gas 6. Heat 25 g (1 oz) (2 tablespoons) of the butter with the oil in a pan and fry the chopped onion for 5 minutes. Add the rice and cook for a further 2 minutes. Add the chicken stock, bouquet garni, turmeric, salt and pepper and boil for 2 minutes. Transfer the rice to an ovenproof dish, cover with greaseproof (parchment) paper and cook in the preheated oven for 18-20 minutes.

2 Meanwhile, coat the scampi in the seasoned flour. Heat the butter and half of the oil in a pan, add the scampi and fry for 5 minutes. Drain well and keep the scampi warm.

3 Heat the remaining oil in the pan, add the onion and cook for about 4 minutes until soft but not brown. Add the garlic, chopped tomatoes and tomato paste and cook for a further 3 minutes.

4 Stir the white wine into the pan and add the bouquet garni, lemon juice, salt, pepper and paprika. Reduce the heat and simmer for 5 minutes. Remove the bouquet garni.

5 Thicken the mixture with the cornflour (cornstarch) mixed with the water and boil for 1 minute.

6 Return the cooked scampi to the pan and cook for 4 minutes to heat through.

7 Meanwhile, remove the rice from the oven. Discard the bouquet garni. Grease a 1.2 litre (2 pint) (5 cup) ring mould with the remaining butter and spoon in the rice. Pack it down well, then immediately turn out onto a serving dish.

8 Spoon the scampi sauce into the centre of the rice mould and decorate the ring with the unpeeled scampi tails. Just before serving, sprinkle with the chopped parsley and tarragon.

Serves 4

Scampi with Ginger and Spring Onions (Scallions)

150 ml (¼ pint) (⅝ cup) chicken stock
15 ml (1 tablespoon) sherry
10 ml (2 teaspoons) soya sauce
5 ml (1 teaspoon) sugar
30 ml (1 fl oz) (2 tablespoons) oil
6 very thin slices fresh root ginger, roughly chopped
12 spring onions (scallions)
450 g (1 lb) peeled scampi
15 ml (1 tablespoon) cornflour (cornstarch)
30 ml (1 fl oz) (2 tablespoons) water

1 Combine the stock, sherry, soya sauce and sugar in a saucepan, and bring to the boil. Take off the heat and reserve.

2 Heat the oil in a deep frying pan (skillet). Stir-fry the ginger for 1 minute. Then add the spring onions (scallions) and the scampi and stir-fry for 2 minutes.

3 Pour in the stock mixture and bring to a boil. Stir and cook for 3 minutes over a high heat. Add the cornflour (cornstarch) dissolved in the water, and cook for another minute while the sauce thickens. Serve at once.

Serves 4

Scampi with Brandy

450 g (1 lb) peeled scampi
100 (¼ lb) shallots or onions, finely chopped
50 g (2 oz) (¼ cup) butter
3 medium tomatoes, skinned and chopped
50 ml (2 fl oz) (¼ cup) chicken stock
50 ml (2 fl oz) (¼ cup) brandy
salt and pepper
15 ml (1 tablespoon) chopped fresh parsley
150 ml (¼ pint) (⅝ cup) double (heavy) cream

1 Gently fry the scampi and the shallots or onions in the butter for 5 minutes.

2 Add the chopped tomatoes and cook for another 2 minutes. Stir in the chicken stock and bring to the boil.

3 Add the brandy and set light to it, being careful to keep it at a safe distance. When the flames are extinguished, simmer the sauce briskly for 3 minutes, stirring constantly.

4 Remove the pan from the heat and stir in the seasoning and the chopped parsley. Allow it to cool for a few minutes before stirring in the cream. Serve immediately.

Serves 4

Scampi with Brandy is a special treat — the aroma of the brandy and tomato sauce is deliciously appetising!

125

Nasi Goreng

150 ml ($\frac{1}{4}$ pint) ($\frac{5}{8}$ cup) oil
2 onions, finely chopped
1 clove garlic, chopped
2.5 ml ($\frac{1}{2}$ teaspoon) chilli powder
675 g ($1\frac{1}{2}$ lb) (3 cups) cooked rice
225 g ($\frac{1}{2}$ lb) ($1\frac{1}{2}$ cups) peeled
  prawns (shrimps)
salt and pepper

For the Omelette:
30 ml (1 fl oz) (2 tablespoons) oil
4 spring onions (scallions),
  chopped
1 tomato, skinned, deseeded and
  chopped
pinch chilli powder
50 ml (2 fl oz) ($\frac{1}{4}$ cup) soya sauce
4 eggs, beaten
$\frac{1}{2}$ cucumber, sliced

1 Heat the oil in a pan and fry the onion until it is transparent. Add the garlic and chilli powder and fry for 3 more minutes. Stir in the rice and prawns (shrimps). Continue to fry, stirring frequently until the rice turns a pale gold. Season to taste and turn onto a warm dish.

2 Prepare the omelette. Heat the oil and fry the spring onions (scallions) until soft. Add the tomato and cook for 3 minutes. Season with salt, chilli powder and half the soya sauce. Add the eggs, cover and cook over a low heat, until set. Remove from the pan and shred the omelette finely.

3 Arrange the omelette over the rice, sprinkle with the remaining soya sauce and garnish with the sliced cucumber.

Serves 4

White Fish Paella, justly one of Spain's most celebrated dishes, is spectacularly topped with prawns (shrimps)

Mussel, Chicken and Prawn (Shrimp) Pilaff

20 mussels in their shells
770 ml ($1\frac{3}{8}$ pints) ($3\frac{1}{2}$ cups) chicken
  stock
70 ml ($2\frac{1}{2}$ fl oz) ($\frac{1}{3}$ cup) oil
2 onions, chopped
225 g ($\frac{1}{2}$ lb) uncooked chicken
  meat cut into 2.5 cm (1 in) cubes
100 g ($\frac{1}{4}$ lb) ($\frac{2}{3}$ cup) cubed bacon
1.25 ml ($\frac{1}{4}$ teaspoon) dried thyme
1 clove garlic, crushed
1.25 ml ($\frac{1}{4}$ teaspoon) freshly
  ground (milled) black pepper
10 ml (2 teaspoons) salt
275 g (10 oz) ($1\frac{1}{4}$ cups) long grain
  rice
pinch saffron powder
100 g ($\frac{1}{4}$ lb) ($\frac{2}{3}$ cup) cubed garlic
  sausage
175 g (6 oz) whiting, skinned,
  boned and cut into 2.5 cm (1 in)
  pieces

Mussel, Chicken and Prawn (Shrimp) Pilaff is a meaty dish garnished with stuffed green olives as a final touch

100 g (¼ lb) (¾ cup) peeled prawns (shrimps)
1 pimento, sliced
1 green pepper, cooked and sliced
4 king prawns (large shrimps)
15 stuffed green olives
1 lemon, quartered

1 Scrub the mussel shells and remove their beards. Soak them in cold water for 20 minutes. Place them in a saucepan with 70 ml (2½ fl oz) (⅓ cup) stock. Cover and simmer for 5 minutes or until the shells open. Keep 4 mussels intact and remove the remainder from their shells.

2 Preheat the oven to 180°C, 350°F, gas 4. Heat the oil in a flameproof casserole. Brown the onions, chicken pieces and bacon. Add the thyme, garlic, pepper, salt, rice, saffron, garlic sausage, whiting and 700 ml (1¼ pints) (3⅛ cups) stock. Bring the mixture to the boil, stirring continually.

3 Cover with aluminium foil and bake in the oven for 25 minutes.

Remove and stir in the shelled mussels, prawns (shrimps), pimento and half the pepper. Arrange the king prawns (large shrimps) and the remaining pepper on top. Replace the foil and return to the oven for 10 minutes. Serve garnished with the green olives, mussels in their shells and lemon wedges.

Serves 8

White Fish Paella

50 ml (2 fl oz) (¼ cup) oil
2 onions, chopped
1 clove garlic, crushed
275 g (10 oz) (1¼ cups) long grain rice
pinch powdered saffron
800 ml (1⅜ pints) (3¼ cups) chicken stock
350 g (¾ lb) any firm white fish, skinned, boned and roughly flaked
1 red pepper, deseeded and sliced
1 green pepper, deseeded and sliced

1.25 ml (¼ teaspoon) freshly ground (milled) black pepper
6.25 ml (1¼ teaspoons) salt
100 g (¼ lb) (1 cup) peeled prawns (shrimps)
4 king prawns (large shrimps)
15 ml (1 tablespoon) chopped parsley

1 Preheat the oven to 190°C, 375°F, gas 5. Heat the oil in a flameproof casserole. Gently fry the chopped onion until it is transparent. Add the garlic and rice. Stirring constantly, fry the rice until it is a pale gold.

2 Stir the saffron into the stock and pour this over the rice. Add the fish, peppers and seasoning.

3 Boil the paella for 5 minutes, reduce the heat and simmer for a further 15 minutes until the liquid has been soaked up. The rice should be moist but not soupy.

4 Remove from the heat and stir in the prawns (shrimps). Cover and place in the oven for 10 minutes.

5 Decorate the paella with the king prawns (large shrimps) and garnish with the chopped parsley.

Serves 4-6

Japanese Sweet 'n Sour Prawns (Shrimps)

225 g (½ lb) (1 cup) long grain rice
salt and pepper
12 king prawns (large shrimps), peeled
20 ml (1½ tablespoons) cornflour (cornstarch)
30 ml (1 fl oz) (2 tablespoons) oil
1 onion, chopped
1 slice ginger, 5mm (¼ in) thick, chopped
2 cloves garlic, crushed
1 red pepper, deseeded and chopped
15 ml (1 tablespoon) soya sauce
5 ml (1 teaspoon) honey
5 ml (1 teaspoon) vinegar
150 ml (¼ pint) (⅝ cup) saké (rice wine) or dry sherry

1 Cook the rice in boiling salted water for 20 minutes, drain and check the seasoning.

2 Meanwhile, coat the prawns (shrimps) in the cornflour (cornstarch). Heat the oil in a pan and fry the onion until tender. Add the ginger, garlic and pepper and stir-fry for 2 minutes. Add the prawns (shrimps) and cook for 1 minute more.

3 Add the soya sauce, honey, vinegar, and saké or sherry to the pan and boil for 1 minute. Check the seasoning and serve with the boiled rice.

Serves 4

Tip: You can vary the sweet 'n sour sauce slightly: try substituting pineapple juice for the saké or sherry.

Prawn (Shrimp) and Mackerel Salad

225 g (½ lb) (1 cup) long grain rice
225 g (½ lb) (1½ cups) peeled prawns (shrimps)
225 g (½ lb) smoked mackerel fillets, skinned and cut in pieces

Prawn (Shrimp) and Mackerel Salad, a colourful medley of delicious seafood, peas, and red peppers

2 sticks celery, sliced
100 g (¼ lb) (1 cup) cooked peas
1 red pepper, deseeded and diced
50 g (2 oz) (½ cup) sliced mushrooms

For the Dressing:
45 ml (2 fl oz) (3 tablespoons) salad oil
15 ml (1 tablespoon) soya sauce
15 ml (1 tablespoon) vinegar
pinch pepper and garlic salt
1 small onion, finely chopped

1 Cook the rice in boiling salted water for 20 minutes, drain and rinse with cold water to remove the starch. Drain again and place in a large serving bowl.

2 In another bowl, combine the prawns (shrimps), mackerel, celery, peas, pepper and mushrooms. Blend this mixture with the rice in the serving bowl.

3 Blend the ingredients for the dressing. Pour the liquid over the salad, toss well and serve.

Serves 6

Tips: Of course, any smoked fish, such as herrings, eels, and cooked smoked haddock, can be used instead of the smoked mackerel. And the vegetables can be varied to suit what is available – try cooked French beans, cucumber, sweetcorn or cooked carrots. You can even use fruits instead of vegetables – pineapple, peach and apple cubes would make an excellent alternative.

Mussel Pilaff

225 g (½ lb) (1 cup) long grain rice
30 ml (1 fl oz) (2 tablespoons) oil
1 clove garlic, crushed
1 small onion, chopped
225 g (½ lb) cooked white fish, cut in small pieces
salt and pepper
24 mussels, cooked and in their shells
4 red chillies
juice 1 lemon

1 Cook the rice in boiling salted water until tender.

2 Meanwhile, heat the oil in a pan, add the garlic and onion and cook for 2 minutes. Add the fish and stir to mix. Cover the pan with a lid and cook for 5 minutes.

3 Drain the rice and add to the pan. Mix well, season to taste and keep the mixture hot.

4 Reserve 12 of the mussels in their shells. Shell the rest, add them to the pan and blend. Transfer the mixture to a serving dish and decorate with the red chillies and the reserved mussels. Sprinkle with the lemon juice.

Serves 6

Brochettes de Moules

18 mussels, washed and scrubbed
18 button mushrooms
18 cubes cooked ham, 5 mm (¼ in) in size
25 g (1 oz) (4 tablespoons) flour
2 eggs, beaten
50 g (2 oz) (1 cup) breadcrumbs
oil for deep frying

Mussel Pilaff makes a few mussels go a long way — it is cheap, colourful, easy to make and treats your family to a filling meal

For the Marinade:
juice 1 lemon
30 ml (1 fl oz) (2 tablespoons) oil
5 ml (1 teaspoon) soya or Worcestershire sauce
salt and pepper
1 clove garlic, crushed

1 Soak the mussels in cold water for 20 minutes. Meanwhile, mix the ingredients for the marinade. Open the mussels with a knife, discard the shells and wash the mussels thoroughly. Add them to the marinade and leave to soak for 5 minutes.

2 Discard the stalks of the mushrooms. Thread each of 6 kebab skewers with 3 cubes of ham, 3 mushroom caps and 3 mussels. Coat the brochettes with the flour, then the beaten egg and finally the breadcrumbs.

3 Heat the oil to 190°C, 375°F, and fry for 30 seconds until golden. Drain well and serve as an appetizer with a tartare or hot tomato sauce.

Serves 6

Tip: As an alternative to ham cubes, try using scallops. Cubes of white fish make another good substitute, but the brochettes should be cooked for 1 minute if using raw fish.

Paella Valencia

1 set chicken giblets
1½ litres (2½ pints) (6 cups) water
1 onion, studded with 2 cloves
2 sticks celery
1 leek, chopped
3 cloves garlic, crushed
3 green peppers
8 tomatoes
2 onions
225 g (½ lb) chorizo
225 g (½ lb) small frozen squid, thawed
8 clams or cockles
8 whole scampi
8 large prawns (shrimps)
16 mussels in their shells
one 1.2 kg (2½ lb) chicken, jointed
salt and pepper
5 ml (1 teaspoon) paprika
100 ml (4 fl oz) (½ cup) oil
pinch saffron
225 g (½ lb) (1 cup) long grain rice
100 g (¼ lb) (1 cup) peas, blanched
100 g (¼ lb) green beans, blanched
bouquet garni

1 Place the chicken giblets in a large pan, cover with the water and add the onion studded with the cloves, the celery, the leek and 1 clove of garlic. Bring to the boil and simmer for 30 minutes.

2 Deseed the peppers and cut them into thin strips. Deseed and chop the tomatoes and chop the 2 onions. Slice the chorizo slantways.

3 Clean the squid and discard the inedible ink sac and skin. Cut the bodies across into rings and shred the tentacles. Bring a pan of salted water to the boil, add the pieces of squid and boil for 10 minutes to blanch. Drain and refresh in cold water. Drain again.

4 Clean the shellfish in cold

Brochettes de Moules are an unusual way of serving mussels on long kebab skewers deep-fried until crisp and golden

water and scrape the shells of the mussels with a knife to remove any barnacles.

5 Split both chicken legs in 2 and the breasts into 3 pieces to give 10 chicken pieces. Season the chicken pieces with salt, pepper and paprika.

6 Heat the oil in a large flame-proof and ovenproof paella pan, add the chicken pieces and cook them for about 10 minutes until golden, turning the chicken once and covering the pan.

7 Lift the chicken from the pan and keep it warm. Add the chorizo and cook for 4 minutes. Add the squid, peppers, tomatoes, chopped onion and saffron. Cover

with a lid and simmer for 10 minutes.

8 Add the rice and chicken pieces. Strain the giblet stock and add 750 ml (1¼ pints) (3 cups) of the liquid to the mixture. Cover and cook for 20 minutes.

9 Preheat the oven to 220°C, 425°F, gas 7.

10 Add the clams or cockles, whole scampi, prawns (shrimps), mussels, remaining garlic, peas and beans. Pour in 150 ml (¼ pint) (⅝ cup) of the giblet stock, cover and cook in the preheated oven for 15 minutes. After this time, add the bouquet garni and return the pan to the oven for a further 5 minutes.

11 Remove the bouquet garni and serve the paella straight away in the pan.

Serves 8

Scallops

There are three types of scallops available: Deep Sea being the largest, Bay scallops slightly smaller and Cape, the smallest and most delicate in flavour. They can either be bought in the shells (see box on "How to Shell Scallops"), or shelled and cleaned, by the gallon or frozen. Scallops have white flesh and orange roes, and the shells, which can be bought separately from the fishmonger to use as serving dishes, are pinkish-brown. Scallops can be poached, baked, grilled (broiled), added to chowders, soups and stews, and served individually on croûtons or wrapped in crisp bacon as an hors d'oeuvre.

Scallops in Cream and Sherry

12 scallops in shells, or 450 g (1 lb) shelled
10 ml (2 teaspoons) butter
10 ml (2 teaspoons) flour
150 ml ($\frac{1}{4}$ pint) ($\frac{5}{8}$ cup) milk
1 small onion, chopped
100 g ($\frac{1}{4}$ lb) (1$\frac{1}{4}$ cups) sliced mushrooms
pinch dried thyme
150 ml ($\frac{1}{4}$ pint) ($\frac{5}{8}$ cup) dry sherry
1 egg yolk
45 ml (2 fl oz) (3 tablespoons) single (light) cream
salt and pepper
pinch paprika pepper
25 g (1 oz) (3 tablespoons) grated Parmesan cheese
5 ml (1 teaspoon) lemon juice
small pinch cayenne pepper
10 ml (2 teaspoons) chopped parsley

1 Shell the scallops (see box).

2 Melt the butter, add the flour and cook for 1 minute. Gradually add the milk, bring to the boil and simmer for 3 minutes, stirring.

3 Simmer the onion, mushrooms, thyme and sherry for 5 minutes. Stir in the white sauce.

4 Mix the egg yolk and cream and stir it into the sauce. Bring to the boil, remove from the heat and add the seasoning, paprika and Parmesan.

5 Put the scallops in a pan and just cover with cold water. Bring to the boil, reduce the heat and poach very gently for 6 minutes.

6 Drain the scallops. Reserve 6 corals, slice the scallops and arrange them in 6 scallop shells. Pour over the sauce and grill (broil) for a few minutes to glaze.

7 Top with the reserved corals and sprinkle with lemon juice, cayenne and parsley.

Serves 6

Scallops in Cream and Sherry are a tasty way to start a meal or they can be served with salad as a main course in their own right

How to Shell Scallops

1 Preheat the oven to 150°C, 300°F, gas 2. Scrub the closed shells with cold water.

2 Place the scallops on a baking (cookie) sheet in the oven for about 5 minutes until the shells open.

3 Cut through the hinge muscles and remove them; detach the rounded shells. Clean these thoroughly for use as hors d'oeuvre dishes.

4 Scrape away the beard-like fringe from around the edible flesh and remove the black intestinal thread.

5 Slip a sharp knife under the flesh and remove the white meat and coral intact.

Coquilles Bretonnes

8 scallops in shells, or 350 g (¾ lb) shelled
50 g (2 oz) (4 tablespoons) butter
50 g (2 oz) (¼ cup) chopped shallot
200 ml (6 fl oz) (¾ cup) dry white wine
salt and pepper
100 ml (4 fl oz) (½ cup) double (heavy) cream
25 g (1 oz) (4 tablespoons) flour
1 egg yolk

1 Shell the scallops (see box), separate the white meat and coral and soak them in cold water.

2 Melt half the butter and sauté the shallots for 2 minutes. Add the drained scallops, wine, seasoning and water to cover. Add the cream, bring to the boil and poach gently for 6 minutes.

3 Remove the scallops from the liquor.

4 Melt the remaining butter, add the flour and cook for 2 minutes. Gradually stir in the strained liquor, bring to the boil and simmer gently for 10 minutes. Cool slightly and beat in the egg yolk.

5 Put a little sauce into 4 scallop shells and arrange the sliced scallops on top. Pour over the remain-

Scallops with Brandied Grapes are a more sophisticated dish for the connoisseur of good food, and make a delicious starter

ing sauce and grill (broil) for a few minutes to glaze and lightly brown.

Serves 4

Scallops with Brandied Grapes

225 g (½ lb) (1½ cups) black grapes
15 ml (1 tablespoon) brandy
pinch powdered cinnamon
450 g (1 lb) shelled scallops
1 small shallot, chopped
bouquet garni
300 ml (½ pint) (1¼ cups) dry white wine
juice 1 lemon
salt and pepper
10 ml (2 teaspoons) butter
10 ml (2 teaspoons) flour
15 ml (1 tablespoon) chopped parsley

1 Halve and deseed the grapes and mix with the brandy and cinnamon.

2 Place the scallops, shallot, bouquet garni, wine, lemon juice and seasoning in a saucepan. Bring to the boil, cover and poach very gently for 6 minutes. Add the grapes and brandy.

3 Melt the butter, add the flour and cook for 1 minute. Gradually add the strained cooking liquor, bring to the boil and simmer for 2-3 minutes.

4 Add the strained ingredients and heat gently. Transfer to a serving dish and garnish with parsley.

Serves 6

Scallops in Saffron Cream

16 scallops in their shells, or
    550 g (1¼ lb) shelled
1 egg yolk
good pinch powdered saffron
75 g (3 oz) (½ cup) grated
    Parmesan cheese
30 ml (1 fl oz) (2 tablespoons)
    single (light) cream
salt and pepper
50 g (2 oz) (¼ cup) butter
50 ml (2 fl oz) (¼ cup) whisky

1 Shell the scallops and clean them (see box on page 1079). Preheat the oven to 200°C, 400°F, gas 6.

2 Remove the corals from the scallops and crush them to a paste in a bowl. Add the egg yolk, saffron, Parmesan, cream and seasoning to taste, and blend together well.

3 Melt the butter in a frying pan (skillet) and sauté the scallops over a high heat for 1 minute. Pour in the whisky, heat it through and transfer the contents of the pan to a medium sized ovenproof dish.

4 Pour the cream mixture over the scallops and bake in the preheated oven for 20 minutes. Serve immediately.

Serves 4

Skewered Scallops with Sour Cream Dressing

1 red pepper, deseeded
2 small onions, peeled
12 scallops, shelled
16 mussels, shelled
4 crayfish, shelled and halved
12 large prawns (shrimps),
    shelled
60 ml (2¼ fl oz) (4 tablespoons) oil
15 ml (1 tablespoon) chopped
    fresh fennel

For the Dressing:
225 ml (8 fl oz) (1 cup) cultured
    sour cream

15 ml (1 tablespoon) tomato
    paste
pinch cayenne
10 ml (2 teaspoons) chopped
    fresh parsley
5 ml (1 teaspoon) chopped fresh
    dill
salt and pepper

1 First prepare the dressing: mix together the sour cream, tomato paste, cayenne, parsley, dill and seasoning. Transfer it to a serving dish and chill well.

2 Cut the red pepper into 2.5 cm (1 in) cubes. Quarter the onions and separate into leaves.

3 Thread the prepared scallops, mussels, crayfish, prawns (shrimps), pepper and onions alternately onto 4 long skewers.

4 Mix the oil, fennel and seasoning, and brush liberally over the skewered shellfish.

5 Cook under a hot grill (broiler) for about 10 minutes until just cooked, turning frequently and brushing with the oil mixture.

6 Serve the skewers immediately, with the chilled dressing and a crisp salad.

Serves 4

Wholemeal Seafood Flan

225 g (½ lb) shelled scallops
100 g (¼ lb) white fish fillets,
    (haddock, cod, whiting)
300 ml (½ pint) (1¼ cups) milk
100 g (¼ lb) canned salmon
40 g (1½ oz) (3 tablespoons) butter
50 g (2 oz) (½ cup) button
    mushrooms, thinly sliced
25 g (1 oz) (4 tablespoons) flour
25 g (1 oz) (¼ cup) grated Gruyère
    cheese
50 g (2 oz) (⅓ cup) grated
    Parmesan cheese
15 ml (1 tablespoon) brandy
1.25 ml (¼ teaspoon) powdered
    mace
salt and pepper

For the Pastry:
175 g (6 oz) (1½ cups) wholemeal
    flour

good pinch salt
40 g (1½ oz) (3 tablespoons) lard
    (shortening)
40 g (1½ oz) (3 tablespoons) butter

1 Preheat the oven to 200°C, 400°F, gas 6.

2 Make the pastry: sieve the flour and salt into a bowl. Rub in the fat until the mixture resembles fine breadcrumbs. Add cold water to bind and stir it in with a round bladed knife. Knead lightly on a floured surface.

3 Roll out the pastry and use it to line a 20 cm (8 in) flan ring. Trim the edges, prick the base all over and line with greaseproof (parchment) paper. Fill with baking beans and bake on a baking (cookie) sheet for 15 minutes. Remove the paper and beans and return to the oven for a further 5 minutes. Cool on a wire rack. Reduce the oven to 180°C, 350°F, gas 4.

4 Put the scallops, white fish and milk into a pan, bring to the boil and poach gently for 5 minutes. Strain, reserving the milk.

5 Roughly chop the scallops, skin the white fish and salmon and remove any bones, and flake roughly.

6 Make the milk up to 300 ml (½ pint) (1¼ cups) with water. Melt the butter in a pan and fry the mushrooms for 2 minutes. Add the flour and cook for 1 minute. Remove from the heat and gradually add the milk. Stirring, bring to the boil and simmer for 2 minutes.

7 Add the Gruyère, 25 g (1 oz) (3 tablespoons) of the Parmesan cheese, brandy, mace and seasoning.

8 Fill the pastry case with the fish and pour over the sauce. Sprinkle with the remaining Parmesan and return to the oven for 10-15 minutes, until the cheese is golden-brown. Serve hot.

Serves 4

Tip: Any types of shellfish and fish can be used in place of the scallops, white fish and salmon in this recipe. It is an ideal way of using up leftovers.

Coquilles Orientales

8 scallops in their shells, or 350 g
 (¾ lb) shelled
150 ml (¼ pint) (⅝ cup) dry white
 wine
15 ml (1 tablespoon) wine
 vinegar
bouquet garni
salt and pepper
225 g (½ lb) button onions
15 ml (1 tablespoon) oil
15 ml (1 tablespoon) butter
1 clove garlic, crushed
5 ml (1 teaspoon) clear honey
2.5 ml (½ teaspoon) arrowroot
5 ml (1 teaspoon) soya sauce
15 ml (1 tablespoon) tomato
 paste
50 g (2 oz) (⅓ cup) seedless raisins

*Coquilles Orientales presents
scallops the Chinese way in a
sweet and sour sauce with onions,
honey and plenty of raisins*

1 Shell the scallops (see box on
page 1079).

2 Place the scallops in a pan with
the wine, vinegar, bouquet garni
and seasoning. Bring to the boil
and poach gently for 3 minutes.
Drain, reserving the liquor.

3 Blanch the onions in boiling
salted water for 8 minutes and
drain them.

4 Heat the oil and butter in a
frying pan (skillet) and sauté the
garlic and scallops for 4 minutes.
Remove with a slotted spoon.
Add the onions to the pan and fry
for 3 minutes, or until golden.
Remove from the pan.

5 Boil the strained liquor with
the honey for about 6 minutes,
until evaporated by half.

6 Mix the arrowroot to a thin
cream with a little water and add
to the liquor with the soya sauce,
tomato paste and raisins. Bring
to the boil, stirring, and simmer
for 2 minutes.

7 Return the scallops and
onions to the sauce and heat
through gently. Season to taste
and transfer to a heated serving
dish. Serve as a starter with
brown bread and butter.

Serves 4

Tip: Pipe a border of creamed
potato around the edge of two
scallop shells and fill with the
scallop mixture, to serve two as a
main course.

Tropical Prawns (Shrimps)

350 g (¾ lb) unpeeled king prawns
  (large shrimps)
25 g (1 oz) (2 tablespoons) butter
5 ml (1 teaspoon) curry powder
1 banana, mashed
50 g (2 oz) (⅓ cup) canned
  pineapple in juice
2 or 3 drops chilli sauce
salt and pepper
15 ml (1 tablespoon) oil
2 spring onions (scallions),
  chopped
15 ml (1 tablespoon) rum
1 egg yolk
30 ml (1 fl oz) (2 tablespoons)
  double (heavy) cream
15 ml (1 tablespoon) coconut
  strands, toasted

1 Boil some salted water in a pan, add the prawns (shrimps) and poach gently for 5 minutes. Drain, remove the heads and peel.

2 Melt the butter in a pan, add the curry powder and fry for 1 minute. Add the mashed banana. Drain the pineapple, reserving the juice, and dice the fruit. Add to the pan and cook for 3 minutes.

3 Add the chilli sauce, salt and pepper to taste and 45 ml (2 fl oz) (3 tablespoons) of the pineapple juice. Set aside.

4 Heat the oil in a frying pan (skillet) and fry the spring onions (scallions) and prawns (shrimps) lightly. Add the rum and ignite with a taper. Transfer to the banana sauce.

5 Mix together the egg yolk and cream and beat it into the sauce. Heat the mixture through, stirring continuously.

6 Transfer the prawn (shrimp) mixture to a heated serving dish and sprinkle with the coconut.

Serves 2

Hawaiian Prawn (Shrimp) Salad, a tempting dish which may be served at a buffet party or on less formal occasions

Hawaiian Prawn (Shrimp) Salad

15 ml (1 tablespoon) butter
15 ml (1 tablespoon) oil
5 ml (1 teaspoon) curry powder
2.5 ml (½ teaspoon) paprika
2 spring onions (scallions),
  sliced
1 stick celery, diced
100 g (¼ lb) (⅔ cup) canned
  pineapple pieces in juice
1 lime
450 g (1 lb) (3 cups) shelled
  prawns (shrimps)
few slices English cucumber
few lettuce leaves
½ red pepper, sliced

1 Heat the butter and oil in a frying pan (skillet), stir in the curry powder and paprika and cook for 1 minute.

2 Add the spring onions (scallions) and celery and stir-fry for 1 minute. Drain the pineapple and add to the pan with 30 ml (1 fl oz)

(2 tablespoons) of the juice, the juice of half the lime and the prawns (shrimps). Season and stir-fry for 3 minutes. Cool.

3 Serve on a bed of cucumber and lettuce, garnished with the remaining lime and the pepper.

Serves 4

Sole Celeste

4 Dover sole or flounder, 350 g (¾ lb) each
50 g (2 oz) (½ cup) flour, seasoned with salt and pepper

Sole Celeste is one of the many recipes that show how well prawns (shrimps) combine with whole white fish

2 eggs, beaten
150 g (5 oz) (2½ cups) fresh white breadcrumbs
oil for deep frying
225 ml (8 fl oz) (1 cup) mayonnaise, mixed with 15 ml (1 tablespoon) each chopped gherkins, capers and parsley
225 g (½ lb) cooked peeled prawns (shrimps)
1 lemon, cut in half decoratively
sprigs of parsley

1 Remove the brown skin from the fish, then wash and dry them.

2 Cut down the middle of the fish on the skinned side. Scrape the fish away from the bone in the same manner as for filleting, but leaving the fish intact around the edges, thus forming two 'pockets'. Snip the ends of the bones inside the pocket with scissors so that later they may be removed easily.

3 Fold the edges of the pockets back and coat the fish lightly in seasoned flour. Dip in the egg and coat in breadcrumbs.

4 Heat the oil to 190°C, 375°F. Fry the fish for 6-8 minutes until golden. Drain on absorbent paper.

5 Arrange the fish on a heated serving dish and very carefully remove the bones. Fill the gap with the prepared tartare sauce and top with the prawns (shrimps). Garnish with lemon and parsley.

Serves 4

Prawn (Shrimp) Salad Supreme

50 g (2 oz) ($\frac{1}{3}$ cup) raisins
100 g ($\frac{1}{4}$ lb) ($\frac{1}{2}$ cup) long grain rice
1 egg
good pinch mustard powder
150 ml ($\frac{1}{4}$ pint) ($\frac{5}{8}$ cup) olive oil
20 ml (4 teaspoons) tomato
  ketchup (catsup)
salt and pepper
pinch cayenne pepper
2 slices pineapple, chopped
100 g ($\frac{1}{4}$ lb) cooked ham cut in
  matchstick strips
50 g (2 oz) ($\frac{1}{4}$ cup) canned
  crabmeat
150 g (6 oz) (1 cup) cooked whole
  prawns (shrimps)
juice 1 lemon
15 ml (1 tablespoon) brandy
15 ml (1 tablespoon) chopped
  chervil

1 Soak the raisins for $\frac{1}{2}$ hour in a bowl of tepid water. Drain.

2 Boil the rice in salted water until just tender. Rinse thoroughly and drain. Cool.

3 To make the mayonnaise: break the egg, discarding the white and placing the yolk in a clean mixing bowl. Beat the egg yolk with the mustard until combined. Add the olive oil in small amounts, beating well all the time. When the mayonnaise is thick and smooth add the tomato ketchup (catsup) and season well with salt, pepper and cayenne.

4 Add the raisins, pineapple and ham strips to the rice in a salad bowl. Flake the crabmeat, reserving the canned liquor if possible. Add the crabmeat to the salad.

5 Peel all the prawns (shrimps) except for 4 reserved to garnish. Blend the peeled prawns (shrimps) into the rice salad.

6 Mix together the crab liquor, lemon juice and brandy, and season lightly with salt and pepper. Stir in the chopped chervil. Pour the dressing over the salad and toss lightly to blend it in well. Decorate with the whole cooked prawns (shrimps) and serve with the mayonnaise.

Serves 6

Prawn (Shrimp) Salad Supreme also contains ham, crabmeat, raisins and pineapple, mixed into boiled rice

Prawn (Shrimp) Toasts

1 shallot, chopped
1 slice fresh ginger root, about
  $\frac{1}{2}$ cm ($\frac{1}{4}$ in) thick, chopped
225 g ($\frac{1}{2}$ lb) ($1\frac{1}{2}$ cups) peeled
  prawns (shrimps)
5 ml (1 teaspoon) sherry
5 ml (1 teaspoon) cornflour
  (cornstarch)
salt and pepper
2 eggs, beaten
4 slices slightly stale white
  bread
75 ml (3 fl oz) ($\frac{3}{8}$ cup) oil

1 Mince the shallot and ginger root with the prawns (shrimps) to form a thick paste.

2 Place the mixture in a bowl and stir in the sherry, cornflour (cornstarch) and salt and pepper to taste. Mix in half the beaten egg smoothly.

3 Cut the crusts off the bread and then cut each slice into 4 triangles. Spread each piece with some of the prawn (shrimp) mixture. Brush them lightly with the rest of the beaten egg.

4 Heat the oil in a deep frying pan (skillet) and fry the bread triangles quickly, turning once, until golden-brown on each side. Remove from the pan and drain on absorbent paper. Serve at once.

Serves 4

Poseidon Cocktail

200 ml (6 fl oz) (¾ cup) mayonnaise
pinch curry powder
2.5 ml (½ teaspoon) castor sugar
100 g (¼ lb) (¾ cup) peeled prawns
  (shrimps)
2 slices pineapple, diced
1 large apple, peeled, cored and
  diced
salt and pepper
4 crisp lettuce leaves
pinch paprika
sprig parsley

1 Beat the mayonnaise with the curry powder and sugar.

2 Stir in the peeled prawns (shrimps), diced pineapple and apple. Season lightly with salt and pepper.

3 Shred the lettuce leaves and divide them between 4 glass serving dishes. Pile ¼ of the prawn (shrimp) mixture on each one.

4 Dust the top of each cocktail with a little paprika and garnish with a little parsley.

Serves 4

Garlic Grilled Prawns (Shrimps)

450 g (1 lb) fresh prawns
  (shrimps)
3 cloves garlic
100 ml (4 fl oz) (½ cup) olive oil
salt and pepper

1 Shell and devein the prawns (shrimps). Finely chop or crush the garlic and mix it with the oil. Season with a little salt and pepper.

2 Marinate the prawns (shrimps) in the oil for 1-2 hours, turning them from time to time.

3 Remove the prawns (shrimps) from the marinade, spear on 4 skewers and grill (broil) for 10-15 minutes until cooked.

Serves 4

Prawn (Shrimp) and Mushroom Cocktail

50 g (2 oz) (1¼ cups) sliced button
  mushrooms
juice and grated rind ½ lemon
100 g (¼ lb) (¾ cup) peeled prawns
  (shrimps)
150 ml (¼ pint) (⅝ cup) mayonnaise
4 drops chilli sauce
2.5 ml (½ teaspoon) paprika
1 spear chicory (Belgian endive)

1 Toss the sliced mushrooms in the lemon juice. In a bowl, mix together the mushrooms, prawns (shrimps) and mayonnaise. Blend in the chilli sauce and a little paprika.

2 Wash the chicory (Belgian endive) and cut it into thin slices

Poseidon Cocktail blends prawns (shrimps) with pineapple, to make a cocktail to delight the god of the sea

across the spear. Divide the shredded chicory (Belgian endive) between 4 small salad bowls.

3 Divide the mushroom and prawn (shrimp) mixture between the salad bowls. Top each one with a little grated lemon rind to decorate. The salads may be chilled, before serving with thinly-sliced brown bread, as an hors d'oeuvre.

Serves 4

Tip: Any green salad vegetable can replace the chicory (Belgian endive); try lettuce or watercress.

Poultry

All kinds of chicken and fowl, turkeys, ducks, geese, and guinea fowl are classed as poultry. They are available fresh or frozen (and sometimes smoked), either whole or as separate joints, so ensuring a good all-year-round supply. Most poultry is sold oven-ready — drawn, plucked and trussed — but should you have to prepare a freshly-killed bird yourself, there are full Step-by-step photo guides are on the following pages

Chicken Roast & Braised

Roast Chicken with Almonds

50 g (2 oz) (⅓ cup) currants
1½ kg (2½-3 lb) chicken, oven-ready
salt and pepper
sprig of thyme
100 g (¼ lb) (½ cup) butter
45 ml (3 tablespoons) water
200 g (7 oz) (1⅓ cups) long grain rice
about 300 ml (½ pint) (1¼ cups) chicken stock (bouillon) – about the equivalent to 1½ times the volume of the rice
50 g (2 oz) (⅓ cup) shelled almonds
25 g (1 oz) (1 tablespoon) pine kernels

1 Wash the currants and leave them to soak in a bowl of tepid water. Preheat the oven to 200°C, 400°F, gas 6.

2 Cut open the gizzard and remove the stone-filled pouch. Remove the spleen from the liver, being careful not to let it split open, and discard. Cut away any greenish parts which may be sticking to the liver and which would give a bitter taste. Wash and dry the chicken and giblets.

3 Season the inside of the chicken with salt and pepper. Put in the sprig of thyme, 25 g (1 oz) (2 tablespoons) of butter and the liver. Rub over the chicken a further 25 g (1 oz) (2 tablespoons) butter. Season the outside. Place the bird in a roasting pan. Pour the water into the pan, put it in the oven and let it cook for 1 hour. Baste the bird from time to time and turn it around so it cooks evenly.

4 Thirty minutes before the chicken is ready, measure the rice. Boil the stock (bouillon), adding all the prepared giblets. Melt the remaining butter in a stewpan. Add the dry rice and cook over moderate heat. Stir with a wooden spoon until the grains become transparent. Pour in the boiling stock (bouillon), cover the pan and simmer until all the liquid is absorbed.

5 Place the almonds in a non-stick frying pan (skillet) and heat, stirring frequently until they are golden-brown.

6 Warm a serving dish and sauceboat. Drain the currants.

7 When the rice is cooked, tip it onto the serving dish. Add the currants and pine kernels and mix them carefully into the rice. Spread the browned almonds on top.

8 Drain the chicken and place it on top of the rice.

9 Pour 2-3 tablespoons of hot water into the roasting pan. Stir vigorously with a spoon to dissolve all the meat juices. Pour the liquid into the sauceboat and serve hot.
Serves 4

Roast Chicken with Almonds — served on a bed of almonds, pine kernels and raisins

Chicken in Wine with Mushrooms

1½ kg (3½ lb) chicken, oven-ready
75 g (3 oz) (⅓ cup) butter
1 clove garlic
2 onions
sprig thyme
1 bay leaf, imported
¼ litre (8 fl oz) (1 cup) dry white
   wine
salt and pepper
250 g (good ½ lb) mushrooms,
   wiped and trimmed
juice 1 lemon
12 g (about ½ oz) canned truffle,
   drained (optional)
300 ml (½ pint) (1¼ cups) single
   (light) cream

1 Brown the chicken in 50 g (2 oz) (4 tablespoons) butter. Peel and chop the garlic and the onions. Put the chicken, together with the garlic and onions, in a large pan with the sprig of thyme, bay leaf and the white wine. Season with salt and pepper, cover and cook gently for about 1 hour.

2 About 20 minutes before the end of the cooking time, heat the remaining butter in a pan, add the strained lemon juice and heat, stirring continuously, without letting the mixture colour. Add the mushrooms, then enough cold water just to cover them. Reduce (evaporate) the liquid to about half its quantity, with the lid off the pan. As soon as the mushrooms are tender, take them off the heat.

3 Cut the truffle, if used, in strips. Remove the chicken from the pan and place on a hot serving dish. Discard the bay leaf and thyme.

4 Reduce (evaporate) the cooking juices a little, then stir in the cream. Pour the sauce over the chicken. Decorate the dish with the strips of truffle, if used, and arrange the drained mushrooms all round.

Serves 6

Scandinavian Roast Chicken

Traditionally, the chicken is wrapped up with pine needles and the parcel is left for 24 hours for the flavour to infuse. However, some needles may be poisonous.

24 juniper berries
1½ kg (3 lb) chicken, oven-ready
2.5 ml (½ teaspoon) salt
pepper
4 shallots
40 g (1½ oz) (3 tablespoons) butter

1 Pound the juniper berries in a mortar or work in a blender and put aside half until the following day.

2 Insert a little of the remaining crushed juniper berries in the chicken and rub the outside with the rest. Season with salt and pepper.

3 Preheat the oven to 200°C, 400°F, gas 6.

4 Peel the shallots and chop them coarsely.

5 Heat the butter in a frying pan (skillet). As soon as it stops frothing, add the shallots and brown them.

6 Add the reserved crushed juniper berries. Cook the mixture gently for 1 minute over a low heat, stirring all the time.

7 Pour half the juniper- and shallot-flavoured butter into a roasting pan. Place the chicken on top, and baste with the rest of the butter. Put the chicken into the oven and cook for 45-60 minutes, turning and basting the chicken from time to time.

8 Serve very hot straight from the oven.

Serves 4

Tip: Scandinavians serve this dish with potatoes baked in ashes and then basted with cream.

Chicken with Mustard

1½ kg (3 lb) chicken, oven-ready
200 ml (7 fl oz) (⅞ cup) oil
salt and pepper
1 egg
25 ml (1½ tablespoons) French
   (Dijon-style) mustard
50 g (2 oz) (1 cup) dry white
   breadcrumbs
30 ml (2 tablespoons) white
   vinegar
5 ml (1 teaspoon) capers, drained
   and chopped
Small bunch parsley, finely
   chopped

1 Preheat the oven to 170°C, 325°F, gas 3.

2 Put the chicken in a roasting pan. Baste it with 30 ml (2 tablespoons) of oil. Season it with salt and pepper. Cook for 30 minutes in the oven.

3 Boil some water in a small saucepan. Hard-boil the egg for 10 minutes. Put it into cold water. Shell it. Halve it. Remove the yolk and place the yolk in a bowl. (Use the white for other purposes.)

4 When the chicken has been cooking for 30 minutes, take it out of the oven. Spread 15 ml (1 tablespoon) of the mustard over the bird. Sprinkle the breadcrumbs over it. Put it back into the roasting pan and cook for a further 15 minutes.

5 Add the rest of the mustard to the egg yolk. Blend in the vinegar. Add the rest of the oil a little at a time, stirring continuously with a wooden spoon. Add the chopped capers and parsley to the sauce. Add salt and pepper to taste and mix again.

6 Warm a serving dish and a sauceboat. Place the chicken on it. Pour the sauce into a sauceboat and serve very hot.

Serves 4

Scandinavian Roast Chicken, with juniper berries, a deliciously different way with chicken

141

Chicken Stuffed with Ham

2 kg (4 lb) chicken
50 g (2 oz) bacon fat
30 ml (2 tablespoons) olive oil

For the stuffing:
125 g (good ¼ lb) bacon, slightly
   salted
1 onion
2 shallots
small bunch parsley
125 g (good ¼ lb) lean veal
2 cloves garlic
pinch mixed spice
1.25 ml (¼ teaspoon) dried
   (powdered) thyme
pinch ground (crushed) bay leaf
100 g (¼ lb) (1 cup) dry white
   breadcrumbs
45 ml (3 tablespoons) milk
1 egg
salt and pepper
2-4 slices cooked ham (gammon)

For the garnish:
1 kg (2 lb) green peppers
1 kg (2 lb) tomatoes
2 onions
2 cloves garlic
few sprigs parsley

1 Wash, drain and wipe the chicken. Prepare the giblets (see pages 126-127) and reserve the zard, first removing stone-filled pouch, and liver. Wash and dry the chicken.

2 Make the stuffing. Dice the bacon. Heat some water in a saucepan and as soon as it is boiling, put in the bacon pieces and blanch them for about 5 minutes. Drain them, cool them in cold water, and dry them.

3 Peel the onion and cut in quarters. Peel the shallots. Wash and dry the parsley.

4 Work in a blender or through a mincer (grinder) the following stuffing ingredients: the bacon, lean veal, chicken gizzard and liver, the onion, shallots and parsley.

5 Peel and finely chop the cloves of garlic. Add them to the rest of the stuffing ingredients, together with the mixed spice, thyme and bay leaf.

6 Rub the dry breadcrumbs through a sieve. Moisten them with the milk and then squeeze out any excess liquid.

7 Add the whole egg to the breadcrumbs and mix well. Fold into the stuffing ingredients. Season with salt and pepper to taste and mix well to obtain an even consistency.

8 Wrap the stuffing in the slices of ham, and slide them into the chicken. Sew up the opening with a trussing needle and thread so that the stuffing does not escape.

9 Cut the bacon fat into small pieces. Heat the oil in a large flameproof casserole. Add the diced bacon fat and melt over a low heat. Put the chicken into the casserole and brown it over a moderate heat, so that it is sealed on all sides. Cover the pan and leave the chicken to cook for about 45 minutes.

10 Meanwhile, prepare the garnish. Wash and dry the peppers. Cut them in half, remove the membranes and take out the seeds. Cut them into strips. Skin the tomatoes by placing in a bowl of boiling water, let stand for 1-2 minutes, then drain and skin; take out the seeds and dice the pulp. Peel the onions and cut them in quarters. Peel and crush the garlic. Wash, dry and chop the parsley.

11 When the chicken has cooked for about 45 minutes, add the onions, green peppers and garlic. Season with salt and pepper to taste and fry for 15 minutes.

12 Then mix in the tomatoes and chopped parsley. Cover and finish the cooking (about 15 minutes).

Chicken Stuffed with Ham — a tasty stuffing made with bacon, veal, spices and herbs

13 Heat a serving dish.

14 Arrange the chicken on the hot dish, surround it with the garnish and serve very hot.

Serves 6

Chicken stuffed with Raisins

150 g (5 oz) (1 cup) seedless raisins
(100 ml) (½ cup) dry sherry
1 large onion
350 g (12 oz) (2¼ cups) long grain
   rice
45 ml (3 tablespoons) oil
100 g (4 oz) (¾ cup) flaked
   almonds
pinch ginger
pinch powdered saffron
1.25 ml (¼ teaspoon)
   chilli powder
pinch mixed spice
salt and pepper
2 kg (4 lb) chicken, oven-ready
75 g (3 oz) (⅓ cup) butter
   or margarine

1 Wash the raisins and soak them for 30 minutes in the dry sherry.

2 Peel and chop the onion. Measure the amount of rice and boil twice its volume of water.

3 Heat the oil in a stewpan. Add the flaked almonds and chopped onion and fry them until golden.

4 Add the rice to the onion and almond mixture and fry, stirring constantly with a wooden spoon, until the grains of rice are opaque. Pour in the boiling water, cover the pan and cook over a very low heat for about 18 minutes.

5 Mix the spices in a bowl – ginger, saffron, chilli and mixed spice. Add a little salt and pepper. When the rice is cooked, mix in the spices and raisins. Preheat the oven to 200°C, 400°F, gas 6.

6 Fill the inside of the chicken with part of the prepared rice and keep the rest hot in either a bain

marie, or a warm oven.

7 Sew up the opening in the chicken so that the stuffing does not leak out.

8 Melt the fat in a roasting tin, add the chicken and roast for about 1½ hours, or until cooked. Baste the bird occasionally during roasting.

9 Put the cooked chicken on a flat serving dish, surrounded by the rice which has been kept hot. Serve hot.

Serves 6

Chicken with Cider

2 kg (4 lb) chicken
1¼ kg (2½ lb) cooking (green)
   apples
100 g (¼ lb) (1 cup) walnuts,
   shelled
10 g (2 tablespoons) parsley,
   chopped
50 g (2 oz) bacon
1 small onion
75 g (3 oz) (1½ cups) fresh white
   breadcrumbs
1 egg
2.5 ml (½ teaspoon) ground
   (powdered) cinnamon or ginger
15 g (1 tablespoon) dark brown
   sugar
100 g (¼ lb) (½ cup) butter or
   margarine
2-3 shallots
sprig fresh thyme
2 cloves
salt and pepper
½ bottle dry cider
150 ml (¼ pint) (⅝ cup) single
   (light) cream

1 Preheat the oven to 190°C, 375°F, gas 5.

2 Peel, core and quarter the apples. Place them in a bowl of lightly salted water to prevent browning.

3 Roughly chop the shelled walnuts.

4 Remove the rind from the bacon and chop it finely. Peel and dice the onion. Melt 25 g (1 oz) of

the fat in a frying pan, and fry the bacon and onion gently until they are softened.

5 Rinse two-thirds of the apples to remove the salty water. Shred (grate) the apples into a bowl, add the bacon, onions, walnuts, parsley, breadcrumbs, beaten egg, half of the cinnamon, seasoning and half of the sugar. Mix well. Stuff the chicken with this mixture, and sew it up with a trussing needle, to prevent the stuffing coming out during cooking.

6 Put the chicken in the roasting tin and spread it with half of the fat. Put into the oven and roast for about one and three-quarter hours, or until the chicken is cooked. 15 minutes before the end of cooking, rinse the remaining apple quarters and place them in the roasting pan around the chicken. Pour over the cider, and baste both the chicken and apples with the cider.

7 Meanwhile, peel and chop the shallots finely. Heat the rest of the fat in a large pan. Add the chopped shallots and fry for 5-6 minutes on a low heat, then add the cloves, pepper and remaining sugar. Stir in the cream, and heat gently for 5 minutes.

8 When the chicken is cooked, remove it from the roasting pan with the apples. Skim off any excess fat from the pan juices, then gradually pour the juices into the sauce.

9 Serve the chicken on a warmed plate surrounded by the apple quarters, with the sauce poured over it.

10 When the chicken is cooked, add the cream and shake the pan to mix the sauce well. Taste and adjust the seasoning with salt and pepper and a pinch of ground (powdered) cinnamon or ginger.

11 Transfer the chicken to a hot serving dish, or carve and arrange the pieces on a hot serving dish, surrounded by the apple quarters and the sauce. Serve immediately.

Serves 6

Chicken Portions

Chicken with Caramelized Apples

4 chicken pieces
3 onions
45 ml (3 tablespoons) oil
salt and pepper
5 ml (1 teaspoon) paprika
2.5 ml (½ teaspoon) ground
  (powdered) ginger
5 ml (1 teaspoon) ground
  (powdered) coriander seeds
pinch ground (powdered)
  saffron
½ litre (1 pint) (2½ cups) water
1 kg (2 lb) firm dessert apples
50 g (2 oz) (¼ cup) butter

1 Lightly fry the peeled and sliced onions in oil. Add the chicken joints and brown.

2 Season the chicken with the salt, pepper, paprika, ginger, coriander and saffron. Pour in the water and simmer for 30 min.

3 Meanwhile, wash and dry the apples. Cut them in half without peeling, and core them. Heat the butter in a frying pan (skillet). Add the apple halves and brown them over a brisk heat.

4 Preheat the oven to 180°C, 350°F, gas 4.

5 After the chicken has simmered for 30 minutes, place the pieces in an ovenproof dish. Add the caramelized apple halves. Pour over the cooking juices from the pan. Cover the dish with foil and pierce a few holes in it. Place the dish in the oven and let the chicken cook for 30 minutes more. Serve at once.

Serves 4

Chicken with Green Peppers and Paprika Rice

225 g (½ lb) bacon, sliced
50 g (2 oz) (¼ cup) butter
1¼ kg (2½ lb) oven-ready chicken,
  cut up into serving pieces
1.25 ml (¼ teaspoon) salt
freshly ground (milled) black
  pepper
1 large onion, peeled and
  chopped
5 ml (1 teaspoon) flour
225 ml (8 fl oz) (1 cup) wine, red or
  white
1 bay leaf, imported
500 ml (1 pint) (2½ cups) chicken
  stock (bouillon)
3 green peppers, halved, cored
  and deseeded
5 ml (1 teaspoon) paprika
225 g (½ lb) (1 cup) long grain rice

1 Preheat the oven to 180°C, 350°F, gas 4. Gently fry the bacon in a deep frying pan (skillet) or stewpan. When the fat has run from the bacon, remove it and pour all but 15 ml (1 tablespoon) of the fat from the pan. Put half the butter in the pan, add the chicken pieces and brown them evenly on all sides. Remove the pieces and season them with salt and pepper.

2 Fry half the onion in the same fat for 3 minutes or until soft. Stir in the flour and cook the roux slowly for a few minutes; then stir in the wine and the bay leaf. Cook over a high heat to reduce (evaporate) the wine to about 100 ml (4 fl oz) (½ cup). Add 100 ml (4 fl oz) (½ cup) of the stock (bouillon) and bring to the boil.

3 Put the chicken pieces, bacon and any juices left in the pan in a casserole, cover with a lid and cook in the oven for 50 minutes or until the chicken is tender.

4 Heat the remaining butter in a pan and add the green peppers cut into 2.5 cm (1 in) squares and the remaining onion. Fry over a moderate heat for 5 minutes, then stir in the paprika and the rice. Stir over a moderate heat for 3 minutes, then add the remaining chicken stock (bouillon), boiling; cover and simmer for 20 minutes. Discard the bay leaf.

5 Serve the chicken from the casserole, with the rice served separately.

Serves 4

Chicken Waterzoi

2 large carrots
8 leeks
4 stalks celery
50 g (2 oz) (¼ cup) butter
salt and pepper
bunch parsley
2 kg (4 lb) chicken, oven-ready
1½ litres (1¼ pints) (3 cups) chicken
  stock (bouillon)
3 egg yolks
200 ml (7 fl oz) (7⅞ cup)
  double (heavy) cream
juice of 1 lemon

1 Peel the carrots; trim and clean the leeks and celery. Wash them, dry and chop finely. Heat the butter in a stewpan, add the prepared vegetables and leave to soften over a low heat for about 15 minutes. Season lightly. Wash the parsley, dry, chop and add three-quarters of it to the pan of vegetables.

2 Cut the chicken in pieces (see pages 112-113. Put half the vegetables into a casserole. Cover with the chicken pieces and then with the remaining vegetables. Place over a low heat for 10 minutes, then gradually pour in the chicken stock. Cover and cook slowly for at least 50 minutes or until the chicken pieces are very tender.

3 Place the pieces of chicken on a heated serving dish. Beat the egg yolks with the cream and the juice of the lemon. Pour this liaison into the casserole whilst stirring with a wooden spoon. Heat for a few minutes, stirring continuously, but do not allow to boil. Pour the thickened vegetable soup into a hot tureen and sprinkle with the remaining chopped parsley.

4 Serve some of the soup in wide soup bowls, topping each one with a piece of chicken.

Serves 6

Grilled Chicken

Grilled (Broiled) Chicken with Onion

1.5 kg (3 lb) chicken, oven-ready
30 ml (2 tablespoons) oil
salt and pepper
40 g (1½ oz) (2½ tablespoons) butter
  or margarine
2 onions
8 small tomatoes
15 ml (1 tablespoon) strong made
  mustard
15 ml (1 tablespoon) double
  (heavy) cream or top of milk
150 g (5 oz) (2½ cups) stale, white
  breadcrumbs
½ carton cress or watercress

1 Cut up the chicken (see pages 112-113).

2 Heat the grill (broiler). Preheat the oven to 200°C, 400°F, gas 6.

3 Baste the chicken with half of the oil. Season with salt and pepper. Place it under the grill (broiler), skin side up, and grill (broil) it on both sides, turning it a quarter of a turn every 2 minutes. Total time is about 8 minutes each side.

4 Place the chicken in an oven-proof dish and cook in the oven for 30 minutes.

5 Peel and grate the onions. Melt the fat in a frying pan (skillet). Add the grated onion and cook over a low heat until soft, with the consistency of a purée.

6 Wash and dry the tomatoes; slice them in half, and cover them in the rest of the oil. Put them on a roasting pan, add salt and pepper, and put them in the oven to cook.

7 Tip the onion purée into a bowl. Add the mustard and

cream or top of the milk. Mix them well. Put the breadcrumbs on a large plate.

8 When the chicken has been cooking for 30 minutes, drain it. Cover it with the onion and mustard mixture. Then coat both sides with the breadcrumbs, pressing them on well. Put it back in the roasting pan and baste it with the cooking juices. Let it cook for another 10 minutes.

9 Cut the cress if used. Wash and drain the cress or watercress. Warm a serving dish.

10 When the chicken is cooked, put it on the serving dish. Place the baked tomatoes and cress round it. Pour the juices from the dish over the chicken and serve hot.

Serves 4

Grilled (Broiled) Chicken with Mustard

1½ kg (3 lb) frying chicken, cut
  into serving pieces
65 g (2½ oz) (5 tablespoons) butter
10 ml (2 tablespoons) mild
  mustard
5 ml (1 teaspoon) Worcestershire
  sauce
5 ml (1 teaspoon) chopped
  rosemary
30 ml (2 tablespoons) finely
  chopped parsley
2.5 ml (½ teaspoon) salt
freshly ground black pepper

1 Preheat the oven to 200°C, 400°F, gas 6. Put the chicken pieces into a buttered fireproof dish and dot with 25 g (1 oz) (2 tablespoons) butter. Bake in the oven for 20 minutes.

2 Mix the remaining butter with the rest of the ingredients. Brush half the mixture over the chicken pieces and grill (broil) for 12 minutes. Turn the chicken over, brush with the remaining butter mixture, and grill (broil) for a

further 12-15 minutes or until the chicken is tender.

3 Serve with a green salad.
Serves 4

Provençal Split Chicken

1.5 kg (3 lb) chicken, oven-ready
3 shallots
2 cloves garlic
3 lemons
15 ml (1 tablespoon) crushed
  thyme and rosemary
75 ml (5 tablespoons) oil
salt and pepper
small bunch watercress

1 Cut up the chicken (see pages 112-113).

2 Peel the shallots and the garlic. Chop them finely. Squeeze 2 of the lemons and pour the juice into a bowl; add the shallots and garlic, the thyme and rosemary and the oil. Add salt and pepper. Beat the marinade with a fork.

3 Place the prepared chicken flat in a deep dish. Pour over the marinade and let the bird marinate for 3 hours in a cool place.

4 Heat the grill (broiler). Drain the chicken and reserve the marinade. Place the bird in the grill (broiler) pan, skin side down. Put it under the grill (broiler) and grill (broil) it under a high heat. Turn the bird after about 15 minutes. Baste it with the marinade and let it cook for a further 15 minutes.

5 Warm a serving dish. Place the well-browned chicken on it, spoon over the cooking juices and serve very hot, garnished with lemon quarters and small bunches of watercress.

Serves 4

Spatchcock
The French phrase for this method of preparing a chicken is *en crapaudine*: the split bird has its legs and wings tucked in to resemble a flattened toad – *crapaud* being the French word for a toad.

Chicken Stews

Rumanian Chicken Stew

1½ kg (3 lb) chicken pieces
5 ml (1 teaspoon) salt
black pepper
1.25 ml (¼ teaspoon) dried
  marjoram
2.5 ml (½ teaspoon) paprika
50 g (2 oz) (4 tablespoons) butter
  or margarine
30 ml (2 tablespoons) oil
2 onions
2 carrots
1 leek
450 g (1 lb) canned butter beans
100 ml (4 fl oz) (½ cup) stock
5 ml (1 teaspoon) lemon juice

1 Dry the chicken pieces and rub them with the salt, pepper, marjoram and paprika mixed together.

2 Heat half the fat and the oil in a frying pan (skillet). Fry the chicken pieces for about 10 minutes, turning them as necessary to brown all over. Peel the onions and cut into rings. Peel the carrots and slice them. Trim off the green part and wash the leek well to remove soil, then cut it into rings. Drain the beans.

3 Heat the remaining fat in a clean pan. Add the onion slices and fry until they are golden-brown. Add the carrots, leek and beans and cook over a low heat for 15 minutes. Add the chicken pieces and the stock. Cover the pan with its lid. Simmer for 1 hour or until tender.

4 Taste for seasoning and adjust if necessary. Add the lemon juice and serve at once.

Serves 4-6

Chicken Fricassée with Walnuts

3 shallots
75 g (3 oz) (¾ cup) shelled walnuts
1½ kg (3 lb) chicken, oven-ready
75 g (3 oz) (6 tablespoons) butter
  or margarine
25 g (1 oz) (2 tablespoons) flour
15 ml (1 tablespoon) paprika
100 ml (4 fl oz) (½ cup) dry white
  wine
½ litre (1 pint) (2½ cups) stock
salt and pepper
15 ml (1 tablespoon) tomato
  concentrate (paste)

1 Peel the shallots and chop them finely. Chop the walnuts.

2 Cut up the chicken into serving pieces (see pages 112-113).

3 Heat the fat in a sauté pan and when hot, brown the pieces of chicken, 2 or 3 at a time. Then add the shallots and leave them to brown. Sprinkle with the flour and the paprika. Stir and cook for 2 minutes.

4 Add the white wine and stock together with the salt and pepper. Add the tomato concentrate (paste) and the walnuts. Blend well together, bring to the boil, then cover the pan, reduce the heat, and simmer for 40 minutes.

5 Heat a serving dish.

6 Taste and adjust the seasoning. Pour the fricassée into the serving dish and serve hot.

Serves 4

Rumanian Chicken Stew – a homely chicken and vegetable stew

Fricassée of Chicken with Paprika

1.2 kg (2½ lb) chicken, oven-ready
salt and pepper
3 medium onions
45 ml (3 tablespoons) lard
5 ml (1 teaspoon) paprika
5 ml (1 teaspoon) caraway seeds
250 ml (8 fl oz) (1 cup) chicken
   stock
300 ml (½ pint) (1¼ cups) fresh
   tomato sauce (see below)
8 medium potatoes
150 g (5 fl oz) (generous ½ cup)
   natural yogurt
15 ml (1 tablespoon)
   double (heavy) cream
7 g (1 tablespoon) flour

1 Cut the chicken into 8 pieces (see pages 112-113) and season.

2 Peel the onions and cut into thin slices.

3 Heat the lard in a sauté pan. Add the sliced onions and the chicken pieces. Cook until golden-brown, stirring often, and until the chicken is done (about 15 minutes).

4 When the chicken and onions are brown, sprinkle them with the paprika. Add the caraway seeds and stir for 1 minute with a wooden spoon to incorporate them.

5 Add the stock and the tomato sauce. Season with salt and pepper and cook over a low heat for 1 hour.

6 Peel and wash the potatoes. Steam or boil them.

7 Heat a deep serving dish.

8 Drain the pieces of chicken, arrange them on the serving dish and surround with the cooked potatoes.

9 Mix together the yogurt, the cream and the flour and pour into the sauce. Blend over a low heat, without boiling, stirring with a wooden spoon until the sauce thickens (3-4 minutes).

10 Pour the sauce over the chicken pieces and serve hot.

Serves 4

Poached Chicken

Chicken Mousse

2 chicken joints
300 ml (½ pint) (1¼ cups) chicken
   stock
150 ml (¼ pint) (⅝ cup) creamy milk
1 bayleaf, imported
few peppercorns
2-3 slices onion
2 hard-boiled (hard-cooked) eggs

For the béchamel sauce:
7 g (¼ oz) (½ tablespoon) butter
7 g (¼ oz) (1 tablespoon) flour
salt and pepper
7 g (¼ oz) powdered gelatin
bunch watercress
1 medium onion
150 ml (¼ pint) (⅝ cup) double
   (heavy) cream
few sprigs parsley

1 Put the chicken joints in a pan and add enough chicken stock to cover. Bring to the boil, then reduce the heat and poach, with the lid on, until the chicken is tender – about 30 minutes for legs, 25 minutes for breast meat. Drain, reserving 150 ml (¼ pint) (⅝ cup) of the stock. Put the milk in a pan, together with the bayleaf, peppercorns and slices of onion and heat just to boiling point; take off the heat and set aside to infuse for about 10 minutes. Strain, reserving the milk.

2 Slice the hard-boiled (hard-cooked) eggs and place them in the bottom of a lightly oiled 20 cm (8 in) ring mould.

3 Make the béchamel sauce: melt the fat in a pan, stir in the flour to make a roux and cook for 1 minute, stirring all the time. Take the pan off the heat and blend in half the reserved milk. Stir in the rest of the milk until smooth. Return the pan to the heat and cook until the sauce thickens, stirring continuously.

Add salt and pepper to taste and leave to cool.

4 In a pan, dissolve the gelatin in a little of the reserved chicken stock and leave for about 5 minutes or until spongy. Then heat gently until the gelatin is completely dissolved, stirring all the time. Take the pan off the heat and cool slightly.

5 Wash and chop half the watercress; peel and slice the onion; stiffly whip the cream.

6 Remove the meat from the chicken joints; put in a blender and work with the rest of the chicken stock to a smooth puree. Add this mixture to the cooled béchamel sauce.

7 When the gelatin is on the point of setting but still liquid, stir it into the sauce (it is important to blend in the gelatin so it sets evenly and without jellied [gelled] lumps). Cut and fold in the cream and chopped watercress as lightly as possible. Check the seasoning, then pour the mousse into the mould and place it in the refrigerator to set.

8 When firm, place your chosen serving dish on top of the mould, invert, tap sharply on the bottom and the mousse should slide out without damage. Garnish the centre with the remaining watercress, the onion slices and parsley. Serve chilled.

Serves 4

Fresh Tomato Sauce
Peel and chop 1 carrot and 1 onion; fry in 25 g (1 oz) (2 tablespoons) fat for 5 minutes. Stir in 15 g (½ oz) (2 tablespoons) flour, then add 450 g (1 lb) skinned and chopped tomatoes, 300 ml (½ pint) (1¼ cups) stock, 1 bay leaf, 5 g (½ teaspoon) sugar, salt and pepper to taste. Bring to the boil, cover and simmer 45 minutes; sieve, reheat and check seasoning. Use as required.

Makes about 400 ml (¾ pint) (2 cups)

Chicken Mousse and Chicken with Orange Sauce – two mouth-watering dishes to make using poached chicken joints

Chicken with Orange Sauce

4 chicken joints
1 bay leaf, imported
few peppercorns
1 litre (2 pints) (5 cups) chicken
  stock or water
few sprigs watercress

For the orange sauce:
25 g (1 oz) (3 tablespoons) butter
  or margarine
25 g (1 oz) (4 tablespoons) flour
½ litre (1 pint) (2½ cups) cooking
  liquid (see recipe)
juice and grated rind 2 oranges
15 ml (1 tablespoon) medium
  sherry
salt and pepper

1 Put the chicken joints, bay leaf and peppercorns in a pan and add enough chicken stock or water to cover. Bring to the boil, reduce the heat and poach, with the lid on, for 30-45 minutes or until the chicken is tender. Strain, reserving ½ litre (1 pint) (2½ cups) of the cooking liquid. Keep the chicken hot.

2 To make the sauce: melt the fat in a small pan, stir in the flour to make a roux and cook gently for 1 minute, stirring all the time. Take the pan off the heat and blend in half the reserved cooking liquid. Stir in the rest of the liquid until smooth and return the pan to the heat. Cook the sauce until it thickens, stirring continuously. Add the juice and grated rind of the oranges, the sherry and salt and pepper to taste.

3 Place the chicken joints on a warmed serving dish, pour over the sauce and garnish with watercress sprigs and segments of the oranges.

Serves 4

Cold Chicken Tonnato is a delicious standby for hot weather eating. This version is derived from the classic Italian recipe, Veal in Tuna Fish Sauce (Vitello Tonnato)

Chicken Tonnato

1 onion
1 stalk celery
4 whole chicken breasts, skinned
  and boned
½ litre (1 pint) (2½ cups) chicken
  stock
salt and pepper
pinch thyme
few parsley stalks
½ bay leaf, imported
150 ml (¼ pint) (⅝ cup) white wine
  (optional)

For the sauce:
210 g (7½ oz) (1 cup) canned tuna
  fish
6 canned flat anchovy fillets
2 tomatoes
400 ml (¾ pint) (2 cups)
  mayonnaise
30 ml (2 tablespoons) lemon juice
45 g (3 tablespoons) capers

For the garnish:
few anchovy fillets
few capers
crisp lettuce leaves

1 Peel and halve the onion.

Wash well and halve the celery.

2 Place the chicken breasts, chicken stock, onion, celery, seasoning, herbs, wine and enough water to cover in a large pan and bring to the boil. Simmer very gently for 20-30 minutes, depending on the size of the chicken breasts, until tender and cooked.

3 Remove the chicken breasts from the pan with a draining spoon and leave to cool.

4 To make the sauce: drain the tuna fish and anchovy fillets. Wash and thinly slice the tomatoes. In a blender, work the mayonnaise, tuna fish, anchovy fillets, lemon juice and capers until smooth and well combined.

5 Place the cooled chicken breasts on a serving dish and spoon the sauce over them to cover. Garnish with more anchovy fillets and capers and arrange tomato slices round them. Serve on a bed of crisp lettuce leaves and any remaining sauce.

Serves 4

Chicken Cutlets with Mushrooms and Almonds

125 g (¼ lb) (½ cup) butter
  or margarine
120 g (¼ lb) (1 cup + 2 tablespoons)
  flour
300 ml (½ pint) (1¼ cups) chicken
  stock (in which the chicken
  was poached)
350 g (¾ lb) (6 cups) mushrooms
white flesh only from 1.2 kg
  (2½ lb) chicken, poached in
  stock
150 g (5 oz) cooked ham
3 eggs
250 ml (8 fl oz) (1 cup) double
  (heavy) cream
30 ml (2 tablespoons) finely
  ground almonds
30 ml (2 tablespoons) brandy
salt and pepper
5 ml (1 teaspoon) paprika
pinch mixed spice
75 g (3 oz) (1 cup) dried white
  breadcrumbs
100 g (¼ lb) (¾ cup) flaked almonds
50 ml (3 tablespoons) white port

1 Melt one-third of the fat in a small pan, add 60 g (2¼ oz) (good ½ cup + 1 tablespoon) flour, and stir over a low heat to make a white roux.

2 Mix the roux with the stock and cook for 10 minutes on a very low heat, stirring frequently with a wooden spoon.

3 During this time, trim the bottom of the mushroom stalks, wash the mushrooms briefly, dry and coarsely chop one-third of them. Slice the rest finely.

4 Heat 15 ml (1 tablespoon) fat, add the chopped mushrooms, and fry until all the liquid from them has evaporated.

5 Dice the white chicken flesh and chop the cooked ham.

6 Break 1 egg into a bowl and beat in half the cream and the ground almonds.

7 Take the pan of sauce off the heat and stir in the egg and cream liquid, the chopped mushrooms, chopped ham, diced chicken and the brandy. Season with salt, pepper, paprika and mixed spice.

8 Return the pan to a low heat for 3 minutes, mixing well with a wooden spoon.

9 Lightly butter a large dish, pour in this mixture to a depth of about 3 cm (1¼ in) and leave to cool and set completely.

10 Heat 25 g (1 oz) (2 tablespoons) fat in a small pan and fry the sliced mushrooms.

11 Preheat the oven to 200°C, 400°F, gas 6.

12 Cut the cold meat mixture into four and shape each piece into an oval cake about 2 cm (¾ in) thick. Curve one of the sides and make it thinner at one end so as to make the cakes into the shape of a cutlet.

13 Break the remaining eggs into a bowl and beat well together.

14 Dip the "cutlets" into the rest of the flour, then in the beaten egg, and coat them with the breadcrumbs.

15 Heat the rest of the fat in a frying pan (skillet), add the egg and breadcrumbed cutlets and brown on each side over not too brisk a heat.

16 Put the flaked almonds to brown in the hot oven, then switch off the heat but leave the door closed.

17 Heat a serving dish.

18 Drain the cutlets on absorbent paper and arrange them on the hot serving dish.

19 Put the cutlets into the still hot oven, but with the door open.

20 Stir the port into the fat left over from cooking the cutlets, scraping the bottom of the pan with a wooden spoon, and cook for 2 minutes on a brisk heat. Add the rest of the cream, season with salt and pepper, and stir on a brisk heat until the mixture thickens.

21 Take the serving dish from the oven, surround the cutlets with the sliced mushrooms and coat with the sauce. Sprinkle with flaked almonds and serve very hot.

Serves 4

Chicken Sautés

Sautéed Chicken in Cream Sauce

1.2 kg (2½ lb) chicken pieces
salt and pepper
30 ml (2 tablespoons) oil
25 g (1 oz) (2 tablespoons) butter
225 g (½ lb) (4 cups) button
  mushrooms
3 shallots
100 ml (4 fl oz) (½ cup) dry
  white wine
200 ml (7 fl oz) (⅞ cup) double
  (heavy) cream

1 Season the chicken pieces.

2 Heat the oil and fat in a sauté pan over a high heat. Seal the pieces of chicken in the fat for about 15-20 minutes, without letting them brown. Turn the pieces and let them cook over a low heat for 15 minutes, without a lid.

3 Meanwhile, trim, wash, dry and slice the mushrooms. Peel the shallots and grate them.

4 Heat a serving dish. Remove the chicken pieces from the pan. Arrange them on the serving dish and keep them warm.

5 Put the mushrooms into the pan. Fry them for 5 minutes but don't let them brown. Then add the shallots and let them soften for 2 minutes over a low heat. Add the white wine. Stir in all the cooking juices at the bottom of the pan and let the liquid reduce (evaporate) by about half over a high heat.

6 Add the cream. Stir vigorously and let the mixture reduce (evaporate) by about half its quantity over a high heat. Taste the sauce and adjust the seasoning. Coat the chicken with the sauce and serve hot.

Serves 4

Sautéed Chicken in Rich Cream Sauce

1½ kg (3 lb) chicken, oven-ready
salt and pepper
30 ml (2 tablespoons) oil
50 g (2 oz) (¼ cup) butter
350 g (¾ lb) (6 cups) mushrooms
3 shallots
100 ml (4 fl oz) (½ cup) dry
   white wine
1 egg yolk
juice ½ lemon
pinch ground (powdered)
   nutmeg
20 g (¾ oz) (3 tablespoons) flour
300 ml (½ pint) (1¼ cups) double
   (heavy) cream
75 g (3 oz) (¾ cup) grated cheese

1 Cut up the chicken (see pages 112-113). Season with salt and pepper.

2 Pour the oil in a frying pan (skillet). Add half the butter and heat. When hot put in the chicken pieces and sauté for about 10 minutes on each side.

3 Meanwhile, trim the mushroom stalks. Wash the mushrooms quickly, dry and slice them. Peel and chop the shallots.

4 Remove the chicken pieces from the frying pan (skillet) after 10 minutes or so and keep them warm. Add the mushrooms to the same frying pan (skillet) and fry them for 5 minutes. Then add the shallots and soften over a low heat for 2 minutes.

5 Pour in the white wine and stir, scraping the bottom of the pan to dissolve the cooking juices; then reduce (evaporate) the liquid to about half its quantity over a high heat.

6 Preheat the oven to 220°C, 425°F, gas 7.

7 Put the egg yolk into a cup. Mix it with the lemon juice and nutmeg. Using a fork work the rest of the butter thoroughly with the flour on a plate.

8 Add the kneaded butter to the sauce bit by bit, whisking vigorously. Boil it for 1 minute, then add the egg and lemon mixture, still whisking the mixture, and without letting it boil. Stir in the cream.

9 Arrange the chicken pieces in a heated ovenproof serving dish. Coat them with the cream sauce. Sprinkle with the grated cheese and put the dish in the oven to brown. When golden and bubbling on top, serve the chicken at once.

Serves 4

Sautéed Chicken with Grape Juice

1.2 kg (2½ lb) chicken, oven-ready
salt and pepper
30 ml (2 tablespoons) chicken
   (poultry) fat
2 shallots
few tarragon leaves
12 mushrooms
100 g (¼ lb) rashers (slices)
   smoked bacon
few sprigs parsley
2 cloves garlic
70 ml (2 fl oz) (¼ cup) natural grape
   juice
30 ml (2 tablespoons) double
   (heavy) cream

1 Cut up the chicken (see pages 112-113) and season with salt and pepper

2 Heat the poultry fat in a stewpan and when it is hot put in the chicken pieces, skin side down, and cook over a slow heat for about 15 minutes; then turn and cook for 15 minutes more.

3 Peel and chop the shallots. Wash the tarragon leaves, dry and chop them finely. Trim, wash, dry and chop the mushrooms. Cut the bacon into thin strips.

4 Wash and dry the parsley. Peel the garlic. Chop the parsley and garlic together. When the chicken is cooked arrange it on a dish and sprinkle with the parsley and garlic. Keep warm.

5 Put the shallots, tarragon, mushrooms and bacon into the pan in which the chicken was cooked. Cook slowly for about 10 minutes, then add the grape juice and cook for a further 10 minutes. Then add the cream, bring to the boil and reduce (evaporate) to about half its volume.

6 Pour the sauce over the chicken and serve very hot.

Serves 4

Sautéed Chicken in Rich Cream Sauce

Sautéed Chicken with Mushrooms

     ☆

1¼ kg (2½ lb) chicken pieces
salt and pepper
100 g (¼ lb) (1 cup) flour
30 ml (2 tablespoons) oil
30 g (1 oz) (2 tablespoons) butter
  or margarine
225 g (½ lb) (4 cups) mushrooms
3 shallots
100 ml (4 fl oz) (½ cup)
  brandy
100 ml (4 fl oz) (½ cup)
  dry white wine
225 g (8 oz) canned tomatoes,
  drained
sprig tarragon
¼ litre (8 fl oz) (1 cup)
  chicken stock

1 Season the pieces of chicken and roll them in the flour.

2 Put the oil and fat into a sauté pan; over a high heat brown the chicken for about 10 minutes, then turn and brown on the other side for another 10 minutes.

3 While the chicken is cooking, trim the mushroom stalks. Wash, dry and slice the mushrooms. Peel and finely chop the shallots.

4 Take the pieces of chicken out of the pan as they are cooked: the quicker-cooking wings first, then the legs, etc. The wings shouldn't take longer than 15 minutes, the legs about 20 minutes. Keep them warm. Add the mushrooms to the pan and fry quickly. Add the shallots, reduce the heat and soften them for 1 minute.

5 Pour in the brandy and flame (set fire to it). Add the wine and stir to dissolve the meat juices.

6 Chop the drained tomatoes roughly and add them to the pan. Chop the tarragon. Add the tarragon and the stock. Let the mixture reduce (evaporate) over a high heat, uncovered, for 10 minutes.

7 Warm a serving dish. Arrange the pieces of chicken on it. Taste and adjust the seasoning of the sauce. Cover the chicken with the sauce and serve hot.

Serves 4

Turkey Roasts and Stews

All kinds of turkey products – both cooked and uncooked, are available to cooks today, thus offering plenty of scope for inventive dishes as well as for evergreen favourites.

Uncooked Turkey

Whole turkeys (fresh or frozen) can reach giant proportions but for most of us a mini bird of between 3-4 kg (6-8 lb), oven-ready, is a popular choice. Just right for family gatherings or picnics, when value for money is often an important consideration.

Apart from whole birds, turkey can be also be bought as:

Portions: breasts, drumsticks, thighs (some already boned and stuffed), wings (either whole or the tips only), and chops (similar to noisettes of lamb).

Turkey roasts: these are boned and rolled white and red meat roasts, wrapped in pork fat and deep frozen – thaw and cook as for ordinary roasts.

Assorted packs of minced and chunked meat, giblets and livers are also available. These are ideal for making stews, casseroles, soups and stocks, or for pâtés and risotto.

Cooked Turkey Products

For lazy cooks, there is a choice of various cooked boneless turkey rolls: some are already sliced, others can be cured or smoked. All will give plenty of lean meat with no wastage. Some convenience foods may also be cooked.

Convenience foods

There are a whole host of these turkey products – uncooked, ready-cooked, and others requiring nothing more than heating through, or deep frying. Choose from turkey meat loaves and pâtés, burgers, crispy fries, fingers, croquettes and sausages.

Stuffing a Turkey

If stuffing a turkey for roasting, allow about 450 g (1 lb) stuffing for the neck end of a bird weighing up to 7 kg (14 lb) – double the quantity for larger birds – and allow about 450-900 g (1-2 lb) for the body cavity, according to the size of the bird. Vary the flavours if using two stuffings: chestnut or veal forcemeat, say, for the neck end and sausagemeat for the body cavity.

Roasting a Turkey

There are many theories on the best way to roast a turkey, but whichever way you choose, make sure the breast is amply covered with softened fat (butter, margarine or dripping) to keep it moist and tender during cooking. For extra flavour lay rashers (slices) of bacon on top as well.

Cover the bird with several thicknesses of greased paper or foil to prevent the flesh drying out and toughening, but remove the coverings for the last 30-40 minutes so the bird can crisp and brown, and be basted with its cooking juices.

Wrap foil round the leg ends so they don't burn during roasting, then dress them with paper turkey frills for serving at the table.

Roast Turkey with Chipolatas (Link Sausages)

450 g (1 lb) fresh chestnuts
4 large potatoes
3½-4 kg (7-8 lb) turkey
salt and pepper
60 ml (2¼ fl oz) (¼ cup) oil
100 g (¼ lb) (½ cup) butter or
  margarine

3 large onions
450 g (1 lb) carrots
100 ml (4 fl oz) (½ cup) dry white wine
10 g (2 teaspoons) sugar
350 g (¾ lb) button (pearl) onions
350 g (¾ lb) lean bacon rashers (slices)
450 g (1 lb) chipolatas (link sausages)
100 ml (4 fl oz) (½ cup) chicken stock

1 Preheat the oven to 200°C, 400°F, gas 6.

2 Peel the chestnuts and cook until tender (see opposite).

3 Peel the potatoes.

4 Stuff the turkey with the potatoes, truss securely with kitchen thread (see pages 102-103), then sprinkle salt and pepper all over the bird. Put the turkey in a roasting pan, pour over half the oil, then dot with half the fat. Roast in the pre-heated oven until golden brown.

5 Meanwhile, peel the large onions and 2 carrots and slice finely. Place them around the turkey, continue roasting until the vegetables are browned, then add the wine. Continue roasting for about 1½ hours or until the turkey is tender, basting frequently. Cover with foil if the skin becomes too brown during cooking.

6 Meanwhile, peel and dice the remaining carrots. Put in a pan with enough water just to cover, then add salt, half the sugar and 25 g (1 oz) (2 tablespoons) fat. Cover with foil and cook over high heat until the carrots are tender and have absorbed all the liquid. Do not allow the carrots to become brown.

7 Peel the small onions, then caramelize them with water and the remaining sugar and fat as for the carrots.

8 Cut the bacon into neat strips and blanch in boiling water for 3 minutes. Drain, rinse under cold running water, then drain again.

9 Slice the chipolatas (link sausages) into 3 cm (1¼ in) lengths.

10 Heat the remaining oil in a frying pan (skillet), add the bacon

and fry until brown. Add the chipolatas (link sausages) and fry until brown, then drain off any excess fat. Add the caramelized carrots and onions and stir well to mix. Drain the chestnuts and add to the pan to heat through. Transfer the mixture to an oven-proof dish and keep hot in the oven.

11 To test if the turkey is cooked, prick the thickest part of the thigh: the juices should run clear. Remove the trussing thread from the turkey, and take out the potatoes. Put the turkey on a warmed serving platter and keep hot.

12 Transfer the roasting pan to the top of the stove and skim off the fat from the cooking juices. Add the stock, then boil until the liquid is reduced (evaporated) by a quarter. Taste and adjust the seasoning, then pour through a

fine sieve (strainer) into a sauce boat.

13 Arrange the chipolata (link sausage) and vegetable garnish around the turkey and serve hot with the sauce separate.

Serves 8

Cooking Fresh Chestnuts
Slit the brown outer skin and put the chestnuts into cold water. Bring to the boil and cook for 5 minutes, then drain and remove the outer and inner skins. Return the chestnuts to the pan, cover with stock and simmer for about 30 minutes or until tender.

Roast Turkey with Chipolatas (Link Sausages) – garnished with chestnuts, sausages, carrots, onions and bacon strips

Turkey Roast with Fruit Sauce

25 g (1 oz) (2 tablespoons) butter
  or margarine
2¾ kg (5½ lb) white turkey roast
1 red pepper
1 small green pepper
1 onion
225 g (8 oz) canned mandarin
  oranges in juice
225 g (8 oz) canned sweetcorn

For the sauce:
5 g (2 teaspoons) cornflour
  (cornstarch)
reserved juice from mandarin
  oranges
reserved juice from canned
  sweetcorn
15 ml (1 tablespoon) vinegar
4 g (1 teaspoon) sugar
5 ml (1 teaspoon) Worcestershire
  sauce
15-30 ml (1-2 tablespoons) sherry

1 Preheat the oven to 190°C, 375°F, gas 5. Spread the fat over the turkey roast then wrap it in foil to make a parcel. Place in a roasting pan and roast for 1½ hours.

2 Wash, deseed and core the peppers; peel and chop the onion. Drain the mandarins and corn, reserving the juices. Mix the mandarins, corn, peppers and onion together.

3 To make the sauce: mix the cornflour with a little water to make a smooth paste. Blend the juice from the mandarins and corn with the vinegar, sugar, Worcestershire sauce, sherry and cornflour and heat until thickened, stirring well. Add the fruit and vegetables.

4 Remove the turkey roast from the oven and unwrap the foil. Pour a little of the sauce all over and round the turkey and cover again with the foil.

5 Replace the turkey in the oven and cook for a further 1-1½ hours or until the turkey is tender and cooked through.

6 Unwrap the turkey and place it on a serving dish surrounded by its fruity sauce and serve the rest of the sauce separately.

Serves 6-8

Turkey en Croûte with Ratatouille

25 g (1 oz) (2 tablespoons) butter
  or margarine
2¾ kg (5½ lb) white turkey roast
1 lb shortcrust pastry,
  home-made or frozen and
  thawed

For the stuffing:
1 medium onion
75 g (3 oz) (1½ cup) white button
  mushrooms
1 egg
175 g (6 oz) (3 cups) fresh white
  breadcrumbs
pinch thyme
pinch sage
10 g (2 tablespoons) finely
  chopped parsley
salt and pepper to taste

For the ratatouille:
225 g (½ lb) courgettes
2 aubergines
1 red pepper
1 green pepper
2 medium onions
4 tomatoes
oil for frying

For the garnish:
parsley sprigs

1 Preheat the oven to 170°C, 325°F, gas 3.

2 Spread the fat over the turkey roast, then wrap in foil to make a parcel and place in a roasting pan. Put in the oven and roast for about 2 hours.

3 To make the stuffing: peel and finely chop the onion. Wipe and finely chop the mushrooms. Beat the egg. Mix the stuffing ingredients together with enough of the beaten egg to bind them all.

4 Wash all the vegetables for the ratatouille. Trim and slice the courgettes; slice and chop the aubergines; deseed and core the peppers and cut the flesh into strips; peel and chop the onions; quarter the tomatoes.

5 Remove the turkey from the oven and open up the foil. Leave until cool enough to handle, then remove the string and the outer layer of skin. Spread some of the stuffing in a thick layer over the turkey roast but leaving the ends free.

6 Roll out the pastry thickly (5-8 mm, ¼-⅜ in) into a large oblong to fit the roast and its stuffing. Place the turkey roast, upside down, on the pastry, so you can spread stuffing on the other side as well.

7 Spread over the remaining stuffing, dampen the ends of the pastry and fold it over to make a "pastry parcel", seal the edges and ends together well, then turn it over again so the lengthwise join is underneath. Increase the oven heat to 190°C, 375°F, gas 5.

8 Brush the parcel with the remaining beaten egg, and decorate the top with leaves from any remaining pastry. Brush the leaves with egg and then bake the parcel on a greased baking sheet for about 35 minutes or until the pastry is golden-brown and the turkey is cooked. Serve either hot or cold, garnished with sprigs of parsley.

9 For the ratatouille: heat the oil and fry the courgettes, aubergines, peppers and onion until softened and slightly browned. Add the tomatoes and cook for a further 5 minutes. Season to taste and serve.

Serves 6-8

Turkey Roast with Fruit Sauce – the mandarin oranges provide a delicious contrast of flavours

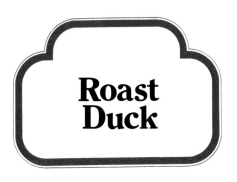

Roast Duck

Of the numerous breeds of edible duck available, probably none is superior to the famous large white Aylesbury ducks. These were formerly bred in large numbers in Aylesbury, Buckinghamshire (hence the name), as well as other English counties and elsewhere.

Aylesbury ducks can weigh as much as 3½ kg (7 lb), but for the cook, the smaller ducklings, up to 2 kg (4 lb), are preferable because they are more tender and less fatty. Ducks more than 1 year old – known as breeders – are too tough for roasting although they can be boiled or braised and used for pies.

If a duck is excessively fatty, pinch the skin together between your forefingers, so it's clear of the flesh, and pierce all over with a sharp knife. This will ensure the fat can run out freely, without the meat juices escaping.

Signs of Quality
You can tell a good-quality duck by the following points: young birds have a clean smell, their feet are a bright yellow colour, the bill and feet are pliable, and there should be plenty of flesh round the breast.

Estimating Quantities
As the ratio of bone to flesh is so much greater in a duck than in other poultry such as chicken, allowance must be made for this when estimating the weight of bird to buy. The following chart is a guide to the average number of portions that can be carved from different weights of bird:

Weight of Bird – undrawn but plucked	Portions without bone – each about 100g (¼ lb)
2¼ kg (4½ lb)	6
2¾ kg (5½ lb)	7¼
3¼ kg (6½ lb)	9¾

Duck with Peaches

1 kg (2 lb) can peach halves
½ lemon
2.2 kg (4½ lb) duck, oven-ready
salt and pepper
2 cloves
pinch cinnamon
50 ml (2 fl oz) (¼ cup) white vinegar
40 g (1½ oz) (3 tablespoons) butter
pinch cayenne pepper

1 Drain the peach halves, reserving the syrup. Squeeze the half lemon, reserving the juice.

2 Season inside the duck with salt and pepper and fill it with 6 half peaches, the cloves, cinnamon and salt and pepper. Then add 30 ml (2 tablespoons) vinegar.

3 Heat the butter in a large pan and when it begins to brown, add the duck.

4 Brown the bird over a low heat, turning it frequently until it is golden-brown on all sides. Cover and leave to cook for about 50 minutes.

5 Add the rest of the vinegar, the other peach halves, sliced, the lemon juice and 150 ml (¼ pint) (⅝ cup) of the reserved peach syrup, and finish the cooking (another 20-25 minutes).

6 Before serving, heat a serving dish and sauce-boat. Put the duck in the centre of the dish. Surround it with the peaches.

7 Adjust the seasoning of the sauce, and boost it with a pinch of cayenne pepper. Pour the sauce into the sauce-boat. Serve the duck and sauce simultaneously.

Serves 6

Duck with Peaches – duck dressed up with a succulent but simple sauce made with canned peaches

Braised Duck with Apricots

2½ kg (5 lb) duck, oven-ready
salt and pepper
pinch (powdered) allspice
50 g (2 oz) (4 tablespoons) butter
  or margarine
15 ml (1 tablespoon) oil
300 ml (½ pint) (1¼ cups) chicken
  or white stock
150 ml (¼ pint) (⅝ cup) dry white
  wine
450 g (1 lb) fresh apricots, or
  canned apricot halves, drained
juice and grated rind 1 lemon
5 ml (1 teaspoon) white vinegar
15 ml (1 tablespoon) apricot
  brandy (optional)
30 ml (2 tablespoons) brandy
  (optional)

1 Preheat the oven to 190°C, 375°F, gas 5.

2 Rub the flesh of the prepared duck with salt, pepper and allspice.

3 Heat the fat and oil in a large frying pan (skillet), then put in the duck and brown on all sides. Lift it out of the frying pan (skillet) and place in a large flameproof casserole.

4 Pour the stock and wine into the frying pan (skillet) and heat until the liquid reaches boiling point. Remove from the heat and pour this mixture over the duck. Cover the casserole and place in the preheated oven for 1½-2 hours.

5 Meanwhile, wash and halve the apricots, discarding the stones (pits). After the duck has been cooking for 1 hour, add half the fresh or canned apricots to the roasting pan. Baste them with the stock mixture, and leave to cook.

6 When the duck is cooked, lift it onto a serving dish and keep warm. Strain the cooking liquid and skim off all but 15 ml (1 tablespoon) of the fat. Rub the cooked apricots through a sieve (strainer) and reserve the purée.

7 Pour the cooking juices into a small pan, and heat briskly until the liquid has reduced (evaporated) by one-third. Stir in the apricot purée, the lemon rind

and juice, and the white vinegar.

8 Arrange the remaining apricot halves round the duck. Bring the brandies to the boil and immediately pour them over the duck. If liked, the brandy can be set alight for effect. Serve at once, with the sauce in a sauce-boat.

Serves 4

Roast Duckling with Turnips

1.5 kg (3 lb) duckling, oven-
  ready
salt and pepper
100 g (¼ lb) (½ cup) butter
2 carrots
2 onions
2 tomatoes
few sprigs parsley
2 cloves garlic
some chicken giblets
sprig thyme
½ bayleaf, imported
100 ml (4 fl oz) (½ cup)
  reisling
200 ml (6 fl oz) (¾ cup) water
1 kg (2 lb) small turnips
15 g (4 teaspoons) sugar
200 g (7 oz) shallots
15 ml (1 tablespoon)
  cornflour
30 ml (1 fl oz) (2 tablespoons)
  Madeira or dry sherry

1 Preheat the oven to 220°C, 425°F, gas 7. Season the duck inside and outside with salt and pepper. Truss it (see pages 102-103) then spread it with 25 g (1 oz) (2 tablespoons) butter. Place it on one side in a roasting pan.

2 Peel and wash the carrots and the large onions and cut them into large dice. Wash and quarter tomatoes. Wash the parsley. Peel and crush the garlic.

3 When the duck starts to brown, place the giblets round it, together with the carrots and onions. Let them brown slightly. When it has been cooking for 25 minutes, turn the duck onto its other

side. With a small ladle, remove the fat which has run from the duck. Add the tomatoes, parsley, garlic, thyme and bayleaf. Pour in 85 ml (3½ fl oz) (7 tablespoons) white wine and the water. Cook for another 25 minutes, basting with juices.

4 Peel and wash the turnips, cutting them into wedges. Place them in a heavy frying pan (skillet) with 40 g (1½ oz) (3 tablespoons) butter, a pinch of salt, half the sugar and just enough water to cover the turnips. Cover with foil. Bring to the boil and cook over a moderate heat. The turnips should be cooked when all the water has evaporated and they are coated with a sticky brown glaze.

5 Take the duck from the oven and turn it on its back; cook for another 20 minutes, basting several times. If it begins to brown too much, cover it with foil.

6 Peel the shallots or baby (pearl) onions and glaze them in the remaining butter and sugar in the same way as for the turnips.

7 When the duck is cooked, put it on a serving dish or in a casserole and keep warm. Pass the cooking juice through a fine mesh strainer into a saucepan. Skim off the fat. Mix the cornflour (cornstarch) with the rest of the white wine. Pour this mixture into the saucepan and mix with a whisk. Cook for 5 minutes, then add the Madeira to the sauce.

8 Mix together the glazed turnips and the shallots or baby (pearl) onions. Pour the sauce over them. Simmer gently for 4-5 minutes and serve with duck.

Serves 4

Roast Duck with Turnips – a homely meal well suited to serving in an earthenware casserole

Roast Goose

A mature goose weighs between 6-7 kg (12-14 lb), so choose smaller, younger birds to be sure of tenderness. You can recognize tenderness by the pliability of the breastbone and light orange-coloured beak of a young bird.

Before roasting a goose, pinch together the skin on the breast, then prick all over with a fork; this will allow the natural fat to run out during cooking.

Roast Goose with Prune and Apple Stuffing

4-4½ kg (8-9 lb) goose, oven-ready
salt and black pepper
pinch garlic salt
pinch ground (powdered) ginger
goose giblets
1 large carrot
1 large onion
little melted goose fat
25 g (1 oz) (2 tablespoons) tomato concentrate (paste) diluted with 30 ml (1 fl oz) (2 tablespoons) vinegar
1.25 ml (¼ teaspoon) gravy browning
pinch mace
50 ml (2 fl oz) (¼ cup) melted goose fat (optional)
25 g (1 oz) 4 tablespoons) flour (optional)

For the Stuffing:
225 g (½ lb) small sharp eating apples
225 g (½ lb) (1½ cups) canned prunes, with the juice
1 egg
225 g (½ lb) (4 cups) fresh brown breadcrumbs
50 g (2 oz) (4 tablespoons) melted butter
pinch mixed spice
25 g (1 oz) (2 tablespoons) brown sugar
juice and grated rind 1 lemon

1 Wash, clean and wipe the bird. Thoroughly season it inside and out with salt, pepper, garlic salt and ginger. Prick the skin without touching the flesh (see page 182) to allow the seasoning to penetrate. Leave to stand for 20 minutes.

2 Make the stuffing: peel, core and quarter the apples. Drain the canned prunes, reserving the juice. Remove the stones (pits) from the prunes. Beat the egg. In a bowl, blend the brown breadcrumbs, melted butter, beaten egg, spice, sugar and juice and grated rind of the lemon. Gently but thoroughly combine the prunes and apples with this mixture.

3 Spoon some of the stuffing inside the cavity of the goose and the rest inside the neck cavity (turn the bird on its back to do this). Fold the neck flap over the backbone and secure it with a skewer or kitchen thread. Preheat the oven to 190°C, 375°F, gas 5.

4 Wash the giblets, put them in a pan and cover with cold water. Bring to the boil and then drain and rinse in cold water. Peel and quarter the carrot and onion. Lay them with the giblets in a roasting pan and place the goose on top. Brush a little melted goose fat all over the bird. Roast in the preheated oven for 1 hour, basting from time to time with a little water and the fat of the goose. After 1 hour, turn the bird on its side and cook for a further 15 minutes. Then turn it on the other side and cook for 15 minutes more. Reduce the oven temperature to 170°C, 325°F, gas 3 for the rest of the cooking time. The goose should be ready after a total cooking time of 2½ hours. To test if the bird is cooked, pierce the thickest part of the leg with a skewer: the juices should run clear.

5 When cooked, lift the goose from the pan and drain all its juice into the pan. Keep the goose warm while making the gravy.

6 Remove all the fat from the roasting pan, leaving only the meat juices. Pour the juices into a saucepan. Dilute 150 ml (¼ pint) (⅝ cup) of the reserved prune juice with 150 ml (¼ pint) (⅝ cup) water and add this mixture to the meat juices. Stir in the tomato concentrate (paste) and vinegar, the gravy browning, salt, pepper and the mace. Bring to the boil and boil for 15 minutes. Strain into a bowl.

7 The gravy can be served thin and clear as it is. If preferred, it can be thickened as follows. Mix the melted goose fat and the flour together in a pan and cook until a light brown. Draw the pan off the heat and gradually add the gravy. Return the pan to the heat, bring to the boil and cook for 3 minutes until thickened. Strain the gravy.

8 Carve the goose (see page 167) by removing the legs first; then slice the breast and leg meat as for duck, cutting 4 thin slices from each breast. Garnish each portion with some of the stuffing and serve the gravy separately.

Serves 4

Roast Goose with Apple and Walnut Stuffing

450 g (1 lb) fresh chestnuts
2½ kg (5 lb) goose

For the Stuffing:
450 g (1 lb) (2 cups) pork sausagemeat
2 onions
2 sticks (stalks) celery
50 g (2 oz) (½ cup) shelled walnuts
2 cooking (green) apples
1 egg
50 g (2 oz) (¼ cup) butter or margarine
2 g (1 teaspoon) dried sage
salt and pepper

1 Peel the chestnuts and cook until tender (see page 141).

2 To make the stuffing, fry the sausagemeat gently for about 10 minutes until lightly coloured, stirring occasionally. Remove from the heat and drain off the excess fat.

3 Peel the onions and chop finely. Chop the celery and walnuts. Peel and core the apples, then slice finely. Beat the egg.

4 Melt half the fat in a pan, add the onions, celery and walnuts and fry gently until softened and lightly coloured. Add the apples and cook for a few minutes more.

5 Remove the pan from the heat, then stir in the sausagemeat, beaten egg, sage and salt and pepper to taste.

6 Preheat the oven to 200°C, 400°F, gas 6.

7 Spoon the stuffing into the cavity of the goose, then truss securely with kitchen thread (see pages 102-103). Place the goose on a rack in a roasting pan, prick all over with a skewer, then brush with the remaining fat.

8 Roast in the preheated oven for 1¾ hours or until the juices run clear when the thickest part of the thigh is pierced with a skewer.

9 Five minutes before the end of the cooking time, drain the chestnuts and heat through in a pan of hot water.

10 When the goose is cooked, remove the thread and place the goose on a warmed serving platter. Drain the chestnuts and arrange around the goose.

11 Serve hot with giblet gravy, chestnuts and brussels sprouts.

Serves 6

Roast Goose—straightforward to cook and a splendid dish to serve. A tart sauce like gooseberry helps to take the edge off the natural fattiness of the bird

Poultry Stuffings

Cranberry Stuffing

1 medium onion
25 g (1 oz) (⅛ cup) butter or margarine
225 g (½ lb) cranberries, fresh or frozen and thawed
25 g (1 oz) (⅛ cup) honey or sugar
225 g (8 oz) pork or beef sausagemeat
100 g (¼ lb) fresh white breadcrumbs
1 beaten egg
salt and pepper
good pinch cinnamon
pinch pepper
juice and grated rind 1 orange
5 g (1 tablespoon) freshly chopped parsley

1 Peel the onion and chop finely. Melt the fat in a sauté pan and sauté the onion for 5 minutes until soft but not coloured. Add the cranberries and fry for 2 minutes until lightly cooked. Remove the pan from the heat, add the honey or sugar, and cool.

2 In a bowl combine the sausagemeat, crumbs and beaten egg. Season with salt, pepper, the juice and rind of 1 orange, and parsley.

3 Stir in the cranberry mixture as lightly as possible so as not to crush the cranberries too much.

Use for turkey, capon and guinea fowl.

Apricot Stuffing

50 g (2 oz) dried apricots
100 ml (⅕ pint) (½ cup) dry cider
1 medium onion
50 g (2 oz) (¼ cup) margarine or fat
150 g (¼ lb) (1 cup) fresh white breadcrumbs
4 g (1 tablespoon) fresh chopped mint and parsley
100 g (¼ lb) pork or beef sausagemeat, or mixture of both
1 egg
salt and black pepper
pinch mace
pinch allspice

1 Soak the dried apricots in the cider for 2 hours, then drain, reserving the liquid, and chop the apricots. Peel the onion and chop.

2 Heat the fat in a pan and brown the onion slightly for 2 minutes; add the crumbs and apricots, cook for 5 minutes, then remove the pan and cool.

3 Combine all the stuffing ingredients in a bowl, together with the reserved liquid, and blend thoroughly to form a smooth but firm paste.

Use for ducks, geese and guinea fowl

Lemon, Rice and Sultana Stuffing

1 medium onion
75 ml (⅛ pint) (5/16 cup) oil
75 g (3 oz) long grain rice
50 g (2 oz) white mushrooms
225 ml (⅜ pint) (1 cup) hot water
1 chicken stock cube
salt and pepper
50 g (2 oz) sultanas
grated rind and juice 1 lemon

1 Peel and chop the onion. Heat the oil in a heavy-based pan and sauté the onion for 3 minutes without colouring. Add the rice, stirring it into the oil, and cook until translucent – about 5 minutes.

2 Wash, drain and slice the mushrooms, and add to the rice mixture; cook for 1 minute only. Pour in the hot water and crumble in the stock cube. Season to taste with salt and pepper and boil for 20 minutes.

3 Scald and drain the sultanas and stir into the rice mixture, together with the lemon juice and grated rind.

Use for ducks, geese and guinea fowl

Potato and Onion Stuffing

50 g (2 oz) (4 tablespoons) butter or margarine
100 g (¼ lb) (½ cup) onion, chopped
175 g (6 oz) cooked potato, diced
225 g (½ lb) sausagemeat
salt and pepper
1 egg, beaten
pinch sage and parsley

1 Heat the fat in a pan, add the onions and sauté them until tender but not brown. Add the diced cooked potato, toss together and then leave to cool.

2 Blend the sausagemeat with salt and pepper, the beaten egg and the sage and parsley. Incorporate the cooled potato mixture and season to taste.

Use with all types of poultry

Roast Rib of Beef

Beef has always enjoyed a sumptuous reputation – it became famous as the 'roast beef of Olde England' and was even knighted by King Henry VIII, after which the two hindquarters, including the legs, rump, sirloin and wing ribs, were always referred to as *Baronne de Boeuf*.

Beef is very nutritious and a good source of energy. It is rich in protein, vitamin B and iron. The price of beef varies with the cut. The most expensive are usually the most tender and can be quickroasted, fried or grilled (broiled). Tougher cheaper cuts require slower cooking methods to soften them but are just as nutritious.

Beef is extremely versatile and can be prepared and cooked in so many ways. You can roast, fry, grill (broil), casserole, pot-roast, stew, boil, braise, stuff, smoke or salt it. It can be minced (ground) and made into hamburgers, or baked *en croûte* in a pastry case. Of course, the method of cooking you use will depend on the cut and quality of the beef and how much you can afford to spend.

Choosing Beef
When choosing beef, always take the colour and texture into account. The lean flesh should be light rosy or cherry red in colour, whereas the fat should be a creamy yellow. The lean meat should be marbled with fat – this is always a sign of good quality, tender meat. There should be a minimum of gristle. The texture will determine the tenderness of the meat – the most tender cuts such as sirloin spring back when touched.

Cuts of Beef
Different cuts will require different methods of cooking. Always be sure that you choose the right one. Cuts vary from one country to another, and even between areas and districts. The British, American and Australian cuts which you can use are often different. Many cuts such as rib, chuck, leg, skirt, blade, shin, silverside and brisket are very similar indeed, if not the same. The main differences lie in the cutting and terminology used, especially

with steaks. The American equivalent of British fillet steak is tenderloin. As well as sirloin steak, they also have T-bone, Porterhouse, pin bone, and Club or Delmonico (rib eye) steaks. All these steaks are now becoming popular in Britain and also in Australia.

Storing Beef
Store raw meat loosely wrapped, in a cool place or refrigerator. Beef will keep in a refrigerator for 2-3 days. The most economical way to buy beef is in bulk if you have a freezer. The recommended storage time in a freezer is 8 months. Always thaw out frozen meat either in the refrigerator or at room temperature slowly. Never immerse in hot water to speed the process up. Once thawed, you should never refreeze the beef.

Seasoning Beef
Always season beef before cooking, especially roasting or grilling (broiling), with salt and freshly ground (milled) black pepper. For additional flavour you can season the beef with herbs or spices. Try rubbing the joint with garlic, onion, herbs or spices before cooking, or insert a clove of garlic or a small piece of onion into the meat itself.

Improving the Texture and Flavour of Beef
One way to improve the texture and flavour of cheaper cuts of meat is to marinate them for several hours. Try using wine, beer or cider or an acidic mixture of fruit juices and vinegar. You can tenderize a tough steak or joint with a ready made tenderizer which most supermarkets sell. These tenderizing powders are usually prepared from extract of figs, pawpaws and pineapple – the fresh juice of these fruits works equally well.

Larding Beef
You can lard tough, cheaper cuts of meat with a larding needle to tenderize them. Just push a larding needle through the meat with the grain, thread with fat and pull back through. This is explained in the step-by-step photo guide to larding on page 606. Introducing the fat into the flesh will make the meat more moist and lubricate it during cooking.

Steaks

The most popular and well-known steak cuts are – in usual order of costliness – fillet, sirloin, rib, and rump. Being very expensive, fillet is graded into several different cuts.

An average beef fillet is 45-50 cm (18-20 in) in length and tapers in width from 10 cm (4 in) to 2.5 cm (1 in). A whole fillet weighs from 3-4½ kg (6-9 lbs) untrimmed, and when prepared for cooking, a fillet will weigh on average 1¾-2 kg (3½-4 lb).

The Châteaubriand is taken from the head of the fillet. A piece 10 cm (4 in) is cut off, weighing from 350 g to 500 g (12-16 oz). It is wrapped round with a cloth, and flattened until it is 5 cm (2 in) thick, widening to double its original size at 20 cm (8 in) in diameter. When cooked it is served in slices, and is always for two.

The Coeur de Filet or Medaillon steak is cut 2½ cm (1 in) thick, and weighs 250 g (½ lb). It is cut from the heart of the fillet, and is also flattened to a diameter of 7.5 cm (3 in). The fillet steak is cut from the middle of the fillet, 6.5 cm (2½ in) thick, about 10 cm (4 in) in diameter, and weighs 200 g (7 oz).

Sirloin steaks are tender and flavoursome. Entrecôte means 'between the ribs' but the term now includes any sirloin steak. Porterhouse is another cut of the sirloin. Rib steaks are a luxury, large and tasty. The famous T-bone steak cut includes part of the fillet and sirloin. Rump steak is often hung to mature, producing a fine flavour. The tenderest cut of rump steak is a point steak.

The Tournedos is also cut from the middle of the fillet. It is tied in a scalded rasher of bacon before cooking. It is cut 4 cm (1½ in) thick, 7.5 cm (3 in) in diameter, and weighs 150 g (5 oz). Filet Mignon is cut from the thin end in a triangular shape, and weighs 100 g (¼ lb). This end of the fillet is also used for Strognoff where the steak is cut into strips 2.5 cm × 5 mm (1 × ¼ in), or raw for Steak Tartare.

The cooking times will vary with the method used and the type and thickness of steak, but in general 2 minutes cooking (1 minute each side) produces a rare steak, 4 minutes a medium steak, and 8-12 minutes a well-done one. Grilling (broiling) is suitable for the best types of steak, while cheaper cuts may be fried very quickly.

Apollo Steaks

30 ml (2 tablespoons) oil
4 sirloin or rump steaks

For the Sauce:
1 lamb's kidney, skinned, cored and sliced
25 g (1 oz) (2 tablespoons) butter or margarine
1 large onion, sliced
2 tomatoes, skinned, deseeded and chopped
1 green pepper, deseeded and chopped

Juicy Apollo Steaks are dressed with a richly flavoured sauce of kidneys, green pepper, tomato and onion

150 ml (¼ pint) (⅝ cup) red wine
150 ml (¼ pint) (⅝ cup) beef stock
salt and pepper
pinch oregano

1 Fry the sauce ingredients, except the wine, stock and seasonings, in a saucepan for 5 minutes until they are tender. Add the wine and stock, and season with salt, pepper and a pinch of oregano. Bring to the boil and simmer for 5 minutes to thicken.

2 Heat the oil in a frying pan (skillet) and fry the steaks for 2-8 minutes or according to taste. Pour the sauce over them and serve immediately. Serve with buttered new potatoes and a green or mixed salad.

Serves 4

Steak au Poivre Vert

4 sirloin steaks, 1 cm (½ in) thick
50 ml (2 fl oz) (¼ cup) oil
pinch salt
50 g (2 oz) (4 tablespoons) butter
45 ml (3 tablespoons) brandy
100 ml (4 fl oz) (½ cup) dry sherry
  or dry Madeira wine
1 medium onion, chopped
25 g (1 oz) (2 tablespoons) green
  peppercorns, canned
30 ml (2 tablespoons) soya sauce
5 ml (1 teaspoon) vinegar
150 ml (¼ pint) (⅝ cup) single
  (light) cream
pinch paprika
5 g (1 tablespoon) chopped fresh
  parsley

1 Trim the steaks of any excess fat and sinew. Brush with a little oil and season very lightly with salt.

2 Heat the rest of the oil and butter in a frying pan (skillet) and quickly fry the steaks on both sides to sear the flesh, for about 2 minutes. Pour in the brandy and set it alight. Almost immediately pour in the sherry or Madeira to put out the brandy flames. Remove the steaks and keep them warm while cooking the sauce.

3 To the mixture in the pan add the onion, peppercorns, soya sauce, and vinegar. Boil for 4 minutes. Add the cream and paprika and boil briskly for another minute.

4 Return the steaks to the sauce to reheat for a minute on each side. Serve immediately, garnished with the chopped parsley.

Serves 4

*Steak au Poivre Vert has
the real taste
of luxury, with brandy to flame,
wine, and mildly spicy
green peppercorns*

Tips: Green peppercorns are the fresh berries of the spice more commonly used in its dried form as black or white ground (powdered) pepper. They are usually only available in canned form, and have a mild and aromatic flavour.

The given cooking times for the sirloin steak are designed for a rare-cooked steak of 1 cm (½ in) thick. Thicker steaks should be fried for twice the given length of time, or beaten with a rolling pin or meat mallet to the given thickness. For a medium-cooked steak, fry for 4 minutes. For a well-cooked steak, cover the pan (skillet) while frying for 4 or 5 minutes.

Entrecôte Bordelaise

4 sirloin steaks, about 3 cm (1½ in)
  thick
30 ml (2 tablespoons) oil
salt and pepper
5 g (1 tablespoon) chopped fresh
  parsley

For the Bordelaise Sauce:
4 shallots or 1 onion, chopped
200 ml (6 fl oz) (¾ cup) good red
  wine
bouquet garni
45 ml (3 tablespoons) meat juice
200 ml (6 fl oz) (¾ cup) beef stock
15 g (½ oz) (1 tablespoon) tomato
  concentrate (paste)
15 g (½ oz) (1 tablespoon) beef fat
15 g (½ oz) (2 tablespoons) flour

1 Brush the steaks with the oil and grill (broil) them for 8-12 minutes according to taste, turning once. Reserve the meat juices and keep the steaks warm.

2 To make the sauce, boil the shallot or onion in the wine, with the bouquet garni, for 5 minutes. Stir in the meat juice, beef stock and tomato concentrate (paste).

3 Make a roux by melting the beef fat and cooking the flour in it for 2 minutes. Remove from the heat and gradually stir in the wine and stock mixture to form a smooth sauce. Simmer very gently for 20 minutes.

4 Season the steaks lightly with salt and generously with freshly ground (milled) black pepper. Pour the sauce over them and garnish with chopped parsley. Serve immediately.

Serves 4

Steak Manzanilla

2 rump steaks, about 225 g
  (½ lb) each
30 ml (2 tablespoons) oil
salt and pepper
2 slices Cheddar cheese,
  ½ cm (⅛ in) thick
pinch paprika
4 anchovy fillets
2 stuffed green olives, sliced

1 Brush the steaks with oil and season with a little salt and plenty of freshly ground (milled) black pepper. Grill (broil) the steaks under high heat for 3-4 minutes on each side according to taste.

2 Place a slice of cheese on each steak, sprinkle with paprika and grill (broil) until the cheese is melted and just starting to brown.

3 Place the steaks on a warmed serving dish. Decorate each steak with a cross of anchovy fillets, and slices of stuffed olive. Serve immediately.

Serves 2

Steak à l'Orange

4 sirloin steaks, 2 cm (¾ in) thick
24 black peppercorns, crushed
rind 1 orange, cut in matchstick
  strips
15 ml (1 tablespoon) oil
150 ml (¼ pint) (⅝ cup) dry sherry
4 fresh mint leaves

150 ml (¼ pint) (⅝ cup) single
  (light) cream

For the Marinade:
juice 2 oranges
2 cloves garlic, peeled and
  crushed
5 g (1 teaspoon) fresh root ginger,
  finely chopped
30 ml (2 tablespoons) soya sauce
50 ml (2 fl oz) (¼ cup) oil
30 ml (2 tablespoons) cider
  vinegar

1 Trim the steaks and rub the crushed black peppercorns into them.

2 Thoroughly blend the orange juice, garlic, ginger, soya sauce, oil, and vinegar to make a marinade. Soak the steaks in it for 20 minutes and then remove

Steak Manzanilla is an unusual idea featuring cheese and anchovies, which would also suit cheaper steak cuts

them, reserving the marinade.

3 Meanwhile boil the orange rind for 8 minutes. Drain and rinse the strips in cold water and add them to the leftover marinade.

4 Fry the steaks in the oil until done to taste. Remove and keep warm. Pour the marinade into the pan and boil for 4 minutes to reduce. Add the sherry and mint leaves and boil for 3 minutes; then stir in the cream and boil 3 more minutes. Pour the sauce over the steaks and serve at once.

Serves 4

Sirloin with Peppercorns and Garlic

four 350 g (¾ lb) sirloin steaks,
  2.5 cm (1 in) thick
12 black peppercorns
4 cloves garlic, thinly sliced
75 ml (2½ fl oz) (⅓ cup) oil
salt

1 Trim the fat from the steaks. Crush the peppercorns, using a rolling pin, and then sprinkle over both sides of the steaks, pressing well into the meat.

2 Make several slits in the surface of the steaks and insert the slices of garlic into the slits. Brush the steaks with oil and then cook them under a grill, over a charcoal fire, or in a frying pan (skillet). Cook for 2 minutes on both sides for underdone meat, 4 minutes for medium or 8 minutes for well-done.

3 Season with salt and serve with watercress, French fries and a pat of garlic butter.

Serves 4

Rump Steak Royal

1 kg (2 lb) rump steak in 1 piece
salt
5 g (1 teaspoon) crushed
  peppercorns
45 ml (3 tablespoons) oil
2 cloves garlic, peeled and
  chopped

Sirloin with Peppercorns and Garlic — try this deliciously different way of serving your steaks

50 g (2 oz) (4 tablespoons) peanut
  butter
150 ml (¼ pint) (⅝ cup) medium
  vermouth

1 Season the steak with salt and peppercorns.

2 Heat the oil in a frying pan (skillet) and shallow fry the steak. Cook for 6 minutes on either side for underdone meat, 12 minutes for medium, 14 minutes for well-done.

3 Remove the steak from the pan and keep warm on a dish.

4 Mix the garlic and peanut butter and put in the frying pan (skillet). Add the vermouth, stir and boil for 4 minutes. Pour over the steak.

5 Serve the whole steak and cut into 3 or 4 portions in front of the guests. Serve with a lettuce and orange salad.

Serves 3-4

Tournedos with Anchovy Butter

6 rashers (slices) streaky bacon
   (scalded)
6 tournedos steaks, 150 g (5 oz)
   each, 4 cm (1½ in) thick
salt and freshly ground (milled)
   pepper
oil for frying steaks
6 green olives
6 anchovy fillets
25 ml (2 tablespoons) tomato
   ketchup (catsup)

For the Anchovy Butter:
100 g (¼ lb) (½ cup) butter
5 g (1 tablespoon) chopped
   parsley
juice ½ lemon
4 anchovy fillets, finely chopped

For the Croutons:
6 slices bread
25 g (1 oz) (2 tablespoons) butter
25 ml (1 fl oz) (⅛ cup) oil

1 Prepare the anchovy butter by creaming the butter with the parsley, lemon juice and anchovy fillets to form a paste. Roll the paste into a cylinder, wrap in greaseproof (parchment) paper, and chill for 1 hour.

2 Make the croutons by cutting six bread circles using a plain cutter of 6.5 cm (2½ in). Put the butter and oil in a frying pan (skillet) and fry the bread on both sides until golden. Place the croutons on a dish and keep warm.

3 Tie a rasher of streaky bacon round each steak and season. Heat some oil in the frying pan (skillet) and fry the steaks for 4-10 minutes, depending on whether you want the steaks rare, medium or well-done. If

Tournedos with Anchovy Butter combines succulent steak with piquant anchovies, topped by green olives

preferred, brush the steaks with oil, and grill (broil). Remove the bacon. Place on the croutons.

4 When ready to serve, cut slices off the roll of anchovy butter and place one on each steak. Place a green olive on each, surrounded by an anchovy fillet, and trickle a little tomato ketchup (catsup) round as decoration. Serve at once with Pommes Allumettes (thin chips) as illustrated.

Serves 6

Steak Mignonette

4 slices of 150 g (5 oz) fillet steak,
   cut from the thin end
1 medium onion
25 g (1 oz) (2 tablespoons) butter

169

4 mushrooms
150 ml ($\frac{1}{4}$ pint) ($\frac{5}{8}$ cup) port
25 g (1 oz) (2 tablespoons) tomato
  concentrate (paste)
pinch thyme
pinch cinnamon
75 ml ($2\frac{1}{2}$ fl oz) ($\frac{1}{3}$ cup) whipping
  cream
salt and pepper
25 ml (1 fl oz) ($\frac{1}{8}$ cup) oil
8 stuffed olives, sliced

1 Flatten the steaks to 12.5 ×
5 cm (5 × $2\frac{1}{2}$ in).

2 Chop the onion and fry gently
in the butter for 4 minutes until
tender without colouring. Chop
the mushrooms and add, and
cook for 1 minute. Then add
the port, tomato concentrate
(paste), thyme and cinnamon.
Boil for 5 minutes. Stir in the
cream, season and put aside.
Keep warm.

3 Heat the oil in a frying pan
(skillet). Quickly cook the steaks
for 1 minute on each side.

4 Put in a dish, pour half of
the sauce over the steaks and
sprinkle with the sliced stuffed
olives. Serve the remainder of
the sauce separately. Serve garnished with braised chicory
(endive).

Serves 4

Brandy Steak with Mandarin Rice

175 g (6 oz) ($\frac{3}{4}$ cup) long grain rice
salt and pepper
25 g (1oz) (2 tablespoons) butter
300 g (11 oz) canned mandarin
  oranges
4 fillet steaks, 150 g (5 oz) each,
  4 cm ($1\frac{1}{2}$ in) thick
4 rashers (slices) streaky bacon
  (scalded)
25 g (1 oz) (2 tablespoons) butter
30 ml (2 tablespoons) oil
60 ml (4 tablespoons) brandy
100 ml (4 fl oz) ($\frac{1}{2}$ cup) single
  (light) cream

*Brandy Steak with Mandarin
Rice, tender tournedos are
flamed in brandy and flavoured
with mandarin oranges*

1 Wash the rice and cook in
salted boiling water for 20
minutes. Drain, and stir in the
butter. Season and keep warm.

2 Meanwhile, heat the mandarin
oranges in their syrup and drain.
Keep the juice. Add the oranges
to the rice. Keep warm.

3 Season the steaks, and tie a
rasher (slice) of bacon around
each. Heat the butter and oil in a
frying pan, and shallow fry the
steaks for 2-3 minutes on each

side, if you like them rare. Cook
for longer if you prefer. If you want
the steaks well done, put a lid on.

4 Pour the brandy into the frying
pan and flame the steaks.
Remove the steaks, discard the
bacon, and put them on a dish
and keep warm.

5 Pour the cream into the frying
pan, and mix with the meat
juices, and boil for 2 minutes to
make a smooth sauce. Remove
from the heat, add 15 ml (1 tablespoon) of the mandarin juice and
pour over the steaks. Serve at
once with the mandarin rice, and
a green salad.

Serves 4

Steak Tartare

Steak Tartare is the name given to a delicious, unusual and highly digestible dish of raw steak.
You should use fillet steak – preferably the thin, tail end – but you can use sirloin or rib, both of which are very tender. Make sure the meat is absolutely fresh: locally killed beef is best. Allow 150 g (5 oz) (good ½ cup) meat for a generous portion per person, and make sure it is passed through a mincer (grinder) twice.

600 g (1¼ lb) (2½ cups) minced (ground) fillet steak
salt and freshly ground (milled) black pepper
100 g (¼ lb) (½ cup) shallots, finely chopped
10 g (2 tablespoons) chopped parsley
8 anchovy fillets, chopped
15 g (1 tablespoon) capers
15 g (1 tablespoon) gherkins (dill pickles), chopped
15 g (1 tablespoon) pearl onions
150 ml (¼ pint) (⅝ cup) vinaigrette sauce
150 ml (¼ pint) (⅝ cup) mayonnaise
4 eggs

1 Season the minced (ground) steak with salt and freshly ground (milled) black pepper. Divide it into 4 portions and shape each into a ball. Place each in the centre of a dinner plate, flatten slightly and make a small cavity in the centre.

Steak Tartare is a classic dish in which diners garnish raw fillet steak according to their individual tastes

2 Either surround each portion with, or serve separately, the shallots, parsley, anchovy fillets, capers, gherkins (dill pickles) and pearl onions. Serve a bowl each of vinaigrette sauce and mayonnaise.

3 Carefully break each egg and separate the white from the yolk. Leave the yolk in half the shell and place in the centre of each steak.

4 Allow your guests to help themselves to the various garnishes and sauces.

Serves 4

Tip: Serve Tartare with a crisp salad. Try lettuce and chicory (Belgian endive), or potato or orange and watercress or Waldorf Salad, which combines celery, crisp eating apples and walnuts.

Roast Beef

There are two methods of roasting beef. The old-fashioned method roasts the meat at a high temperature. This sears the outside of the joint and keeps the meat juices inside. The moisture acts as a heat conductor and so the joint stays moist and juicy long after cooking. Lovers of underdone beef also claim that it has more flavour this way. An alternative is to start the cooking on a high temperature and sear the joint for 20 minutes, then lower the temperature for the remainder of the cooking time.

The second method which is commonly used in America roasts the meat at a low temperature. This way, the meat is cooked throughout and it is difficult to obtain an underdone, juicy, red joint. You will probably find it best to sear your joint first, then lower the temperature.

Basic rules for Roasting
There are some basic rules for roasting and, if you follow them, you should always have good results. They are:

1 Always season the joint lightly with salt and freshly ground (milled) pepper.

2 Always handle the meat very gently and never pierce it with a knife or skewer. It is important that the meat juices should stay intact.

3 Always smother your meat with plenty of fat – a mixture of butter and lard is best. Use 25 g (1 oz) fat for every 450 g (1 lb) meat. Baste the meat frequently with the fat during cooking.

4 If you can, stand the joint on a rack or grille or trivet above a roasting pan to catch the juices. An alternative is to place the joint on a bed of root vegetables (carrots, celery and onions) or meat bones. The vegetable and meat juices can be used as a base for the gravy.

5 Always use a meat thermometer if you like your meat well-done. It is essential to obtain good results. Insert it into the meat but take care that it does not touch the bone.

6 Always preheat the oven before roasting to 220°C, 425°F, gas 7. Cook the meat on the middle shelf and sear it at the high temperature. Then, if you like your beef underdone, continue cooking it at this temperature. If you prefer well-done beef, lower the temperature to 190°C, 375°F, gas 5.

Serving Roast Beef
The traditional way to serve roast beef is with roast potatoes, Yorkshire puddings and horseradish sauce and mustard. You can make a delicious gravy from the meat juices and vegetable water. Rest the joint for 15 minutes before carving – keep it warm in the bottom of the oven – and garnish with sprigs of watercress.

Suitable Cuts of Meat
Sirloin, wing rib or loin, forerib and middlerib are all suitable for roasting. If these are too expensive, try topside or round which are cheaper and slightly tougher cuts.

Roasting Times
Sirloin, rib and the better cuts of beef should be seared for 20 minutes in a hot oven. Then, if you like your meat underdone, roast it a further 10 minutes for every 450 g (1 lb). For well cooked meat, allow 15-20 minutes per 450 g (1 lb). Topside and the cheaper cuts need 20 minutes also.

Yorkshire Pudding

2 eggs
150 g (5 oz) (1¼ cups) plain flour, sifted
300 ml (½ pint) (1¼ cups) water, or milk and water mixed
pinch salt

1 Beat the eggs well together, then stir in the flour. Add the liquid and beat for 3 to 4 minutes to obtain a smooth batter. Season with the salt and leave the batter to rest for 1 hour.

2 If your oven is not already hot, preheat it to 190°C, 375°F, gas 5.

3 Place a teaspoonful of the meat fat and juices in the bottom of each patty tin (muffin pan) and heat in the oven for 5 minutes. Then half-fill them with batter and bake for 15-20 minutes until well-risen and golden.

Makes 6-8

Horseradish Sauce

75 g (3 oz) fresh horseradish root, peeled and washed
45 ml (3 tablespoons) wine vinegar
salt and pepper
pinch sugar
300 ml (½ pint) (1¼ cups) milk
75 g (3 oz) (1½ cups) fresh white breadcrumbs

1 Grate the horseradish and soak in the wine vinegar for 1 hour. Season with the salt and pepper and sugar.

2 Heat the milk in a saucepan and bring to the boil. Stir in the breadcrumbs and leave them to soak for 10 minutes. Blend in the horseradish mixture and serve the sauce with roast beef.

Makes about 300 ml (½ pint) (1¼ cups)

Tip: For a change, try making horseradish sauce in the Hungarian way. Just mix the horseradish and vinegar mixture into 300 ml (½ pint) (1¼ cups) white sauce.

Roast Rib of Beef, served with Yorkshire Pudding and Horseradish Sauce, is a meal fit for an English king

Meatballs with Courgettes (Zucchini)

50 g (2 oz) (⅓ cup) chick peas,
   cooked or canned and drained
450 g (1 lb) (2 cups) lean minced
   (ground) beef
1 clove garlic, peeled and
   crushed
50 g (2 oz) (1 cup) fresh
   breadcrumbs
50 g (2 oz) (⅓ cup) hazelnuts, finely
   chopped
1 egg, beaten
1 small green chilli pepper,
   finely chopped
5 g (1 tablespoon) chopped
   parsley
pinch cumin
salt and pepper
15 g (½ oz) (2 tablespoons) flour
60 ml (2 fl oz) (¼ cup) oil

For the Sauce:
30 ml (2 tablespoons) oil
1 onion, chopped
1 clove garlic, peeled and
   crushed

*Meatballs with Courgettes
(Zucchini) includes other unusual
vegetables — chick peas,
hot chilli pepper and hazelnuts*

4 courgettes (zucchini), sliced
4 tomatoes, skinned, deseeded
   and chopped
150 g (5 oz) (1¼ cups) peas, fresh or
   frozen
300 ml (½ pint) (1¼ cups) water
1 chicken stock cube
5 g (1 tablespoon) mixed mint
   and parsley, chopped

1 Preheat the oven to 200°C,
400°F, gas 6.

2 Mash the chick peas with a
fork. Place them in a mixing bowl,
and add the beef, garlic, breadcrumbs, hazelnuts, beaten egg
and chilli pepper. Blend together
well and add the parsley, cumin,
salt and pepper. Shape into 8
slightly flattened balls and dust
with the flour.

3 Heat the oil in a frying pan
(skillet) and fry the meatballs for
6-8 minutes. Drain and keep hot.

4 To make the sauce, pour away
the oil in which the meatballs
were cooked and wipe the pan
clean. Heat 30 ml (2 tablespoons)
oil and gently fry the onion for 4
minutes, until soft but not brown.
Add the garlic, courgettes (zucchini), tomatoes and peas. Pour
on the water and crumble in the
stock cube. Bring to the boil, add
the parsley and mint and season
to taste. Transfer to a casserole,
add the meatballs, and place in
the oven for 20 minutes.

Serves 4

Tips: Try using equal quantities
of minced (ground) pork and beef
for a good texture as well as a
delicious flavour.

For economy, replace 150 g
(5 oz) (good ½ cup) minced (ground)
meat with 65 g (2½ oz) texturized
vegetable protein.

Meatballs can be braised in the
oven or deep fried and any kind of
cereal binder can be used, such as
matzo meal, oats, cooked rice or
rusk.

174

Beef Italienne

675 g (1½ lb) piece fillet steak
4 strips bacon fat
75 ml (3 fl oz) (⅜ cup) oil
1 carrot, 1 onion and 2 celery
  sticks, sliced

For the Gravy:
150 ml (¼ pint) (⅝ cup) white wine
225 ml (8 fl oz) (1 cup) water
1 stock cube
bouquet garni
5 g (1 teaspoon) cornflour
  (cornstarch)

1 Prepare the fillet by removing the tough skin carefully with a knife to avoid damaging the meat. Lay the bacon fat along the fillet and secure with string, tied at intervals of 2.5 cm (1 in).

2 Preheat the oven to 200°C, 400°F, gas 6.

3 Heat the oil in a frying pan (skillet) and brown the meat all over for 8 minutes to seal.

4 Transfer the meat to a roasting pan and add the carrot, onion and celery.

5 Roast for 40 minutes. Remove from the oven, discard the bacon fat, string, and vegetables. Place on a serving dish and keep hot.

6 To the juices in the roasting pan, add the wine, 150 ml (¼ pint) (⅝ cup) water, stock cube, and bouquet garni and simmer for 15 minutes. Thicken with cornflour (cornstarch) mixed with the remaining water. Boil for 3 minutes, season and strain.

Serves 6

Beef Italienne could be the star turn at a special dinner — superb fillet beef, flamboyantly garnished

Tip: As the photograph shows, the Beef Italienne may be garnished in several ways.

With small strips of fresh noodle paste deep fried until crisp and golden and arranged in heaps around the dish.

With globe artichokes, boiled in water and lemon juice, after the outside leaves and hairy choke have been removed. The artichokes may be filled with a duxelles of ham, mushrooms, onion and breadcrumbs, sautéed for 5 minutes.

The dish may be decorated with a few button mushrooms, which have been scribed with the point of a knife blade, and then blanched in water with lemon juice or wine.

The garnishes should be prepared before the fillet is cooked.

Braised Beef

Braised meat is first seared in hot fat to seal in the juices, and then barely covered with a water-based liquid and cooked gently until tender. For additional flavour, the meat can be soaked in a marinade before it is cooked; the marinade liquid should always include vinegar, wine or fruit juice for the best flavour.

Beef Olives with Ham

4 thin slices braising steak, 150 g (5 oz) each, from leg or shoulder
4 thin slices cooked ham
1 small onion, chopped
1 clove garlic, chopped
few sage leaves, chopped
10 g (2 tablespoons) chopped parsley
salt and pepper
110 g (4¼ oz) (8½ tablespoons) butter

Beef Olives with Ham uses less expensive beef dressed up with a garnish of button mushrooms and onions

100 ml (4 fl oz) (½ cup) oil
1 onion, coarsely chopped
1 carrot, coarsely chopped
7 g (1 tablespoon) flour
150 ml (¼ pint) (⅝ cup) red wine
300 ml (½ pint) (1¼ cups) brown stock
10 g (1 tablespoon) capers
150 g (5 oz) (⅝ cup) long grain rice
225 g (½ lb) (2 cups) button (pearl) onions
225 g (½ lb) (4 cups) button mushrooms

1 Preheat the oven to 180°C, 350°F, gas 4.

2 Beat the steaks until very thin. Place a slice of ham on each steak. Mix together the chopped onion garlic, sage and half the parsley and divide the mixture between the steaks. Sprinkle with salt and pepper.

3 Roll up the steaks tightly and secure with string or wooden cocktail sticks (toothpicks).

4 Heat 35 g (1¼ oz) (2½ tablespoons) of the butter and half the oil together in a pan, add the meat and fry briskly for 5 minutes.

5 Transfer the meat to a casserole dish. Add the chopped vegetables to the pan, and fry gently, covered, for about 8 minutes or until soft. Sprinkle in the flour and cook for 1-2 minutes or until brown. Stir in the wine and stock and bring to the boil. Pour the contents of the pan over the meat, add the capers and season to taste. Cover the dish and cook in the oven for 1¼ hours.

6 Meanwhile, prepare the garnish. Boil the rice in salted water for 18 minutes, drain and blend in 50 g (2 oz) (4 tablespoons) of the butter and salt and pepper. Heat the rest of the oil and butter in a pan and sauté the onions for 3 minutes until brown. Add the mushrooms and cook for 1 minute more. Cover the vegetables with water and boil for 6 minutes. Drain.

7 When the meat is cooked, arrange the rice on a warmed serving dish, place the meat on top and garnish with the mushrooms and onions and the rest of the parsley.

Serves 4

Braised Beef Home-style

1 kg (2 lb) braising beef from leg,
  in 1 piece
1 onion, finely sliced
1 clove garlic, peeled and
  quartered
1 bouquet garni
50 ml (2 fl oz) ($\frac{1}{4}$ cup) brandy
300 ml ($\frac{1}{2}$ pint) (1$\frac{1}{4}$ cups) dry white
  wine
100 g ($\frac{1}{4}$ lb) ($\frac{1}{2}$ cup) butter
2 onions, chopped
200 ml (7 fl oz) ($\frac{7}{8}$ cup) stock
pinch mixed spice
salt and pepper
450 g (1 lb) carrots, sliced
450 g (1 lb) French beans

*Braised Beef Home-Style
provides a hearty mixture of
lean beef and vegetables
to satisfy a hungry family*

1 Place the meat in a bowl, and
add the sliced onion, garlic, bouquet garni, brandy and two-
thirds of the wine. Leave to marinate for 3 hours.

2 Drain the meat, reserving the
marinade, and dry. Melt half the
butter in a flameproof casserole,
add the meat and fry briskly until
browned all over. Add the
chopped onion and fry until
golden-brown. Strain the
reserved marinade and add it to
the pan with the stock, mixed
spice and salt and pepper to taste.

Cover and cook gently for 2 hours.

3 Melt the remaining butter in a
separate pan, add the carrots and
fry gently until browned. Add just
enough water to cover, then cook
gently until the carrots are
tender. Cook the beans in salted
water until tender, then drain.

4 When the meat is cooked, add
the vegetables to the casserole,
cover and cook for a further 15
minutes.

5 Drain the meat and carve into
neat slices. Arrange on a warmed
serving dish and surround with
the vegetables and gravy. Serve
hot with roast potatoes.

Serves 6

Beef Stews

Stews and casseroles provide the best methods of cooking tougher cuts of beef. They all involve slow cooking at a low heat with a measured volume of liquid: (that is, one cup meat to one cup liquid) although you can use a pressure cooker. You can use a covered pan on the stove and simmer at 85°C, 180°F, but for best results, cook in a casserole in an oven pre-heated to 180°C, 350°F, gas 4.

The cooking liquor should be slightly acid, to help tenderize the meat. Include a little wine, cider, beer, tomato concentrate (paste) or fruit juice. The meat can be marinated first, and the marinade included in the cooking liquor. For a better flavour, fry the meat quickly in fat to brown it and seal in the juices. Root vegetables and onions which are added for flavour should be lightly fried, too, before you add stock and any aromatic herbs you may wish to include. Flour for thickening can be added when the meat is browned, or as a roux stirred into the cooking liquor when the stew is nearly done. A stew cooked with pulses or beans makes a meal in itself.

Cuts suitable for stewing come from muscular areas, such as leg and shoulder. Buttock steak, silverside, flank, skirt, clod and chuck steak are all good and economical. Beef offal (variety meats) lend themselves to slow cooking. Oxtail provides a rich stew and ox kidney and liver, which tend to be strongly flavoured, are often cooked with stewing beef or bacon.

Stews have the great merit of being suitable for cooking in advance, for reheating or freezing. Many casseroles improve with reheating because their sauce continues its work of tenderizing even as it cools.

Beef from Burgundy

100 ml (4 fl oz) (½ cup) oil
1 kg (2 lb) silverside, cut into 2.5 cm (1 in) cubes
1 carrot, thinly sliced
1 large onion, thinly sliced
25 g (1 oz) (4 tablespoons) flour
500 ml (1 pint) (2½ cups) dry red wine
salt and pepper
2 cloves garlic, peeled and crushed
1 bouquet garni
100 g (¼ lb) (1 cup) small (pearl) onions, peeled
15 g (½ oz) (1 tablespoon) sugar
50 g (2 oz) (¼ cup) butter
100 g (¼ lb) streaky bacon rashers (slices), cut in strips
100 g (¼ lb) (1 cup) mushrooms, chopped

1 Heat three-quarters of the oil in a stewpan, put the pieces of beef into it and brown over a high heat. Remove the meat, then pour out any remaining oil and add the slices of carrot and onion. Let them brown lightly, then add the flour and cook it, stirring constantly with a wooden spoon.

2 Mix in all the wine. Bring it to the boil and allow at least a third of it to evaporate on a high heat. Return the meat to the pan and add enough cold water to cover it. Add salt, pepper, the garlic and the bouquet garni. Cover and cook gently for 2½ hours.

3 Put the small (pearl) onions in a pan with the sugar, the butter and enough water to cover. Cover and cook until the water has evaporated. When a golden caramel mixture remains, roll the small onions in it and put to one side.

4 Heat the rest of the oil in a pan and lightly fry the bacon. Drain and reserve. Fry the mushrooms in the same oil and reserve.

5 When the stew is cooked, sieve (strain) the sauce, then return it to the pan. Add the small (pearl) onions, bacon and mushrooms and cook for a further 10 minutes.

Serves 6

Czardaz Beef with Caraway Rice

30 ml (1 fl oz) (2 tablespoons) oil
1 kg (2 lb) stewing beef, cut into 2.5 cm (1 in) cubes
3 sticks celery, chopped
1 large onion, sliced
150 ml (¼ pint) (⅝ cup) water
½ beef stock cube
450 g (1 lb) (2⅔ cups) canned pineapple cubes, with juice
5 g (1 tablespoon) chopped parsley
good pinch sugar
15 g (½ oz) (1 tablespoon) tomato concentrate (paste)
few drops Worcestershire sauce
salt and pepper
350 g (¾ lb) (1½ cups) long grain rice
25 g (1 oz) (2 tablespoons) butter
10 g (2 teaspoons) caraway seeds

1 Preheat the oven to 180°C, 350°F, gas 4.

2 Heat the oil in a frying pan (skillet). Brown the meat in it, remove and place in a casserole. Add the celery and the onion to the oil and fry for 3 minutes, then add to the casserole.

3 Pour the water into a pan, bring to the boil and crumble in the stock cube. Drain the pineapple and add the juice to the stock with the parsley, sugar, tomato concentrate (paste), Worcestershire sauce and salt and pepper to taste. Pour over the meat in the casserole, cover, and Cook for 1½ hours, adding more stock if necessary.

4 15 minutes before the end of cooking, add the pineapple.

5 To cook the rice, first place it in a sieve (strainer) and wash it thoroughly under cold running water. Remove any discoloured grains. Place it in a large pan of boiling, slightly salted water. Boil for 12 minutes or until the rice is tender. Drain and return to the pan to dry. Gently stir in the butter and the caraway seeds.

Serves 6

Czardas Beef with Caraway Rice is a fruity casserole with a Russian flavour which will delight your family and friends

All about Pork

Sautéed Pork Cutlets

Pork has a distinctive flavour which is quite different from other meats. As well as giving us tasty joints and chops, the pig also provides us with bacon, gammon, ham and many types of sausage.

Choosing Pork

The lean meat should always be pale pink in colour, without gristle and firm to the touch. It should be marbled a little with milky-white fat, and the outer fat should be firm and white. If you are buying a joint with skin or rind, make sure that there are no hairs and that it is not too thick. If you like crackling on your roast, ask the butcher to score the rind for you.

Storing Pork

Pork is available all the year round, fresh or frozen. Of course, if you have a freezer you would be well advised to buy in bulk. Joints and chops will store in a freezer for about 4 months. Pork can be stored in a refrigerator for 2-3 days, or in a cool place for about 24 hours.

Cuts of Pork

Pork is available in a variety of cuts and should always be cooked thoroughly. It can be roast, grilled (broiled), fried, casseroled, cured, boiled and made into sausages. Here are the best known cuts:

Loin: This is usually considered to be the choicest cut, it is also the most expensive. It can be roasted whole on the bone or boned, rolled and stuffed. It is also cut up into loin and chump chops. When roasting loin, allow 225 g (½ lb) on the bone per person, and 100-175 g (4-6 oz) boned per person.

Fillet: This is another expensive cut which is lean and tender. It is usually roasted either on the bone or boned and stuffed. It comes from the top end of the hind leg and can also be cut into steaks.

Leg: This is a very large joint which is often cut in two and then roasted. It can be roasted on the bone or stuffed and rolled. Generally, it has more flavour when roasted on the bone.

Spare Ribs: These are usually associated in most people's minds with Chinese and Oriental cooking. However, they are growing ever more popular in the West.

They are usually roasted or marinated or grilled (broiled). They should not be confused with spare rib chops which come from the belly.

Chops: Chump and loin chops both come from the loin and are about 2.5 cm (1 in) thick. They are usually grilled (broiled), fried or baked. Sometimes they include the kidney as well.

Cutlets: These lean pieces of meat are taken from the spare rib and have very little bone. Like chops, they can be fried, grilled (broiled) or casseroled.

Blade: This is a cheaper joint which can be roasted or braised on or off the bone.

Belly: This is a very fatty cut which can be roasted as a joint or cut into slices. Because it is so fat, it is cheap and sold either fresh or salted.

Hand: This joint comes from the foreleg and is sold both fresh and salted. It is suitable for roasting, braising and stewing. If you are a crackling lover, this is the cut for you as it has a very large area of rind.

Sucking Pig: This is a young pig which is slaughtered between three weeks and two months. It can be spit-roasted.

Sauces and Flavourings

Pork is traditionally served with apple or gooseberry sauce. Spices such as cloves and paprika go well with pork in either a marinade or a tart apple sauce. Herbs such as thyme, sage, rosemary and garlic all enhance the flavour of pork. Pork is a favourite meat in oriental dishes and is often served with ginger, soya sauce or pineapple. You can make a delicious marinade for a joint or chops with these ingredients. Or why not try cooking your roast the Italian way? Just make some small cuts in the lean meat and insert some slivers of garlic. Sprinkle with oregano and roast as normal. The end result tastes and looks delicious. Or you can try making a sticky glaze for a roast joint with honey, orange or pineapple juice and spices such as powdered cloves, ginger or cinnamon.

Chops and Cutlets

Both loin and chump pork chops come from the loin. Pork chops can be grilled (broiled), fried or casseroled in many different ways. In this section, we give you recipes for all three. Pork chops are most economical when served in a sauce or casserole to make them go further.

Fruity Pork Chops

four 175 g (6 oz) pork chops
salt and pepper
50 ml (2 fl oz) (¼ cup) oil
pinch oregano
½ red pepper, cut in strips
100 g (¼ lb) (½ cup) long grain rice
225 g (½ lb) green grapes, halved

1 Sprinkle the pork chops with salt and freshly ground (milled) black pepper.

2 Heat the oil in a frying pan (skillet) and gently fry the chops until brown on both sides. Sprinkle in the oregano.

3 Add the strips of red pepper and fry until soft.

4 Meanwhile, cook the rice in boiling salted water until tender, but still firm.

5 Add the halved grapes to the pork and peppers and heat through.

6 Arrange the rice on a heated serving dish and pile the chops in the centre. Spoon the peppers and grapes over the top and serve.

Serves 4

Fruity Pork Chops are served on a bed of plain rice with sautéed strips of red pepper and juicy green grapes

Joints of Pork

The following recipes show just how many ways there are of serving roast pork apart from with the traditional apple sauce and crackling.

Pork with Pineapple

75 g (3 oz) (6 tablespoons) butter
70 ml (2½ fl oz) (⅓ cup) oil
1 kg (2 lb) best end of pork
salt and pepper
150 ml (¼ pint) (⅝ cup) water

1 small pineapple, cut into
  chunks, or 225 g (½ lb) canned
  pineapple pieces, drained

For the Gravy:
15 ml (1 tablespoon) flour
70 ml (2½ fl oz) (⅓ cup) water
30 ml (1 fl oz) (2 tablespoons)
  Worcestershire sauce
70 ml (2½ fl oz) (⅓ cup) pineapple
  juice
15 ml (1 tablespoon) cornflour
  (cornstarch)

1 Preheat the oven to 190°C, 375°F, gas 5. Melt the butter in a saucepan and combine it with the oil.

2 Remove the back spine bone from the joint and all the rind from the pork itself. Season the meat with salt and pepper and brush all over with half the butter

Pork with Pineapple – crisp, roast best end of pork with fresh or canned pineapple chunks in a delicious, golden gravy

and oil mixture. Place the pork on a rack in a roasting pan and roast in the oven for 1½ hours or until the meat is well cooked. Baste from time to time with the water, to ensure the meat does not dry out.

3 Meanwhile heat the remaining butter and oil in a pan and fry the pineapple pieces for 3 minutes on both sides or until it is golden. Remove from the pan and keep warm.

4 When the meat is cooked, prepare the gravy. Remove most of the fat from the meat juice. Add the flour and stir over a low heat for 3-4 minutes until browned. Add the water, Worcestershire sauce, and the pineapple juice. Bring to the boil and simmer for 5 minutes, stirring all the time. Thicken with the cornflour (cornstarch) mixed with a little water. Check the seasoning.

5 Place the meat on a heated serving tray, surround it with the pineapple pieces and, just before serving, pour over the gravy.

Serves 8

Braised Leg of Pork

1½ kg (3 lb) joint of pork, from the
  thick part (cushion) of the leg
300 ml (½ pint) (1¼ cups) dry white
  wine
70 ml (2½ fl oz) (⅓ cup) brandy
2 shallots, sliced
1 clove garlic, crushed
2 carrots, sliced
1 bay leaf
sprig thyme
sprig parsley
salt and pepper
25 g (1 oz) (2 tablespoons) fat
25 g (1oz) (½ cup) brown
  breadcrumbs
50 ml (2 fl oz) (¼ cup) water
5 ml (1 teaspoon) cornflour
  (cornstarch)

1 Preheat the oven to 230°C, 450°F, gas 8. Trim the pork all round. Remove all the rind and some of the fat.

2 Place it in a large bowl and cover it with the wine, brandy, shallots, garlic, carrots, bay leaf, thyme and parsley. Cover and allow the meat to marinate for 6 hours, turning it from time to time.

3 Wipe it, season it to taste with salt and pepper and place it in a roasting pan. Add the fat and sear the meat in the oven for 30 minutes. Strain off any excess fat.

4 Reduce the heat to 180°C, 350°F, gas 4. Add the vegetables and herbs and baste the meat with the marinating liquor from time to time, until it is cooked. The cooking time will depend on the weight of the leg. Allow at least 30 minutes per 450 g (1 lb). When cooked, sprinkle the meat with the brown breadcrumbs.

5 Strain the juices into a saucepan. Season, add the water and boil it for 5 minutes. If necessary, thicken with the cornflour (cornstarch) mixed with a little water.

Serve the sauce in a gravyboat with the meat.

Serves 8-10

Pork with Rosemary

1 kg (2 lb) lean boned shoulder or
  loin of pork
salt and pepper
150 g (5 oz) ($\frac{5}{8}$ cup) butter
1 carrot, sliced
1 large onion, chopped
1 stick celery, diced
350 g ($\frac{3}{4}$ lb) mushrooms
300 ml ($\frac{1}{2}$ pint) ($1\frac{1}{4}$ cups) water
150 ml ($\frac{1}{4}$ pint) ($\frac{5}{8}$ cup) dry white
  wine
2 sprigs rosemary
1 clove garlic, crushed

1 Preheat the oven to 190°C, 375°F, gas 5. Season the meat.

Pork with Rosemary – an unusual way of serving a joint by pot-roasting in white wine with mushrooms and celery

2 Melt half of the butter in a flameproof casserole. Add the meat and brown it on all sides. Remove the casserole from the heat.

3 In a separate pan heat the remaining butter. Add the carrot and sauté for 5 minutes. Add the onion and celery and sauté for a further 5 minutes. Finally add the mushrooms, cover and cook on a low heat for 2 minutes.

4 Pour the contents of the pan into the casserole. Add the water, wine, one rosemary sprig and the garlic. Check the seasoning. Cover and cook in the oven for $1\frac{1}{2}$ hours or until the meat is well cooked.

5 Serve garnished with the second sprig of rosemary.

Serves 6

Oriental Pork

Sweet'n Sour Pork

450 g (1 lb) pork tenderloin,
  cubed
30 ml (1 fl oz) (2 tablespoons)
  sherry
15 ml (1 tablespoon) soya sauce
1.25 ml (¼ teaspoon) sugar
5 mm (¼ in) piece fresh root
  ginger, grated
salt and pepper
4 celery sticks, sliced
1 red pepper, deseeded and diced
8 spring onions (scallions), cut
  into 5 cm (2 in) pieces
¼ English cucumber, cut into
  wedges
45 ml (2 fl oz) (3 tablespoons) oil
225 g (½ lb) canned pineapple
  chunks with juice

50 g (2 oz) (6 tablespoons)
  cornflour (cornstarch)
50 ml (2 fl oz) (¼ cup) vinegar
100 ml (4 fl oz) (½ cup) sweet white
  wine
15 ml (1 tablespoon) brown sugar
oil for deep frying

1 Mix the pork with the sherry, soya sauce, sugar and ginger. Add pepper to taste and mix well. Marinate for 30 minutes.

2 Fry the vegetables in the oil until soft but not brown. Drain the pineapple reserving the juice and add the chunks to the pan. Stir-fry for 2 minutes.

3 Mix 30 ml (2 tablespoons) of the cornflour (cornstarch) with the vinegar, and stir in to the pan with pineapple juice, wine and sugar. Season and simmer for 2 minutes, stirring.

4 Heat the oil for deep frying. Remove the pork from the marinade and add the marinade to the sauce.

5 Coat the pork in the remaining

Pork and Bamboo Shoots. Sliced pork tenderloin stir-fried with onion and garlic in a pineapple and ginger sauce

cornflour (cornstarch) and fry it in the hot oil. Drain well.

6 Serve the pork on a bed of fried noodles with the sauce poured over.

Serves 4

Pork and Bamboo Shoots

45 ml (2 fl oz) (3 tablespoons) oil
1 onion, chopped
1 clove garlic, crushed
450 g (1 lb) pork tenderloin,
  thinly sliced
225 g (½ lb) bamboo shoots, thinly
  sliced
5 ml (1 teaspoon) cornflour
  (cornstarch)
2.5 ml (½ teaspoon) powdered
  ginger
5 ml (1 teaspoon) soya sauce
2.5 ml (½ teaspoon) anchovy
  essence
150 ml (¼ pint) (⅝ cup) pineapple
  juice
pepper

1 Heat the oil in a frying pan (skillet) and fry the onion and garlic until soft but not brown. Add the pork and stir-fry until browned.

2 Add the bamboo shoots to the pan, cover and cook gently for 10 minutes.

3 Mix the cornflour (cornstarch), ginger, soya sauce and anchovy essence with enough pineapple juice to make a smooth paste. Add to the pan with the remaining juice and simmer gently, uncovered, for 15 minutes.

4 Season with pepper and serve with boiled rice and Kumquat pickle.

Serves 4

Sweet 'n Sour Pork — traditional Chinese Food, which is becoming increasingly popular in countries all over the world. Serve it on a bed of fried noodles, with fried rice, boiled noodles and chopped mangoes

Barbecued Pork Cutlets

50 ml (2 fl oz) ($\frac{1}{4}$ cup) oil
6 pork cutlets
50 g (2 oz) (4 tablespoons) butter
1 small onion, chopped
100 ml (4 fl oz) ($\frac{1}{2}$ cup) water
25 g (1 oz) (2 tablespoons) brown
  sugar
2.5 ml ($\frac{1}{2}$ teaspoon) made
  mustard
salt and pepper
15 ml (1 tablespoon) vinegar
15 g ($\frac{1}{2}$ oz) (1 tablespoon) tomato
  concentrate (paste)
2 tomatoes, skinned, deseeded
  and chopped
5 ml (1 teaspoon) Worcestershire
  sauce
70 ml (2$\frac{1}{2}$ fl oz) ($\frac{1}{3}$ cup) tomato
  ketchup (catsup)
pinch paprika

1 Heat the oil and fry the pork cutlets until well browned on both sides.

2 Meanwhile, make the barbecue sauce. Melt the butter in a saucepan and fry the onion until soft. Add the water and stir in the brown sugar, mustard, seasoning and vinegar. Bring to the boil, then simmer for 5 minutes.

3 Add all the remaining ingredients, stir well and simmer for 15 minutes.

4 Serve the pork cutlets with the barbecue sauce on a bed of plain boiled rice.

Serves 6

Tips: You can make the sauce more interesting by adding sliced mushrooms or peppers. If you like red-hot food, why not add a few drops of chilli sauce? Or you can make a more fruity version with cooked plums, pineapple or fresh chopped peaches and apricots.

You can remove the meat from the chops, of course, and use it skewered as kebabs. Or why not try marinating the chops in soya sauce, pineapple juice, oil and garlic for a more oriental flavour?

Pork in Cider brings the flavour of the countryside to your dinner table with its fresh vegetables and fruity taste

Pork in Cider

100 ml (4 fl oz) ($\frac{1}{2}$ cup) oil
2 carrots, diced
2 onions, diced
1 clove garlic, crushed
2 shallots, chopped
1 stick celery, thinly sliced
50 g (2 oz) ($\frac{1}{2}$ cup) flour
3 tomatoes, skinned, deseeded
  and chopped
300 ml ($\frac{1}{2}$ pint) (1$\frac{1}{4}$ cups) dry cider
bouquet garni
225 g ($\frac{1}{2}$ lb) (1 cup) canned,
  creamed corn kernels
salt and pepper
six 225 g ($\frac{1}{2}$ lb) pork cutlets
15 ml (1 tablespoon) chopped
  parsley

1 Heat half of the oil in a saucepan and gently fry the carrots, onions, garlic, shallots and celery until tender.

2 Sprinkle in half of the flour, stir and cook for 1 minute. Add the tomatoes and cider and bring to the boil. Add the bouquet garni and corn kernels and season with

salt and pepper. Simmer for 15-20 minutes.

3 Coat the cutlets in the remaining seasoned flour and heat the rest of the oil in a pan. Shallow fry the cutlets for about 10 minutes until browned on both sides.

4 Preheat the oven to 180°C, 350°F, gas 4.

5 Remove the cutlets from the pan and arrange in an ovenproof dish. Cover with the sauce and check the seasoning. Bake in the covered ovenproof dish for 20 minutes.

6 Sprinkle with parsley and serve with boiled new potatoes.

Serves 6

Tip: If you have no cider, you can always use apple juice or white wine or a mixture of both. Fresh sliced applies will increase the fruity flavour. Fresh corn on the cob or canned corn kernels will give the casserole a more crunchy texture.

Pork with Rice and Peppers is an easy and tasty dish to prepare which is ideal for quick, filling family meals

Pork with Rice and Peppers

6 pork cutlets
50 g (2 oz) ($\frac{1}{2}$ cup) seasoned flour
50 ml (2 fl oz) ($\frac{1}{4}$ cup) oil
1 onion, chopped
1 green pepper, deseeded and cut in strips
1 red pepper, deseeded and cut in strips
1 clove garlic, crushed
100 ml (4 fl oz) ($\frac{1}{2}$ cup) water
salt and pepper
175 g (6 oz) ($\frac{3}{4}$ cup) long grain rice
50 g (2 oz) (4 tablespoons) butter

1 Coat the pork cutlets in the seasoned flour. Heat the oil in a frying pan (skillet) and cook the cutlets for about 10 minutes until browned on both sides.

2 Remove the cutlets and keep warm. Sauté the onion, green and red peppers and garlic until soft. Then return the cutlets to the pan and add the water and seasoning. Bring to the boil, then simmer, covered with a lid, for 20 minutes.

3 Meanwhile, cook the rice in boiling salted water until tender. Drain and place in a buttered mould. Press it down firmly and trim out on to a serving dish.

4 Surround the moulded rice with the cutlets, peppers and onions and serve immediately.

Serves 6

Tips: You can use either pork chops or cutlets for this dish. It tastes especially delicious if served in a tomato sauce. Just add some skinned, deseeded and chopped tomatoes, tomato concentrate (paste), sliced mushrooms and a pinch of basil. For a special occasion, try substituting white wine or dry sherry for the water.

188

Pork Chops with Cider Cream Sauce

4 pork chops
15 g (½ oz) (2 tablespoons) flour
salt and pepper
50 g (2 oz) (4 tablespoons) butter
1 large onion, chopped
175 g (6 oz) (1½ cups) sliced
  mushrooms
300 ml (½ pint) (1¼ cups) dry cider
50 ml (2 fl oz) (¼ cup) double
  (heavy) cream
15 ml (1 tablespoon) chopped
  parsley

1 Coat the pork chops in half the flour seasoned with salt and pepper. Melt the butter in a large frying pan (skillet) and fry the pork chops slowly until cooked through. Remove the chops from the pan and keep them warm.

2 Add the onion to the meat cooking juices and fry gently for 3 minutes.

3 Stir in the mushrooms and cook for another 3 minutes.

4 Stir in the rest of the flour and cook for 1 minute. Take the pan off the heat and stir in the cider to make a smooth sauce. Return the pan to the heat and stir for 1 minute.

5 Over a low heat, stir in the cream and season with salt and pepper. Heat to just below boiling point. Pour the sauce over the pork chops, garnish with the chopped parsley, and serve at once.

Serves 4

Pork Chops a l'Orange

4 thick pork chops
1 onion, finely chopped
50 g (2 oz) (4 tablespoons) butter
60 ml (2¼ fl oz) (4 tablespoons) oil
50 g (2 oz) (1 cup) fresh
  breadcrumbs
salt and pepper

Pork Chops with Cider Cream Sauce – an impressive combination, enriched with thick cream and sliced mushrooms

good pinch dried sage
grated rind and juice 1 orange
30 ml (2 tablespoons) flour
300 ml (½ pint) (1¼ cups) chicken
  stock

1 Cut a pocket in each pork chop by making a slit in the same direction as the bone, cutting from the fat side through to the bone.

2 Gently fry the chopped onion in half of the butter and oil for 5 minutes until softened but not browned.

3 Stir in the breadcrumbs, salt and pepper to taste, sage, and the grated orange rind, so that the mixture absorbs the cooking fats and forms a thick paste. If necessary, remove from the heat and use the milk to bind the mixture.

4 Preheat the oven to 170°C, 325°F, gas 3. Stuff ¼ of the breadcrumb mixture into each chop, securing if necessary with a cocktail stick. Arrange the chops in an ovenproof dish and keep warm.

5 Heat the rest of the butter and oil in the pan, scraping up any residue. Fry the flour for 3 minutes. Remove from the heat and stir in the stock and orange juice and bring to the boil, stirring all the time.

6 Pour the sauce over the chops, cover, and cook in the oven for 15 minutes. Serve with buttered green beans.

Serves 4

Stuffed Pork with Aubergines (Eggplants)

1.2 kg (2½ lb) boneless loin of
  pork, rind and some fat
  removed
salt and pepper
450 g (1 lb) onions, chopped
1 clove garlic, crushed
30 ml (1 fl oz) (2 tablespoons) oil
8 tomatoes, skinned, deseeded
  and chopped
5 ml (1 teaspoon) chilli powder
50 g (2 oz) (⅓ cup) seedless raisins
175 g (6 oz) cooked rice
1 egg, beaten
150 ml (¼ pint) (⅝ cup) dry white
  wine
150 ml (¼ pint) (⅝ cup) stock
2 aubergines (eggplants), peeled
  and sliced
25 g (1 oz) (¼ cup) flour
oil for deep frying

1 Preheat the oven to 190°C,
375°F, gas 5. Cut the pork almost in
half lengthways and season.

2 Fry the onions and garlic in the
oil until soft. Add the tomatoes
and chilli powder and simmer for
5 minutes. Add the raisins.

3 Blend half the tomato mixture
with the rice and egg and place
the stuffing on the pork. Fold over
the meat and tie at intervals.
Place in a roasting pan and cook
in the oven for 1 hour.

4 Pour out the fat which has col-
lected in the roasting pan. Mix the
remaining tomato mixture with
the wine and stock and add to
the pan. Return to the oven for
30 minutes or until the meat is
cooked. Baste occasionally,
adding more wine to the sauce if
it becomes too thick.

5 Meanwhile, soak the aubergines (eggplants) in salted water
for 15 minutes, then drain and dry.
Coat in the flour and deep fry until
golden. Keep warm.

6 Remove the string from the
joint and place the meat in a serving dish. Pour the sauce round it
and add the aubergine (eggplant)
slices.

Serves 6-8

*Stuffed Pork with Aubergines
(Eggplants). A tomato
and chilli mixture is used in both
the sauce and the filling*

Pork with Prune and Almond Stuffing

1 kg (2 lb) boned fillet of pork,
  rind and some fat removed
salt and pepper
100 g (¼ lb) (½ cup) long grain rice

For the Stuffing:
100 g (¼ lb) (¾ cup) stoned (pitted)
  prunes, cooked
50 g (2 oz) (½ cup) flaked almonds
100 g (¼ lb) (2 cups) fresh
  breadcrumbs
1 egg
pinch mixed spice

For the Gravy:
300 ml (½ pint) (1¼ cups) stock
½ beef stock cube
5 ml (1 teaspoon) cornflour
  (cornstarch)
100 ml (4 fl oz) (½ cup) port or dry
  sherry (optional)

1 Preheat the oven to 190°C,
375°F, gas 5.

2 Spread the meat flat and season the inside. Combine the
ingredients for the stuffing and
place along the centre of the
meat. Roll up and secure with
string. Season the outside of the
meat and roast in the preheated
oven for 1¼ hours, basting from
time to time with a little water.

3 Meanwhile, cook the rice in
boiling salted water until tender.
Drain and keep warm.

4 Place the stock in a pan,
crumble in the stock cube and
bring to the boil. Add the cornflour (cornstarch), mixed with a
little water, and cook for a few
minutes more. Season the gravy
and add the port or sherry, if used.

5 Place the rice on a serving dish
and lay the roast pork on the top.
Serve with the gravy and apple
sauce.

Serves 6

Tip: You can substitute other
nuts such as chopped walnuts for
the almonds in the stuffing.

Pork with Prune and Almond ▶
*Stuffing, on a bed of
rice, is served with a deliciously
rich wine-flavoured gravy*

Crown Roast of Pork

2 loins of pork, each containing
   8 chops, chined
50 g (2 oz) (4 tablespoons) melted
   butter
1 onion, finely chopped
2 sticks celery, finely chopped
225 g (½ lb) (1 cup) pork
   sausagemeat
100 g (¼ lb) (2 cups) fresh
   breadcrumbs
5 ml (1 teaspoon) rosemary
30 ml (2 tablespoons) finely
   chopped parsley
2.5 ml (½ teaspoon) thyme
salt and pepper
50 ml (2 fl oz) (¼ cup) chicken
   stock

1 Remove the chine bone from the loins. Cut 4 cm (1½ in) of the fat away from the ends of the bones. Trim away the sinew from between the bones.

2 Bend the 2 loins round to form the crown and secure with string. Place the crown in a roasting pan and brush all over the outside with the melted butter. Wrap pieces of aluminium foil round the ends of the bones to prevent them burning.

3 Preheat the oven to 180°C, 350°F, gas 4. Prepare the stuffing: heat the remaining butter in a frying pan (skillet) add the onion and celery and fry until they are soft.

4 Add the sausagement and cook until all the fat has run out of the meat. Drain the excess fat from the pan.

5 Stir in the breadcrumbs, rosemary, parsley, thyme, seasoning and stock and mix.

6 Place the stuffing in the centre of the crown and cover the stuffing with a circle of foil.

7 Roast the crown in the oven, allowing 30 minutes per 450 g (1 lb).

8 Before serving, remove the pieces of foil and place a cutlet frill on the end of each bone. Serve the crown roast garnished with peas and roast potatoes.

Serves 8

Loin of Pork
Spanish-style

450 g (1 lb) haricot beans, soaked
   overnight
2 cloves garlic, crushed
1 bay leaf
50 ml (2 fl oz) (¼ cup) olive oil
2 onions, sliced
1 kg (2 lb) boned loin of pork,
   cubed
225 g (½ lb) chorizo (spicy Spanish
   sausage), cut in 2 cm (¾ in) slices
225 g (½ lb) smoked streaky
   bacon, cut in small strips
3 tomatoes, skinned, deseeded
   and chopped
15 ml (1 tablespoon) paprika
pinch saffron
1 litre (1¾ pints) (4½ cups) boiling
   water
salt and pepper
350 g (¾ lb) runner beans,
   trimmed and cut in 3 cm (1¼ in)
   lengths
small round cabbage, quartered
6 eggs

1 Drain the haricot beans, rinse and place in a pan. Cover with fresh cold water and add 1 clove of garlic and the bay leaf. Bring to the boil, reduce the heat and simmer for 1 hour.

2 Heat the oil in a pan and add the onion, pork, chorizo, bacon, the remaining garlic and the tomatoes. Add the paprika and saffron and cook gently for 7 or 8 minutes, stirring constantly.

3 Pour in the boiling water, season with salt and pepper and cook over a low heat for 45 minutes.

4 When the haricot beans have cooked for 1 hour, drain and add them to the pork and simmer for a further 30 minutes.

5 Add the runner beans and cabbage and cook for 20 minutes.

6 Meanwhile, cook the eggs in boiling water for 10 minutes, cover with cold water and then remove the shells.

7 Transfer the pork mixture to a heated serving dish and garnish with the hard-boiled eggs. Serve very hot.

Serves 6

Pork Orloff

50 g (2 oz) (4 tablespoons)
   margarine
few bacon rinds
1½ kg (3 lb) loin of pork in 1 piece
1 onion
1 carrot, sliced
1 bay leaf
bouquet garni
salt and pepper
45 ml (3 tablespoons) grated
   Parmesan cheese
25 g (1 oz) (2 tablespoons) butter,
   cut in pieces

For the Purée:
50 g (2 oz) (4 tablespoons)
   margarine
15 ml (1 tablespoon) oil
4 onions, chopped
450 g (1 lb) mushroom caps, diced
150 ml (¼ pint) (⅝ cup) thick white
   sauce
150 ml (¼ pint) (⅝ cup) double
   (heavy) cream
pinch grated nutmeg
45 ml (3 tablespoons) grated
   Parmesan cheese

1 Heat the margarine in a pan, add the bacon rinds and pork and cook until browned. Add the onion, sliced carrot, bay leaf, bouquet garni and seasoning and then cover with water. Cover the pan and cook slowly for 1¼ hours.

2 Meanwhile, make the purée. Heat the margarine and oil in a pan and gently fry the chopped onion for 10 minutes, without browning. Add the diced mushrooms and cook for 1 minute.

3 Strain off the fat and add the white sauce and cream. Mix well and season with salt, pepper and nutmeg. Stir in the cheese and cook for 3 minutes. Cool.

4 Preheat the oven to 230°C, 450°F, gas 8. Lift the pork from the pan and carve it into thick slices. Spread each slice with purée and replace the slices to resemble the original joint.

5 Cover with the remaining purée and sprinkle with the grated Parmesan cheese and the pieces of butter. Return to the oven for 5-10 minutes to brown.

Serves 6-8

Pickled Pork with Saffron Rice

1½ kg (3 lb) pork loin, boned
15 ml (1 tablespoon) saltpetre
450 g (1 lb) sea salt
5 ml (1 teaspoon) powdered
  ginger
salt and pepper
4 cloves
450 g (1 lb) (2 cups) long grain rice
1.25 ml (¼ teaspoon) powdered
  saffron
50 g (2 oz) (4 tablespoons) butter

1 Buy the pork loin the day before the dish is to be served. Rub saltpetre over it. Put a layer of sea salt in an earthenware bowl. Lay in the meat and cover it with the rest of the salt. Leave it for 24 hours in a cool place.

2 Remove the pork from the salt, wash it thoroughly in cold water and dry it.

3 Preheat the oven to 190°C, 375°F, gas 5. Spread out a cloth and put the meat onto it, fat side down. Sprinkle with the ginger and pepper to taste. Roll it up, seasoned side inside, tying it tightly with string.

4 Using the point of a very sharp knife, cut the fat in criss-cross lines forming a diamond pattern. Stud the meat with the 4 cloves and season with pepper.

5 Pour 100 ml (4 fl oz) (½ cup) of warm water into a roasting pan containing a rack. Place the meat on the rack and roast in the oven for about 1¼ hours or until cooked through.

6 Put the rice into a pan with 1.2 litres (2 pints) (5 cups) cold water, the saffron and salt to taste. Cover and cook for 20 minutes, until the rice is tender and the water absorbed. Add the butter, season with pepper and fluff up with a fork.

7 Arrange the sliced pork on the rice to serve.

Serves 8

Tip: You can use ordinary table or cooking salt for curing the pork instead of sea salt.

Boned Blade of Pork with Apricot and Walnut Stuffing

2 kg (4 lb) blade or shoulder of
  pork, boned
1 onion, finely chopped
15 g (½ oz) (1 tablespoon) butter
50 g (2 oz) (⅓ cup) dried apricots,
  soaked in water overnight and
  finely chopped
12 walnut halves, finely chopped
50 g (2 oz) (1 cup) fresh white
  breadcrumbs
15 ml (1 tablespoon) chopped
  parsley
salt and pepper
1 egg
15 ml (1 tablespoon) oil
5 ml (1 teaspoon) salt

1 Preheat the oven to 230°C, 450°F, gas 8. Score the rind of the pork with a very sharp knife.

2 Fry the onion gently in the butter until lightly golden.

3 Mix together the apricots, walnuts, onion, breadcrumbs, parsley and salt and pepper to taste. Mix in the egg.

4 Place the stuffing on the inner side of the meat. Roll up the meat and tie tightly with string. Place in a greased roasting pan, brush with the oil and rub the salt into the skin.

5 Roast for 30 minutes or until the surface has crackled. Turn the oven to 190°C, 375°F, gas 5, and roast for a further hour.

Serves 6

Flemish Pork with Red Cabbage

1 kg (2¼ lbs) best end rib of pork,
  or loin
salt and pepper
good pinch mixed spice
60 ml (2¼ fl oz) (4 tablespoons) oil
1 small red cabbage, shredded
1 onion, chopped
1 clove garlic, finely chopped

100 ml (4 fl oz) (½ cup) vinegar
2 apples, peeled, cored and
  thinly sliced
15 ml (1 tablespoon) sugar
5 ml (1 teaspoon) chopped
  parsley
½ beef stock cube dissolved in
  300 ml (½ pint) (1¼ cups) water
15 ml (1 tablespoon) tomato
  concentrate (paste)
10 ml (2 teaspoons) cornflour
  (cornstarch), mixed with water

1 Preheat the oven to 190°C, 375°F, gas 5. Remove the rind from the pork and season with salt, pepper and mixed spice. Brush with oil and place on a rack in a roasting pan. Roast in the preheated oven for 1¼ hours, basting frequently with 225 ml (8 fl oz) (1 cup) water.

2 Place the cabbage in an earthenware bowl with the onion, garlic, vinegar and 550 ml (1 pint) (2½ cups) water. Leave to stand for 15 minutes.

3 Add the apples to the cabbage with the sugar and seasoning. Transfer to a stainless steel pan, bring to the boil and simmer for 20 minutes.

4 Transfer the pork to a serving dish. Surround with the cabbage in its liquid and sprinkle with parsley.

5 Pour off the fat from the roasting pan, retaining the meat juices. Add the stock and tomato concentrate (paste), bring to the boil and simmer for 5 minutes. Add the cornflour (cornstarch) to the pan and simmer for 1 minute, stirring. Season and strain into a sauce boat or jug to serve.

Serves 6

Tips: To save time, instead of pickling a best end or loin of pork, you can buy a gammon or back bacon joint. If you are not a lover of red cabbage, don't ignore this recipe. You can substitute white Savoy cabbage and omit the vinegar. However, if you do use red cabbage and want to make this dish extra special, use red wine instead of water.

Pork Piedmontese

50 ml (2 fl oz) (¼ cup) oil
675 g (1½ lb) lean pork, cut into cubes
15 g (½ oz) (2 tablespoons) flour
15 g (½ oz) (1 tablespoon) tomato concentrate (paste)
300 ml (½ pint) (1¼ cups) water
150 ml (¼ pint) (⅝ cup) dry white wine
85 ml (3 fl oz) (⅜ cup) single (light) cream
juice 1 lemon
pinch oregano
salt and pepper
3 medium courgettes (zucchini)

For the Stuffing:
100 g (¼ lb) calves liver
salt and pepper
15 g (½ oz) (2 tablespoons) flour
30 ml (1 fl oz) (2 tablespoons) oil
1 onion, chopped
50 g (2 oz) bacon, finely sliced
50 g (2 oz) mushrooms, finely sliced

Pork Portuguese, served with rice pilaff, is a tasty way of serving pork in white wine with tomatoes, celery and peppers

15 ml (1 tablespoon) Parmesan cheese
50 ml (2 fl oz) (¼ cup) dry white wine
85 ml (3 fl oz) (⅜ cup) double (heavy) cream

1 Preheat the oven to 180°C, 350°F, gas 4. Heat the oil in a pan. Add the meat and brown for 12 minutes. Sprinkle in the flour and stir. Cook for one minute, then add the tomato concentrate (paste), water and wine. Bring to the boil and simmer for 15 minutes. Stir in the cream, lemon juice and oregano. Season and transfer to a casserole. Bake in the preheated oven for one hour or until the meat is tender.

2 Meanwhile cut the courgettes (zucchini) in half lengthways. Cook them for 5 minutes in boiling salted water. Drain and keep warm.

3 If necessary remove the mem-

brane from the liver. Cut it into small cubes and roll in seasoned flour.

4 In a separate pan, heat the oil. Add the onion and sauté until it is soft. Add the bacon, liver, mushrooms and Parmesan cheese and cook for 5 minutes on a moderate heat. Pour in the wine and cream. Stir and simmer for a further 5 minutes. Check the seasoning.

5 With a spoon scoop out the seeds from the courgette (zucchini) halves. Place them on a warm serving dish and spoon the stuffing mixture into the cavities. Surround with the hot pork casserole and serve.

Serves 6

Tips: You can use this tasty stuffing for other vegetables besides courgettes (zucchini). Try using it in aubergines (eggplants) or even red and green peppers. To give it an even richer, more distinctive flavour, substitute a fortified wine such as sherry or port for the white wine.

Pork Paupiettes Braised in Beer

450 g (1 lb) lean loin of pork
salt and pepper
25 g (1 oz) (2 tablespoons) fat
100 g (¼ lb) carrots
450 g (1 lb) small onions
25 g (1 oz) (4 tablespoons) flour
15 ml (1 tablespoon) tomato
  concentrate (paste)
400 ml (14 fl oz) (1¾ cups) brown
  stock
300 ml (½ pint) (1¼ cups) light beer
bouquet garni

For the Stuffing:
30 ml (2 tablespoons) chopped
  onion
15 ml (1 tablespoon) oil
50 g (2 oz) (1 cup) white
  breadcrumbs
5 ml (1 teaspoon) chopped
  parsley
pinch thyme
½ egg to bind
25 g (1 oz) chopped apricots
25 g (1 oz) chopped walnuts
10 ml (2 teaspoons) butter

1 Cut the meat across the grain into 4 thin slices and pound them. Trim to approximately 12.5 cm × 10 cm (5 in × 4 in) and chop the trimmings into small pieces. Season the meat slices.

2 Prepare the stuffing. Sauté the onion in the oil until it is soft. Combine the onion with all the other ingredients and mix in the chopped pork trimmings. Spread a quarter of the stuffing down the centre of each meat slice. Roll them up and secure with string.

3 Heat the fat in a pan. Add the paupiettes and lightly brown them all over. Then add the carrots and onions and continue cooking until the meat is golden all over. Remove from the heat.

4 Drain off the fat and pour 25 g (1 oz) (2 tablespoons) into a clean pan. Add the flour and stir on a low heat until you have a brown roux. Mix in the tomato concentrate (paste) and allow to cool. Boil the stock and add it to the pan with the beer. Bring the sauce to the boil, remove any scum, season and pour over the meat.

5 Add the bouquet garni, cover and allow to simmer on a low heat for 1-1½ hours.

6 Remove the string and place the paupiettes on a warm serving dish. Surround with the vegetables and pour over the sauce.

Serves 4

Pork Alentago

675 g (1½ lb) lean pork tenderloin,
  boned
200 ml (6 fl oz) (¾ cup) dry white
  wine
2 cloves garlic, crushed
2 bay leaves
5 ml (1 teaspoon) paprika
salt and pepper
2 slices bacon, diced
4 slices white bread
1 clove garlic, halved
30 ml (1 fl oz) (2 tablespoons) oil
275 g (10 oz) canned mussels or
  clams, drained

1 Cut the pork into 2.5 cm (1 in) cubes.

2 Combine the wine, garlic, bay leaves and paprika in a bowl. Season with the salt and pepper and add the pork. Cover tightly with plastic or foil and refrigerate for 24 hours.

3 Fry the bacon in a heavy frying pan (skillet) until the fat runs out.

4 Drain the pork cubes, dry them thoroughly and brown in the bacon fat. Cover and cook over a very low heat for 30 minutes.

5 Strain the marinade and add the liquid to the pan. Simmer uncovered for 20 minutes.

6 Meanwhile, remove the crusts from the bread and rub with the garlic clove. Heat the oil in a pan and sauté the bread until it is brown. Place the bread slices in a shallow casserole and keep warm.

7 Add the mussels or clams to the pork and marinade and heat through. Pour the pork and shellfish over the bread and serve.

Serves 4

Pork Canton

675 g (1½ lb) lean minced pork
50 g (2 oz) (½ cup) chopped onions
salt and pepper
1.25 ml (¼ teaspoon) fresh root
  ginger, chopped
1 egg, beaten
30 ml (1 fl oz) (2 tablespoons) oil

For the Sauce:
50 g (2 oz) (½ cup) chopped onion
2 sticks celery, diced
30 ml (2 tablespoons) cornflour
  (cornstarch)
1.25 ml (¼ teaspoon) fresh root
  ginger, chopped
25 g (1 oz) (2 tablespoons) sugar
15 ml (1 tablespoon) soya sauce
225 ml (8 fl oz) (1 cup) chicken
  stock
100 ml (4 fl oz) (½ cup) peach juice
50 ml (2 fl oz) (¼ cup) vinegar
225 g (½ lb) canned peaches,
  drained and diced

1 Combine the pork, onion, salt, pepper and ginger in a bowl. Bind with the beaten egg.

2 Roll the mince mixture into balls approximately 4 cm (1½ in) in diameter.

3 Heat the oil in a frying pan (skillet) and cook the meatballs for about 10 minutes or until done. Remove the meat from the pan and drain well.

4 Prepare the sauce. Drain all but 15 ml (1 tablespoon) of fat from the pan. Sauté the onion and celery in the fat until the onion is transparent.

5 Combine the remaining ingredients, except the peaches, and pour into the pan. Stir and cook until the sauce is thick and clear.

6 Finally add the meatballs and diced peaches. Cover and simmer gently for 10 minutes to allow the sauce flavour to impregnate the meat. Serve with hot rice or noodles.

Serves 6

Pork Paupiettes Braised in Beer are stuffed with fruit, nuts and herbs and cooked in a tasty, beer-flavoured stock

Saté

This is a traditional Indonesian dish of small pork kebabs served with a spicy peanut sauce, always featured among the many accompaniments on an Indonesian rice table.

450 g (1 lb) pork fillet
50 ml (2 fl oz) ($\frac{1}{4}$ cup)
  soya sauce
50 ml (2 fl oz) ($\frac{1}{4}$ cup) sherry
1 clove garlic, crushed
1 thin slice fresh root ginger,
  finely chopped
5 ml (1 teaspoon) curry
  powder
30 ml (1 fl oz) (2 tablespoons) oil
100 g ($\frac{1}{4}$ lb) ($\frac{2}{3}$ cup) fresh peanuts,
  finely chopped
5 ml (1 teaspoon) honey
few drops chilli sauce
5 ml (1 teaspoon) tomato ketchup
  (catsup)
5 ml (1 teaspoon) lemon juice
50 g (2 oz) ($\frac{1}{4}$ cup) peanut butter
5 ml (1 teaspoon) cornflour
  (cornstarch)

1 Cut the pork into 3 cm (1$\frac{1}{4}$ in) cubes. Mix together the soya sauce, sherry, garlic, ginger, curry powder and oil, and marinate the pork pieces in this for 3 hours, basting from time to time.

2 Strain the meat from the marinade and thread the pieces on to kebab skewers. Grill (broil) the kebabs, turning frequently, until browned on all sides.

3 Meanwhile, pour the marinade into a saucepan and add the rest of the ingredients except the cornflour (cornstarch). Heat gently, stirring to blend them into a smooth sauce. Thicken if required with the cornflour (cornstarch) mixed with a little water.

4 Take the cooked pork from the kebab skewers. Arrange the meat around a heated serving dish, and pour the peanut sauce into the middle. Use cocktail sticks to dip

A traditional Indonesian Rice Table with the famous Saté (foreground), Indonesian Rice (centre), king prawns, curried chicken and bean sprouts

the meat pieces into the sauce. Serve with Indonesian Rice.

Serves 4

Indonesian Rice

100 g ($\frac{1}{4}$ lb) ($\frac{1}{2}$ cup) long grain rice
pinch turmeric
30 ml (1 fl oz) (2 tablespoons) oil
50 g (2 oz) ($\frac{1}{3}$ cup) fresh peanuts,
  skinned
5 ml (1 teaspoon) cumin seeds
25 ml (1$\frac{1}{2}$ tablespoons) desiccated
  coconut
salt and pepper

1 Boil the rice in salted water with a pinch of turmeric. Rinse and drain.

2 Heat the oil in a frying pan (skillet). Add the rice and stir-fry for 3 minutes. Add the other ingredients, stir well and fry for another 3 minutes.

Serves 4

Veal in Vermouth and Tuna Sauce

Veal is the meat of the young milk-fed calf of up to 3 months in age, although animals of up to 1 year may be sold as veal.

Dutch veal is considered the best and the meat is very popular in Italy, Northern France and in Holland.

Veal is at its best from May to September. When choosing veal, the flesh should be pale pink, moist, firm and smell pleasant. The fat should be white and slightly pinkish. The connective tissue should be gelatinous (which will disappear during cooking) but not hard or bubbly. If very white meat is desired for a fricassée, or blanquette, the veal may be soaked in salted water to remove the blood, and even bleached with a little lemon juice in the water.

The joints of veal are similar to beef, with shin, cushion (topside), under-cushion (silverside and thick flank) and thick rump being cut from the leg. Shin is used for stews and the famous dish of Osso Buco. The cushions and thick rump are used for roasts, braising or escalopes. Rump and loin can also be roasted, braised or made into escalopes. Best rib and middle rib are used grilled (broiled) or sautéed. Shoulder and breast can be used for roasts or stews, and neck for piemeat or stews. Use top rib for sautées or braising and shank for stock and Osso Buco.

The liver and kidneys are renowned for their high quality. Calf's head and feet may be boiled and served with a sharp vinaigrette sauce.

Veal is an expensive meat and is probably best known for the world-famous Wiener Schnitzel. To make a Wiener Schnitzel escalope, only 75 g (3 oz) of meat is used. It is flattened out and cooked very briefly in a mixture of oil and butter.

The meat has very little fat and tends to be rather bland and lacking in flavour. For this reason, interesting sauces are often made to go with veal, and pot roasting on a bed of vegetables, or braising, is a better, more tasty way to cook veal than a simple roast.

Veal Joints

Veal in Vermouth and Tuna Sauce

1 kg (2 lb) boned rolled leg of veal
25 g (1 oz) (2 tablespoons) butter
25 ml (1 fl oz) ($\frac{1}{8}$ cup) oil
300 ml ($\frac{1}{2}$ pint) (1$\frac{1}{4}$ cups) water

For the Marinade:
$\frac{1}{2}$ litre (17$\frac{1}{2}$ fl oz) (2$\frac{1}{4}$ cups) dry vermouth
30 ml (1 fl oz) (2 tablespoons) vinegar
1 large onion, sliced
1 large carrot, sliced
2 cloves garlic, peeled and chopped
salt and pepper
pinch basil

For the Sauce:
150 g (5 oz) tuna fish
4 anchovy fillets
3 egg yolks
yolks of 2 hard-boiled eggs
juice 1 lemon
15 ml (1 tablespoon) olive oil
7 ml ($\frac{1}{2}$ tablespoon) wine vinegar
salt and pepper
1 pickled cucumber, sliced
25 g (1 oz) (2 tablespoons) capers

1 Mix the marinade ingredients and leave the veal to marinate for 2 hours. Remove the meat and dry with absorbent paper.

2 Put the butter and oil in a saucepan and brown the meat. Add the marinade and water, bring to the boil and simmer for 1 hour. Allow to cool in the marinade. If convenient, this part may be done the day before.

3 Remove the meat, and wipe it.

4 Strain the marinade and reduce (evaporate) by fast boiling until 300 ml ($\frac{1}{2}$ pint) (1$\frac{1}{4}$ cups) remains. Cool.

5 Make the sauce by mixing the tuna fish, anchovy fillets, egg

yolks, hard-boiled egg yolks, lemon juice, olive oil and vinegar. Add the marinade and blend to a smooth, thick sauce, in a liquidizer if possible. Season with salt and pepper, and add the pickled cucumber and capers.

6 Cut the veal in thin slices, arrange on a dish, and pour on the sauce. Serve with a rice salad.

Serves 6-8

Veal Vesuvio

15 g ($\frac{1}{2}$ oz) (1 tablespoon) butter
15 g ($\frac{1}{2}$ oz) (2 tablespoons) flour
150 ml ($\frac{1}{4}$ pint) ($\frac{5}{8}$ cup) stock
300 ml ($\frac{1}{2}$ pint) (1$\frac{1}{4}$ cups) milk
pinch salt, nutmeg, pepper
juice 1 lemon
50 g (2 oz) (4 tablespoons) corn kernels
1 kg (2 lb) boned rolled breast of veal
175 g (6 oz) slices ham
few sprigs watercress
salt and pepper
50 ml (2 fl oz) ($\frac{1}{4}$ cup) oil
300 ml ($\frac{1}{2}$ pint) (1$\frac{1}{4}$ cup) water

1 To make the sauce, make a roux and add the stock. Boil for 10 minutes, add the milk, seasoning and lemon juice. Simmer for 5 minutes. Add the corn kernels.

2 Preheat the oven to 200°C, 400°F, gas 6.

3 Unroll the meat, spread with the ham slices, reserving one for decoration, and watercress leaves. Spread with half of the sauce and season. Roll the meat and tie with string. Season and brush with oil.

4 Roast the meat for 1 hour. Add 300 ml ($\frac{1}{2}$ pint) (1$\frac{1}{4}$ cups) water to the pan, and cook for $\frac{1}{2}$ hour, basting with the liquid. When cooked, place the meat on a dish.

5 Reheat the remaining sauce and pour over the meat. Decorate with the slice of ham and sprigs of watercress.

Serves 6-8

Veal Vesuvio is a real test for your culinary skills, but the end result makes it all very worthwhile

Escalopes and Steaks

Veal escalopes (scallops), which come from the leg of the calf, are considered particularly choice cuts since they contain no fat or gristle. They are cut about 5mm ($\frac{1}{4}$ in) thick and are then usually beaten with a mallet or rolling pin until very thin.

Scaloppines and escalopes (scallops) are similar cuts of veal but differ in the way in which they are cut from the main joint: scaloppines are cut against the grain of the meat whereas escalopes (scallops) are cut with it.

We have included in this section one recipe which uses veal loin steaks. The loin is a prime cut and so the steaks can be very expensive; pork loin steaks would make a suitable alternative, but the cooking time should be lengthened to ensure that the meat is cooked through.

Veal Steaks with Jerusalem Artichokes

50 ml (2 fl oz) ($\frac{1}{4}$ cup) oil
50 g (2 oz) (4 tablespoons) butter
six 225 g ($\frac{1}{2}$ lb) veal loin steaks,
   1 cm ($\frac{1}{2}$ in) thick

For the Sauce:
1 onion, chopped
bouquet garni
150 ml ($\frac{1}{4}$ pint) ($\frac{5}{8}$ cup) dry
   vermouth
1 stock cube
150 ml ($\frac{1}{4}$ pint) ($\frac{5}{8}$ cup) water
juice $\frac{1}{2}$ lemon
15 g ($\frac{1}{2}$ oz) (1$\frac{1}{2}$ tablespoons)
   cornflour (cornstarch)

For the Garnish:
50 g (2 oz) (4 tablespoons) butter
1 kg (2 lb) Jerusalem artichokes,
   cut in halves
1 onion, chopped

1 Heat the oil and butter in a pan, add the veal steaks and fry for 12-14 minutes over a low heat and covered with a lid. Turn the steaks over once or twice during the cooking time. Remove the steaks and keep them warm.

2 Make the sauce. Using the fat left from cooking the meat, fry the onion for 5 minutes and then remove surplus fat. Add the bouquet garni and vermouth and boil for 8 minutes.

3 Dissolve the stock cube in the water, add the stock to the pan and boil for 4 minutes more. Season to taste and add the lemon juice.

4 Mix the cornflour (cornstarch) with 90 ml (4 fl oz) (6 tablespoons) water and add to the sauce. Boil for 1 minute until thickened. Strain the sauce and pour a little of the sauce over the veal.

5 For the garnish, heat the butter in a pan and sauté the Jerusalem artichokes for 6 minutes, covered with a lid. Add the chopped onion and cook for 2 minutes more. Drain off the fat, add 100 ml (4 fl oz) ($\frac{1}{2}$ cup) of the sauce and simmer for 5 minutes. Season.

6 Serve the veal steaks with the garnish and pour the rest of the sauce into a sauce-boat.

Serves 6

Wiener Schnitzel

4 veal escalopes (scallops)
40 g (1$\frac{1}{2}$ oz) (6 tablespoons) plain
   flour, seasoned
1 egg, beaten
50 g (2 oz) ($\frac{3}{4}$ cup) fine dried
   breadcrumbs
50 g (2 oz) ($\frac{1}{4}$ cup) butter
4 slices lemon

1 Place the veal escalopes (scallops) between 2 sheets of dampened greaseproof (parchment) paper and beat with a mallet or rolling pin until very thin, 3 mm ($\frac{1}{8}$ in).

2 Coat the veal with the seasoned flour, then dip in the beaten egg and the breadcrumbs until thoroughly coated.

3 Melt the butter in a large frying pan (skillet). Add the veal and fry over a moderate heat until golden-brown on both sides, turning once during cooking.

4 Transfer the veal to a warmed serving dish and serve immediately, garnished with the lemon slices. Serve with new potatoes tossed in parsley and a green salad.

Serves 4

Veal Escalopes (Scallops) in Marsala

4 veal escalopes (scallops)
50 g (2 oz) (4 tablespoons) butter
100 ml (4 fl oz) ($\frac{1}{2}$ cup) Marsala
200 ml (6 fl oz) ($\frac{3}{4}$ cup) gravy or
   thickened stock
pinch cayenne pepper

1 Place the veal escalopes (scallops) between 2 sheets of dampened greaseproof (parchment) paper and beat with a mallet or rolling pin until they are 3 mm ($\frac{1}{8}$ in) thick.

2 Heat the butter in a frying pan (skillet) and fry the escalopes until well browned. Transfer them to a warmed serving dish and keep hot.

3 Add the Marsala to the fat in the pan and boil for 5 minutes, stirring well. Add the gravy or stock and cayenne, mix well and pour the sauce over the veal.

Serves 4

Veal Escalopes (Scallops) Milanese

1 bunch asparagus
4 veal escalopes (scallops)

50 g (2 oz) (¼ cup) butter
5 ml (1 teaspoon) arrowroot
60 ml (4 tablespoons) white port
45 ml (2 fl oz) (3 tablespoons)
  single (light) cream
sprig tarragon, finely chopped
pinch paprika
salt and pepper

1 Cook the asparagus in boiling salted water for 15-20 minutes.

2 Meanwhile, place the veal escalopes (scallops) between 2 sheets of dampened greaseproof (parchment) paper and beat with a mallet or rolling pin until very thin. Heat the butter in a frying

Veal Steaks with Jerusalem Artichokes is a dish that shows how well veal combines with less familiar vegetables

pan (skillet) and fry the escalopes over a low heat for 5-8 minutes on each side or until cooked through.

3 Mix the arrowroot and the port. Drain the escalopes (scallops) and arrange them on a heated serving dish. Keep hot.

4 Pour the cream into the frying pan (skillet) and stir well to mix with the pan juices. Add the tar-

ragon. Boil for 2 minutes, then add the arrowroot mixed with the port. Simmer, stirring, until thickened. Add the paprika and the salt and pepper to taste.

5 Drain the asparagus and arrange round the escalopes (scallops). Pour the sauce over the top and serve very hot.

Serves 4

Tip: The asparagus must be very carefully drained to ensure that no extra water is added to the sauce – otherwise it will become diluted.

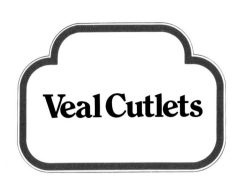

Veal Cutlets

Veal cutlets can either be grilled (broiled) or fried. It is important to differentiate between cutlets and chops – many people confuse the two. Cutlets are taken from the best rib part of the animal; chops from the loin. Cutlets usually weigh about 275 g (10 oz) and are 1 cm ($\frac{1}{2}$ in) thick. Frying is the best method of cooking them. Season the cutlets with salt and pepper, dredge with flour and brown the cutlet on both sides. Then fry gently, covered with a lid, for 15 minutes. Use clarified butter or oil and butter mixed for the best results and flavour. When the cutlets are cooked, drain off the butter, remove the cutlets and pour a little white wine, sherry or Madeira into the pan. Add some demi-glace sauce and boil for 5 minutes. Serve with the cutlets.

Veal Cutlets Provençale

4 tomatoes
salt and pepper
45 ml (3 tablespoons) olive oil
four 225 g ($\frac{1}{2}$ lb) veal cutlets
50 g (2 oz) ($\frac{1}{2}$ cup) flour
100 g ($\frac{1}{4}$ lb) ($\frac{1}{2}$ cup) butter
50 g (2 oz) ($\frac{3}{8}$ cup) green olives,
  stoned (pitted) and blanched
1 clove garlic, peeled and
  crushed
1 bunch parsley, chopped

1 Preheat the oven to 190°C, 375°F, gas 5.

2 Wash the tomatoes and place them in an ovenproof dish. Sprinkle with salt and pepper and pour in the oil. Place in the oven for about 10 minutes.

3 Tenderize the cutlets by beating with a mallet or rolling pin. Season with salt and pepper and dredge with flour.

4 Melt half of the butter in a frying pan (skillet) and fry the cutlets for about 5 minutes on each side until browned and cooked.

5 Arrange the cutlets in a dish, place the olives and baked tomatoes around the edges. Keep warm.

6 Melt the rest of the butter in a pan and fry the garlic and parsley for a minute, stirring all the time. Pour this butter mixture over the cutlets and serve at once.

Serves 4

Veal Cutlets with Mushrooms

100 g ($\frac{1}{4}$ lb) ($\frac{1}{2}$ cup) butter
350 g ($\frac{3}{4}$ lb) ($3\frac{3}{4}$ cups) sliced
  mushrooms
salt and pepper
four 225 g ($\frac{1}{2}$ lb) veal cutlets
30 ml (2 tablespoons) brandy
100 ml (4 fl oz) ($\frac{1}{2}$ cup) single
  (light) cream
5 g (1 tablespoon) chopped
  parsley

1 Melt the butter in a frying pan (skillet). Add the sliced mushrooms and salt and pepper and fry until tender. Remove from the pan and keep warm.

2 Season the cutlets with salt and pepper and place in the pan. Fry gently until browned on both sides and cooked through.

3 Warm the brandy and pour it over the cutlets. Set alight and, when the flames die down, transfer the cutlets to a heated serving dish and keep warm.

4 Add the cream to the pan and boil for 2 minutes to thicken, stirring all the time. Taste the sauce and correct the seasoning.

5 Arrange the mushrooms around the veal cutlets. Pour the sauce over the cutlets and sprinkle with the chopped parsley. Serve very hot with sautéed potatoes.

Serves 4

Tip: Veal cutlets are delicious when dredged with flour and fried and served on a bed of French beans, as shown in the picture. Pour the butter and meat juices over the veal and sprinkle with chopped parsley. This makes a very quick and easy meal to prepare.

Veal Cutlets Portuguese

six 225 g ($\frac{1}{2}$ lb) veal cutlets
salt and pepper
50 g (2 oz) ($\frac{1}{2}$ cup) flour
50 ml (2 fl oz) ($\frac{1}{4}$ cup) oil
1 onion, sliced
1 red pepper, deseeded and sliced
2 tomatoes, skinned, deseeded
  and chopped
2 cloves garlic, peeled and
  chopped
pinch rosemary
50 g (2 oz) ($\frac{1}{4}$ cup) corn kernels
150 ml ($\frac{1}{4}$ pint) ($\frac{5}{8}$ cup) dry sherry
150 ml ($\frac{1}{4}$ pint) ($\frac{5}{8}$ cup) water
1 chicken stock cube
salt and pepper
pinch paprika

1 Sprinkle the cutlets with salt and pepper and dredge with flour. Heat the oil in a frying pan (skillet) and fry the cutlets for 5 minutes on each side until browned. Transfer the cutlets to a shallow ovenproof dish and keep warm.

2 Preheat the oven to 190°C, 375°F, gas 5.

3 Fry the onion in the same pan for 5 minutes until soft. Add the sliced pepper and fry for a further 2 minutes. Add the tomatoes, garlic, rosemary and corn kernels and stir well. Pour in the sherry and water and sprinkle in the stock cube. Season with salt and pepper and paprika, and boil for 5 minutes.

4 Pour the sauce over the veal and braise gently in the oven for 35 minutes, covered with a lid. Serve with plain boiled rice.

Serves 6

Stuffed Veal

These dishes use escalopes (scallops) in a different way by stuffing them with interesting fills, rolling them up into little parcels, and then gently braising them. The long slow cooking means that it is not necessary to use expensive cuts and the escalopes (scallops) can be cut from any part.

Veal Paupiettes

150 g (5 oz) lean pork or veal
  trimmings
1 egg
300 ml (½ pint) (1¼ cups) whipping
  cream
4 veal escalopes (scallops), 175 g
  (6 oz) each
salt, pepper and nutmeg
25 g (1 oz) (2 tablespoons) butter
200 ml (6 fl oz) (¾ cup) white wine

1 Chop and mince the pork or veal trimmings. Put in a bowl, add the egg and mix well. Stir in 50 ml (2 fl oz) (¼ cup) of the cream and chill to make a firm paste.

2 On a wet board, beat the escalopes (scallops) to make them very thin. Season with salt, pepper and nutmeg.

3 Spread the stuffing on the escalopes (scallops), roll up and tie with string.

4 Heat the butter and brown the paupiettes all over.

5 Add the rest of the cream and the white wine and stir carefully. Bring to the boil and simmer the paupiettes for 1 hour.

6 Remove the paupiettes. Discard the string and keep hot.

7 Reduce (evaporate) the sauce to 300 ml (½ pint) (1¼ cups) by fast boiling, and pour over the paupiettes.

Serves 4

Hungarian Veal Paupiettes

100 g (¼ lb) (½ cup) sausagemeat
100 g (¼ lb) (½ cup) ham, minced
1 egg
salt and pepper
6 escalopes (scallops), 100 g (¼ lb)
  each
50 g (2 oz) (½ cup) flour
50 ml (2 fl oz) (¼ cup) oil
450 g (1 lb) carrots
100 g (¼ lb) streaky bacon rashers
  (slices)
50 g (2 oz) (4 tablespoons)
  margarine
200 ml (6 fl oz) (¾ cup) white wine
225 g (½ lb) button (pearl) onions
300 ml (½ pint) (1¼ cups) stock
5 g (1 tablespoon) chopped
  parsley

1 Blend the sausagemeat, minced ham, egg and seasoning to a smooth paste. Chill.

2 On a wet board, flatten the escalopes (scallops) by beating to make them thin. Spread the filling on each escalope (scallop). Roll up and tie with string, and dip in flour.

3 Heat half of the oil in a pan and brown the paupiettes for 4 minutes, covered with a lid. Remove and put in a casserole.

4 Slice the carrots. Cut the bacon into strips.

5 Heat the margarine and rest of the oil and fry the bacon for 1 minute, then add the carrots. Sauté for 3 minutes, then add the bacon and carrots to the veal.

6 Add the white wine and bring to the boil. Cover the dish and simmer for 1 hour.

7 Meanwhile, boil the button (pearl) onions in stock for 2 minutes.

8 Remove the paupiettes, discard the string.

9 Reduce (evaporate) the sauce by fast boiling to 300 ml (½ pint) (1¼ cups).

10 Serve the paupiettes surrounded by the bacon, carrots and onions. Pour over the sauce. Sprinkle with parsley.

Serves 6

Veal with Olives

2 large onions chopped
50 g (2 oz) (¼ cup) butter
100 g (¼ lb) (⅔ cup) calves' liver
100 g (¼ lb) (⅔ cup) streaky bacon
100 g (¼ lb) (1 cup) olives, stoned
  (pitted)
100 g (¼ lb) veal trimmings
50 g (2 oz) (1 cup) breadcrumbs
1 egg
salt and pepper
6 veal escalopes (scallops),
  175 g (6 oz) each
1 carrot, chopped
15 ml (1 tablespoon) flour
100 ml (4 fl oz) (½ cup) white wine
225 ml (8 fl oz) (1 cup) stock
25 g (1 oz) (2 tablespoons) tomato
  concentrate (paste)
bouquet garni

1 Fry one chopped onion in 25 g (1 oz) (2 tablespoons) of the butter and brown lightly. Put in a bowl. Briefly fry the calves' liver to brown and remove.

2 Mince the bacon, one third of the olives, veal trimmings and liver, and add to the onions. Add the breadcrumbs and egg.

3 On a wet board, beat the escalopes (scallops) to make them thin. Spread with the stuffing. Roll up and tie with string.

4 Brown the paupiettes all over in the remainder of the butter. Remove and put in a casserole.

5 Fry the other chopped onion and carrot and brown. Stir in the flour and brown. Add the white wine, stock and tomato concentrate (paste). Add the bouquet garni, salt and pepper.

6 Pour over the paupiettes and cook for 1 hour. Add the remainder of the olives 10 minutes before the end.

7 Remove the paupiettes. Discard the string, and arrange on a dish. Reduce (evaporate) the sauce to 300 ml (½ pint) (1¼ cups) and pour over.

Serves 6

Hungarian Veal Paupiettes, stuffed with sausagemeat, would win plenty of compliments from guests at the dinner table

Cold Veal

Cold Veal Galantine

one 225 g (½ lb) aubergine
  (eggplant)
450 g (1 lb) (2 cups) minced
  stewing veal
225 g (½ lb) (1 cup) minced pork
50 g (2 oz) (¼ cup) minced bacon
1 onion, chopped
50 g (2 oz) (1 cup) fresh
  breadcrumbs
5 g (1 tablespoon) chopped
  parsley
salt and pepper
pinch curry powder
pinch garlic salt
1 egg, beaten
6 slices cucumber
3 radishes, sliced

1 Preheat the oven to 200°C,
400°F, gas 6.

2 Bake the aubergine (eggplant)
in its skin for 15 minutes. Cut in
two and scoop out the pulp. Mix in
a bowl with the meat, onion,
breadcrumbs and parsley, salt
and pepper, curry powder and
garlic salt. Blend in the beaten
egg.

3 Place the meat mixture in a
greased, oblong bread tin. Stand
the tin on a baking tray (cookie
sheet) half-filled with water and
bake for 1½ hours. Cool and turn
out on to a dish. Garnish with the
cucumber and radishes.

Serves 6

Veal Roulade

six 100 g (¼ lb) veal escalopes
salt and pepper
25 g (1 oz) (4 tablespoons) flour
50 ml (2 fl oz) (¼ cup) oil

For the Stuffing:
150 g (5 oz) (1 cup) diced liver ·
1 onion, chopped
25 g (1 oz) (4 tablespoons) flour
1 egg, beaten
12 asparagus tips, canned or
  frozen

For the Chaudfroid Sauce:
300 ml (½ pint) (1¼ cups) white
  sauce
150 ml (¼ pint) (⅝ cup) chicken
  stock
10 g (2 teaspoons) ground
  gelatine

1 Beat each escalope thinly with
a mallet or rolling pin. Season and
dredge with flour.

2 Heat the oil in a frying pan
(skillet) and fry the escalopes
for 5 minutes each side. Then cool.

3 Fry the diced liver in the same
pan for 4 minutes, add the onion
and cook for a further 4 minutes.
Stir in the flour and cook for
1 minute.

4 Mince (grind) the stuffing mixture finely – twice if necessary –
and blend with the beaten egg.

5 Spread this liver stuffing over
each escalope, roll up tightly and
wrap in foil. Chill overnight, then
unwrap and place on a rack.

6 Heat the white sauce. Heat the
stock and add the gelatine.
Simmer for 2 minutes. Blend half
of the jelly stock with the white
sauce and put the remainder
aside for glazing and allow to cool.

7 Coat each stuffed veal roll
evenly with the chaudfroid sauce.
Leave to cool and set. Then brush
with the aspic jelly. Decorate each
roll with two asparagus tips and
serve.

Serves 6

*Cold Veal Galantine makes a
tasty summer lunch;
it is also ideal for picnics
and buffet parties*

All about Joints of Lamb

Roast Shoulder of Lamb

Lamb used to be referred to as 'spring lamb' when it was only home-produced. However, the advent of refrigeration meant that it could be shipped around the world and eaten at all times of the year. Lamb is only called 'lamb' from five months to a year and a half, after that it is referred to as mutton.

Choosing Lamb

You should always look carefully at the colour and texture of the meat when buying lamb. Good quality lamb is light pink and lean with firm fat – the younger the animal, the paler the meat. In an older animal it may be light red. The colour of the fat varies too. Freshly killed young lamb, available in the spring and early summer, has a creamy fat, while the fat of imported lamb is firm and white.

Cuts of Lamb

The cuts of lamb, unlike beef, are international and thus the same throughout the world. Lamb is easy to cook as it has a distinctive flavour and natural fat. Thus most cuts are tender and not tough. In England, the United States and Australia, most people prefer their lamb well cooked. However, in France and Europe it is usually eaten slightly underdone and still pink in the centre. Lamb is very versatile and most cuts can be cooked by both dry and moist cooking methods. In this issue we concentrate on the joints of lamb. These are traditionally roasted but they can also be boiled and pot-roasted.

Loin: This is a prime cut which is usually roasted, either on the bone or boned, stuffed and rolled. The loin is also cut up and served as chops. Other cooking methods for loin are pot-roasting and braising. When cooking loin, you should allow 350 g (¾ lb) per person on the bone, and 100-175 g (4-6 oz) off the bone.

Leg: This is another joint which is usually roasted, braised or pot-roasted. It is often boned and stuffed but the meat can also be cut off the bone and used in stews and casseroles, pies and kebabs. If you intend to roast a leg joint,

always allow 350 g (¾ lb) meat on the bone per person.

Shoulder: This is a large joint which is often more flavoursome than the leg. It is also inclined to be more fatty. Shoulder can be stuffed with various exciting stuffings and roasted. Allow 350 g (¾ lb) on the bone per person.

Breast of Lamb: This is a cheap and rather fatty cut which is often boned, stuffed and rolled. It is then roasted or braised, stewed or boiled. You should allow 225-350 g (8-12 oz) per person, on the bone.

Best End of Neck: This is inexpensive and probably the most versatile joint of all. It is the cut next to the loin and can be roasted, stewed or braised. Allow 350 g (¾ lb) per person.

Chops: These are cut from the loin; the ones nearest to the leg are known as the chump chops. They are usually grilled (broiled) or fried but they are also often used in casseroles. Allow 1-2 chops per person.

Cutlets: These come from the best end and can be grilled (broiled) or fried. They have little lean meat and a longish bone. Allow 1-2 per person.

Neck, Middle and Scrag End: These are all cheap cuts which are suitable for stews and casseroles. They have little meat and a high proportion of fat and bone. Allow 225-350 g (8-12 oz) meat on the bone per person.

Sauces and Stuffings

Roast lamb is traditionally served with mint sauce or jelly, redcurrant jelly, Cumberland or onion sauce. Lamb is delicious when stuffed. Be adventurous and try some new fruity stuffings, made with apricots, prunes, apples and dried fruit. Rice can be used for stuffing lamb – try mixing it with herbs and nuts for a change from the usual thyme and parsley or sage and onion.

Crown Roast of Lamb

This is a very special and well-known lamb dish which always looks impressive at dinner parties. Most butchers will prepare a

crown roast for you if you give them a couple of days' warning. It consists of two pieces of best end which are usually taken from opposite sides of the animal. It is served stuffed in the centre and the bones are decorated with cutlet frills.

Roasting Lamb

Lamb joints are usually roasted. Always roast with the thickest layer of fat on top so that the joint will be automatically basted during cooking. You can try dusting the basted skin of the lamb with seasoned flour. This will absorb excess fat and make the top crisp and golden.

Herbs and Lamb

Herbs go very well with lamb and you should try roasting or casseroling it with different herbs and combinations. Thyme, oregano, marjoram, basil, savory, rosemary, parsley and mint all enhance its flavour. Garlic is also a good flavouring – try rubbing your joint with it, or inserting a clove into the meat itself. Do not overdo the flavouring as lamb has a rather delicate flavour and you may disguise it altogether. Herbs should only be used to complement it.

Storing Lamb

The cheapest way to buy lamb, of course, is to buy in bulk and store it in your freezer. However, if you cannot afford to do this, uncooked meat should keep in the refrigerator for 3-4 days. It will keep best if placed immediately below the freezing compartment. Do not store the lamb in its wrapping paper. Instead, put it on a plate and cover with some thin polythene – leave the ends open for ventilation. Always wrap cooked lamb before placing in a refrigerator, otherwise it will dry out. If you do not have a refrigerator, store the meat in a very cool place and wrap it well to protect it from flies.

Two examples of the varied dishes which can be made from lamb joints: a stuffed roast leg, and cutlets from the best end served with caper sauce

208

Leg of Lamb

Traditionally served, a roast leg of lamb with roast potatoes, peas, mint sauce, redcurrant jelly, or cranberry sauce, is very popular.

We also realise that you may want to know of other unusual ways of cooking a leg of lamb and so we offer you many different and interesting recipes. We show you how to add a delicate flavour by inserting slivers of garlic into cuts in the flesh. In another recipe we explain how to lard a leg of lamb with bacon strips to give a gamey venison flavour. Lamb can be marinated and spread with a sauce made with sour cream before cooking as a change. Or it can be served, Spanish-style, with tomatoes and olives and flavoured with rosemary.

You will know when a leg of lamb is cooked because the juice will run clear if the meat is pierced with a sharp knife. If you use a meat thermometer, the internal temperature of the meat (not near a bone) should read 87°C, 180°F.

To calculate cooking times, allow 20 minutes per 450 g (1 lb), and 20 minutes over for a joint on the bone. Allow 25 minutes if the joint is boned, and 30 minutes if the joint is boned and stuffed and make sure you add the weight of the stuffing to the weight of the joint. When you buy a leg of lamb, allow 350 g (¾ lb) for each person for meat on the bone, and 100 g-175 g (4-6 oz) if the joint has been boned.

Pot Roast Lamb

salt and pepper
2 kg (4 lb) leg of lamb, boned, rolled and tied
2 cloves garlic
50 g (2 oz) (4 tablespoons) butter
30 ml (2 tablespoons) oil

3 carrots, sliced
3 onions, sliced
3 leeks, sliced
450 ml (16 fl oz) (2 cups) beef stock
450 g (1 lb) (2 cups) cooked flageolet or lima beans
350 ml (12 fl oz) (1½ cups) water
7 ml (½ tablespoon) cornflour (cornstarch)

1 Season the leg of lamb and insert slices of garlic into cuts in the flesh.

2 Heat 25 g (1 oz) (2 tablespoons) butter and the oil in a casserole, and brown the lamb all over for 8 minutes. Remove. Brown the carrots, onions and leeks in the same fat for 5 minutes. Pour off the fat. Return the lamb to the casserole. Add the stock and bring to the boil, and simmer for 2 hours.

3 Reheat the beans in the rest of the butter and season with salt and pepper. Keep warm.

4 When the meat is cooked, remove from the casserole and keep warm. Pour off the fat, add 300 ml (½ pint) (1¼ cups) of the water and boil for 5 minutes. Thicken with the cornflour (cornstarch) mixed with the rest of the water. Boil for 5 minutes, strain and season.

5 To serve, slice the meat and arrange on a dish, surrounded by the beans. Serve the sauce separately.

Serves 8

Roast Lamb with Lemon Sauce

1½ kg (3 lb) leg of lamb
2 cloves garlic, sliced
salt and pepper
50 ml (2 fl oz) (¼ cup) oil
50 g (2 oz) (4 tablespoons) butter
2 carrots, sliced
2 sticks celery, sliced
1 onion, chopped
2 lemons

275 ml (9 fl oz) (1⅛ cup) water
100 g (¼ lb) (½ cup) sugar
15 ml (1 tablespoon) vinegar
7 ml (½ tablespoon) cornflour (cornstarch)

1 When buying the leg of lamb, ask the butcher to cut out the aitchbone (pelvic bone) and to trim the knuckle.

2 Preheat the oven to 200°C, 400°F, gas 6.

3 Make cuts in the flesh and insert the slices of garlic. Season the leg, smother with the oil and butter and place in a roasting tin on a bed of carrots, celery, onion, 1 sliced lemon and the aitchbone.

4 Roast for 1¼ hours (allowing 20 minutes per 450 g (1 lb) and 20 minutes over) basting from time to time. When cooked, rest the meat for 15 minutes, then remove and place on a clean dish and keep warm.

5 Make the gravy. During the roasting time, cut the other lemon into segments, and simmer for 8 minutes in 225 ml (8 fl oz) (1 cup) of the water with the sugar and vinegar.

6 When the joint has been removed, put the roasting tin on top of the stove over a gentle heat for 2 minutes to allow the sediment to settle. Carefully pour off the fat, leaving the sediment and juices. Cook for 3 minutes until brown, then add 300 ml (½ pint) (1¼ cups) of lemon liquid (add water if necessary to make up the amount). Stir and scrape the tin to loosen the browned sediment, and cook for 8 minutes. Thicken with the cornflour (cornstarch) mixed with 45 ml (3 tablespoons) of the water. Cook for 5 minutes to clear. Strain.

7 To serve, decorate the leg of lamb with a frill round the bone, and pour a little sauce over it. Arrange the lemon segments on top. Serve the rest of the sauce separately. Serve with boiled rice, sprinkled with chopped parsley.

Serves 6

An unusual and different way of serving roast leg of lamb is on a bed of beans

Braised Lamb in Wine

4 cloves garlic
2 kg (4 lb) leg of lamb
100 ml (4 fl oz) (½ cup) oil
2 onions, chopped
2 carrots, diced
100 ml (4 fl oz) (½ cup) white wine
1 litre (1¾ pints) (4½ cups) stock
bouquet garni
salt and pepper

1 Preheat the oven to 200°C, 400°F, gas 6.

2 Cut each clove of garlic into four and insert each into a gash cut in the leg of lamb.

3 Heat the oil in a frying pan (skillet) and brown the lamb on all sides for 8 minutes. Remove and place in a casserole.

4 Brown the onions and carrots and add to the lamb.

5 Pour the white wine and stock into the casserole. Add the bouquet garni, salt and plenty of pepper and bring to the boil. Cover and put in the oven for 2 hours.

6 When the meat is cooked, remove from the casserole and keep warm. Strain the liquid from the casserole into a saucepan. Remove the fat and boil until only 300 ml (½ pint) (1¼ cups) remains.

7 The lamb may be served sliced, with a little sauce poured over it, or whole to be carved at table.

Serves 6-8

Festive Leg

225 g (½ lb) canned pineapple
rings with juice
2 kg (4 lb) leg of lamb
salt and pepper
glacé cherries for decoration

1 Preheat the oven to 200°C, 400°F, gas 6.

2 Remove the juice from the can of pineapple rings.

3 Put the lamb in a roasting tin and pour the pineapple juice over. Season with salt and pepper.

4 Roast in the preheated oven, allowing 20 minutes per 450 g (1 lb) and 20 minutes over, basting occasionally with the juice.

5 When cooked, place on a dish and garnish with halved pineapple rings with a cherry between each. Serve with roast potatoes.

Serves 6-8

Stuffed Leg of Lamb

25 g (1 oz) (2 tablespoons)
currants
75 g (3 oz) (6 tablespoons) butter
1 onion, chopped
4 apples, peeled, cored and diced
175 g (6 oz) (¾ cup) long grain rice
salt and pepper
2 kg (4 lb) leg of lamb, boned
100 ml (4 fl oz) (½ cup) oil
100 ml (4 fl oz) (½ cup) stock
juice 1 lemon

1 Preheat the oven to 200°C, 400°F, gas 6.

2 Soak the currants in water.

3 Heat the butter in a frying pan (skillet). Fry the onion gently, add the apples and cook until all the liquid evaporates.

4 Boil the rice for 10 minutes.

5 Mix the onion and apples with the drained currants and the rice. Season with salt and pepper. Stuff the leg with the mixture and sew up the opening. Season and brush with oil.

6 Roast for 2¼ hours in all, 35 minutes at 200°C, 400°F, gas 6 and for 1 hour 40 minutes with the temperature reduced to 180°C, 350°F, gas 4.

7 When the leg is cooked, remove from the pan and put on a serving dish. Make a gravy with the juices in the pan and the stock and flavour with lemon juice.

Serves 6-8

Normandy Lamb

1 clove garlic
2 kg (4 lb) leg of lamb
salt and pepper
5 ml (1 teaspoon) thyme
75 g (3 oz) (6 tablespoons) butter
225 ml (8 fl oz) (1 cup) cider
5 ml (1 teaspoon) flour
50 ml (2 fl oz) (¼ cup) calvados,
(apple brandy) or brandy
150 ml (5 fl oz) (⅝ cup) single
(light) cream

1 Preheat the oven to 200°C, 400°F, gas 6.

2 Insert the clove of garlic, peeled, into the knuckle end of the leg of lamb with the point of a knife. Salt and pepper the meat generously and sprinkle with thyme. Rub in well so that the flavours sink into the meat.

3 Heat the butter, reserving 5 ml (1 teaspoon), in a casserole. Add the lamb and brown all over for 8 minutes. Cover and cook, allowing 20 minutes per 450 g (1 lb) and 20 minutes over, basting with half of the cider from time to time.

4 Blend the 5 ml (1 teaspoon) flour with the 5 ml (1 teaspoon) butter for a "beurre manié" to thicken the gravy later on.

5 When the lamb is cooked, pour on the calvados (apple brandy) or brandy and flame. Then place the meat on a serving dish and keep warm.

6 Pour the remainder of the cider into the pan. Boil for 2 minutes, scraping the casserole to loosen the browned sediment.

7 Add the cream and stir for 1 minute, then add the "beurre manié" and cook gently until it thickens.

8 Serve the sauce separately with the lamb.

Serves 6-8

---

*Stuffed Leg of Lamb. The
stuffing is
a tasty mixture of raisins,
apple and onion*

Glazed Lamb with Sherry Sauce

1.75 kg (3½ lb) boned leg of
  lamb
150 g (5 oz) streaky bacon,
  chopped or minced
50 g (2 oz) (1 cup) breadcrumbs
1 egg, beaten
salt and pepper
pinch dried thyme and rosemary
300 ml (½ pint) (1¼ cups) dry sherry
300 ml (½ pint) (1¼ cups) water
3 carrots, cleaned and chopped
2 sticks celery, chopped
few sprigs each fresh parsley
  and tarragon
1 clove garlic, crushed
30 ml (2 tablespoons) oil
50 g (2 oz) (4 tablespoons) butter
150 ml (¼ pint) (⅝ cup) sour cream
15 ml (1 tablespoon) made
  mustard
1 egg yolk
5 ml (1 teaspoon) chopped fresh
  parsley

1 Ask the butcher to bone the leg of lamb for you. Mix the bacon, breadcrumbs, egg, seasoning and herbs to a paste and use it to stuff the leg. Tie the meat into shape with fine string and marinate it for 5 hours or overnight in the sherry, water, vegetables, fresh herbs and garlic, turning it from time to time to soak all sides.

2 Preheat the oven to 200°C, 400°F, gas 6. Drain the joint from the marinade and dry it. Brush it with the oil and butter, season with a pinch of salt and pepper, and roast for 35 minutes.

3 Meanwhile drain the vegetables from the marinade, reserving both. Place the vegetables under the joint and continue to roast for 15 minutes.

4 Reduce the oven temperature to 180°C, 350°F, gas 4. Pour the marinade around the joint, cover and cook for 1 hour.

5 Mix the sour cream, mustard, egg yolk and parsley. Remove the meat from the oven and pour the vegetables and cooking liquid into a pan. Turn the oven up to 220°C, 425°F, gas 7. Spread the sour cream mixture over the joint and return to the oven for 10 minutes until it is golden-brown.

6 Meanwhile boil the marinade to reduce (evaporate) it to a thicker consistency. Strain the vegetables out and pour the sauce into a sauce-boat. Serve the meat on a heated dish with the sauce.

Serves 8

Leg of Lamb Minorca

1.75 kg (3½ lb) leg of lamb
2 cloves garlic
salt and pepper
2 sprigs fresh rosemary
2 onions, chopped
3 carrots, quartered
30 ml (2 tablespoons) oil
75 g (3 oz) (6 tablespoons) butter
300 ml (½ pint) (1¼ cups) rosé wine
25 g (1 oz) (2 tablespoons) tomato
  concentrate (paste)
100 g (¼ lb) (1 cup) sliced button
  mushrooms
12 stuffed green olives
15 g (½ oz) (1½ tablespoons)
  cornflour (cornstarch)
45 ml (3 tablespoons) water
12 small tomatoes

1 Remove the aitchbone (pelvic bone) or ask the butcher to do it for you, and keep it. Cut the garlic into slivers and insert them into slits on the surface of the meat. Season with salt and pepper, and rosemary sprigs.

2 Preheat the oven to 190°C, 375°F, gas 5. Place the onions and carrots in a roasting pan with the bone. Brush the joint with oil and 50 g (2 oz) (4 tablespoons) of the butter and set it on the vegetables. Roast for 45 minutes.

3 Add the wine and tomato concentrate (paste), cover and continue to cook for 45 minutes.

4 Remove the meat from the roasting pan and keep it warm. Take the bone and carrots from the liquid. Boil the liquid to reduce (evaporate) it.

5 Fry the mushrooms in the rest of the butter for 5 minutes. Add to the sauce with the green olives. Thicken the sauce with the cornflour (cornstarch) dissolved in the water.

6 Grill (broil) the tomatoes for 5 minutes. Arrange them around the joint on a serving dish. Impale 2 tomatoes on a kebab skewer with a few stuffed olives and stick it into the meat to decorate. Pour the sauce over the joint and serve.

Serves 6-8

Lamb Espagnola

2 kg (4 lb) leg or shoulder of lamb
2 cloves garlic, crushed
5 ml (1 teaspoon) mixed dried
  herbs
few sprigs fresh rosemary
60 ml (4 tablespoons) sherry
60 ml (4 tablespoons) water
12 small onions or shallots,
  peeled
6 stuffed green olives, sliced

1 Place the lamb in a roasting pan. Spread the crushed garlic and dried herbs evenly over the surface and arrange rosemary sprigs on top and underneath. Pour the sherry over the meat and leave it to stand for 3 hours.

2 Preheat the oven to 190°C, 375°F, gas 5. Add the water to the roasting pan and arrange the peeled, whole onions around the joint. Roast in the oven for 20 minutes per 450 g (1 lb) and 20 minutes more, basting from time to time.

3 Set the lamb on a heated serving dish and arrange the onions around it. Stir the sliced olives into the cooking juices and pour the liquid over the joint.

Serves 6-8

*Leg of Lamb Minorca. The
joint is covered
with a sauce of mushrooms
and olives*

Shoulder of Lamb

Shoulder of lamb is a popular cut which has a higher proportion of fat than the leg but greater flavour. The joint is sold both on the bone and with the bones removed, ready for stuffing.

Shoulder of lamb can be used in four main ways: cut into blade-bone chops which can be grilled (broiled) or braised; as a stuffed joint to be roasted or braised; cut into cubes for stews, curries or blanquettes; and minced to make meatballs, burgers or sausages which can be grilled (broiled), fried or baked.

For the traditional roast joint, allow 350 g (¾ lb) weight on the bone per person and a cooking time of 20 minutes per 450 g (1 lb) plus an extra 20 minutes. Spread the meat with a little butter and oil and season with salt and pepper. Roast at 200°C, 400°F, gas 6 for the first 30 minutes, then reduce the temperature to 180°C, 350°F, gas 4 for the rest of the cooking time.

Lamburgers Capucine

725 g (1½ lb) (3 cups) minced raw
  shoulder of lamb
1 onion, chopped
1 egg
salt and pepper
50 g (2 oz) (1 cup) breadcrumbs
25 g (1 oz) (¼ cup) flour
4 slices (rashers) bacon, scalded
50 g (2 oz) (4 tablespoons) butter
50 ml (2 fl oz) (¼ cup) oil
100 g (¼ lb) (1 cup) sliced
  mushrooms
1 green pepper, sliced

1 Combine the meat, onion, egg, seasoning, breadcrumbs, and flour and shape into 4 burgers. Wrap each with a rasher (slice) of bacon and secure with kitchen thread.

2 Heat the butter and oil in a pan, add the lamburgers, cover with a lid and cook for 8-10 minutes, turning from time to time until golden-brown and cooked through.

3 Lift from the pan, remove the thread and place on a warmed serving plate. Fry the mushrooms and pepper in the same pan for 4 minutes and use to garnish the lamburgers.

Serves 4

Variation

Preheat the oven to 200°C, 400°F, gas 6. Combine the lamb, onion, eggs, seasoning, breadcrumbs and flour in the same way as for the lamburgers. Cut four thick slices from a marrow (large zucchini) and remove the seeds. Parboil the rings in salted water, drain and place in a casserole dish. Fill the rings with the lamb mixture, cover and bake in the preheated oven for 20 minutes.

Andorran Shoulder of Lamb

2 kg (4 lb) shoulder of lamb,
  bones and fat removed
25 g (1 oz) (2 tablespoons) butter
30 ml (1 fl oz) (2 tablespoons) oil
225 ml (8 fl oz) (1 cup) stock
225 ml (8 fl oz) (1 cup) dry white
  wine
100 ml (4 fl oz) (½ cup) anisette

For the Stuffing:
225 g (½ lb) sausagemeat
1 egg, beaten
15 ml (1 tablespoon) brandy
  (optional)
100 g (¼ lb) (1 cup) chopped
  mushrooms
2 sprigs thyme, finely chopped
sprig rosemary, finely chopped
15 ml (1 tablespoon) chopped
  parsley
1 shallot, chopped
1 clove garlic, peeled and
  chopped

salt and pepper
25 g (1 oz) (2 tablespoons) butter
15 ml (1 tablespoon) oil

For the Tomato Sauce:
45 ml (3 tablespoons) oil
1 onion, chopped
700 g (1½ lb) tomatoes, skinned
  and chopped
1 clove garlic, peeled
1 chilli, deseeded and chopped
1 sugar lump
1 sprig thyme

1 To make the stuffing, mix all the ingredients, except the butter and oil, together in a bowl.

2 Heat the butter and oil in a pan, add the stuffing and cook for 7-8 minutes until golden-brown.

3 Spread the lamb flat on the work surface. Spread the stuffing over the meat, taking it to within 3 cm (1¼ in) of the edge. Roll up the meat and secure with kitchen string.

4 Heat the butter and oil in a heavy-bottomed pan and fry the meat until golden-brown all over. Pour in the stock and white wine, cover and leave to cook over a low heat for 2¼ hours.

5 Meanwhile, prepare the tomato sauce. Heat the oil in a pan add the onion, tomatoes, garlic, chilli, sugar and thyme and season with salt and pepper. Cook over a high heat until golden-brown, then reduce the heat, cover and cook over a low heat for 40 minutes.

6 Pour the sauce through a fine conical strainer, cover and return to a low heat. If the sauce becomes too thick, add a few spoonfuls of the cooking liquor from the meat.

7 When the meat is cooked, transfer it to a heated serving dish and pour the sauce into a sauceboat.

8 Just before serving, warm the anisette, sprinkle it over the meat and set it alight. Serve with rice, noodles or French beans.

Serves 6-8

---

*In front, Roast Shoulder of
Lamb and, behind,
Andorran Shoulder of Lamb and
Lamburgers Capucine*

Loin of Lamb

The loin of a lamb is half of the saddle, cut lengthways through the spine. It is a meaty and well-flavoured cut and is hence quite expensive. It may be roasted on the bone or with the bone removed – the butcher will do this for you. When boned, with the long flap of the breast, it is sometimes stuffed and rolled, tied in shape with string and roasted. It is also used without the breast flap.

Beswick Lamb

1½ kg (3 lb) loin of lamb, boned
25 g (1 oz) (2 tablespoons) butter
30 ml (1 fl oz) (2 tablespoons) oil
450 g (1 lb) garden peas
1 sprig mint
6 spring onion (scallion) bulbs
50 ml (2 fl oz) (¼ cup) sherry
juice 1 orange

For the Stuffing:
2 slices bacon, chopped
2 lamb's kidneys, skinned, cored and chopped
50 g (2 oz) (4 tablespoons) butter
1 onion, finely chopped
100 g (¼ lb) (1 cup) chopped mushrooms
salt and pepper
5 ml (1 teaspoon) tomato concentrate (paste)
50 g (2 oz) (1 cup) fresh breadcrumbs

1 To make the stuffing, fry the chopped bacon and kidney in the butter for 3 minutes. Then stir in the onion and cook another 3 minutes. Add the mushrooms and fry 2 minutes. Season, stir in the tomato concentrate (paste) and the breadcrumbs, and stir to bind all ingredients together to a loose mixture, adding a little melted butter if necessary. Allow the stuffing to cool.

Beswick Loin of Lamb is served with peas and redcurrant jelly for a dinner party or an extra special occasion

2 Preheat the oven to 200°C, 400°F, gas 6. Spread the stuffing on the inside of the loin of lamb, roll up the meat and tie it with fine string. Place it in a roasting pan, brush with butter and oil and season. Roast it for 1-1½ hours.

3 Boil the peas in salted water with a sprig of mint and the spring onion (scallion) bulbs until tender. Drain and pile the peas on a heated serving dish.

4 When the meat is cooked, carve it into slices and arrange them on the bed of garden peas.

5 Strain off excess fat from the cooking juices. Pour the sherry and orange juice into the roasting pan and boil for 3 minutes. Season to taste. Pour the sauce into a sauce-boat and serve with the meat, peas, and some redcurrant or cranberry jelly.

Serves 8

Kebabs and Grills

Shish kebab are the Turkish words for cooked meat (kebab) on the skewer (shish). In Turkey and all over the Middle East people eat shish kebab at home, in cafés, and even from street vendors. There, lamb is the most usual meat and a shish kebab of lamb's liver and kidneys is considered the greatest delicacy. In Turkey the meat is separated by pieces of mutton fat. In England we use pieces of bacon. The fat from the bacon is needed to moisten the chunks of lean meat as they are grilled (broiled) and the kebabs need to be brushed with oil.

The meat is usually mixed with vegetables, such as onions, mushrooms, green peppers and tomatoes. If using small whole tomatoes it is wise to put them on either end of the skewer so that they receive less heat and remain firm. Fruit makes an interesting addition, and chunks of pineapple, firm apricots and pieces of peach or apple grill well.

Kebabs are always marinated in a mixture of wine, oil and vinegar with additions of garlic and herbs. Using a marinade helps to tenderize the meat as well as impart extra flavour. It is important that the cubes of meat should be the same size so that they will be cooked at the same time.

Lemon Kebabs

2 rashers (slices) streaky bacon
550 g (1¼ lb) leg of lamb, cut in
  2.5 cm (1 in) cubes
4 onions, quartered
2 tomatoes, quartered
1 green pepper
8 bay leaves
8 mushrooms
50 ml (2 fl oz) (4 tablespoons) oil

Lemon Kebabs are colourful and ideal to prepare for a party or when your friends drop in unexpectedly

5 ml (1 teaspoon) cornflour
(cornstarch)
45 ml (1½ fl oz) (3 tablespoons)
  water
225 g (½ lb) (1 cup) long grain rice,
  boiled
25 g (1 oz) (2 tablespoons) butter

1 Scald the bacon in boiling water for ½ minute. Drain and dry on absorbent paper. Cut into strips 2.5 cm (1 in) wide.

2 Soak the lamb cubes (which may be cut in half if preferred) and the bacon strips in the marinade for 3 hours. Drain and dry on absorbent paper.

3 Impale on skewers the lamb and bacon alternately with the onions, tomatoes, green pepper, bay leaves, and mushrooms.

4 Brush the kebabs with oil.

5 Cook under a grill (broiler) or over charcoal for 8 minutes.

6 Meanwhile, boil the marinade for 5 minutes until 300 ml (½ pint) (1¼ cups) is left. Thicken with the cornflour (cornstarch) mixed with water and cook for 2 minutes until clear. Season.

7 Serve the kebabs on a bed of plain boiled rice mixed with the butter and seasoned, with the sauce separately.

8 To serve each guest, place some rice on a plate and then arrange the meat and garnish on the rice, removing the skewer carefully.

Serves 4

All about Lamb Stews and Casseroles

Spring Hotpot

Lamb Stews

Stews have the great merit of being suitable for cooking in advance, for reheating or freezing.

A stew is a combination of meat and vegetables cooked on top of the stove. There are three kinds of stew, one brown and two white. For the brown stew the meat is always seared first to seal the juices. It is then thickened by flour sprinkled on the meat or by a roux or cornflour (cornstarch).

The stew may be given a good brown colour by the addition of 1.25 ml (¼ teaspoon) of commercial "browning", made from caramel, or you can use the same amounts of black treacle and vinegar to darken the stew without sweetening it.

In a white stew, the meat is first boiled in water. A roux is added to the stew and diluted with the stock, mixed with some milk. The stew may be further enriched with cream or a liaison of egg yolks and cream.

The other type of white stew is a fricasée in which the meat is lightly pan fried to sear, but not to colour. The meat is then dredged with flour and liquid added.

A sauté is another variety of stew in which the meat is cooked as dry as possible. The meat is browned and cooked, with a lid on, in its own juices until almost tender.

Stews are cooked on top of the stove and it is necessary to use a heavy cast-iron dish. However, even with one, it is difficult with a gas cooker to prevent the meat burning.

If you do not have a suitable dish, it may be best to start the stew in a saucepan on top of the stove, and then to put the meat and vegetables in an ovenproof dish and finish the cooking in the oven.

Haricot Bean Lamb Stew

550 g (1¼ lb) stewing lamb
25 g (1 oz) (2 tablespoons) lard (shortening)
2 rashers (slices) streaky bacon
8 button onions
1 clove garlic, crushed
25 g (1 oz) (¼ cup) flour
900 ml (1½ pints) (3¾ cups) stock
salt and pepper
bouquet garni
225 g (½ lb) (1⅓ cups) dried haricot beans, soaked overnight
1 carrot, chopped
1 large onion, chopped
15 g (½ oz) (1 tablespoon) tomato concentrate (paste)
15 ml (1 tablespoon) vinegar
15 ml (1 tablespoon) chopped parsley

1 Cut the meat into cubes.

2 Heat the lard (shortening) in a pan and add the bacon, diced (keep the bacon rind to cook with the beans) and the button onions. Colour slightly and remove from the pan.

3 In the same pan, brown the meat. Drain off half the fat, add the garlic and flour and stir for 1 minute.

4 Add the stock and bring to the boil. Season, skim off any scum. Add the bouquet garni, cover with a lid and simmer for 1½ hours.

5 Preheat the oven to 180°C, 350°F, gas 4.

6 Drain the soaked haricot beans, reserving the liquid. Put the beans in clean water and bring to the boil. Throw the water away. Put the beans in an ovenproof dish with the chopped carrot, onion, bacon rinds, tomato concentrate (paste) and vinegar. Add some of the original liquid to cover and bake in the oven for 1 hour. When the beans are tender, remove the bacon rinds, and season with salt and pepper.

7 To serve, either combine the beans with the meat in one dish, or serve separately, sprinkled with chopped parsley.

Serves 4

Lamb and Pasta Stew

salt and pepper
2 courgettes (zucchini), cut in chunks
50 ml (2 fl oz) (¼ cup) oil
4 chump chops
1 onion, chopped
25 g (1 oz) (¼ cup) flour
25 g (1 oz) (2 tablespoons) tomato concentrate (paste)
300 ml (½ pint) (1¼ cups) stock
juice 2 oranges
15 ml (1 tablespoon) thin strips of orange peel
225 g (½ lb) pasta wheels
15 ml (1 tablespoon) chopped fresh mint
few mint leaves

1 Sprinkle salt on the courgettes (zucchini) and leave for ½ hour. Wash off the bitter juices and dry.

2 Preheat the oven to 180°C, 350°F, gas 4.

3 Heat the oil and brown the chops. Remove from the pan and place in an ovenproof dish.

4 In the same pan, fry the onion for 3 minutes; stir in the flour and cook for 1 minute. Add the tomato concentrate (paste) and cook for 1 minute. Stir in the stock and orange juice and boil for 15 minutes. Season with salt and pepper and strain over the chops.

5 Meanwhile, blanch the strips of orange peel in boiling water for 6 minutes. Drain and add to the meat.

6 Put the meat in the oven to cook for 1 hour.

7 During this time, boil the pasta for 8 minutes. Drain and add to the stew with the courgettes (zucchini) 15 minutes before the end of the cooking time.

8 When ready to serve, check the seasoning, sprinkle with chopped mint and garnish with a few whole leaves for decoration.

Serves 4

Lamb and Pasta Stew is a good way of serving lamb with mint and oranges which makes an ideal lunch or supper dish

Lamb and Prawns Spanish-style

50 ml (2 fl oz) (¼ cup) oil
1 kg (2 lb) boned middle lamb
  cutlets, cut in small, thin slices
1 large onion, sliced
12 stuffed olives, sliced
2 cloves garlic, chopped
300 ml (½ pint) (1¼ cups) water
150 ml (¼ pint) (⅝ cup) medium
  sherry
1 bay leaf
pinch saffron
100 g (¼ lb) (½ cup) long grain rice
225 g (½ lb) tomatoes, skinned,
  deseeded and chopped
1 small red pepper, deseeded
  and chopped
175 g (6 oz) (1⅛ cups) peeled
  prawns
175 g (6 oz) (1½ cups) sliced
  mushrooms
salt and pepper
15 ml (1 tablespoon) chopped
  parsley

1 In a large sauté pan, heat the oil and cook the lamb for 8 minutes, covered with a lid.

2 Add the onion, cook for 1 minute, then add the olives, garlic, water, sherry, bay leaf and saffron, and bring gently to the boil. Reduce the heat and simmer for ½ hour.

3 Add the rice, tomatoes and pepper and simmer for 20 minutes.

4 Add the prawns and mushrooms, season and cook for 4 minutes more. Sprinkle with the chopped parsley and serve.

Serves 6

Lamb Bourguignonne

900 g (2 lb) lean shoulder of
  lamb, cut in 2½ cm (1 in) cubes
50 ml (2 fl oz) (¼ cup) oil
3 rashers (slices) bacon, diced
2 onions, chopped

Lamb Bourguignonne is a dish for special occasions which is marinated in red wine then served on a bed of rice

25 g (1 oz) (2 tablespoons) tomato
  concentrate (paste)
5 ml (1 teaspoon) molasses or
  dark treacle
150 g (5 oz) (⅝ cup) long grain rice
50 g (2 oz) (4 tablespoons) butter
6 mushrooms, sliced
salt and pepper
pinch mixed spice

For the Marinade:
300 ml (½ pint) (1¼ cups) red wine
150 ml (¼ pint) (⅝ cup) water
1 bay leaf
2 cloves garlic, crushed
bouquet garni
30 ml (1 fl oz) (2 tablespoons)
  vinegar

1 Mix the ingredients for the marinade. Place the lamb in a bowl, pour over the marinade and leave to soak for 3 hours.

2 Lift the meat from the marinade and dry it. Heat the oil in a pan and cook the lamb and bacon for about 6 minutes until browned. Add the onions and cook for a further 3 minutes.

3 Add the marinade, tomato concentrate (paste) and molasses or treacle and bring to the boil. Reduce the heat and simmer for 1½ hours.

4 Meanwhile, cook the rice in boiling salted water, drain and mix with half of the butter.

5 Sauté the mushrooms in the rest of the butter for 2 minutes.

6 When the stew has finished cooking, discard the bay leaf and bouquet garni. Add the mushrooms, check the seasoning and add a pinch of mixed spice. Arrange the boiled rice on a serving dish and pour the lamb bourguignonne over it.

Serves 6

Winter Specials

Classic Quiche

Pressure Cookers

To cook with pressure is to experience nothing less than a revolution in your kitchen. Within minutes you can create tender, appetizing and nutritious meals with all the natural goodness sealed in. Your fuel bills decrease, vegetables retain their natural colour, and because a complete meal can be prepared in the one cooker, washing up is made easier.

It is essential that you read and understand the manufacturer's instructions before using your cooker. They will tell you how to assemble and clean it; how much water to use; how to bring your cooker to pressure and the cooking time required for foods ranging from jams to puddings. There are a number of different makes of cooker on the market with varying pressures. In all our recipes we have given a 6.75 kg (15 lb) pressure, so if your cooker doesn't have this measure, find a similar recipe in your manual and adjust the cooking accordingly.

Once pressure is reached, you should reduce the heat to low and begin to calculate your cooking time. It is essential that the timing is accurate, not only to prevent the cooker boiling dry but to get the best results: one minute extra in the pressure cooker can ruin a meal.

Always remember to reduce the pressure before opening your cooker. Take it to the sink and let cold water run over the sides until there is little or no steam coming from the steam escape. Once you have mastered these uncomplicated procedures, you will be in a position to experiment with the endless variety of dishes which can be cooked to perfection in this speediest of cooking processes.

Latin American Vegetable Stew

1 litre (1¾ pints) (4½ cups) water
1 herb stock cube
100 g (¼ lb) chick peas
100 g (¼ lb) butter beans
100 g (¼ lb) lentils
1 green pepper, deseeded and roughly chopped
1 red pepper, deseeded and roughly chopped
200 g (7 oz) (1 cup) frozen corn kernels
6 stalks celery, sliced
3 carrots, peeled and diced
30 ml (2 tablespoons) tomato paste
225 g (½ lb) peeled tomatoes
bouquet garni
salt and pepper
15 ml (1 tablespoon) cornflour (cornstarch)

1 Place the water in the cooker and crumble in the herb stock cube. Bring the water slowly to the boil. Add the chick peas, butter beans and lentils. Cover and bring to 6.75 kg (15 lb) pressure in the usual way. Cook for 30 minutes. Reduce the pressure under cold water.

2 Add the peppers, corn kernels, celery, carrots, tomato paste, tomatoes and bouquet garni. Season and return to 6.75 kg (15 lb) pressure. Cook for 2 minutes. Reduce the pressure under cold water.

3 Mix the cornflour (cornstarch) with a little water to a smooth paste. Stir it into the cooker over a gentle heat and simmer for a few minutes. Check the seasoning, turn the stew into a warmed casserole dish and serve.

Serves 6-8

Tip: This is a basic vegetable stew and you can use virtually any vegetables you choose. Try adding Brussels sprouts, cauliflower florets, French beans, mushroom caps or asparagus tips but remember to add extra water. Potatoes, turnips or other large root vegetables should be quartered and cooked for 4 minutes.

Boiled Brisket Polish-style

1 kg (2 lb) brisket of beef
3 onions
4 medium carrots
1 small cabbage
salt and pepper
1 bay leaf
peppercorns

For the Sauce:
25 g (1 oz) (2 tablespoons) soft margarine
25 g (1 oz) (4 tablespoons) flour
salt and pepper
300 ml (½ pint) (1¼ cups) milk
15 ml (1 tablespoon) dry mustard
10 ml (2 teaspoons) sugar
15 ml (1 tablespoon) vinegar

1 Trim the meat of excess fat. Leave the onions whole and cut the carrots into quarters lengthways. Cut the cabbage into quarters.

2 Place the meat in the pressure cooker with enough water to just cover, if possible, but don't fill the pan more than half-full when the meat and water have been added. Add the seasoning, bay leaf and peppercorns and cook at 6.75 kg (15 lb) pressure for 20 minutes.

3 Reduce the pressure with cold water and lift off the weights and cover. Skim the liquid and add the vegetables. Bring the cooker up to pressure again and continue to cook for 5 minutes.

4 Reduce the pressure and serve the joint whole or in overlapping slices. Arrange the vegetables around the dish and pour over a spoonful of the stock. Keep warm.

5 Make the mustard sauce. Put the margarine, flour, seasoning and milk in a saucepan and slowly bring to the boil, whisking continuously. Cook for a further 2-3 minutes.

6 Blend the mustard, sugar and vinegar to a smooth cream and stir it into the sauce. Serve the sauce separately.

Serves 4

Latin American Vegetable Stew is full of the natural goodness of high-protein beans and fresh tasty vegetables

Carrot and Orange Soup

675 g (1½ lb) carrots
1 medium onion
2 sticks celery
1 litre (1¾ pints) (4½ cups) chicken stock
salt and pepper
1 bay leaf
15 g (½ oz) (1½ tablespoons) cornflour (cornstarch)
juice and grated rind 1 orange
freshly grated nutmeg
50 ml (2 fl oz) (¼ cup) single (light) cream

1 Peel and slice the carrots. Peel and chop the onion. Scrub the celery, remove the leaves and chop.

2 Place the vegetables in the cooker with 300 ml (½ pint) (1¼ cups) of the stock, salt and pepper, and the bay leaf. Cover and bring the cooker to 6.75 kg (15 lb) pressure. Cook for 5 minutes. Reduce the pressure under cold water.

3 Pass the vegetables and stock through a sieve, or blend them in a liquidizer, to make a smooth purée.

4 Blend the cornflour (cornstarch) with the rest of the stock. Return the vegetable purée and the stock to the pan with the orange rind and juice and the nutmeg. Adjust the seasoning and stir over heat until at simmering point.

5 Pour the soup into serving bowls and put about 5 ml (1 teaspoon) of cream in the middle of each bowl. Lightly swirl the surface with the tip of a knife and serve immediately.

Serves 6-8

Chicken Tropicana, garnished with toasted strands of coconut, is an exotic dish from the Polynesian islands

Chicken Tropicana

50 g (2 oz) (¼ cup) lard
4 chicken joints
1 large onion, sliced
350 g (¾ lb) (2 cups) canned pineapple cubes in syrup
150 ml (¼ pint) (⅝ cup) chicken stock
10 ml (2 teaspoons) ground ginger
5 ml (1 teaspoon) desiccated coconut
5 ml (1 teaspoon) Worcestershire sauce
salt and pepper
10 ml (2 teaspoons) cornflour (cornstarch)
toasted coconut strands and chopped fresh parsley to garnish

1 Heat the lard in the open pressure cooker and fry the chicken joints until lightly browned all over. Drain them from the cooker.

2 Fry the onion for about 3 minutes in the lard until it is softened. Drain the onion from the cooker and place it with the chicken pieces. Pour off excess fat from the cooker.

3 Drain the syrup from the canned pineapple and mix the syrup with the stock, ginger, coconut, Worcestershire sauce and seasoning. Pour the mixture into the pressure cooker and add the pineapple cubes, chicken joints and onion.

4 Close the cooker and bring it to 6.75 kg (15 lb) pressure. Cook for 5 minutes. Reduce the pressure under cold water. Transfer the chicken to a heated serving dish.

5 Dilute the cornflour (cornstarch) with a little water and stir it into the sauce in the open cooker. Stir constantly until the sauce thickens. Pour it over the chicken. Garnish the dish with toasted coconut strands and chopped fresh parsley, and serve at once.

Serves 4

Carrot and Orange Soup takes no time at all to make using a pressure cooker. Serve it with a swirl of cream

Fig Pudding

225 g (½ lb) figs
1 large cooking (green) apple
100 g (¼ lb) (½ cup) brown sugar
grated rind 1 lemon
50 ml (2 fl oz) (¼ cup) milk
100 g (¼ lb) (2 cups) fresh
 breadcrumbs
2 eggs, beaten
75 g (3 oz) (¾ cup) flour
pinch salt
100 g (¼ lb) (½ cup) melted
 margarine
1.1 litre (2 pints) (5 cups) water
juice 1 lemon

1 If the figs are very hard, soak them for 1 hour in boiling water and chop them roughly. Peel, core and chop the apple. Place the figs, apple, sugar and lemon rind in a bowl and mix well.

2 Warm the milk and pour it over the breadcrumbs. Add the beaten eggs and stir well before mixing with the figs and apple. Sift the flour and salt into the bowl and stir in the melted margarine.

3 Position the trivet in the pressure cooker and pour in the water and lemon juice. Pour the pudding mixture into a well-greased 1.1 litre (2 pint) (5 cup) pudding basin. Cover with a double thickness of greaseproof (parchment) paper, tied securely with clean string. A string handle, to facilitate lifting the basin out when hot, can be made by bringing a long end from the knot on one side over to the other. (A fitted lid is not recommended as it tends to cut the contents off from the steam.) The basin should be no more than three-quarters full.

4 Place the basin on the trivet. Position the lid on the cooker but do not adjust the weight or indicator or shut down the pressure valve. Heat gently and leave a gentle stream of steam coming from the steam escape for 15 minutes. Shut down the pressure valve and bring the cooker to 6.75 kg (15 lb) pressure. Cook for 45 minutes. Reduce the pressure under cold water. Serve the pudding with whipped cream.

Serves 4

Whiting in White Wine or Cider

4 whiting, scaled and gutted
15 ml (1 tablespoon) chopped
 parsley
2 mushrooms, sliced
4 spring onions (scallions),
 sliced
50 ml (2 fl oz) (¼ cup) white wine
 or cider
15 ml (1 tablespoon) lemon juice
300 ml (½ pint) (1¼ cups) cold
 water
salt and pepper

1 Place the whiting in the cooker and cover it with the remaining ingredients. Cover and bring to 6.75 kg (15 lb) pressure. Cook for 5 minutes and reduce the pressure under cold water.

2 Transfer the fish to a shallow serving dish and pour the contents of the cooker over them.

Serves 4

Poussins with Mushrooms

2 poussins
25 g (1 oz) (2 tablespoons) butter
100 g (¼ lb) mushrooms
5 ml (1 teaspoon) salt
freshly ground (milled) pepper
150 ml (¼ pint) (⅝ cup) vegetable
 stock
30 ml (2 tablespoons) dry sherry

1 Cut the poussins in half. Melt the butter in the cooker and add the poussins. Cook for about 5 minutes, turning them so that both sides are lightly browned. Slice the mushrooms and add them to the cooker with the salt, pepper and vegetable stock.

2 Seal and bring the cooker to 6.75 kg (15 lb) pressure. Cook for 8 minutes. Reduce the pressure under cold water.

3 Transfer the poussins and mushrooms to a warmed serving dish and keep them hot. Stir the sherry into the liquid in the

cooker. Reheat and strain the sauce over the dish. Serve with boiled asparagus and sautéed potatoes.

Serves 4

Jewish Fish Balls

450 g (1 lb) raw white fish,
 minced
1 egg, beaten
75 g (3 oz) matzo crumbs
1 small onion, finely chopped
salt and pepper
2.5 ml (½ teaspoon) sugar
flour for rolling
450 g (1 lb) carrots, sliced

For the Stock:
450 g (1 lb) fish bones
400 ml (14 fl oz) (1¾ cups) water
15 ml (1 tablespoon) chopped
 onion
1 clove
1 stick celery, diced
bouquet garni
salt and pepper

1 Prepare the stock: place the cleaned fish bones in the cooker with the water. Gradually bring to the boil. Skim thoroughly and add the onion, clove, celery, bouquet garni and seasoning. Bring to 6.75 kg (15 lb) pressure and cook for 10 minutes. Reduce the pressure with cold water and strain the stock.

2 In a bowl, combine the fish, beaten egg, matzo crumbs, onion, seasoning and sugar. Blend well. Roll the mixture into twelve 3.5 cm (1½ in) balls with floured hands. Place them in the cooker with the sliced carrots and strained stock. Seal and bring the cooker to 6.75 kg (15 lb) pressure. Cook for 4 minutes. Reduce the pressure under cold water.

3 Transfer the fish balls to a shallow serving dish and pour the contents of the cooker over them.

Serves 4

Jewish Fish Balls are coated in matzo crumbs, then quickly cooked in a pressure cooker with a delicious fish stock

Savoury Quiche
(Basic Recipe)

2 eggs
300 ml (½ pint) (1¼ cups) milk
pinch salt
pinch nutmeg

1 Beat the eggs for 5 minutes, then blend into the milk. Preheat the oven to 200°C, 400°F, gas 6.

2 Season with salt and nutmeg, then strain and pour into the prepared flan case until about two-thirds full. Bake in the preheated oven for 20 minutes, then reduce the oven temperature to 180°C, 350°F, gas 4 for the remaining 20-25 minutes baking time. Overall cooking time should be about 45 minutes. Serve hot or cold.

Makes enough to fill 20 cm (8 in) diameter flan case

Variations

Bacon Quiche
Sprinkle over flan base 100 g (¼ lb) fried bacon rashers (slices),

derinded and cut up. Pour over custard and bake as basic recipe.

Onion and Cheese Quiche
Sprinkle over flan base 50 g (2 oz) (½ cup) grated cheese, then top with a layer of fried sliced onions. Pour over custard and bake as basic recipe.

Tip: To thicken and enrich basic savoury custard, add 150 ml (¼ pint) (⅝ cup) thick béchamel sauce to basic custard.

Quiche Lorraine

3 thin rashers (slices streaky unsmoked bacon, derinded
25 g (1 oz) (4 tablespoons) butter, melted
1 x 20 cm (8 in) unbaked flan case (pie shell), 4 cm (1½ in) deep
100 g (¼ lb) (1 cup) grated hard cheese
3 eggs, beaten
200 ml (7 fl oz) (⅞ cup) single (light) cream
50 ml (2 fl oz) (¼ cup) milk

Quiche Lorraine – the classic French savoury custard flan

pinch salt and white pepper
pinch grated nutmeg
pinch cayenne pepper, optional

1 Scald the bacon and refresh, then cut into small pieces.

2 Set the oven at 190°C, 375°F, gas 5.

3 Brush melted butter over the bottom of the flan case (pie shell), then place on a greased baking (cookie) sheet. Sprinkle grated cheese over the pastry, then layer with the bacon pieces.

4 In a bowl blend the beaten eggs, cream, milk and the seasonings. Pour half the custard only into the flan case (pie shell). Bake in the preheated oven for 20 minutes, then remove and add the rest of the custard and bake for another 20 minutes longer. Serve hot or cold.

Makes 6 – 8 portions

Tip: Quiche Lorraine lends itself to countless variations: the cheese or bacon can be omitted, or instead of bacon use salt beef or garlic sausage.

231

Omelettes

The term 'omelette' is derived from the latin 'ova mellita', which, in the days of the Roman empire, consisted of a mixture of eggs and honey beaten together and baked.

Preparing the pan

Unless you have a non-stick omelette pan, it is best to prepare the pan you are going to use so that your omelettes are perfect every time. First of all, rub round the inside with coarse salt. Then cover the bottom of the pan with oil and heat it on the cooker for about 5 minutes or until the oil is hot. Tip away the oil. The pan is now ready to use.

Mushroom Omelette

½ lemon
300 g (scant ¾ lb) mushrooms
90 g (3½ oz) (⅓ cup + 1 tablespoon) butter
8 eggs
30 ml (2 tablespoons) cream
salt and pepper
small bunch parsley

1 Squeeze the half lemon.

2 Clean the mushrooms: cut off the base of the stalks and wash the mushrooms rapidly (do not let them soak). Slice them into thin strips. Sprinkle the lemon juice over them.

3 Melt 25 g (1 oz) (2 tablespoons) butter into a frying pan (skillet) and when it begins to turn golden put in the mushrooms. Cook until the juices have boiled away and the mushrooms are golden brown.

4 Cut about 25 g (1 oz) (2 tablespoons) butter into small pieces.

5 Break the eggs into a bowl. Add the pieces of butter, the cream, salt and pepper. Beat with a fork. When the eggs are frothy, stop beating.

6 Warm a serving dish. Wash and chop the parsley.

7 Melt the rest of the butter in the frying pan (skillet) and when it begins to turn golden pour in the egg mixture. Make the omelette.

8 When the omelette is done, i.e. set but still soft, tip 3 spoonsful of mushrooms over it. Fold it into half and slide it onto the serving dish.

9 Pile the rest of the mushrooms onto the dish around the omelette and sprinkle chopped parsley on top.

Serves 4

Mushroom omelette makes an excellent family meal accompanied by fried potatoes and salad

Spanish Omelette with Spiced Sausage

3 onions
2 peppers
450 g (1 lb) tomatoes
2 cloves garlic
100 ml (4 fl oz) (1 cup) oil
1 bouquet garni
salt and pepper
200 g (7 oz) chorizo
   (Spanish sausage)
150 ml (¼ pint) (⅝ cup) white stock
8 eggs

1 Peel the onions. Mince (grind) one and shred the other two. Wash and dry the peppers, and cut them in halves. Remove the pips and cut into thin strips. Skin and chop the tomatoes, discarding the seeds. Peel and crush the garlic.

2 To make the tomato puree: heat 25 ml (1 fl oz) of the oil in a small sauté pan. Add the minced (ground) onion. Cook until golden-brown, then add the tomatoes, the bouquet garni, and half of the crushed garlic. Season with salt and pepper. Cover and cook for 15 minutes over a slow heat.

3 In the meantime, cut the chorizo or other sliced sausage into thin slices.

4 Heat 50 ml (2 fl oz) oil in a frying pan (skillet). Add the chorizo, cook gently, then drain and keep warm.

5 Cook the shredded onions in the same oil until they are golden-brown. Add the peppers and cook until soft. Season with salt and pepper.

6 When the peppers begin to brown, add the rest of the garlic. Cook for another 5 minutes then remove from the heat and keep hot with the chorizo.

7 Pour the tomato purée through a fine strainer. Return to a low heat and thin with the stock. Adjust the seasoning and leave to cook over the low heat.

8 Break the eggs into a mixing bowl. Season with salt and pepper. Beat gently with a fork until frothy.

9 Heat the rest of the oil in a frying pan (skillet). When it is hot, pour in the beaten eggs, and mix, scraping the bottom of the pan with a fork. Before the eggs start to solidify add the onions, the pepper and the chorizo, stirring all the time.

10 When the omelette is cooked, place it on a warmed serving dish. Serve hot with the tomato sauce in a sauce-boat.

Serves 4

Rolled Omelettes

25 g (1 oz) (2¼ tablespoons) flour
3 beaten eggs
75 ml (2½ fl oz) (⅓ cup) milk
25 g (1 oz) (2 tablespoons) butter
pinch of chopped parsley or
   mixed herbs
pinch of salt and pepper

1 Sieve the flour and add the beaten eggs and milk. Season with salt and pepper and strain.

2 Add a pinch of chopped parsley or mixed herbs for flavouring.

3 Melt the butter in an omelette pan (skillet) and, when it is foaming, add the egg mixture. Stir it through and when it is cooked on one side, toss it over like a pancake and cook until golden-brown.

4 Remove the omelette from the pan (skillet) and spread with a filling. Roll up and serve.

Cheshire-Style

1 Sprinkle 50 g (2 oz) (½ cup) grated Cheshire cheese onto the cooked omelette. Add a few drops of Worcestershire sauce.

2 Place under a hot grill (broiler) to melt the cheese.

3 Roll up and serve.

Rolled Herb Omelette

bunch of fresh mixed herbs
   (chives, chervil, tarragon etc.)
6 eggs
salt and pepper
5 ml (1 tablespoon) oil
25 g (1 oz) (2 tablespoons) butter

1 Pick over the mixed herbs. Wash and dry them, then chop finely.

2 Break the eggs into a bowl. Add salt and pepper. Beat with a fork until the eggs are blended but not frothy.

3 Add the chopped herbs and mix in with the fork.

4 Melt the oil and butter together in a frying pan (skillet) until foaming and hot, then pour in the eggs. Stir, in all directions, with a wooden spoon or the back of a fork to prevent the cooked eggs from sticking to the pan.

5 When the omelette is cooked, but the eggs are still creamy, roll it up by tilting the pan and assisting the rolling with the wooden spoon or fork. Slide the rolled omelette to the edge of the pan.

6 Bring a heated serving dish to the edge of the pan. Lift the opposite side of the pan to turn out the omelette.

7 Serve immediately.

Serves 4

Tips: Always heat the serving dish and, if possible, the plates. Omelettes should be served either very hot or cold.

   If intending to serve an omelette cold, cook it more thoroughly. It should be quite set and no longer creamy.

   Cold omelettes make excellent picnic fare. They can also be served as a sandwich filling either whole in a French loaf or sliced and packed into rolls.

Savoury and Sweet Breads

French Baguette

100 ml (4 fl oz) ($\frac{1}{2}$ cup) milk
225 ml (8 fl oz) (1 cup) water
25 ml (1$\frac{1}{2}$ tablespoons) vegetable oil
25 ml (1$\frac{1}{2}$ tablespoons) castor (fine granulated) sugar
50 ml (2 fl oz) ($\frac{1}{4}$ cup) warm boiled water
10 ml (2 teaspoons) dried yeast
550 g (1$\frac{1}{4}$ lb) (5$\frac{5}{8}$ cups) strong white flour
15 ml (1 tablespoon) salt
1 egg white mixed with 15 ml (1 tablespoon) water

For the Starter:
30 ml (1 fl oz) (2 tablespoons) water
15 ml (1 tablespoon) milk
2.5 ml ($\frac{1}{2}$ teaspoon) vegetable oil
2.5 ml ($\frac{1}{2}$ teaspoon) castor (fine granulated) sugar
15 ml (1 tablespoon) warm boiled water
2.5 ml ($\frac{1}{2}$ teaspoon) dried yeast
5 ml (1 teaspoon) salt
50 g (2 oz) ($\frac{1}{2}$ cup) strong white flour

1 To make the starter, mix together the water, milk and oil in a pan, bring them to the boil and allow to cool until lukewarm. In a bowl, dissolve the sugar in the warm boiled water and stir in the yeast. Leave to rest for 6 minutes and add to the milk mixture. Stir in the salt. Add the liquid to the flour in a bowl, cover with a clean cloth and leave in a warm place for at least 12 hours.

2 To make the bread, mix the milk, water and oil in a pan; bring to the boil and cool to lukewarm. Dissolve $\frac{1}{3}$ of the sugar in the warm boiled water and stir in the yeast. Leave in a warm place until it becomes frothy.

3 Sift the flour into a mixing bowl. Make a hole in the middle and pour in the salt, milk mixture, yeast liquid and remaining sugar. Blend in the starter and stir without kneading, until well blended to a soft dough. Leave in a warm place until doubled in bulk.

4 Place the dough on a floured surface, divide into 2 equal parts and roll each into a rectangle of 38 x 25cm (15 x 10in). Roll each piece of dough tightly into a long stick, pinching to seal. Roll the ends to round off.

5 Grease a baking tray (cookie sheet) and place the loaves on it. Cut diagonal slashes along the tops of the loaves. Cover and leave to rise until doubled again in size.

6 Preheat the oven to 220°C, 425°F, gas 7. Bake for 15 minutes. Reduce the oven temperature to 180°C, 350°F, gas 4 and bake for 15 minutes more. Brush the tops of the loaves with the egg white and water mixture and return to the oven for 5 minutes. Cool on a wire rack in an airy place.

Makes 2

Fresh Yeast Rolls

15 g ($\frac{1}{2}$ oz) fresh yeast
300 ml ($\frac{1}{2}$ pint) (1$\frac{1}{4}$ cups) lukewarm water
450 g (1 lb) (4$\frac{1}{2}$ cups) strong white flour
10 ml (2 teaspoons) salt
5 ml (1 teaspoon) castor (fine granulated) sugar
15 ml (1 tablespoon) lard
15 ml (1 tablespoon) milk
30 ml (2 tablespoons) poppy seeds (optional)

1 Blend the yeast with the warm water. Sift the flour, salt and sugar into a large mixing bowl. Rub in the lard. Pour the yeast liquid into the bowl and blend the ingredients together, adding more flour if necessary, until the mixture leaves the sides of the bowl clean.

2 Knead the dough on a floured surface for several minutes until it is smooth and elastic. Cover with a greased polythene bag and leave in a warm place until it has doubled in bulk.

3 Divide the dough into small balls and knead each one lightly. Form the rolls into different shapes, as shown on pages 1476-9.

4 Place the rolls on a greased baking tray (cookie sheet) and leave to rise again. Preheat the oven to 220°C, 425°F, gas 7. Brush the tops of the rolls with milk to glaze, and sprinkle them with poppy seeds, if wished. Bake at the top of the oven for about 15 minutes until crisp and golden-brown. Cool on a rack and serve.

Makes 8-12 rolls

Variation

The same dough can be used to make a white loaf. Instead of dividing the dough, knock back the whole amount, place on a greased baking tray (cookie sheet), cover, and leave to rise again. Glaze with milk and cut a cross in the top. Bake for about 30 minutes.

Garlic Bread and Herb Bread

2 French Baguette loaves
1 or 2 cloves garlic
225 g ($\frac{1}{2}$ lb) (1 cup) butter
10 ml (2 teaspoons) finely chopped fresh parsley
10 ml (2 teaspoons) each: finely chopped fresh chives and tarragon, or chervil and marjoram

1 Cut the loaves at 2$\frac{1}{2}$cm (1 in) intervals just down to the bottom crust. Preheat the oven to 170°C, 325°F, gas 3.

2 Crush the garlic and blend with half of the butter. Spread some on one side of each cut in one loaf.

3 Cream the rest of the butter with the parsley and two other herbs. Spread the other loaf as for the Garlic Bread. Wrap the loaves in kitchen foil and bake for 10 minutes. Serve hot with soups, salads, or cheese.

Serves 6-8

Fresh Yeast Rolls can be made in a variety of attractive shapes; or you can use the dough to make a loaf (right)

Poppyseed Plaits (Braids)

675 g (1½ lb) (6¾ cups) strong
  plain flour
15 ml (1 tablespoon) salt
15 ml (1 tablespoon) lard
7.5 ml (1½ teaspoons) sugar
20 g (¾ oz) fresh yeast
400 ml (14 fl oz) (1¾ cups)
  lukewarm milk and water,
  mixed
milk to glaze
poppy seeds for sprinkling

1 Sieve the flour and salt into a bowl, rub in the lard and stir in the sugar.

2 Blend the yeast with the milk and water and mix with the flour.

3 Turn on to a floured surface and knead for about 10 minutes until smooth and elastic. Divide the dough into two pieces and knead each to a ball. Place in clean bowls, cover and leave in a warm place until doubled in size.

4 Preheat the oven to 200°C, 400°F, gas 6. Knead one ball of risen dough until smooth, divide into three pieces and roll each to a long sausage shape. Starting from the middle, plait (braid) the pieces together to one end. Turn the dough around and plait (braid) to the other end. Pinch the ends together well to seal.

5 For the second loaf: form the ball of dough into four long sausage shapes and pinch them together at the end furthest from you. Plait (braid) by passing the left-hand piece over to the right-hand gap, then pass the right-hand piece over to the left-hand gap. Continue to plait (braid) in this way and pinch the ends together well to seal.

6 Place the two loaves on a greased baking tray (cookie sheet) and leave in a warm place

Plaited (braided) milk bread may be eaten with savoury foods such as cheese or with a pot of home-made jam

for about 30 minutes until doubled in bulk.

7 Brush the loaves with milk and sprinkle with poppy seeds. Bake in the preheated oven for 30-35 minutes. Cool on a wire rack.

Makes 2 loaves

Greek Pitta Bread

1 quantity risen white bread dough (see page 1474)

1 Preheat the oven to 230°C, 450°F, gas 8. Form the risen dough into 5 balls and roll each to an oval, about 5 mm (¼ in) thick. Sprinkle them with flour, lay in a floured cloth and leave in a warm place until risen.

2 Place 2 or 3 oiled baking trays

(cookie sheets) in the oven for a few minutes to get hot. Slip the breads on to the sheets and brush the tops with cold water.

3 Bake for 6-10 minutes, then cool on a wire rack.

Makes 5 pitta breads

Tip: The pitta breads will have a pouch in the middle and, when cut in half, can be filled with salad and meat.

Jewish Bagels

5 ml (1 teaspoon) sugar
225 ml (8 fl oz) (1 cup) lukewarm
  milk
7.5 ml (1½ teaspoons) dried yeast
450 g (1 lb) (4½ cups) flour
5 ml (1 teaspoon) salt
2 eggs, beaten
30 ml (2 tablespoons) honey
30 ml (2 tablespoons) oil
1 egg yolk for brushing
poppy and sesame seeds

1 Dissolve the sugar in the milk, sprinkle the yeast over and leave in a warm place until frothy.

2 Add the yeast mixture to the flour, salt, beaten eggs, honey and oil. Knead until smooth and elastic.

3 Place in a greased bowl and leave in a warm place until doubled in bulk.

4 Preheat the oven to 230°C, 450°F, gas 8. Knead until smooth and divide into 15 pieces. Roll each to a 15 cm (6 in) rope and form into a ring, pinching the ends to seal. Leave on a floured surface for 10 minutes, until puffy.

5 Put the bagels into boiling water for 15 seconds, until puffy. Place them on a greased baking tray (cookie sheet). Beat the egg yolk with 5 ml (1 teaspoon) water, brush over the bagels and sprinkle them with poppy or sesame seeds. Bake for 10-15 minutes, then cool on a wire rack.

6 Serve the bagels warm or cold.

A Castle Roll is just one of many roll shapes to make — eat it with butter, Cheddar cheese and crisp pickled onions

They are delicious split, and filled with cream cheese, smoked fish or pâté.

Makes 15 bagels

Indian Nan Bread

75 ml (2½ fl oz) (5 tablespoons)
  plain yogurt
75 ml (2½ fl oz) (5 tablespoons)
  milk
5 ml (1 teaspoon) sugar
15 ml (1 tablespoon) dried yeast
275 g (10 oz) (2¾ cups) flour
1.25 ml (¼ teaspoon) salt
2.5 ml (½ teaspoon) bicarbonate
  of soda
1 egg, beaten
milk for brushing
sesame seeds for sprinkling

1 Blend the yogurt with the milk and heat to lukewarm. Stir in the sugar, sprinkle the yeast over and leave in a warm place for 10-15 minutes until frothy.

2 Add the yeast mixture to the flour, salt, bicarbonate of soda and egg. Knead on a floured surface until smooth and elastic. Place in a bowl, cover, and leave in a warm place until well-risen.

3 Preheat the oven to 230°C, 450°F, gas 8. Divide the dough into 4 pieces and, with floured hands, knead each to a ball. Flatten each to an oval, about 25 cm (10 in) long, and pull to a 'shoe sole' shape. Place them on greased baking trays (cookie sheets), brush with milk and sprinkle generously with sesame seeds.

4 Bake for about 7 minutes, until golden-brown. Serve the nan breads immediately, keeping them warm if necessary by wrapping them in a clean cloth.

Makes 4 nan breads

Brown Bread

The nutty wholesome flavour of brown wholegrain breads has been enjoyed by more people in the last 10 years than at any other time this century. Whether it is a plain wheatmeal or made with dried fruits, nuts and honey, this bread is a meal in itself.

Wholemeal Bread

350 g (12 oz) (3 cups) wholemeal flour
5 ml (1 teaspoon) salt
10 ml (2 teaspoons) lard
10 ml (2 teaspoons) castor (fine granulated) sugar
225 ml (8 fl oz) (1 cup) lukewarm water
7.5 ml (1½ teaspoons) dried yeast
15 ml (1 tablespoon) milk
30 ml (2 tablespoons) cracked wheat

1 Place the flour and salt in a bowl and rub in the lard. Dissolve the sugar in the lukewarm water and sprinkle over the yeast. Leave to rest in a warm place for 15 minutes or until frothy.

2 Pour the yeast liquid into the flour and mix until the dough leaves the sides of the bowl. Turn the dough on to a floured board and knead until it is smooth and elastic.

3 Return the dough to a clean bowl and cover it loosely with a greased polythene bag. Leave it to rise in a warm place until the dough has doubled in size. Knock back the risen dough and knead until smooth.

4 Divide the dough into 3 equal pieces and form each piece into a roll 38 cm (15 in) long. Gather the rolls together at one end and plait (braid) them, tucking under the ends. Place the plait (braid) on a well-greased baking tray (cookie sheet). Cover with greased polythene and let it rest in a warm place until it has doubled in size.

5 Preheat the oven to 230°C, 450°F, gas 8.

6 Remove the polythene and brush the plait (braid) lightly with milk. Sprinkle it with the cracked wheat and bake in the oven for 20-25 minutes.

Makes 1 loaf

Malt Bread

5 ml (1 teaspoon) sugar
200 ml (6 fl oz) (¾ cup) warm water
15 ml (1 tablespoon) dried yeast
45 ml (3 tablespoons) malt extract
30 ml (2 tablespoons) black treacle (molasses)
25 g (1 oz) (2 tablespoons) margarine
450 g (1 lb) (4½ cups) plain flour
5 ml (1 teaspoon) salt
225 g (½ lb) (1 cup + 2 tablespoons) seedless raisins
30 ml (2 tablespoons) honey

1 Dissolve the sugar in the water and sprinkle over the yeast. Leave in a warm place for 15 minutes until frothy.

2 In a saucepan heat the malt extract, treacle (molasses) and margarine, stirring continually until well blended. Remove from the heat.

3 Sieve the flour and salt into a bowl and mix in the raisins. Stir in the yeast liquid and malt mixture. Work to a soft dough that leaves the bowl clean. Turn the dough out on to a floured board and knead until it is smooth and elastic.

4 Preheat the oven to 200°C, 400°F, gas 6.

5 Divide the dough in half and roll up each piece to make a loaf. Place the loaves in 2 greased 450 g (1 lb) loaf tins (pans) and cover with greased polythene. Leave to prove for 1¼ hours or until they have doubled in size.

6 Remove the polythene and bake the loaves on the middle shelf of the oven for 40-45 minutes. Brush the top with honey and leave them to cool.

Makes two 450 g (1 lb) loaves

Mixed Whole Grain Bread

5 ml (1 teaspoon) sugar
150 ml (¼ pint) (⅝ cup) lukewarm water
15 ml (1 tablespoon) dried yeast
300 ml (½ pint) (1¼ cups) boiling water
70 ml (2½ fl oz) (⅓ cup) honey
15 ml (1 tablespoon) salt
40 g (1½ oz) (3 tablespoons) butter
175 g (6 oz) (1½ cups) wholewheat flour
90 g (3½ oz) (1 cup) rye flour
75 g (3 oz) (1 cup) rolled oats
15 ml (1 tablespoon) grated orange rind

1 Dissolve the sugar into the water and sprinkle over the yeast. Leave in a warm place for 15 minutes or until frothy.

2 In a bowl, stir together the boiling water, honey, salt and butter until well blended. Leave to cool slightly. Stir in the yeast liquid, flours and rolled oats until well mixed. Cover the bowl with a greased polythene bag and leave it in a warm place until it has doubled in size.

3 Knock back the dough and knead in the orange rind. Turn the dough into a well-greased 450 g (1 lb) loaf tin (pan). Cover and leave it to prove in a warm place until it has doubled in size.

4 Preheat the oven to 180°C, 350°F, gas 4. Remove the polythene and bake the loaf for 1 hour.

Makes one 450 g (1 lb) loaf

Wheatmeal Bread can be plaited (braided) or baked in a flowerpot, as well as moulded into more familiar loaf shapes

Granary Bread

275 g (10 oz) (2¾ cups) strong plain flour
275 g (10 oz) (2½ cups) wholewheat flour
15 ml (1 tablespoon) salt
15 ml (1 tablespoon) butter
50 g (2 oz) (⅔ cup) wheatgerm
100 g (¼ lb) (⅝ cup) cracked wheat
5 ml (1 teaspoon) sugar
400 ml (14 fl oz) (1¾ cups) warm water and milk, mixed in equal quantities
10 ml (2 teaspoons) dried yeast
30 ml (2 tablespoons) malt extract
15 ml (1 tablespoon) milk

1 Sift the flours and salt into a mixing bowl. Rub in the butter with your fingertips and mix in the wheatgerm and cracked wheat.

2 Dissolve the sugar in the water and milk and sprinkle in the dried yeast. Leave for about 10 minutes.

3 Make a well in the centre of the flours and pour in the yeast mixture. Add the malt extract and mix well to form a soft dough.

4 Knead the dough on a lightly floured surface for about 10 minutes.

5 Place the dough in an oiled polythene bag and leave until doubled in size. Knead the dough again and shape into a loaf, or divide into two and shape into two loaves. Place in a greased 900 g (2 lb) loaf tin (pan), or use two 450 g (1 lb) tins (pans). Cover and leave to prove until doubled in size.

6 Meanwhile, heat the oven to 220°C, 425°F, gas 7. When risen, brush with milk and bake the bread in the centre of the oven for about 35 minutes. You can, if wished, sprinkle the loaves with cracked wheat for a more attractive appearance and crunchy texture.

Makes two 450 g (1 lb) loaves or one 900 g (2 lb) loaf

Tip: You can buy a special granary flour mix in many delicatessens and supermarkets.

Rye Bread

150 g (5 oz) (1⅜ cups) strong plain flour
200 g (7 oz) (2 cups) rye meal
10 ml (2 teaspoons) salt
5 ml (1 teaspoon) caraway seeds
5 ml (1 teaspoon) sugar
225 ml (8 fl oz) (1 cup) warm water
10 ml (2 teaspoons) dried yeast
a little beaten egg

Rye Bread tastes especially good when served with a creamy cheese and salad. It has a coarse texture and yeasty flavour

1 Place the flours, salt and caraway seeds in a mixing bowl.

2 Dissolve the sugar in the warm water and sprinkle in the yeast. Leave for about 10 minutes until frothy.

3 Make a well in the flour and mix in the yeast mixture to form a stiff dough. Knead well for 10 minutes on a lightly floured surface. Place in an oiled polythene bag and leave in a warm place until doubled in size.

4 Knock back the dough, knead again and shape into an elongated loaf. Make some diagonal slits along the top with a sharp knife and place on a greased bak-

266

2 eggs
275 g (10 oz) (2¾ cups) self-raising
 flour
pinch salt
50 g (2 oz) (⅔ cup) chopped walnuts
100 g (¼ lb) (¾ cup) crystallized
 ginger, chopped
100 g (¼ lb) (¾ cup) dates, chopped
15 walnut halves
30 ml (2 tablespoons) apricot jam,
 melted

1 Preheat the oven to 180°C, 350°F, gas 4.

2 Peel, core and slice the apples and place in a pan with 30 ml (1 fl oz) (2 tablespoons) water. Cover and simmer gently until the apples are soft. Mash the cooked apples with a wooden spoon, then leave to cool.

3 Cream the butter and sugar, then beat in the eggs. Sieve the flour and salt and fold into the mixture. Mix to a soft, dropping consistency with the apple purée.

4 Stir the chopped walnuts, ginger and dates into the mixture and transfer to a greased 900 g (2 lb) loaf tin (pan). Bake in the preheated oven for 1¼ hours. Cool on a wire rack.

Nutty Apple Cake is covered with a delicious mixture of apple slices and chopped nuts in a spicy flavoured syrup

5 Arrange the walnut halves over the cold teabread and brush with the melted apricot jam.

Serves 6-8

Nutty Apple Cake

225 g (½ lb) (2¼ cups) flour
10 ml (2 teaspoons) baking
 powder
1.25 ml (¼ teaspoon) salt
40 g (1½ oz) (3 tablespoons)
 margarine
30 ml (2 tablespoons) sugar
1 egg
150 ml (¼ pint) (⅝ cup) milk
25 g (1 oz) (2 tablespoons) butter
45 ml (3 tablespoons) soft brown
 sugar
1.25 ml (¼ teaspoon) cinnamon
1.25 ml (¼ teaspoon) nutmeg
450 g (1 lb) cooking (green) apples

50 g (2 oz) (¼ cup) demerara sugar
50 g (2 oz) (⅔ cup) chopped nuts

1 Preheat the oven to 180°C, 350°F, gas 4.

2 Sieve the flour, baking powder and salt into a bowl. Rub in the margarine and stir in the sugar.

3 Beat the egg with the milk and stir into the flour to form a soft dough.

4 Combine the butter with the brown sugar and spices, and spread over the base of a 27 x 18 cm (11 x 7 in) shallow cake tin (pan).

5 Peel, quarter, core and thinly slice the apples and arrange over the spicy mixture. Pat out the dough and place it over the apples, pressing it into the corners of the tin (pan).

6 Bake in the preheated oven for 45 minutes, then turn on to a wire rack.

7 Mix together the demerara sugar and chopped nuts and sprinkle on top of the cake while it is still warm. Allow to cool completely.

Serves 6-8

Latticed Apple Cake

175 g (6 oz) (¾ cup) butter
175 g (6 oz) (¾ cup) castor (fine granulated) sugar
4 eggs
grated rind ½ lemon
225 g (½ lb) (2¼ cups) plain flour, sieved
10 ml (2 teaspoons) baking powder

For the Topping:
350 g (¾ lb) apples, peeled, cored and sliced
25 g (1 oz) (2 tablespoons) sugar
100 g (¼ lb) (⅜ cup) apricot jam
225 g (½ lb) marzipan
15 ml (1 tablespoon) icing (confectioners') sugar

1 Preheat the oven to 180°C, 350°F, gas 4. Cream the butter and sugar until light and fluffy. Then beat in the eggs, one at a time. Stir in the lemon rind.

2 Gradually fold in the sieved flour and the baking powder with a metal spoon. Place the mixture in a greased and lined 20 cm (8 in) cake tin (pan). Make a slight well in the centre of the top of the mixture. Bake for about 45 minutes until cooked and golden.

3 Meanwhile, place the apples and sugar in a small pan and cook gently over low heat until soft. Mix in half of the apricot jam. Put aside.

4 Roll out the marzipan, 1 cm (½ in) thick and cut into long strips.

5 When the cake is cooked, remove from the oven and spread the top with the apple mixture. Arrange the marzipan strips in a criss-cross pattern across the top and around the edge to form a border. Place a spoonful of the remaining apricot jam in each gap between the strips.

6 Increase the oven temperature to 200°C, 400°F, gas 6. Bake the cake for a further 10-20 minutes until the marzipan is pale golden.

7 Remove the cake from the tin (pan) and cool, then dust with icing (confectioners') sugar.

Serves 6-8

Latticed Apple Cake, topped with apple purée and apricot jam, is decorated with a lattice of marzipan strips

Apple Gingerbread Cake

100 g (¼ lb) (½ cup) butter
100 g (¼ lb) (½ cup) soft brown sugar
grated rind and juice 1 lemon
2 eggs
100 g (¼ lb) (1⅛ cups) self-raising flour, sieved
2.5 ml (½ teaspoon) salt
2.5 ml (½ teaspoon) grated nutmeg
7.5 ml (1½ teaspoons) ground ginger
6 glacé cherries

For the Topping:
50 g (2 oz) (¼ cup) butter
50 g (2 oz) (¼ cup) soft brown sugar
2 dessert apples, peeled, cored and sliced

1 Preheat the oven to 170°C, 325°F, gas 3. Cream the butter, soft brown sugar, lemon rind and juice until fluffy. Beat in the eggs, one at a time.

2 Fold in the sieved flour, salt, nutmeg and ginger with a metal spoon.

3 Make the topping: cream the butter and sugar and spread the mixture across the base and sides of a 20 cm (8 in) cake tin (pan). Arrange the apple slices across the base. Fill the tin (pan) with the cake mixture, then bake for about 45 minutes until cooked.

4 Turn out the cake on to an attractive serving dish and decorate with the glacé cherries.

Serves 6-8

Tips: You can serve this cake either cold at teatime with lashings of cream, or hot as a dessert with cream or custard.

Apple Gingerbread Cake has a delicious, sticky glazing and is topped with golden apple slices and glacé cherries

Cherry and Walnut Christmas Cake

fat for greasing
175 g (6 oz) (½ cup) glacé cherries
50 g (2 oz) preserved ginger
100 g (¼ lb) (1½ cups) walnuts
225 g (½ lb) (1⅓ cups) raisins
175 g (6 oz) (1 cup) ground
    almonds
350 g (12 oz) (1½ cups) butter
350 g (12 oz) (1½ cups) castor (fine
    granulated) sugar
4 eggs
5 ml (1 teaspoon) vanilla essence
350 g (12 oz) (3¾ cups) flour
5 ml (1 teaspoon) baking powder

For the Sherry Almond Paste:
100 g (¼ lb) (⅔ cup) ground almonds
50 g (2 oz) (¼ cup) castor (fine
    granulated) sugar
50 g (2 oz) (⅜ cup) icing
    (confectioners') sugar
10 ml (2 teaspoons) dry sherry
a little lightly beaten egg white
icing (confectioners') sugar for
    dusting
45 ml (3 tablespoons) apricot jam

For the Snow Icing:
275 g (10 oz) (2 cups) icing
    (confectioners') sugar
5 ml (1 teaspoon) softened butter
2.5 ml (½ teaspoon) vanilla
    essence
15 ml (1 tablespoon) milk

1 Preheat the oven to 150°C, 300°F, gas 2. Grease and line a 20 cm (8 in) square cake tin (pan) and grease again.

2 Wash, dry and halve the cherries. Roughly chop the ginger and walnuts and mix with the raisins and ground almonds.

3 Cream the butter and sugar until light and fluffy. Beat in the eggs and vanilla essence. Sieve the flour with the baking powder and fold in with the fruit mixture.

4 Turn the mixture into the prepared cake tin (pan) and bake in the preheated oven for 30 minutes. Reduce the oven temperature to 140°C, 275°F, gas 1, and bake for a further 2½ hours. Leave to cool in the tin (pan).

5 Make the Sherry Almond Paste: mix the ground almonds

with the sugars and stir in the sherry. Add enough egg white to form a firm paste.

6 Lightly dust the table with icing (confectioners') sugar and roll out the almond paste to a square a little larger than the top of the cake.

7 Melt and sieve the apricot jam and brush over the top of the cake. Place the almond paste on top. Cut a very thin slice from each side of the cake, removing the crust and trimming the almond

Cherry and Walnut Christmas Cake is less rich in flavour and lighter in colour than most other festive fruit cakes

paste at the same time.

8 Make the Snow Icing: sieve the sugar into a bowl and add the butter and vanilla. Gradually beat in the milk until the icing is of a smooth coating consistency, adding a little extra milk if necessary.

9 Spread the icing over the top of the cake and swirl it with a knife. Leave to set.

Makes one 20 cm (8 in) cake

Tip: To test if the cake is cooked, insert a warmed skewer in the centre. If any mixture clings to the skewer, the cake is not yet cooked.

Almond Cakes

Crisp and crunchy almond fancies that melt in your mouth are quick and easy to prepare and taste delicious with freshly brewed coffee.

Japonaise Fancies

2 egg whites
100 g ($\frac{1}{4}$ lb) ($\frac{1}{2}$ cup) castor (fine granulated) sugar
50 g (2 oz) ($\frac{1}{2}$ cup) ground almonds

1 First prepare the basic mixture. Place the egg whites in a bowl and whisk until they form stiff peaks. Add 50 g (2 oz) ($\frac{1}{4}$ cup) of the castor (fine granulated) sugar and beat to a strong meringue.

2 Mix the ground almonds with the remaining sugar and fold them gently into the meringue. This mixture is sufficient to make 6 Almond Nibbles, 8 Almond Cream Fancies or 8 Chocolate Surprises. Now, preheat the oven to 180°C, 350°F, gas 4.

Almond Nibbles
1 Fill a piping (decorator's) bag fitted with a 2.5 cm (1 in) plain nozzle with the mixture and pipe 12 fingers on a greased baking (cookie) sheet. Dust with castor (fine granulated) sugar and sprinkle them with 25 g (1 oz) ($\frac{1}{4}$ cup) of chopped almonds. Bake for 20 minutes or until they are just beginning to colour. Cool.

2 Melt 25 g (1 oz) of chocolate and use it to drizzle half the fingers. Whip 150 ml ($\frac{1}{4}$ pint) ($\frac{5}{8}$ cup) of double (heavy) cream. Sandwich the fingers, chocolate drizzled ones uppermost, with the whipped cream.

Almond Cream Fancies
1 Fill a piping (decorator's) bag fitted with a 2.5 cm (1 in) plain nozzle with the mixture and pipe

Almond Nibbles, Almond Cream Fancies and Chocolate Surprises are all made from the basic japonaise fancy mixture

16 buttons on to a greased baking (cookie) sheet. Dust them with castor (fine granulated) sugar and sprinkle them with 50 g (2 oz) ($\frac{3}{8}$ cup) of flaked almonds. Bake for 20 minutes and cool on a rack.

2 Melt 50 g (2 oz) of chocolate and use it to drizzle over each biscuit. When the chocolate sets, sandwich the buttons together with 150 ml ($\frac{1}{4}$ pint) ($\frac{5}{8}$ cup) of whipped double (heavy) cream and decorate each one with a glacé cherry.

Chocolate Surprises
1 Fill a piping (decorator's) bag fitted with a plain nozzle with the mixture and pipe 16 buttons onto a greased baking (cookie) sheet.

Dust with castor (fine granulated) sugar and sprinkle them with 50 g (2 oz) ($\frac{1}{2}$ cup) of chopped almonds. Bake for 20 minutes. Cool.

2 Melt 100 g ($\frac{1}{4}$ lb) of chocolate. Dip half the buttons in the chocolate and shake off the excess. Allow the chocolate to set and sandwich the buttons with 150 ml ($\frac{1}{4}$ pint) ($\frac{5}{8}$ cup) of whipped double (heavy) cream.

Lemon Macaroon Tartlets

sweet shortcrust (pie crust) made with 225 g ($\frac{1}{2}$ lb) ($2\frac{1}{4}$ cups) flour
grated rind 1 lemon

50 g (2 oz) (½ cup) ground almonds
100 g (¼ lb) (½ cup) sugar
5 ml (1 teaspoon) ground rice
1 egg, beaten
100 g (¼ lb) (⅜ cup) apricot jam
50 g (2 oz) (½ cup) flaked almonds
few pistachio nuts, chopped

For the Glaze:
apricot jam
lemon water icing

1 Preheat the oven to 190°C, 375°F, gas 5. Roll out the pastry and use it to line 16 deep fluted tartlet tins (pans).

2 Mix the lemon rind, almonds, sugar, rice and egg to a smooth paste.

3 Prick the pastry with a fork and spot each one with a little apricot jam. Fill the tartlets with the almond paste and sprinkle with flaked almonds. Bake for 20 minutes. Cool.

Jam, Fruit and Lemon Macaroon Tartlets are just three ways of using the macaroon mixture. Try other shapes and designs

4 Glaze each tartlet with hot apricot jam and lemon water icing. Sprinkle with chopped pistachio nuts and return to the oven for 30 seconds to set the icing.

Makes 16

Jam Macaroon Tartlets

sweet shortcrust (pie crust)
    made with 225 g (½ lb) (2¼ cups)
    flour
50 g (2 oz) (½ cup) ground almonds

100 g (¼ lb) (½ cup) sugar
5 ml (1 teaspoon) ground rice
1 egg
100 g (¼ lb) (⅜ cup) apricot jam
castor (fine granulated) sugar
    for dusting
15 ml (1 tablespoon) flaked
    almonds

1 Preheat the oven to 190°C, 375°F, gas 5. Roll out the pastry and use it to line 8 round tartlet tins (pans) and 8 small 'boat-shaped' tins (pans). Prick the pastry with a fork.

2 Mix the almonds, sugar, rice and egg to a smooth paste. Place 5ml (1 teaspoon) of the apricot jam in each pan and fill with the almond paste. Dust each with castor (fine granulated) sugar and sprinkle a few flaked almonds over each 'boat.' Bake for 20 minutes. Cool.

Makes 16

Fruit Macaroon Tartlets

sweet shortcrust (pie crust)
    made with 225 g (½ lb) (2¼ cups)
    flour
50 g (2 oz) (½ cup) ground almonds
100 g (¼ lb) (½ cup) sugar
5 ml (1 teaspoon) ground rice
1 large egg
100 g (¼ lb) mixed dried fruits
100 g (¼ lb) apples, peeled, cored
    and chopped
castor (fine granulated) sugar
    for dusting

1 Preheat the oven to 190°C, 375°F, gas 5. Roll out the pastry and use it to line 16 small tartlet tins (pans). Prick the pastry with a fork.

2 Mix the almonds, sugar, rice and egg to a smooth paste.

3 Place a little of the mixed fruits and chopped apple in each tin (pan). Top with the macaroon mixture and smooth the top. Sprinkle each tartlet with a little castor (fine granulated) sugar and bake for 20 minutes.

Makes 16

Labour Savers

All about Home-Freezing

Orange Bombe

A freezer can be a godsend, saving you both time and money – ideal for the busy working wife and mother who can cook meals in advance and freeze them until needed. Another advantage is that you can buy in bulk and thus save money on food bills. Seasonal vegetables and fruit can be bought when they are cheap and plentiful and frozen for use later in the year.

Care and Maintenance
Freezers more or less look after themselves, but you should have your freezer serviced annually and clean it thoroughly at least once every 6 months. Remove all the packages inside and wrap them in thick sheets of newspaper or blankets to keep them in their frozen state, otherwise they will thaw. Cut off the electricity supply to the freezer and fill it with large bowls of boiling water. Then scrape off the ice from the bottom and sides of the freezer, using a plastic scraper. Wipe the inside dry with a clean cloth and turn on the current. When the temperature drops, return the frozen packages to the freezer.

Emergencies
A common worry among new freezer-owners is what to do in the event of a power cut or breakdown, or even when moving house. You can, of course, insure the contents of your freezer against such exigencies. The first rule to remember in the event of a power failure is *not* on any account to open the freezer door. If the door remains closed and no warm air is allowed to enter, the contents will stay frozen for at least 12 hours. Food which has started to thaw but is still full of ice crystals may be safely refrozen, as with bread, unfilled pastry, plain cakes and fruit. However, all fish, meat and poultry, and pre-cooked foods which have thawed, should be eaten straight away or thrown out. If you are moving house, just pack newspaper and blankets around the packages inside and move the freezer with its contents intact.

Equipment and Packaging
Always make sure that food is correctly wrapped before freezing. Polythene bags, aluminium foil, plastic airtight containers, waxed freezer paper and tin foil containers are all suitable for freezing. Always label these studiously with the name of the contents and when frozen. Remember that one frozen package looks very like another and it may be difficult to distinguish a frozen curry from a rich tomato sauce, or a meat pie from a fruit one. Casseroled meals can be frozen in strong fireproof dishes which saves time when reheating. Don't throw away ice-cream containers, yogurt cartons and margarine tubs – they all make useful containers. You can make packages airtight with a special freezer tape – the common adhesive tape will not work. Always squeeze out as much air as possible before sealing polythene bags. Separate individual items such as rissoles or croquettes with waxed paper. When you freeze liquids, allow 1 cm ($\frac{1}{2}$ in) at the top of the container for expansion on freezing.

Freezing Vegetables and Fruit
Vegetables should be frozen only if really fresh and unblemished. Most vegetables need to be blanched in boiling water before freezing. The length of time will depend on the individual vegetable. Best quality fruit can be frozen whole, but it is better to purée over-ripe fruit before freezing. You can use the purées for pie and crumble fillings as well as drinks and mousses. Always wash fruit and vegetables thoroughly before freezing. You can prepare them ready for cooking; for example, apples, carrots and runner beans are best sliced, cauliflower divided into florets and mushrooms and Brussels sprouts left whole. Soft fruits such as strawberries and raspberries which do not freeze well and tend to go mushy, may be better puréed.

Freezing Meat
You can save money if you buy meat in bulk for your freezer. Many butchers and home-freezer centres sell whole or half-carcasses as well as discount bulk packs. When freezing meat, trim off any excess fat and don't freeze bones unnecessarily – they take up valuable space. Place waxed or greaseproof (parchment) paper between steaks, chops, hamburgers and individual portions to prevent them freezing in a solid lump. Wrap the meat completely in clingfilm or aluminium foil and seal in polythene bags. You can either cook the meat in its frozen state or thaw it first. Steaks, chops and hamburgers are easily and quickly cooked while frozen, but it is probably better to thaw large joints before roasting. This takes, per 450g (1lb), about 6 hours in a refrigerator or 3 hours at room temperature.

Freezing Poultry
Take extra care with frozen poultry, especially when thawing. Always clean and truss the bird before freezing and pack in a sealed polythene bag. All poultry and game birds must be *completely* thawed before cooking – thaw in the polythene wrapping either in the refrigerator or at room temperature.

Freezing Fish
Only freeze freshly caught fish within 12 hours of being caught. Scale and gut the fish and remove the head and tail. Rub with a little olive oil and seal in a polythene bag or airtight container. Thaw whole fish before cooking – this is not necessary with fillets and steaks.

Freezing Cooked Foods
Always cool cooked foods before placing in the freezer. When freezing cooked meat, make sure that it does not come into contact with fresh meat or poultry. Undercook, rather than overcook, dishes which are to be frozen, allowing for the fact that they will need reheating at a later date. Aluminium foil dishes and plastic containers are generally best for freezing cooked foods. If you have to add an egg yolk or some cream to a dish, it is best to do so after freezing. Among those foods which should not be frozen are: mayonnaise, custard, hard-boiled eggs, soft meringue, salad vegetables and stuffed poultry, also soufflés and mousses which contain gelatine.

You can freeze almost anything from sweet and savoury pies to fresh fruit and vegetables and even bread loaves

Deep-fried Chicken Balls

675 g (1½ lb) cooked chicken, minced
50 g (2 oz) (¼ cup) minced pork fat
4 water chestnuts, minced
1 spring onion (scallion), minced
1 thin slice fresh root ginger, minced
1 egg
15 ml (1 tablespoon) cornflour (cornstarch)
2.5 ml (½ teaspoon) salt
15 ml (1 tablespoon) sherry
oil for deep frying
150 ml (¼ pint) (⅝ cup) coating batter

1 In a bowl, mix the chicken, fat, water chestnuts, spring onion (scallion), ginger, egg, cornflour (cornstarch), salt and sherry until smooth. Form the mixture into balls, 4 cm (1½ in) in diameter.

2 Heat the oil for deep frying. Dip the chicken balls, a few at a time, in the batter and fry them in the oil until light golden-brown. Drain and leave to cool. Place in a rigid container. Seal, label and freeze. To serve, re-fry the chicken balls in oil, heated for deep frying, until dark golden-brown. Drain and serve.

Serves 4

Fried Vegetables

oil for frying
275 g (10 oz) canned bamboo shoots, drained and sliced
1 green pepper, deseeded and sliced
1 leek, sliced
225 g (½ lb) bean sprouts
2 sticks celery, sliced

For the Sauce:
30 ml (2 tablespoons) vinegar
25 g (1 oz) (2 tablespoons) sugar
15 ml (1 tablespoon) tomato ketchup (catsup)
10 ml (2 teaspoons) cornflour (cornstarch)
50 ml (2 fl oz) (¼ cup) water

1 Heat the oil in a pan and fry all the vegetables, stirring frequently, for 3 minutes. Blend all the sauce ingredients and pour them over the vegetables. Stir over a moderate heat until the sauce thickens. Serve.

2 To freeze: leave to cool before pouring the mixture into a rigid container. Seal, label and freeze. Thaw the vegetables in the refrigerator before reheating. Serve with the Deep-fried Chicken balls and fried egg noodles.

Serves 6

Creamed Chinese Chicken

one 1.5 kg (3 lb) chicken
45 ml (3 tablespoons) seasoned flour
25 g (1 oz) (2 tablespoons) butter
25 g (1 oz) (¼ cup) blanched almonds
225 g (½ lb) bamboo shoots, sliced
salt and pepper
150 ml (¼ pint) (⅝ cup) chicken stock
100 ml (4 fl oz) (½ cup) sour cream

1 Preheat the oven to 180°C, 350°F, gas 4. Dust the chicken with seasoned flour. Melt the butter in a large pan and brown the chicken all over. Transfer the chicken to a large ovenproof casserole, lined with a double layer of aluminium foil.

2 Cut the almonds into strips and brown them lightly in the pan. Add them to the casserole with the bamboo shoots, seasoning and stock. Cover and cook in the oven for 1 hour. Then, remove the lid and pour the sour cream over the chicken, mixing it well with the gravy. Baste and cook for 30 minutes more before serving.

3 To freeze: allow the chicken to thoroughly cool in the casserole. Fold the tin foil over the top and place it in the freezer until firm. Lift the chicken and foil intact from the casserole and place it in a polythene bag. Seal and label before returning it to the freezer.

4 To serve: replace the chicken wrapped in foil in a casserole and leave it to thaw in the refrigerator overnight. Place it in the oven set at 180°C, 350°F, gas 4 for 25-30 minutes. Serve with boiled rice.

Serves 4-5

Chinese Walnut Chicken

45 ml (3 tablespoons) oil
100 g (¼ lb) chopped walnuts
350 g (¾ lb) chicken, cooked and cut into strips
pinch salt
1 large onion, sliced
4 celery stalks, thinly sliced
300 ml (½ pint) (1¼ cups) chicken stock
15 ml (1 tablespoon) cornflour (cornstarch)
30 ml (2 tablespoons) dry sherry
5 ml (1 teaspoon) sugar
45 ml (3 tablespoons) soya sauce
275 g (10 oz) canned water chestnuts, drained and sliced
225 g (½ lb) canned bamboo shoots, drained

1 Heat the oil in a pan and fry the walnuts until golden. Remove and drain. Add the chicken and fry for a few minutes. Remove and sprinkle with salt. Place the onion, celery and half of the stock in the same pan and cook for 5 minutes. Mix the cornflour (cornstarch) with the sherry, sugar, soya sauce and remaining stock. Add to the pan, stirring continuously until the sauce comes to the boil and thickens. Add the water chestnuts, bamboo shoots and walnuts with the chicken and heat through. Serve.

2 To freeze, allow the mixture to cool before transferring it to a rigid container. Seal, label and freeze. Thaw in the refrigerator and reheat in a pan.

Serves 4

Creamed Chinese Chicken and Chinese Walnut Chicken are pictured with Deep-fried Chicken Balls and Fried Vegetables

265

Ragoût de Boeuf à l'Orange

30 ml (2 tablespoons) oil or bacon fat
675 g (1½ lb) stewing steak, cubed
12 button onions
15 ml (1 tablespoon) flour
100 ml (4 fl oz) (½ cup) red wine
bouquet garni
1 clove garlic, crushed
550 ml (1 pint) (2½ cups) stock
salt and pepper
5 sticks celery, sliced
50 g (2 oz) (⅜ cup) walnuts
25 g (1 oz) (2 tablespoons) butter
30 ml (2 tablespoons) shredded orange rind, blanched

1 Heat the oil or fat and fry the meat until well-browned. Remove and keep warm. In the same pan, cook the onions gently until golden-brown. Stir in the flour and cook over a low heat for 2-3 minutes.

2 Add the wine, bouquet garni, garlic and stock and bring to the boil. Season to taste, stir in the meat and reduce the heat. Cover with a lid and cook for 1½-2 hours gently, stirring occasionally.

3 If you wish to eat this dish straight away, or at least part of it, fry the celery and walnuts in the butter and add to the ragoût. Serve at once, garnished with the orange shreds.

4 To freeze: do not add the celery and walnuts, but cool the cooked ragoût before placing in a plastic or foil container. Seal, label and freeze. When ready to use, thaw the ragoût overnight in the refrigerator and reheat slowly over a low heat, stirring well. Cook the walnuts and celery as outlined above, and add to the ragoût. Serve, sprinkled with orange shreds, with boiled rice and green vegetables.

Serves 4

Tip: You can make this dish even more special by adding a little cheap brandy or cognac. This will ensure that it becomes a well-deserved favourite, especially at dinner parties.

Pheasant with Walnut Sauce

one 1.5 kg (3 lb) oven-ready pheasant
salt and pepper
50 g (2 oz) (¼ cup) butter
juice 4 oranges
150 ml (¼ pint) (⅝ cup) grape juice
150 ml (¼ pint) (⅝ cup) vermouth
225 g (½ lb) (2 cups) shelled walnuts
10 ml (2 teaspoons) tea leaves
150 ml (¼ pint) (⅝ cup) boiling water
25 g (1 oz) (4 tablespoons) flour

1 Preheat the oven to 200°C, 400°F, gas 6. Season the pheasant, inside and outside, with salt and pepper. Place it in a shallow ovenproof dish with 25 g (1 oz) (2 tablespoons) of the butter, the orange and grape juice, vermouth and walnuts.

2 Make the tea by infusing it in the boiling water for several minutes. Strain it and pour over the pheasant. Cover the dish and braise in the oven for about 40 minutes until the pheasant is cooked. Keep the pheasant and nuts warm and strain off the cooking liquid into a small saucepan.

3 Make a beurre manié with the flour and remaining butter. Bring the liquid to the boil and gradually beat in the beurre manié until the sauce thickens. Cook gently for 5 minutes, then stir in the shelled walnuts.

4 Either serve the pheasant at once, surrounded by the walnut sauce, or freeze until needed. To freeze: place the cooked pheasant and the walnut sauce in a rigid plastic or foil container, cool, seal and freeze.

5 To thaw: place in the refrigerator overnight and heat in a casserole in an oven preheated to 180°C, 350°F, gas 4. Serve with fresh green vegetables and boiled new potatoes.

Serves 4

Tip: This dish is especially attractive if garnished with halved and deseeded grapes.

Bitter Sweet Lamb

1 kg (2 lb) lamb neck chops
1.1 litres (2 pints) (5 cups) water
30 ml (2 tablespoons) malt vinegar
30 ml (2 tablespoons) chopped parsley

For the Sauce:
60 ml (4 tablespoons) orange marmalade
30 ml (2 tablespoons) tomato ketchup (catsup)
10 ml (2 teaspoons) dry mustard
grated rind and juice 1 orange
150 ml (¼ pint) (⅝ cup) chicken stock
10 ml (2 teaspoons) cornflour (cornstarch)

1 Place the lamb chops, water and vinegar in a pan and bring to the boil. Cover the pan, reduce the heat and simmer for 15 minutes. Drain the chops, discarding the liquid.

2 In another pan, heat the marmalade, ketchup (catsup), mustard, orange rind and juice and stock. Bring to the boil, stirring well.

3 When the sauce boils, add the lamb chops, cover the pan and simmer for 45 minutes until the lamb is cooked and tender.

4 Remove the lamb chops and keep warm. Blend the cornflour (cornstarch) with a little water and stir into the sauce. Heat gently, stirring until the mixture thickens. Pour the sauce over the lamb and, if it is to be eaten straight away, sprinkle with the chopped parsley and serve with boiled rice.

5 To freeze: place the lamb chops and the sauce in a rigid plastic or foil container and seal. Label and freeze until needed.

6 To serve: thaw the dish for 12 hours in the refrigerator. Reheat gently over a low heat or in a moderate oven, stirring occasionally.

Serves 4

Pheasant with Walnut Sauce is perfect for a dinner party; just thaw and leave to reheat while you mingle with guests

Celery Mornay

2 heads celery
salt
25 g (1 oz) (2 tablespoons) butter
25 g (1 oz) (¼ cup) flour
550 ml (1 pint) (2½ cups) milk
pepper
5 ml (1 teaspoon) made mustard
175 g (6 oz) (1½ cups) grated cheese
100 g (¼ lb) lean bacon, chopped
  (optional)

1 Prepare the celery: remove the leaves and outer sticks and cut the heads in half lengthways. Place in salted water and bring to the boil. Simmer for 35 minutes until tender but not soft.

2 Meanwhile, melt the butter in a pan. Stir in the flour and cook for 1 minute. Remove the pan from the heat and stir in the milk little by little, beating to make a smooth sauce. Add the pepper and mustard. Return to the heat and bring to the boil. Stir in the cheese until it is completely blended, and the sauce is thickened but not stiff.

3 Drain the celery and place it in a serving dish. Pour the sauce over the top. If wished, grill (broil) or fry the bacon until crisp, and scatter over the dish.

4 If the dish is to be served at once, place it under the grill (broiler) for 5-10 minutes until the top is golden-brown. Serve.

5 To freeze: cover the dish with foil, seal, label and freeze. When required, thaw for 12 hours in a refrigerator. Preheat the oven to 180°C, 350°F, gas 4, and bake the dish, uncovered, for 20-30 minutes until heated through. Finish off under the grill (broiler) if necessary to brown the top.

Serves 4

Celery Mornay is equally good served as a starter, or as a vegetable dish to accompany grilled (broiled) meat or fish

Bacon Braid

225 g (½ lb) streaky bacon slices
225 g (½ lb) potatoes
100 g (¼ lb) onions
100 g (¼ lb) carrots
25 g (1 oz) (2 tablespoons) butter
5 ml (1 teaspoon) dried mixed
  herbs
15 ml (1 tablespoon) fresh
  chopped parsley
pepper
375 g (13 oz) puff pastry, frozen
  and thawed
1 egg, beaten

1 Discard the rind and cartilage from the bacon and cut it into small pieces.

2 Peel and dice the potatoes. Peel and chop the onions. Scrape and dice the carrots.

3 Fry the bacon and the vegetables in the butter for about 8 minutes. Add the dried herbs, parsley, and pepper to taste. Leave to cool.

4 Roll the pastry out on a floured board to make a rectangle of about 28 x 33cm (11 x 13 in). Trim off any uneven edges.

5 Arrange the cooked vegetable mixture in a row down the middle of the pastry, leaving 2 cm (¾ in) at the ends and about 10 cm (4 in) bare at each side. Make slanted cuts in the uncovered side pieces from the edge to near the filling, about 2.5 cm (1 in) apart.

6 Fold the cut pieces over the filling alternately, to form a plaited (braided) effect. Tuck the ends up neatly. Brush beaten egg over the top of the braid. Preheat the oven to 220°C, 425°F, gas 7. Place the braid on a greased baking (cookie) sheet and bake for 20 minutes. Reduce the heat to 180°C, 350°F, gas 4 and cook for 15 minutes more.

7 To freeze: allow to cool, wrap in foil, label and freeze. When required, preheat the oven to 180°C, 350°F, gas 4, and cook the frozen plait on a lightly greased baking (cookie) sheet for 30-40 minutes. Serve hot or cold.

Serves 4

Bacon Braid is tasty and nourishing, an ideal lunch-time or picnic recipe — you can make and freeze several at once

Stuffed Courgettes (Zucchini)

4 large courgettes (zucchini)
25 g (1 oz) (2 tablespoons) finely chopped onion
25 g (1 oz) (2 tablespoons) butter
50 g (2 oz) (1 cup) parsley and thyme stuffing
2 tomatoes, skinned and chopped
50 g (2 oz) (½ cup) grated cheese
pinch nutmeg
salt and pepper
30 ml (2 tablespoons) melted butter

1 Scrub the courgettes (zucchini) and trim off the tops. Plunge them into boiling salted water and cook for 10 minutes. Drain.

2 Cut the courgettes (zucchini) in half lengthways. Scoop out the flesh leaving 5mm (¼ in) thickness

throughout. Fry the flesh with the chopped onion in the butter for 5 minutes over gentle heat.

3 Mix the stuffing with a little boiling water to make a moist but crumbly mixture. Mix the stuffing with the onion and courgette (zucchini) mixture, and add the tomato, grated cheese, and nutmeg. Season.

4 Preheat the oven to 170°C, 325°F, gas 3. Place the courgette (zucchini) shells in a greased ovenproof dish so that they are wedged upright. Divide the mixture between them. Brush with a little melted butter and bake for 15 minutes.

5 To freeze, place the cooked, stuffed courgettes (zucchini) in a freezer container. Seal, label and freeze. When required, preheat the oven to 170°C, 325°F, gas 3. Place the frozen courgettes (zucchini) on a lightly greased baking (cookie) sheet and bake for about 45 minutes, or until heated through. Serve with salad as a snack, or as an accompaniment to roast meat.

Serves 4

Savoury Sausage Roly Poly

1 medium cooking (green) apple
225 g ($\frac{1}{2}$ lb) sausagemeat
30 ml (2 tablespoons) chopped
  onion
30 ml (2 tablespoons) chopped
  parsley
225 g ($\frac{1}{2}$ lb) (2$\frac{1}{4}$ cups) plain flour
2.5 ml ($\frac{1}{2}$ teaspoon) salt
10 ml (2 teaspoons) baking
  powder
100 g ($\frac{1}{4}$ lb) (1 cup) shredded suet
cold water

For Serving:
1 beaten egg

1 Preheat the oven to 200°C, 400°F, gas 6. Peel, core and chop the apple. Place it in a bowl with the sausagemeat, onion and parsley and mix well.

2 Sieve the flour with the salt and baking powder into a clean bowl and mix well. Lightly knead in the shredded suet, adding just enough water to make a soft but not sticky dough. Roll out the dough on a floured board to a rectangle, 23 cm (9 in) wide and 5 mm ($\frac{1}{4}$ in) thick.

3 Spread the sausage mixture over the dough leaving a 2.5 cm (1 in) border all round. Damp the border lightly and roll up the dough like a Swiss (jelly) roll. Seal the ends and the join line. Place the roly poly in a lined and greased 1 kg (2 lb) loaf tin (pan). Make a few slits in the top of the roly poly to allow any steam to escape and bake it in the oven for 20 minutes.

4 If you wish to serve it immediately, bake for a further 20-30 minutes and serve. To freeze, remove it from the oven after the preliminary 20 minutes' cooking. Allow it to cool thoroughly before wrapping it in aluminium foil and placing it in a polythene bag. Seal, label and freeze.

5 To serve, preheat the oven to 200°C, 400°F, gas 6. Place the roly poly on a baking (cookie) sheet and brush it with the beaten egg. Bake it in the oven for 30-40 minutes or until cooked. Serve

*Savoury Sausage Roly Poly
is a useful standby to
have in your freezer to feed
the family or unexpected guests*

with carrots, beans and a bowl of hot onion gravy.

Serves 4

Cheese and Onion Quiches

shortcrust (pie crust) made with
  225 g ($\frac{1}{2}$ lb) (2$\frac{1}{4}$ cups) flour
2 onions, chopped
25 g (1 oz) (2 tablespoons) butter
225 g ($\frac{1}{2}$ lb) Cheddar cheese,
  grated

2 eggs
300 ml ($\frac{1}{2}$ pint) (1$\frac{1}{4}$ cups) single
  (light) cream
salt and pepper
8 slices tomato

1 Preheat the oven to 220°C, 425°F, gas 7. Roll out the pastry on a floured board to a thickness of 3 mm ($\frac{1}{8}$ in) and use it to line eight 9 cm (3$\frac{1}{2}$ in) individual flan tins (pans). Bake them blind for 15 minutes.

2 Fry the onion in the butter until transparent and then divide it, with the grated cheese, between the flan cases. Whip the eggs, cream and seasoning and pour the mixture into the cases. Place a slice of tomato on top of each quiche, and bake them for 30 minutes.

3 They can be eaten immediately, hot or cold. To freeze, leave them to cool and wrap each quiche separately in foil or polythene. Seal and label before placing them in the freezer.

4 To serve, thaw the quiches for 12 hours in the refrigerator. If you wish to reheat them, place them in the oven, preheated to 190°C, 375°F, gas 5, for 10-12 minutes.

Makes 8

Chinese Sausage Pancakes

400 ml (14 fl oz) (1¾ cups) pancake batter
350 g (¾ lb) bean sprouts
4 sausages, cooked and chopped
15 ml (1 tablespoon) soya sauce
30 ml (2 tablespoons) mango chutney
oil for deep frying

For the Sauce:
225 g (½ lb) canned peeled tomatoes
15 ml (1 tablespoon) tomato paste
50 ml (2 fl oz) (¼ cup) vinegar
40 g (1½ oz) (3 tablespoons) brown sugar
1 carrot, grated
2 gherkins, finely chopped
grated rind ½ orange

1 Reserve 100 ml (4 fl oz) (½ cup) of the pancake batter, and use the rest to make 8 pancakes. In a bowl, mix the bean sprouts, chopped sausage, soya sauce and chutney. Divide the mixture between the 8 pancakes and roll each one up, sealing the edges with a little of the reserved batter.

2 Heat the oil for deep frying to 190°C, 375°F. Dip each pancake in the remaining batter so that they are very lightly coated, and fry them in the oil until they are crisp

Chinese Sausage Pancakes are a super snack meal out of the freezer to feed any large and hungry family

and golden-brown. Drain them on absorbent paper.

3 If you wish to eat them immediately, place all the sauce ingredients in a saucepan and mix well. Simmer over a gentle heat for 8 minutes. Place the pancakes on a serving dish and cover them with sauce.

4 To freeze: cool the pancakes before wrapping them individually in aluminium foil. Place them in a rigid container, remembering to label them before placing them in the freezer. Pour the prepared sauce into a freezing container. Seal, label and place it in the freezer.

5 To serve: thaw the sauce overnight in the refrigerator. Place it in a saucepan and gently reheat it. Unwrap the pancakes and deep-fry them in oil just long enough to thaw and reheat them. Place the reheated pancakes on a serving dish and cover them with the sauce.

Serves 4

Rabbit Sauté Flamande

1 large rabbit, cleaned
225 g (½ lb) carrots
2 large onions
50 g (2 oz) (½ cup) flour
salt and pepper
50 ml (2 fl oz) (¼ cup) oil
15 ml (1 tablespoon) finely
  chopped parsley
bouquet garni
15 ml (1 tablespoon) tomato
  paste
300 ml (½ pint) (1¼ cups) chicken
  stock
300 ml (½ pint) (1¼ cups) dry white
  wine
225 g (½ lb) (1¼ cups) dried prunes,
  soaked for 2 hours in warm
  water

1 Joint the rabbit by cutting the back into 3 pieces and separating the hind legs. With a sharp knife, cut the chest flesh away from the ribcage and remove the ribcage.

2 Clean and slice the carrots. Peel and thinly slice the onions. Dust the rabbit pieces in flour seasoned with salt and pepper.

3 Heat the oil in a frying pan (skillet) and fry the rabbit pieces for about 5 minutes on each side, until lightly browned. Drain and remove them from the pan and place in a casserole.

4 Preheat the oven to 180°C, 350°F, gas 4.

5 Fry the onions and carrots for 5 minutes in the oil used to fry the rabbit pieces. Transfer them to the casserole, and add the parsley, bouquet garni, tomato paste, and stock. Pour in the wine, and adjust the seasoning to taste. Strain the soaked prunes and place them in the casserole; cover with a lid. Cook in the oven for 1½-2 hours.

6 If wished, serve at once. To freeze: transfer to a container, seal, label, and freeze. When required, thaw for 12 hours in the refrigerator. Transfer to a casserole and cook for 1 hour in an oven preheated to 180°C, 350°F, gas 4. Place in a serving dish and serve with sautéed potatoes.

Serves 6

Chicken in Curry Yogurt Sauce can be quickly knocked up with frozen chicken joints and a special tasty curry sauce

Chicken in Curry Yogurt Sauce

4 frozen chicken breasts, with
  wings removed
salt, pepper and paprika
25 g (1 oz) (¼ cup) flour
50 ml (2 fl oz) (¼ cup) oil

For the Sauce:
300 ml (½ pint) (1¼ cups) plain
  yogurt
5 ml (1 teaspoon) each: curry
  powder, ground ginger and
  paprika
pinch cayenne pepper and salt
1 clove garlic, crushed
15 ml (1 tablespoon) tomato
  paste
grated rind ½ lemon

1 Mix together all the sauce ingredients and place in a container. Seal, label and freeze.

2 When required, thaw the sauce and the chicken portions in the refrigerator for 12 hours.

3 Season the flour and use it to dust the chicken pieces. Gently fry the chicken pieces in the oil until golden-brown and cooked.

4 Drain the oil out of the pan. Pour the sauce over the chicken, cover and cook gently for 10 minutes. Place the chicken on a serving dish, cover with the sauce, and serve with rice.

Serves 4

Lemon Chicken Pie

25 g (1 oz) (2 tablespoons) butter
1 onion, chopped
1 green pepper, deseeded and
  chopped
50 g (2 oz) (1 cup) button
  mushrooms, halved
20 g (¾ oz) (3 tablespoons) flour
150 ml (¼ pint) (⅝ cup) dry white
  wine or dry cider
150 ml (¼ pint) (⅝ cup) milk
finely grated rind 1 lemon
pinch dried thyme
salt and pepper
450 g (1 lb) (2⅔ cups) diced cooked
  chicken
225 g (½ lb) flaky pastry, frozen
  and thawed
1 egg, beaten

1 Melt the butter and cook the
onion, pepper and mushrooms
until tender. Stir in the flour and
cook for 1 minute. Remove from
the heat and gradually stir in the
wine and the milk.

2 Return the pan to the heat and
bring to the boil. Cook for 1
minute. Stir in the lemon rind,
thyme, seasoning and chicken.
Pour into a 900 ml (1½ pint)
(3¾ cup) pie dish with a funnel.

3 Preheat the oven to 220°C,
425°F, gas 7.

4 Roll the pastry out on a lightly
floured board until it is wider than
the top of the pie dish. Cut a narrow strip of dough and place it
round the rim of the dish. Place
the pastry lid over the pie, mois-
tening the edges to seal. Knock
the edges together and crimp
with a fork.

5 Brush the pie with beaten egg,
bake for 20 minutes, and serve.

6 To freeze: place the uncooked
pie in the freezer and freeze
quickly. Wrap in foil, label and
return to the freezer. To serve,
thaw in the refrigerator for 12
hours. Brush the pie with beaten
egg and bake for 15 minutes in an
oven preheated to 220°C, 425°F,
gas 7. Reduce the oven temperature to 180°C, 350°F, gas 4 and bake
for 20-30 minutes more.

Serves 4

Chicken Ruby

4 chicken joints
25 g (1 oz) (¼ cup) flour
salt and pepper
50 g (2 oz) (¼ cup) butter
350 g (¾ lb) (1½ cups) cranberries
75 g (3 oz) (⅓ cup) sugar
1 onion, chopped
grated rind 1 orange
200 ml (6 fl oz) (¾ cup) orange juice
good pinch each: ground ginger
  and ground cinnamon
carrots and peas to garnish

*Chicken Ruby is an excellent
way to use convenient
chicken pieces, and the sweet 'n
sour sauce can be frozen too*

1 Coat the chicken with seasoned flour. Melt the butter in a
pan and fry the chicken gently
until golden-brown on all sides.
Remove from the pan and keep
warm.

2 Combine the remaining ingredients in the pan and bring to the
boil. Replace the chicken in the
pan and simmer for 30-40
minutes.

3 Serve at once; or place in a container, seal and freeze. When
required, thaw for 12 hours in the
refrigerator. Place in a pan and
cook gently until heated through.
Serve on a bed of rice, garnished
with carrots and peas.

Serves 4

Kipper Pizza

225 g (½ lb) (2¼ cups) self-raising
  flour
2.5 ml (½ teaspoon) salt
40 g (1½ oz) (3 tablespoons) butter
70 ml (2½ fl oz) (⅓ cup) milk
2 tomatoes, sliced
225 g (½ lb) kipper (smoked
  herring) fillets, cut in strips
6 stuffed olives, sliced
100 g (¼ lb) Cheddar, grated

1 Sieve the flour and salt into a
bowl. Rub in the butter until the
mixture resembles fine breadcrumbs and stir in the milk.
Knead to a smooth dough.

2 Roll out the dough on a floured
board to a 23 cm (9 in) round and
place on a baking (cookie) sheet.
Preheat the oven to 200°C, 400°F,
gas 6.

3 Cover the dough with slices of
tomato. Place the fish strips
criss-cross over the tomatoes and
sprinkle with the olives and
cheese. Bake for 15 minutes.

4 If you intend to eat it immediately, continue to cook for a
further 10 minutes. To freeze,
remove the pizza from the oven
after the initial cooking period
and leave it to cool. Place the
pizza unwrapped in the freezer
until hard, then pack it in aluminium foil and place it in a polythene bag. Seal, label and freeze.

5 To serve, place the frozen pizza
in the oven set at 200°C, 400°F,
gas 6 for 20-30 minutes to complete cooking. Brown under the
grill (broiler) just prior to serving.

Serves 4

Crispy Fish Pie

350 g (¾ lb) cod fillets
salt and pepper
1 large onion, sliced
150 ml (¼ pint) (⅝ cup) milk
25 g (1 oz) (2 tablespoons)
  margarine

45 ml (3 tablespoons) flour
75 g (3 oz) (¾ cup) grated cheese
3 large tomatoes
25 g (1 oz) potato crisps (chips)
seasoning

1 Preheat the oven to 190°C,
375°F, gas 5. Cut the fish fillets into
2.5 cm (1 in) strips. Place them in a
greased ovenproof dish and season. Arrange the onion slices over
the top and pour over the milk.
Cover the dish and bake it in the
oven for 40 minutes. Remove from
the oven.

2 Melt the margarine in a pan.
Stir in the flour and cook for 2-3
minutes, stirring all the time.
With a spoon, transfer the liquid
from the cooked fish to the pan.
Bring to the boil, stirring constantly, and cook for 2-3 minutes.
Remove the pan from the heat
and stir in 50 g (2 oz) (½ cup) of the
cheese.

3 Skin and slice the tomatoes.
Arrange them over the fish and
pour over the sauce. Lightly crush
the crisps (chips) and sprinkle
them on top with the remaining
cheese. Return the dish to the
oven for 10-15 minutes.

4 To freeze, cool the dish and
cover it with aluminium foil. Seal
and label before placing it in the
freezer.

5 To serve, remove the pie from
the freezer and thaw for 12 hours
in the refrigerator. Heat in the
oven set at 180°C, 350°F, gas 4, for
20-30 minutes or until lightly
browned.

Serves 4

Haddock and Vegetable Pancakes

fat for frying
300 ml (½ pint) (1¼ cups) pancake
  batter

For the Filling:
225 g (½ lb) haddock fillets
300 ml (½ pint) (1¼ cups) milk
25 g (1 oz) (2 tablespoons) butter

45 ml (3 tablespoons) flour
2.5 ml (½ teaspoon) salt
pepper
100 g (¼ lb) frozen mixed
  vegetables
30 ml (2 tablespoons) capers,
  chopped

For Serving:
150 ml (¼ pint) (⅝ cup) sour cream
pinch paprika

1 Lightly grease a frying pan
(skillet) and heat it until smoking
hot. Quickly pour in enough batter to thinly coat the bottom of
the pan, tilting the pan so that the
bottom is evenly covered. Cook
until the underside of the pancake is golden-brown. Turn and
cook on the other side. Repeat
this process until all the batter is
used, making 8 pancakes in all.
Allow them to cool.

2 Prepare the filling: place the
haddock and milk in a pan. Cover
and poach the fish for 10 minutes.
Drain, reserving the liquid, and
skin and flake the fish.

3 Melt the butter in a clean pan.
Add the flour and cook for 1
minute, stirring continually.
Remove the pan from the heat
and gradually stir in the reserved
liquid, making it up to 300 ml
(½ pint) (1¼ cups) with more milk, if
necessary. Return the pan to the
heat and cook gently, stirring
continuously, until the sauce is
thick and smooth. Stir in the seasoning, vegetables and capers
and cook for a further 5 minutes
before adding the fish.

4 Divide the filling between the
8 pancakes and roll them up
tightly. You can serve them
immediately. To freeze, pack
them into a foil container. Seal
and label the container before
placing it in the freezer.

5 To serve, place the foil container in an oven set at 180°C,
350°F, gas 4, for 25-30 minutes or
until thoroughly heated through.
Place them on a dish and serve
garnished with sour cream and
paprika.

Makes 8

---

*Haddock and Vegetable
Pancakes are served
with sour cream — make the
filling and pancakes in advance*

Chicken Livers Paysanne

50 g (2 oz) ($\frac{1}{4}$ cup) butter
1 onion, chopped
675 g (1$\frac{1}{2}$ lb) chicken livers,
 chopped
5 ml (1 teaspoon) marjoram
10 ml (2 teaspoons) chopped
 parsley
45 ml (3 tablespoons) red wine
225 ml (8 fl oz) (1 cup) sour cream
salt and pepper

1 Melt the butter in a pan and sauté the onion for 2-3 minutes. Add the chicken livers and cook for 5 more minutes, then add the marjoram, parsley, wine and sour cream and season to taste. Simmer for 5 minutes.

2 You can serve this dish immediately but, to freeze, allow it to cool before transferring it to a rigid container. Seal and label before placing it in the freezer. Thaw thoroughly before gently reheating. Serve with hot boiled rice.

Serves 6-8

Pork Casserole

1 kg (2 lb) lean leg of pork
50 g (2 oz) ($\frac{1}{4}$ cup) lard
1 onion, chopped
juice $\frac{1}{2}$ lemon
1 bay leaf
10 ml (2 teaspoons) salt
freshly ground (milled) black
 pepper
300 ml ($\frac{1}{2}$ pint) (1$\frac{1}{4}$ cups) red wine
50 g (2 oz) ($\frac{1}{4}$ cup) plain flour
225 ml (8 fl oz) (1 cup) water
1 chicken stock cube
25 g (1 oz) (2 tablespoons) butter
100g ($\frac{1}{4}$ lb) mushrooms, sliced
2 cloves garlic, crushed
150 ml ($\frac{1}{4}$ pint) ($\frac{5}{8}$ cup) white wine
300 ml ($\frac{1}{2}$ pint) (1$\frac{1}{4}$ cups) sour
 cream

1 Cut the pork into 2.5 cm (1 in) cubes. Melt the lard in a large pan and gently fry the onion for 5 minutes. Add the pork, lemon juice, bay leaf, salt and pepper and half of the red wine. Cover and cook gently for 15 minutes. Transfer the pork to a plate. Add the flour to the pan and stir over a medium heat for 1-2 minutes. Add the remaining red wine, and the water and chicken stock cube. Stirring continuously, gradually bring the mixture to the boil.

2 Melt the butter in a clean pan. Add the mushrooms and crushed garlic and sauté gently for 2-3 minutes. Add the white wine, cover and simmer for 10 minutes.

3 Return the pork to the pan and add the mushroom mixture. Cover and simmer for 15 minutes or until the meat is tender. Check the seasoning. If you wish to serve the casserole immediately, stir in the sour cream and reheat without letting it boil.

4 To freeze, allow the casserole to cool before transferring it to a rigid container. Seal and label before placing it in the freezer. Thaw the casserole in the refrigerator before gently reheating it. Stir in the sour cream and serve with creamed potatoes and braised red cabbage.

Serves 6

Raised Game Pie

75 g (3 oz) (6 tablespoons) lard
200 ml (7 fl oz) ($\frac{7}{8}$ cup) milk
350 g ($\frac{3}{4}$ lb) (3$\frac{3}{8}$ cups) flour, sieved
7.5 ml (1$\frac{1}{2}$ teaspoons) salt
beaten egg

For the Filling:
350 g ($\frac{3}{4}$ lb) sausagemeat
100 g ($\frac{1}{4}$ lb) bacon, cut into small
 strips
175 g (6 oz) lean chuck steak, cut
 into small cubes
meat of 1 cooked pheasant or
 2 pigeons, cut into small pieces
1 onion, finely chopped
100 g ($\frac{1}{4}$ lb) button mushrooms,
 chopped
salt and pepper
30 ml (2 tablespoons) sherry

1 Melt the lard in the milk and bring it to a rolling boil. Make a well in the flour and salt, and pour in the boiling liquid. Work quickly with a wooden spoon to form a fairly soft dough. Use one hand to lightly pinch the dough together and knead until smooth and silky. Place the dough in a bowl covered with a plate or damp tea-towel to retain the heat.

2 Grease a 1.8 litre (3 pint) (7$\frac{1}{2}$ cup) hinged pie mould and place it on a baking (cookie) sheet. Roll out $\frac{2}{3}$ of the pastry on a floured surface to an oval 28 × 25 cm (11 × 10 in). Keep the remaining pastry covered. Drape the rolled pastry over the rolling pin, lift the pin and unroll the dough over the tin (pan). Press the pastry into the tin (pan) to 5 mm ($\frac{1}{4}$ in) above the rim and dampen the edges.

3 Preheat the oven to 200°C, 400°F, gas 6. Line the base and sides of the pastry with the sausagemeat to keep the pastry in good shape. Mix the bacon, steak, pheasant or pigeon, onion and mushrooms together. Season well, fill the pie with the mixture and sprinkle over the sherry. Roll out the pastry to fit the top of the mould. Position it over the filling, pinch the edges together and flute. Brush the lid with the beaten egg.

4 Make a fairly large hole in the centre of the pie and bake it in the preheated oven for 15-20 minutes. Reduce the oven temperature to 180°C, 350°F, gas 4 and bake for a further 1$\frac{1}{2}$ hours, or until the meat is tender when tested with a skewer. If the top of the pie appears to be overbrowning, cover it with foil or greaseproof (parchment) paper. Remove the pie from the oven and allow it to cool.

5 To freeze: wrap the pie in foil and place it in a polythene bag. Seal, label and place it in the freezer. To serve: thaw the pie for 12 hours in the refrigerator.

Serves 6-8

*Raised Game Pie, with its rich
meaty filling encased
in golden hot-water crust pastry,
makes a tasty summer dish*

Sweet Dishes

With all the rush involved in preparing the main course it is a relief to know that the dessert is waiting safely in the freezer. All you have to remember is to give it plenty of time to thaw.

Sorbet Fizz

1 pineapple
300 ml (½ pint) (1¼ cups) orange juice
300 ml (½ pint) (1¼ cups) grapefruit juice
300 ml (½ pint) (1¼ cups) ginger ale
sugar

For Serving:
whipped cream
orange and lemon slices

1 Peel the pineapple and crush it into tiny pieces. Mix it with the fruit juices and ginger ale and sweeten to taste.

2 Pour the mixture into a rigid container. Seal and label it before placing it in the freezer.

3 To serve, remove from the freezer for about 1 hour prior to serving. Spoon the sorbet into individual glasses and decorate with cream and fruit slices.

Serves 8

Rhubarb and Ginger Cream

450 g (1 lb) rhubarb
sugar
2 pieces stem ginger, finely chopped
15 ml (1 tablespoon) ginger syrup
2.5 ml (½ teaspoon) ground ginger
pink colouring

300 ml (½ pint) (1¼ cups) double (heavy) cream, whipped

1 Gently stew the rhubarb in a small amount of water with sugar to taste. Cool, and purée by forcing it through a sieve.

2 Mix together the purée, chopped ginger, ginger syrup, ground ginger and sufficient colouring to give a deep shade of pink. Fold in the whipped cream.

3 Pour the mixture into a rigid container and cover. Seal, label and freeze. To serve, half defrost it in the refrigerator and whisk it well. Spoon the cream into 4 individual glasses and chill.

Serves 4

Caramel Fruit Savarin

7.5 ml (1½ teaspoons) dried yeast
50 ml (2 fl oz) (¼ cup) warm water
50 ml (2 fl oz) (¼ cup) warm milk
225 g (½ lb) (2¼ cups) flour
50 g (2 oz) (¼ cup) sugar
pinch salt
2 eggs
2.5 ml (½ teaspoon) vanilla essence
50 g (2 oz) (¼ cup) softened butter

For the Syrup:
100 g (¼ lb) (½ cup) sugar
150 ml (¼ pint) (⅝ cup) water
85 ml (3 fl oz) (⅜ cup) rum

For the Filling:
175 g (6 oz) grapes
2 oranges
2 dessert apples

For the Topping and Decoration:
175 g (6 oz) (¾ cup) sugar
few clusters of grapes

1 Place the yeast, warm water and milk in a bowl and leave in a warm place until frothy.

2 Sieve the flour, sugar and salt into a bowl. Stir in the yeast mixture and the eggs, beaten with the vanilla essence. Beat until the dough is smooth and thick. Dot the butter over the dough and cover with greased polythene. Leave until the dough has doubled in size.

3 Beat the dough down until it leaves the sides of the bowl clean and place it in a well-greased savarin ring mould (tube pan). Cover again with the greased polythene and leave it to rise to the top of the mould – approximately 45 minutes.

4 Preheat the oven to 200°C, 400°F, gas 6. Bake the savarin at this temperature for 10 minutes. Reduce the temperature to 180°C, 350°F, gas 4 and bake for a further 25-30 minutes.

5 Leave the savarin to cool thoroughly before turning it out of the mould. If you are going to freeze the savarin, wrap it in foil and place it in a polythene bag. Seal and label before placing it in the freezer. To thaw, place in the refrigerator for 12 hours before serving.

6 Make the syrup. Place the sugar and water in a saucepan and heat gently, stirring continually, until the sugar dissolves. Simmer until the syrup thickens. Remove from the heat and stir in the rum. Prick the savarin all over with a fork and spoon over the syrup.

7 Halve the grapes. Remove the rind and pith from the oranges and segment the flesh. Core and chop the apple. Reserve a few grape halves and orange segments for garnishing and combine the remaining fruit. Place the savarin on a serving dish and put the mixed fruit in the centre. Arrange the reserved orange segments and grape halves decoratively on top.

8 Make the topping: heat the sugar gently until it dissolves and simmer until it turns a dark golden colour. Quickly dip the clusters of grapes into the topping and place them on a greased baking (cookie) sheet to cool. Pour the caramel over the savarin. Place the cooled caramelized grapes around the dish and serve.

Serves 8

Caramel Fruit Savarin is topped with fresh fruit and is decorated with deliciously sticky, caramelized grapes

Look 'n Cook Orange Bombe

1 Finely grate the orange rind and squeeze the juice 2 Whisk the egg yolks with the sugar until the mixture is thick and pale. Whisk in the orange rind and juice 3 Whip the cream until it is just thick. Stiffly whisk the egg whites and fold in the egg yolk mixture 4 Fold the whipped cream into the mixture, pour into a polythene freezer container and freeze for about 3 hours. Chill a bombe mould or cake tin (pan) in the refrigerator 5 Whisk the prepared ice-cream until it is smooth, then place two-thirds of it in a clean polythene freezer container. Add the orange food colouring and liqueur to the remaining ice-cream and pour it into a separate container 6 Cut the glacé fruits into small dice 7 Stir the glacé fruits into the plain ice-cream. Return both containers of ice-cream to the freezer and freeze until firm 8 Line the sides of the chilled bombe mould or cake tin (pan) with the orange ice-cream, spreading it firmly with the back of a metal spoon 9 Fill the centre with the fruit ice-cream. Grease the mould edge with lard, lay a piece of greaseproof (parchment) paper over and cover with the lid. If using a cake tin (pan) cover with foil. Return to the freezer 10 and 11 Turn on to a plate and decorate with whipped cream and halved cherries

Orange Bombe

2 oranges
4 eggs, separated
175 g (6 oz) (¾ cup) castor (fine
  granulated) sugar
450 ml (¾ pint) (2 cups) double
  (heavy) cream
few drops orange food colouring
15 ml (1 tablespoon) Grand
  Marnier (optional)
75 g (3 oz) assorted glacé fruits

To Decorate:
150 ml (¼ pint) (⅔ cup) double
  (heavy) cream, whipped
halved glacé cherries

1 Finely grate the orange rind and squeeze the juice.

2 Whisk the egg yolks with the sugar until the mixture is thick and pale. Whisk in the orange rind and juice. Whip the cream until it is just thick. Stiffly whisk the egg whites and fold in the egg yolk mixture. Gently fold in the cream.

3 Pour the mixture into a polythene freezer container and freeze for about 3 hours, until the mixture is beginning to set. Chill a 900 ml (1½ pint) (3¾ cup) capacity bombe mould or cake tin (pan) in the refrigerator.

4 Whisk the prepared ice-cream until it is smooth, then place two-thirds of it in a clean polythene freezer container. Add the orange food colouring and Grand Marnier (if using) to the remaining ice-cream and pour it into a separate container.

5 Cut the glacé fruits into small dice and stir them into the plain ice-cream. Return both containers of ice-cream to the freezer and freeze until firm.

6 Line the base and sides of the chilled bombe mould with the orange ice-cream, spreading it firmly with the back of a metal spoon. Fill the centre with the fruit ice-cream. To cover the bombe mould, grease the edges of the mould with lard, lay a piece of greaseproof (parchment) paper over and cover with the lid. If using a cake tin (pan), cover it with aluminium foil. Return to the freezer until required.

Cream Cheese Meringue Pie is a delicious mixture with a cream cheese filling and fluffy light meringue topping

7 Turn the bombe on to a chilled plate. If using a bombe mould, simply unscrew the knob at the base, which will release the pressure and cause the bombe to slide out. If using a cake tin (pan), dip it into cold water for a few seconds. Decorate the bombe with whipped cream, and halved glacé cherries and serve immediately.

Serves 6

Tip: A variety of fruits and flavourings can be added to the filling of the orange bombe in place of the glacé fruits. Three sliced bananas, 75 g (3 oz) sliced strawberries, 50 g (2 oz) chocolate chips or 50 g (2 oz) finely crushed nut brittle would make delicious alternatives.

Cream Cheese Meringue Pie

shortcrust (pie crust) made with
  100 g (¼ lb) (1 cup + 2
  tablespoons) flour

For the Filling:
200 g (7 oz) canned mandarin
  segments, with juice
45 ml (3 tablespoons) cornflour
  (cornstarch)
25 g (1 oz) (2 tablespoons) sugar
2 large eggs, separated
100 g (¼ lb) (½ cup) cream cheese

For the Meringue:
100 g (¼ lb) (½ cup) castor (fine
  granulated) sugar

1 Preheat the oven to 200°C, 400°F, gas 6. Roll out the pastry and use it to line a 21 cm (8¾ in)

Raspberry Soufflé

oil for greasing
450 g (1 lb) raspberries, fresh or
frozen and thawed
4 eggs, separated
100 g (¼ lb) (½ cup) castor (fine
granulated) sugar
150 ml (¼ pint) (⅝ cup) double
(heavy) cream, whipped
10 ml (2 teaspoons) powdered
gelatine
75 ml (2½ fl oz) (5 tablespoons)
water

For Serving:
45 ml (3 tablespoons) chopped
nuts
150 ml (¼ pint) (⅝ cup) double
(heavy) cream, whipped
5 walnut halves
4 raspberries

1 Tie a double band of greaseproof (parchment) paper around
a 15 cm (6 in) soufflé dish. Lightly
oil the inside of the paper.

2 Purée the raspberries. Add the
egg yolks and sugar to the purée
and whisk until thick and
mousse-like. Fold in the cream.

3 Place the gelatine and water in
a bowl and leave to soften for 5
minutes. Stand the bowl in a pan
of hot water and stir until the
gelatine has dissolved. Stir it into
the raspberry mixture.

4 When the mixture begins to
set, stiffly whisk the egg whites
and fold in carefully with a large
metal spoon. Turn the mixture
into the prepared soufflé dish and
leave in a cool place to set.

5 If you wish to freeze the soufflé,
place it, uncovered, in the freezer
until firm. Wrap it with
aluminium foil, place in a thick
polythene bag, seal, label and
freeze.

6 Thaw the frozen soufflé in the
refrigerator for 8-10 hours.

7 To serve the soufflé, remove
the paper collar and press the
chopped nuts on to the sides. Pipe
a border of whipped cream
around the top and decorate with
the walnut halves and the
raspberries.

Serves 6

---

aluminium foil pie plate. Bake
blind for 15-20 minutes and allow
to cool.

2 Drain the juice from the
canned mandarin segments into
a measuring jug and make up to
300 ml (½ pint) (1¼ cups) with water.
Roughly chop the mandarin
segments.

3 Place the cornflour (cornstarch) in a small pan and gradually stir in the juice and water.
Bring slowly to the boil and
simmer for 2 minutes, stirring
continuously. Remove the pan
from the heat and stir in the sugar.

4 Blend the egg yolks with the
cream cheese, blend in the thickened mixture and stir in the mandarins. Pour the mixture into the
pastry case.

5 To freeze the pie, wrap it in
aluminium foil, seal, label and

*Raspberry Soufflé, a really
eyecatching dessert, will impress
your guests; freeze it in
advance and save yourself time*

freeze. Place the egg whites in a
separate container and freeze.
Thaw the pie and the egg whites
at room temperature.

6 To serve the pie, preheat the
oven to 180°C, 350°F, gas 4. Whisk
the egg whites until stiff, then
whisk in half of the sugar. Fold
in the remaining sugar with a
metal spoon. Spread half of the
meringue over the pie. Transfer
the remainder to a piping
(decorator's) bag fitted with a
large star nozzle and pipe the
mixture decoratively over the
top. Bake in the preheated oven
for 10 minutes, until the meringue
is lightly browned. Serve the pie
warm or cold.

Serves 6

Rum and Chocolate Mousse

175 g (6 oz) plain chocolate
45 ml (3 tablespoons) rum
30 ml (1 fl oz) (2 tablespoons) water
2 eggs, separated
few drops vanilla essence
75 g (3 oz) (⅜ cup) castor (fine granulated) sugar
300 ml (½ pint) (1¼ cups) double (heavy) cream
300 ml (½ pint) (1¼ cups) single (light) cream

1 Line a 20 cm (8 in) soufflé dish with greaseproof (parchment) paper. Melt the chocolate with the rum and water in a bowl over a pan of hot water.

2 Remove the bowl from the heat and mix in the egg yolks and vanilla essence. Cool.

3 Whisk the egg whites until they form soft peaks, then fold in the sugar, a spoonful at a time. Stir the meringue into the chocolate mixture.

4 Place the creams in a bowl and whip until they form peaks. Fold them into the chocolate meringue mixture. Pour the mousse into the prepared soufflé dish. Place the mousse in the freezer until firm. Put it in a polythene bag. Seal and label before returning it to the freezer.

5 To serve, thaw the mousse at room temperature for 30 minutes and decorate it with chocolate curls and piped cream.

Serves 4

Cider Syllabub

550 ml (1 pint) (2½ cups) double (heavy) cream
grated rind and juice 2 lemons
150 ml (¼ pint) (⅝ cup) cider
2 egg whites
50 g (2 oz) (¼ cup) castor (fine granulated) sugar

1 Whip the cream together with the lemon rind until it forms peaks. Beat in the lemon juice and cider.

2 Whisk the egg whites until they are stiff. Add the sugar and whisk again. Fold the meringue mixture into the cream.

3 To freeze, spoon the mixture into a rigid container. Seal and label before placing it in the freezer. To serve, defrost it in the refrigerator for 12 hours. Stir well as the cream and lemon juice may have separated, then spoon it into individual glasses and chill.

Serves 4

Pineapple Banana Snow

10 ml (2 teaspoons) powdered gelatine
300 ml (½ pint) (1¼ cups) water
225 g (½ lb) (1 cup) sugar
5 ml (1 teaspoon) grated lemon rind
2 ripe bananas
50 ml (2 fl oz) (¼ cup) lemon juice
300 ml (½ pint) (1¼ cups) pineapple juice
150 ml (¼ pint) (⅝ cup) evaporated milk
2 egg whites

1 Dissolve the gelatine in a little of the water. Place the remaining water in a saucepan with the sugar and lemon rind. Stir over a gentle heat until the sugar has dissolved, then simmer gently for 5 minutes. Cool and stir in the dissolved gelatine.

2 Place the bananas and lemon juice in a large bowl and mash well. Add the sugar syrup, pineapple juice and evaporated milk. Mix well.

3 Pour the mixture into a freezer container and freeze until nearly firm.

4 Meanwhile, whisk the egg whites until they form soft peaks. Spoon the semi-frozen banana mixture into a bowl. Add the whisked egg whites and beat well. Return to the container, cover

with aluminium foil and freeze. Serve the snow direct from the freezer topped with fresh pineapple.

Serves 4

Surprise Cherry Tarts

shortcrust (pie crust) made with 225 g (½ lb) (2¼ cups) flour
4 egg whites
175 g (6 oz) (¾ cup) castor (fine granulated) sugar
425 g (15 oz) canned cherry pie filling
8 scoops chocolate ice-cream

1 Preheat the oven to 220°C, 425°F, gas 7. Roll out the pastry on a floured board to a thickness of 5 mm (¼ in) and use it to line 8 small individual flan cases. Bake them blind for 15 minutes and allow them to cool.

2 While the flan cases cook, prepare the meringue. Whisk the egg whites until they are stiff, then whisk in the castor (fine granulated) sugar, a spoonful at a time, until the meringue stands in stiff peaks.

3 Fill each flan case with the cherry pie filling and top with a scoop of chocolate ice-cream. Immediately spoon the meringue over each tartlet. Place them on a baking (cookie) sheet and return them to the oven for 1-2 minutes until the meringue is lightly browned. Serve immediately.

4 To freeze: leave the tarts on the baking (cookie) sheet and place them in the freezer until firm. Pack the tarts in a rigid container, taking care not to damage the meringue. Seal and label the container before placing it in the freezer. To serve, remove the tarts from the container and place them in an oven preheated to 230°C, 450°F, gas 8 for 1 minute.

Makes 8

Tip: Make sure that the meringue is taken right to the edge of each tartlet, otherwise the ice-cream will melt during the cooking.

285

Look'n Cook Cherry Surprise Tartlets

1 Roll out the pastry and use it to line 8 small individual flan tins (pans). Bake the flan cases blind before filling each one with cherry pie filling and topping with a scoop of chocolate ice-cream **2** While the tartlets are baking, whisk the egg whites, gradually whisking in the sugar until the meringue is very stiff. Spoon the meringue over each tartlet **3** Place the tartlets on a baking (cookie) sheet and put them in the oven for a few minutes to brown the meringue **4** A finished tart

Frozen Yogurt Ambrosia

150 ml (¼ pint) (⅝ cup) double
  (heavy) cream
100 g (¼ lb) (½ cup) castor (fine
  granulated) sugar
5 ml (1 teaspoon) vanilla essence
300 ml (½ pint) (1¼ cups) natural
  yogurt

For the Ambrosia Topping:
25 g (1 oz) (¼ cup) sunflower seeds
45 ml (3 tablespoons) chopped
  hazelnuts
45 ml (3 tablespoons) roughly
  chopped walnuts
15 ml (1 tablespoon) desiccated
  coconut
50 g (2 oz) (⅔ cup) dried apple
  rings, roughly chopped
50 g (2 oz) (½ cup) dried peaches or
  apricots, roughly chopped

1 Whip the cream until it is just
thick, and fold in the sugar, vanilla and yogurt.

2 Transfer the mixture to a polythene freezer container and place
it in the freezer for 1-2 hours, until
the mixture is icy around the
edges. Whisk until smooth, then
return to the freezer until firm.

3 The topping can be made in
advance and stored in an airtight
jar. Lightly toast the sunflower
seeds and mix with the remaining
topping ingredients. Allow the
ice-cream to soften in the
refrigerator for 30 minutes before
serving. Scoop the ice-cream into
4-6 dessert glasses and sprinkle
with the topping. Serve immediately.

Serves 4-6

Banana-peanut Pops

4 bananas
50 g (2 oz) (¼ cup) smooth peanut
  butter
35 g (1¼ oz) (¼ cup) dried skim milk
15 ml (1 tablespoon) honey
75 ml (2½ fl oz) (⅓ cup) single (light)
  cream
25 g (1 oz) (⅓ cup) chopped peanuts

*Peach Sundae can be quickly
and easily made with
simple ingredients — canned
peaches, ice-cream and sauce*

1 Peel the bananas, wrap them
individually in plastic cling film
and freeze until firm.

2 Blend together the peanut
butter, dried milk, honey and
cream and spread over the frozen
bananas.

3 Roll the bananas in the
chopped peanuts, then freeze
until firm. Thaw slightly before
serving.

Makes 4

Peach Sundae

225 g (½ lb) raspberries, puréed
50 g (2 oz) (¼ cup) sugar
8 canned peach halves, drained
4-8 scoops vanilla ice-cream
4 fan wafers

1 Mix the raspberry purée with
the sugar.

2 Place the peach halves in the
base of 4 dessert glasses and top
with the ice-cream. Pour the
raspberry purée over the top and
add a fan wafer to each.

Serves 4

Cooking with Electrical Equipment

Honey Roast Chicken

Food Mixers

There are two basic types of food mixer: the hand-held whisk and the stand-mounted machine. The hand-held variety is particularly useful when preparing sauces and puddings that require whisking during cooking, or when preparing dishes with several ingredients which require whisking in separate bowls.

Stand-mounted mixers have a variety of optional attachments. **The liquidizer (or blender)** can chop, crumb, purée or blend food in seconds, and is invaluable in the preparation of soups and drinks. (See recipes on pages 1866-1871.)
The dough hook takes the hard work out of bread-making, but don't overload the machine which should be used to knead only 700g (1½lb) dough at a time.
The mincer can cope with both raw and cooked meats to make pâtés, meat loaves, rissoles, *etc.*
The slicer and shredder cuts vegetables and salads to the thickness that you require, and can also be used for grating such foods as nuts, chocolate and cheese.
The cream-maker combines milk and unsalted butter to make cream and ice-cream.
The juice extractor extracts juice from citrus fruits.
The juice separator takes juice from vegetables and fruits other than the citrus types. It is used to make delicious healthy drinks, and also to pulp fruits and vegetables for wine making.

Spoonbread

750 ml (1¼ pints) (3 cups) milk
275 g (10 oz) (1 cup) yellow
 cornmeal
5 ml (1 teaspoon) salt
5 ml (1 teaspoon) baking powder

15 ml (1 tablespoon) soft dark
 brown sugar
25 g (1 oz) (2 tablespoons) butter
3 eggs, separated

1 Preheat the oven to 180°C, 350°F, gas 4.

2 Heat 450 ml (¾ pint) (2 cups) of the milk in a saucepan. When the milk begins to simmer, add the cornmeal and continue to cook, stirring, until the mixture is thick.

3 Remove from the heat and add the salt, baking powder, sugar, butter, egg yolks and remaining milk.

4 Whisk the egg whites until they are stiff and peaking and fold gently into the cornmeal mixture. Turn the mixture into a lightly greased 900 ml (1½ pint) (3¾ cup) soufflé dish.

5 Bake for about 1 hour, until puffed-up and golden-brown. Serve the spoonbread immediately, with knobs of butter.

Serves 6-8

Cheese and Walnut Puffed Omelette

2 eggs, separated
25 g (1 oz) (¼ cup) grated cheese
15 ml (1 tablespoon) finely
 chopped walnuts
salt and pepper
butter for frying

1 Place the egg whites in the mixer bowl and whisk until stiff and peaking.

2 Combine the egg yolks, cheese, walnuts and seasoning and fold gently into the egg whites.

3 Melt the butter in a frying pan (skillet). Pour in the mixture and cook over a medium heat until golden-brown on the underside.

4 Flash the pan under a pre-heated hot grill (broiler) until puffed and golden. Serve immediately.

Serves 1

Tuna Fish Braid

25 g (1 oz) (2 tablespoons) butter
25 g (1 oz) (4 tablespoons) flour
300 ml (½ pint) (1¼ cups) milk
finely grated rind ½ lemon
5 ml (1 teaspoon) lemon juice
200 g (7 oz) canned tuna, drained
75 g (3 oz) (½ cup) canned corn
 kernels, drained
1 tomato, thinly sliced

For the Pastry (Pie crust):
275 g (10 oz) (2¾ cups) flour
5 ml (1 teaspoon) salt
150 g (5 oz) (⅝ cup) margarine
60-75 ml (4-5 tablespoons) water
beaten egg to glaze

1 Preheat the oven to 200°C, 400°F, gas 6.

2 Melt the butter in a pan, stir in the flour and cook for 2 minutes. With the hand-mixer set at a low speed, gradually incorporate the milk. Bring to the boil and simmer for 2 or 3 minutes, whisking continuously. Leave to cool.

3 Meanwhile, make the pastry (pie crust): sieve the flour and salt into the mixer bowl and add the fat, which should be cut into small pieces. 'Rub in' the ingredients with the mixer set at the lowest setting. Sprinkle the water over the mixture and incorporate, with the mixer set at a medium speed. Switch off the machine as soon as the ingredients come together.

4 Add the lemon rind, juice, tuna and corn to the cool sauce.

5 Roll the pastry (pie crust) to an oblong, 30 x 20 cm (12 x 8 in). Mark into three, lengthways. Spoon the filling along the centre section and top with the tomato slices. Make diagonal slashes 1 cm (½ in) apart down the two side sections, then fold the strips of dough across to form a plait (braid).

6 Brush with beaten egg, place on a baking (cookie) sheet and bake for 30-35 minutes,

Serves 4 or 5

*Tuna Fish Braid, served cold
with a fresh, crisp
salad, is the ideal food
for summer lunches and picnics*

Orange and Almond Ring

fat for greasing
100 g (¼ lb) (½ cup) butter
100 g (¼ lb) (½ cup) castor (fine
  granulated) sugar
10 ml (2 teaspoons) finely grated
  orange rind
2 eggs
50 g (2 oz) almonds, chopped
100 g (¼ lb) (1 cup + 2 tablespoons)
  self-raising flour, sifted
canned mandarin orange
  segments
angelica, cut into 'leaves'

For the Orange Frosting:
30 ml (2 tablespoons) melted
  butter
30 ml (2 tablespoons) orange
  juice
175 g (6 oz) (¾ cup) icing
  (confectioners') sugar, sifted

1 Preheat the oven to 180°C,
350°F, gas 4. Lightly grease a
900ml (1½ pint) (3¾ cup) ring mould
(tube pan).

2 Place the butter, sugar and
orange rind in the mixer bowl,
and, with the mixer set at a high
speed, cream the mixture until it
is light and fluffy. Beat in the eggs.

3 Stir in the almonds, then fold in
the flour. Transfer the mixture to
the prepared tin (pan).

4 Bake for 35-40 minutes. Leave
the cake in the tin (pan) for 2 or 3
minutes, then turn on to a wire
rack to cool.

5 Prepare the frosting: with the
mixer set at a low speed, combine
the melted butter and orange
juice. Gradually add the icing
(confectioners') sugar and continue to beat until the mixture is
thick and creamy. Reserve a little
of the frosting for piping. Spread
the remainder over the cold cake.

6 Decorate the cake with mandarin segments, piped buttercream and 'leaves' of angelica.

Serves 8

Apple and Hazelnut Gâteau

100 g (¼ lb) (½ cup) butter
100 g (¼ lb) (½ cup) castor (fine
  granulated) sugar
2 eggs, separated
50 g (2 oz) (½ cup) ground
  hazelnuts, toasted
100 g (¼ lb) (1 cup + 2 tablespoons)
  self-raising flour
pinch salt
15 ml (1 tablespoon) milk

For the Filling:
450 g (1 lb) sharp dessert apples
30 ml (2 tablespoons) apricot jam
juice and grated rind 1 lemon
45 ml (3 tablespoons) sugar
45 ml (3 tablespoons) brandy
300 ml (½ pint) (1¼ cups) double
  (heavy) cream

1 Preheat the oven to 190°C,
375°F, gas 5. Cream the butter and
sugar until light and beat in the
egg yolks. Stir in ¾ of the hazelnuts. Fold in the flour and salt
with the milk. Stiffly whisk the
egg whites and fold in with a
metal spoon.

2 Turn the mixture into a
greased and floured 20 cm (8 in)
cake tin (pan), and bake for 25
minutes, until the cake has
shrunk slightly from the sides of
the tin (pan) and is firm. Cool on a
wire rack.

3 Peel, core and slice the apples,
and place in a small pan with the
jam, lemon rind and juice. Cover
and cook gently until the apples
are soft. Cool.

4 Dissolve the sugar in a small
pan with 45 ml (3 tablespoons)
water, bring to the boil and boil
until syrupy. Stir in 30 ml (2 tablespoons) of the brandy and cool.

5 Whip the cream until thick and
fold in the remaining brandy.

6 Split the cold cake and
sprinkle each half with some of
the syrup. Sandwich the sponges
with some of the cream and the
apples. Moisten the cake with the
remaining syrup.

7 Decorate with the remaining
cream and reserved hazelnuts.

Serves 6-8

Strawberry Orange Soufflé

3 eggs, separated
75 g (3 oz) (⅜ cup) castor (fine
  granulated) sugar
finely grated rind and juice
  1 orange
15 g (½ oz) (2 tablespoons)
  powdered gelatine
450 g (1 lb) fresh or frozen and
  thawed strawberries, puréed
150 ml (¼ pint) (⅝ cup) double
  (heavy) cream

For the Decoration:
40 g (1½ oz) plain chocolate,
  grated
a little whipped cream
3 strawberry halves

1 Tie a double band of greaseproof (parchment) paper around
a 900 ml (1½ pint) (3¾ cup) soufflé
dish.

2 Place the egg yolks, sugar and
orange rind in the mixer bowl,
and, with the mixer set at a high
speed, beat the mixture until it is
very thick and pale.

3 Place the orange juice and
gelatine in a small bowl and leave
to soften for 5 minutes. Stand the
bowl in a pan of hot water and stir
the mixture until the gelatine has
dissolved completely. Whisk the
gelatine mixture into the egg
yolks and sugar, then fold in the
strawberry purée. Leave in a cool
place until beginning to set.

4 With the mixer set at a medium
speed, whip the cream until it is
just thick. Whisk the egg whites
until stiff and peaking, then fold
the cream and egg whites into the
strawberry mixture.

5 Transfer the mixture to the
prepared soufflé dish and leave in
a cool place to set.

6 Remove the paper from the set
soufflé, and press the chocolate
on to the sides. Decorate the top
with whipped cream and halved
strawberries.

Serves 6-8

*Strawberry and Orange Soufflé
is a spectacular dessert
which can be whisked up with no
effort at all in a food mixer*

Tudor Syllabub

150 ml (¼ pint) (⅝ cup) sherry
10 ml (2 teaspoons) finely grated
  lemon rind
15 ml (1 tablespoon) lemon juice
75 g (3 oz) (⅜ cup) castor (fine
  granulated) sugar
1 egg white, lightly beaten
30 ml (2 tablespoons) sugar
300 ml (½ pint) (1¼ cups) double
  (heavy) cream
15 ml (1 tablespoon) milk

1 Place the sherry, lemon rind, juice and castor (fine granulated) sugar in the mixer bowl and leave to stand for at least 3 hours.

2 Meanwhile, frost the rims of 6 dessert glasses by dipping them in the beaten egg white and then in the sugar. Leave them to dry.

3 Add the cream and milk to the sherry mixture, and, with the mixer set at a medium speed, whip the mixture until it stands in soft peaks.

4 Pour the syllabub into the frosted glasses and leave in a cool place for several hours before serving.

Serves 6

Marble Cake

fat for greasing
175 g (6 oz) (¾ cup) margarine
175 g (6 oz) (¾ cup) castor (fine
  granulated) sugar
3 large eggs
150 g (5 oz) (1¼ cups) plain flour
75 g (3 oz) (¾ cup) self-raising flour
15 ml (1 tablespoon) cocoa
  powder
a little milk

Tudor Syllabub is a traditional English dessert which dates back to mediaeval times and still tastes delicious

chocolate, orange and yellow
  food colourings
finely grated rind 1 orange
5 ml (1 teaspoon) orange juice
finely grated rind 1 lemon
5 ml (1 teaspoon) lemon juice
few drops vanilla essence

For the Buttercream:
75 g (3 oz) (⅜ cup) margarine
175 g (6 oz) (¾ cup) icing
  (confectioners') sugar
15 ml (1 tablespoon) cocoa
  powder

1 Preheat the oven to 170°C, 325°F, gas 3. Grease a 20cm (8 in) cake tin (pan), line it with greaseproof (parchment) paper and re-grease.

2 Place the margarine and sugar in a mixer bowl and, with the mixer set at a high speed, cream the mixture until it is light and fluffy. Add the eggs, one at a time, beating well. Sieve the flours together and fold them into the mixture with a large metal spoon.

3 Divide the mixture into 4 portions. Mix the cocoa powder, 5 ml (1 teaspoon) milk and a few drops of chocolate colouring into one portion. Add the orange rind and juice to the second portion, with a few drops of orange colouring. Add the lemon rind and juice to the third portion with a few drops of yellow colouring. Add the vanilla to the last portion.

4 Place spoonfuls of the mixtures alternately in the prepared cake tin (pan). Bake in the preheated oven for about 1¼ hours, until the cake is well-risen and firm to the touch. Remove the cake to a wire rack to cool.

5 Prepare the buttercream: place the margarine, sugar and cocoa powder in the mixer bowl. Incorporate the ingredients with the mixer set at a low speed. Increase the speed and beat the mixture until smooth, adding a little water if necessary.

6 Spread the buttercream over the cake, swirling attractively.

Serves 8

Marble Cake is always a firm favourite with kids who love the different colours and the thick chocolate covering

Apricot and Sultana Loaf

This recipe uses the stand-mounted mixer fitted with the dough hook.

10 ml (2 teaspoons) dried yeast, or
  15 g ($\frac{1}{2}$ oz) fresh yeast
365 ml (13 fl oz) (1$\frac{5}{8}$ cups)
  lukewarm milk
25 g (1 oz) (2 tablespoons) castor
  (fine granulated) sugar
675 g (1$\frac{1}{2}$ lb) (6$\frac{3}{4}$ cups) strong plain
  flour
15 ml (3 teaspoons) salt
25 g (1 oz) (2 tablespoons) lard
1 egg, beaten
75 g (3 oz) (1 cup) dried apricots,
  diced
50 g (2 oz) ($\frac{2}{3}$ cup) sultanas
  (seedless raisins)
beaten egg to glaze

1 If using dried yeast, pour 150 ml ($\frac{1}{4}$ pint) ($\frac{5}{8}$ cup) of the luke-warm milk into a small bowl, stir in 5 ml (1 teaspoon) of the sugar, sprinkle the yeast over and leave in a warm place for 10 minutes until frothy. If using fresh yeast, blend it with the warm milk.

2 Sieve the flour and salt into the mixer bowl. Rub in the lard and stir in the sugar. Make a well in the centre and pour in the yeast, milk and egg.

3 With the mixer set at a medium speed, knead the dough for about 3 minutes, until smooth and elastic. Place the dough in a clean bowl, cover with greased poly-thene and leave in a warm place to rise until doubled in bulk.

4 Preheat the oven to 230°C, 450°F, gas 8. Turn the risen dough on to a lightly floured surface and flatten it out. Sprinkle over the apricots and sultanas (seedless raisins), then fold the dough over to enclose them. Knead until smooth.

5 Flatten the dough into an oblong and fold the edges under to form a smooth roll. Drop the roll, smooth side upwards, into a well-greased 1 kg (2 lb) loaf tin (pan), cover with greased poly-thene and leave in a warm place until doubled in size.

Apricot and Sultana Loaf is a tasty tea-bread which is easily made in a mixer using a dough hook attachment

6 Brush the loaf with beaten egg to glaze and bake for about 25 minutes, until well-risen and golden-brown. The loaf should sound hollow when rapped with the knuckles underneath. Cool on a wire rack.

Makes one 1 kg (2 lb) loaf

Jumblie Cookies

75 g (3 oz) ($\frac{3}{8}$ cup) lard
50 g (2 oz) ($\frac{1}{4}$ cup) margarine

175 g (6 oz) ($\frac{3}{4}$ cup) soft light
  brown sugar
1 egg
225 g ($\frac{1}{2}$ lb) (2$\frac{1}{4}$ cups) self-raising
  flour
50 g (2 oz) ($\frac{2}{3}$ cup) raisins
50 g (2 oz) chocolate chips

1 Preheat the oven to 180°C, 350°F, gas 4.

2 Cream together the lard, mar-garine and sugar with the mixer set at a high speed, until the mix-ture is pale and fluffy. Beat in the egg.

3 Stir the remaining ingredients into the mixture to form a firm dough. Roll into walnut-sized balls and place them on a lightly greased baking (cookie) sheet, about 5 cm (2 in) apart. Press them down lightly with a fork.

4 Bake in the preheated oven for

about 15 minutes, until the biscuits are pale golden. Cool on a wire rack.

Makes 36

Coffee Choux Puffs

150 ml ($\frac{1}{4}$ pint) ($\frac{5}{8}$ cup) water
50 g (2 oz) ($\frac{1}{4}$ cup) margarine
40 g (1$\frac{1}{2}$ oz) (6 tablespoons) flour,
  sieved
2 eggs, beaten
170 ml (6 fl oz) ($\frac{3}{4}$ cup) double
  (heavy) cream
5 ml (1 teaspoon) castor (fine
  granulated) sugar
15 ml (1 tablespoon) coffee
  essence
icing (confectioners') sugar for
  dredging

1 Preheat the oven to 200°C, 400°F, gas 6.

2 Place the water in a small pan with the margarine, and melt over a gentle heat. Bring to a rolling boil and immediately add all the flour. Beat well with a wooden spoon until the mixture forms a ball in the middle of the pan. Allow the mixture to cool slightly.

3 If using a stand-mounted mixer, transfer the mixture to the mixer bowl. With the mixer set at a medium speed, add the eggs a little at a time, until the mixture is soft and just holds its shape.

4 Spoon about 12 small rounds of the mixture on to a lightly greased baking (cookie) sheet and bake in the preheated oven for 20 minutes. Make a slit in the side of each puff with the point of a sharp knife, then return them to the oven for a further 10 minutes. Cool the puffs on a wire rack.

5 Whip the cream until it is just thick, then fold in the sugar and coffee essence. Slit the cold puffs almost in half and spoon or pipe in the cream. Dredge with a little icing (confectioners') sugar before serving.

Makes about 12

12-15 minutes, until golden. Cool on a wire rack.

Makes 40

Coffee-speckled Biscuits

225 g ($\frac{1}{2}$ lb) (1 cup) margarine
100 g ($\frac{1}{4}$ lb) ($\frac{1}{2}$ cup) castor (fine
  granulated) sugar
1 egg
5 ml (1 teaspoon) vanilla essence
23 ml (1$\frac{1}{2}$ tablespoons) instant
  coffee granules
250 g (9 oz) (2$\frac{1}{2}$ cups) flour
5 ml (1 teaspoon) baking powder
1.25 ml ($\frac{1}{4}$ teaspoon) salt

Coffee Choux Puffs, filled with coffee-flavoured whipped cream and dusted with sugar, are easy to make in a food mixer

1 Preheat the oven to 180°C, 350°F, gas 4.

2 Cream together the margarine and sugar with the mixer set at a high speed, until the mixture is pale and fluffy. Beat in the egg, vanilla and coffee granules.

3 Sieve the flour with the baking powder and salt and fold into the mixture with a large metal spoon. Transfer the mixture to a piping (decorator's) bag and pipe 'S' shapes, about 6.5 cm (2$\frac{1}{2}$ in) long, on to an ungreased baking (cookie) sheet.

4 Bake in the preheated oven for

Blenders

For those of you who have always wanted to make exciting soups and pâtés but rarely have the time after a day at the office or looking after the family, a blender is the answer to all your problems. Within minutes you can whip up sauces, pâtés, soups, delicious drinks and desserts or purée vegetables for young children. The amount of time and effort saved is well worth the initial small outlay.

If you are the proud owner of a new blender, make sure that you thoroughly understand the manufacturer's instructions before assembling and using it. Keep the blender out of reach of young children, and on a handy working surface so that it is available for any job at the flick of a switch. Never store anything in the goblet – the machine could be switched on by accident and be damaged.

Most blenders give their best performance when only half-full, so don't overfill your blender goblet. Generally speaking, 2 or 3 short bursts are better than one long one. In any event, blend only for the length of time set out in the manufacturer's instructions. If the mixture is flung to the sides of the goblet, switch off the blender and scrape the mixture back on to the blades.

Always clean your blender as soon as possible after use – once food dries on the blades it is difficult to remove. To clean, half-fill the blender goblet with warm water and switch it to high speed for 20 seconds. Empty and give it a good rinse with warm clean water. Wipe off any surplus liquid and leave it in a warm place to dry. Never immerse the base in water. Use common sense when it comes to what foods you put in your blender. Whole spices, such as cloves, dill seeds and cumin seeds, or whole peppercorns are unsuitable and may damage the blades.

Chilled Mushroom and Lemon Soup

450 g (1 lb) flat mushrooms
thinly pared rind 1 lemon
45 ml (3 tablespoons) lemon juice
1 clove garlic, crushed
5 ml (1 teaspoon) dried thyme
salt
freshly ground (milled) black pepper
900 ml (1½ pints) (3¾ cups) chicken stock
150 ml (¼ pint) (⅝ cup) single (light) cream
chopped parsley for garnishing

1 Wash and dry the mushrooms. Reserve 1 or 2 for garnishing and slice the rest. Put them in a flat dish with the lemon rind, lemon juice, garlic, thyme and seasoning and leave them to marinate for several hours.

2 Place the mushrooms and the marinade in a blender with the stock and blend to a purée. Stir in the cream and adjust the seasoning. Pour the soup into a serving bowl and chill. Serve garnished with the reserved mushrooms and the chopped parsley.

Serves 6-8

Egg and Anchovy Mousse

85 ml (3 fl oz) (⅜ cup) mayonnaise
8 canned anchovy fillets, drained
salt and freshly ground (milled) black pepper
30 ml (2 tablespoons) single (light) cream
5 ml (1 teaspoon) anchovy essence
few drops chilli sauce
4 hard-boiled eggs
1 egg white
1 sliced tomato, parsley or watercress to garnish

1 Put the mayonnaise in the blender goblet with the drained anchovy fillets, seasoning, cream, anchovy essence and chilli sauce. Blend gently until smooth.

2 Cut the eggs into pieces and add them to the blender. Blend for a few seconds until they are finely chopped.

3 Whisk the egg white in a bowl until it is stiff and fold the contents of the blender goblet into it. Check the seasoning and turn it into four 150 ml (¼ pint) (⅝ cup) soufflé dishes. Cover and refrigerate for several hours. Serve garnished with sliced tomato, parsley or watercress.

Serves 4

Hummus bi Tahini

450 g (1 lb) canned chick peas, drained
2 cloves garlic, crushed
2.5 ml (½ teaspoon) ground cumin
2.5 ml (½ teaspoon) salt
45 ml (3 tablespoons) sesame or olive oil
50 ml (2 fl oz) (¼ cup) lemon juice
15 ml (1 tablespoon) chopped parsley or coriander

1 Rub the chick peas through a strainer into the blender goblet. Add the garlic, cumin and salt and replace the lid. Blend, adding the oil and lemon juice alternately, 15 ml (1 tablespoon) at a time, until you have a thick, smooth paste.

2 Transfer the mixture to a serving bowl and refrigerate for 3 hours before serving. Garnish with coriander or parsley leaves and serve with pitta bread and a selection of raw mushrooms, carrot strips, celery strips, pepper slices and cucumber cut into segments.

Serves 4

Hummus bi Tahini, a thick purée of chick peas flavoured with sesame oil, can be served as a dip with fresh vegetables

Chicken Liver Whip

450 g (1 lb) chicken livers
50 g (2 oz) (¼ cup) butter
175 g (6 oz) bacon, diced
1 small onion, chopped
1 clove garlic, crushed
salt
ground (milled) black pepper
100 ml (4 fl oz) (½ cup) sweet
   sherry
10 ml (2 teaspoons) powdered
   gelatine
300 ml (½ pint) (1¼ cups) double
   (heavy) cream, whipped
aspic jelly crystals to make
   150 ml (¼ pint) (⅝ cup) aspic
1 cucumber
1 slice orange
1 black olive

1 Clean the livers and discard the green parts (gall bladders). Melt the butter in a pan and sauté the bacon until crisp. Add the livers and sauté for 5-6 minutes. Add the onion, garlic and seasoning and stir-fry for 1 more minute. Remove from the heat.

2 Heat the sherry and dissolve in the gelatine. Stir the sherry into the pan, then transfer the contents of the pan to a blender. Blend until smooth. Turn the mixture into a bowl and fold in the whipped cream. Turn the whip into a wet 900 ml (1½ pint) (3¾ cup) oval mould. Smooth the top and place in the refrigerator to set. When set, unmould on to a plate.

3 Make up 150 ml (¼ pint) (⅝ cup) of aspic with the aspic jelly crystals, following the instructions on the packet. Wash the mould and pour in the aspic. Cut a few strips of cucumber peel and when the aspic begins to set, arrange the orange slice and cucumber peel in the aspic to represent a flower. Place a sliver of olive in the centre of the orange slice and allow the aspic to set completely before returning the shaped whip to the mould.

4 Chill the whip for 1½ hours before unmoulding. Surround with slices of cucumber and serve.

Serves 6-8

Banana Mousse

450 g (1 lb) bananas
15 ml (1 tablespoon) lemon juice
25 g (1 oz) (2 tablespoons) soft
   brown sugar
150 ml (¼ pint) (⅝ cup) yogurt
50 ml (2 fl oz) (4 tablespoons)
   double (heavy) cream
2 egg whites
15 ml (1 tablespoon) flaked
   almonds
demerara sugar for serving
shortbread biscuits for serving

1 Skin the bananas and cut them up roughly. Put them in a blender goblet with all the remaining ingredients except the egg whites, almonds and demerara sugar. Blend until smooth. Turn the mixture into a bowl.

2 Whisk the egg whites until stiff and fold them with the almonds into the mixture. Turn the mixture into a serving dish. Cover and chill until the mousse thickens and darkens slightly. Sprinkle with demerara sugar and serve with shortbread biscuits.

Serves 4

Golden Vegetable Soup

40 g (1½ oz) (3 tablespoons) butter
2 large onions, sliced
350 g (¾ lb) carrots, roughly
   chopped
2 sticks celery, chopped
50 g (2 oz) bacon pieces
5 ml (1 teaspoon) curry powder
1 litre (1¾ pints) (4½ cups) chicken
   stock
1 bay leaf
225 g (½ lb) canned tomatoes
salt and pepper
a little top of the milk (optional)

1 Melt the butter in a frying pan (skillet) and add the vegetables, bacon and curry powder. Fry for 5 minutes, shaking the pan occasionally. Add the stock, bay leaf and tomatoes. Cover and cook gently for 25-30 minutes

until the vegetables are tender. Discard the bay leaf and cool slightly.

2 Transfer the mixture to the goblet of the blender. (Don't fill it more than half full. If necessary, blend in batches.) Switch to maximum speed and run it for about 20 seconds until really smooth.

3 Return the soup to a rinsed pan, season to taste and thin with a little top of the milk (optional). Bring to the boil and serve hot.

Makes approximately 1.8 litres (3 pints) (7½ cups)

Tomato Cream Soup

15 ml (1 tablespoon) fat
1 small onion, sliced
1 rasher (slice) streaky bacon,
   chopped
1 medium potato, sliced
450 g (1 lb) tomatoes, quartered
2.5 ml (½ teaspoon) sugar
150 ml (¼ pint) (⅝ cup) water
5 ml (1 teaspoon) salt
pinch paprika
pinch cayenne pepper
2.5 ml (½ teaspoon) celery salt
150 ml (¼ pint) (⅝ cup) milk
chopped parsley to garnish

1 Melt the fat in a pan. Add the onion and bacon and fry for about 5 minutes. Add the potato, tomato, sugar and water. Cover and simmer gently until the potato is cooked.

2 Remove the bacon and pour the contents of the pan into a warmed blender goblet. Add the seasonings and blend for 1 minute. Remove the lid and pour in the milk. Blend for a few more seconds and strain the soup into a saucepan. Heat gently before pouring it into serving bowls. Serve sprinkled with parsley.

Serves 3-4

Chicken Liver Whip, flavoured with orange juice, is a rich and tasty pâté which you can whip up in your blender

299

Apricot Delight Whip

225 g (½ lb) canned apricots
5 ml (1 teaspoon) powdered
  gelatine
50 ml (2 fl oz) (¼ cup) syrup from
  the apricots, warmed
juice ½ lemon
30 ml (2 tablespoons) gin
300 ml (½ pint) (1¼ cups) double
  (heavy) cream
15 ml (1 tablespoon) grated
  chocolate

1 Place the apricots in a blender and blend to a purée.

2 Dissolve the gelatine in the warmed apricot syrup and mix with the purée. Add the lemon juice, gin and half of the cream. Blend again lightly.

3 Whip the remaining cream and fold it into the apricot mixture. Pour the whip into 4 serving glasses and place them in the refrigerator for 2 hours or until set. Sprinkle with grated chocolate and serve.

Serves 4

Banana and Chocolate Egg Nog Dessert

100 g (¼ lb) dark chocolate,
  melted
15 ml (1 tablespoon) rum
3 bananas, peeled and sliced
3 egg yolks
25 g (1 oz) (¼ cup) icing
  (confectioners') sugar
300 ml (½ pint) (1¼ cups) double
  (heavy) cream, whipped

1 Place all the ingredients, except the cream, in the blender and blend until smooth. Fold 225 ml (8 fl oz) (1 cup) of the cream into the mixture and divide between 4 sundae glasses. Chill.

2 Pipe rosettes of the remaining cream on top of each glass and serve with sponge fingers.

Serves 4

Sunny Cheesecake

150 g (5 oz) sweetmeal biscuits
  (cookies)
40 g (1½ oz) (3 tablespoons) butter,
  melted
25 g (1 oz) (4 tablespoons)
  powdered gelatine
30 ml (2 tablespoons) warm
  water
225 (½ lb) cream cheese, cut into
  pieces
25 g (1 oz) (2 tablespoons) castor
  (fine granulated) sugar
300 ml (½ pint) (1¼ cups) milk
rind 1 orange
2 eggs, separated
1 orange, segmented
1 glacé cherry

1 In a bowl, mix together the biscuits (cookies) and the butter until the crumbs are very moist. Press them firmly into the bottom of a lightly greased 15 cm (6 in) loose-bottomed cake tin (pan).

2 Dissolve the gelatine in the warm water and place it with the cream cheese, castor (fine granulated) sugar, milk, orange rind and egg yolks in the blender goblet. Blend for 45 seconds.

3 Whisk the egg whites to form stiff peaks and then gently fold in the contents of the blender. Spoon the mixture into the crumb case and refrigerate until firm. Arrange the orange segments on top with a cherry in the centre to represent a flower.

Serves 4-6

Hot Chocolate Mint Drink

1 small bar peppermint cream
  chocolate
300 ml (½ pint) (1¼ cups) hot milk

1 Break the chocolate into pieces and place it in the blender goblet. Pour in the hot milk and blend for 30 seconds. Pour immediately into mugs.

Serves 2

Caramel Crème Brulée

2 egg yolks
2.5 ml (½ teaspoon) vanilla
  essence
40 g (1½ oz) (3 tablespoons) sugar
350 ml (12 fl oz) (1½ cups)
  evaporated milk
demerara sugar

1 Preheat the oven to 180°C, 350°F, gas 4. Place the egg yolks, vanilla essence and sugar in a blender goblet. Heat the evaporated milk to simmering point.

2 Remove the centre cap from the lid of the blender and switch to whip. Gradually pour the hot milk into the goblet, while running, and blend for 30 seconds. Pour the mixture into a fireproof dish and bake for 1 hour or until set.

3 Cool, then chill thoroughly in the refrigerator for several hours. Sprinkle the surface evenly with demerara sugar and slide it under a hot grill (broiler) just long enough to melt the sugar.

Serves 4-6

Gin Fizz

50 ml (2 fl oz) (¼ cup) gin
juice ½ lemon
thin strip lemon rind
10 ml (2 teaspoons) sugar
1 egg white
4 ice cubes
soda water

1 Place all the ingredients except the soda water in a blender goblet and blend for about 15 seconds.

2 Strain the drink into 2 long glasses and fill them with soda water.

Serves 2

Apricot Delight Whip and Banana and Chocolate Egg Nog Dessert are two delicious blender desserts, while making meringues is simple with a mixer

Infra-red Grills

The infra-red grill is a very recent invention which is ideal for two groups of cooks in particular: those who have little time for cooking, and those who have a very limited amount of space for cooking. The infra-red grill cooks food in considerably less time (and hence more economically) than normal methods. It also combines the functions of a grill (broiler), direct-contact griddle, cooking ring, and a small oven, so almost any type of dish can be cooked – and in much less space than that occupied by a cooker with the same facilities. In fact, an infra-red grill on a refrigerator is a whole kitchen in miniature.

Sole Parmigiana

5 fillets sole
30 ml (2 tablespoons) flour,
  seasoned with salt and pepper
1 large egg, beaten
35 g (1¼ oz) (4 tablespoons) grated
  Parmesan cheese
50 g (2 oz) (1 cup) fresh
  breadcrumbs
50 g (2 oz) (¼ cup) butter
15 ml (1 tablespoon) flaked
  almonds

1 Set the grill to number 2.

2 Coat the sole fillets in the seasoned flour and then in beaten egg. Finally coat the fillets with a mixture of grated Parmesan cheese and breadcrumbs.

3 Place the butter in the grill tray and heat until foamy. Place the coated fillets in the butter and cook until golden-brown.

4 Remove the fillets from the pan and place them on a serving dish. Stir the almonds in the butter for a few minutes, and scatter them over the fish. Serve at once.

Serves 5

Potato Cheese Bake

1 kg (2 lb) old potatoes
50 g (2 oz) (¼ cup) butter
salt and pepper
2 onions, sliced
50 g (2 oz) (½ cup) grated cheese

1 Set the grill to number 2.

2 Peel and slice the potatoes.

3 Grease the grill tray with half of the butter. Place a layer of potatoes over the bottom of the tray, season, and top with a layer of onions. Dot with butter and repeat, finishing with a layer of potato. Cover with foil and cook in the grill for 20 minutes.

4 Raise the grill to number 3. Sprinkle grated cheese over the potato and cook for a few minutes until golden-brown.

Serves 4

Infra-grilled Lamb Chops

5 large lamb chops
salt and black pepper
garlic salt (optional)
50 g (2 oz) (¼ cup) butter
15 ml (1 tablespoon) finely
  chopped fresh parsley
finely grated zest 1 lemon
5 ml (1 teaspoon) lemon juice
pinch cayenne pepper

1 Set the grill to number 3.

2 Season the lamb chops lightly with salt and freshly ground (milled) black pepper, and a dusting of garlic salt, if wished. Lightly oil the grill plates and arrange the meat on them. Cook for 8-10 minutes, according to taste.

3 Meanwhile, blend the butter, parsley, lemon zest and juice, and cayenne pepper. When the chops are cooked, arrange them on a bed of rice, and melt the lemon and herb butter over them. Serve immediately.

Serves 5

Apple and Orange Rings

4 oranges
3 dessert apples
25 g (1 oz) (2 tablespoons) soft
  light brown sugar
150 ml (¼ pint) (⅝ cup) sherry
20 g (¾ oz) (1½ tablespoons) butter

1 Set the grill to number 2.

2 Peel the oranges and cut them in 1 cm (½ in) slices. Peel and core the apples and slice them.

3 Arrange the apple and orange slices in the grill tray. Sprinkle them with the sugar and pour over the sherry. Dot with butter and cook in the grill for 5-8 minutes, until the apple is soft. Serve hot or cold.

Serves 4

Spicy Flapjacks

125 g (4½ oz) (9 tablespoons)
  margarine
125 g (4½ oz) (9 tablespoons)
  demerara sugar
4 ml (¾ teaspoon) ground
  cinnamon
good pinch ground nutmeg
200 g (7 oz) (1⅛ cups) rolled oats

1 Set the grill to number 3.

2 In a large bowl, cream the margarine with the sugar to make a pale, fluffy mixture. Blend in the cinnamon and nutmeg.

3 Stir in the oats gradually to make an evenly blended, thick mixture. Grease the grill tray and spread the mixture evenly in it, pressing it down.

4 Grill for 10 minutes until crisp and golden. Allow to cool in the tray. Turn out of the tray, cut into fingers and serve .

Makes about 20

Apple and Orange Rings, Spicy Flapjacks, Infra-grilled Lamb Chops and Sole Parmigiana are cooked in an infra-red grill

Electric Fry-pans

Economical, roomy and easy to use, the electric fry-pan is an invaluable appliance for the busy cook. It is amazingly versatile: you can use it for roasting, braising, stewing, casseroling, steaming and boiling, as well as frying.

Frying and roasting are particularly easy in a fry-pan because you can regulate the temperature and therefore avoid overheating and burning food. Fry-pans are ideal when you are cooking for crowds. You can fry up huge mounds of rice Chinese-style, or roast a large joint or chicken and fry the vegetable garnish at the same time. Potatoes, parsnips and chipolata (link) sausages can be roasted around the joint in the meat juices. When roasting, always remember to cover the fry-pan.

When cleaning and washing your fry-pan after use, *never* immerse it totally in water. Also, take care that the electric socket does not become wet.

Many fry-pans can also be used for slow cooking, which helps to retain the nutrients and flavour of the food. Slow cookers are dealt with on pages 1886-1888, and so this section deals with only the frying and roasting functions of the electric fry-pan.

With a fry-pan, you can cook money-saving meals all in the same pan, and so cut down on fuel costs and washing up dirty pots and pans! This makes cooking fast, exciting and easy – no slaving away for hours over a hot stove. Instead, you can fry up a large omelette with a chunky topping, a colourful risotto or even a stroganoff in a matter of minutes. Quick desserts like bananas flambé, pancakes and apple fritters are all easy to make with a fry-pan.

Honey-Roast Chicken

one 2 kg (4 lb) roasting chicken, trussed and oven-ready
salt and pepper
45 ml (3 tablespoons) oil
30 ml (2 tablespoons) honey
675 g (1½ lb) potatoes, peeled
450 g (1 lb) courgettes (zucchini), sliced
few sprigs watercress

For the Stuffing:
40 g (1½ oz) (¼ cup) almonds, chopped
40 g (1½ oz) (¼ cup) dried apricots, chopped
50 g (2 oz) (1 cup) fresh breadcrumbs
15 ml (1 tablespoon) honey
45 ml (3 tablespoons) melted butter
15 ml (1 tablespoon) chopped onion
10 ml (2 teaspoons) oil
salt and pepper

1 Make the stuffing: mix together the almonds, apricots, breadcrumbs, honey and melted butter. Sauté the onion in the oil until soft. Stir into the stuffing mixture and season.

2 Stuff this mixture into the chicken. Season the chicken.

3 Heat the fry-pan to 180°C, 350°F, and add the oil. Roast the chicken with the lid on the pan for 15 minutes, stirring occasionally, until browned on all sides. Reduce the temperature to 150°C, 300°F, and continue roasting for about 1¼ hours. Turn the chicken occasionally, and brush with the honey during the last 10 minutes of the cooking time.

4 Prepare the potatoes in advance. Bring them to the boil in a pan of salted water and then place them around the chicken for the last 45 minutes of the cooking time. Turn them from time to time in the hot fat. Do not add the courgettes (zucchini) to the fry-pan until the last moment. They only require 4-5 minutes to cook and become golden-brown.

5 Garnish the chicken with sprigs of watercress and serve.

Serves 6

Chicken Shanghai

one 1.5 kg (3 lb) chicken
225 g (½ lb) lean pork tenderloin
45 ml (3 tablespoons) soya sauce
45 ml (3 tablespoons) sherry
25 ml (1½ tablespoons) cornflour (cornstarch)
50 ml (2 fl oz) (¼ cup) oil
small piece root ginger, chopped
1 clove garlic, crushed
450 g (1 lb) shelled shrimps
175 g (6 oz) boiled egg noodles
1 large onion, chopped
1 red pepper, deseeded and sliced
¼ white cabbage, shredded
8 spring onions (scallions), sliced
2 sticks celery, chopped
salt and pepper
100 ml (4 fl oz) (½ cup) stock

1 Skin the chicken and remove the flesh. Cut into 2.5 cm (1 in) cubes. Cut the pork into cubes of the same size.

2 Mix together 30 ml (2 tablespoons) soya sauce, 30 ml (2 tablespoons) sherry and 10 ml (2 teaspoons) cornflour (cornstarch) in a bowl and marinate the meat in this mixture for about 1 hour.

3 Heat the oil in the electric fry-pan at 150°C, 300°F, and fry the ginger and garlic for 2-3 minutes. Add the meat to the pan and brown, tossing constantly, for 5 minutes. Raise the temperature if necessary. Add the shrimps and boiled egg noodles and stir-fry for another 3 minutes. Then add all the chopped vegetables and season with salt and pepper.

4 Stir in the stock and the remaining sherry, soya sauce and cornflour (cornstarch). Cook for several minutes, stirring occasionally, until the sauce thickens. Serve with a crisp green salad and a sweet 'n sour sauce, if wished.

Serves 6

Chicken Shanghai is an exotic and colourful Chinese dish which you can cook in your fry-pan to save washing-up

Look'n Cook Chicken Shanghai

1 The ingredients: chicken, pork, shrimps, celery, spring onions (scallions), soya sauce, sherry, oil, red pepper, root ginger, onion, cornflour (cornstarch), stock, cabbage and egg noodles **2** Skin and remove the chicken flesh and cut into cubes. Trim the pork and cut in similar-sized cubes **3** Mix some soya sauce, sherry and cornflour (cornstarch) together and pour over the meat. Leave for 1 hour **4** Chop the onion and root ginger; deseed and slice the pepper; shred the cabbage and slice the spring onions (scal-

lions) and celery **5** Heat the oil in the fry-pan and fry the ginger and garlic for 2-3 minutes. Add the meat to the pan and cook for 5 minutes until brown **6** Add the cooked egg noodles and shrimps. Stir-fry for 3 minutes **7** Add all the vegetables to the pan and cook for several minutes, stirring. Season to taste with salt and pepper **8** Mix the remaining sherry, soya sauce and cornflour (cornstarch) with the stock and add to the pan. Carry on cooking for several more minutes, stirring until the sauce thickens

Spanish Braised Beef

50 g (2 oz) (¼ cup) butter
15 ml (1 tablespoon) oil
2 onions, chopped
450 g (1 lb) stewing steak, cubed
25 g (1 oz) (4 tablespoons) flour
300 ml (½ pint) (1¼ cups) stock
30 ml (2 tablespoons) tomato
  paste
150 ml (¼ pint) (⅝ cup) red wine
salt and pepper
4 courgettes (zucchini), sliced
225 g (½ lb) French beans
2 potatoes, parboiled and cubed

1 Heat the butter and oil in a fry-pan at 170°C, 325°F, and fry the onions until soft and browned. Add the stewing steak and brown all over. Stir in the flour and cook for 2-3 minutes. Add the stock, tomato paste and red wine and bring to the boil, stirring all the time.

2 Season with salt and pepper and reduce the heat to 110°C, 225°F. Cover with the lid and simmer gently for about 1 hour. Add the courgettes (zucchini), French beans and parboiled potatoes and cook for a further 20 minutes until the meat and vegetables are tender.

Serves 4

Spanish Braised Beef (left) and Italian-style Pork Chops (right) are two of the colourful dishes which you can fry up using your electric fry-pan

Burmese Rice

45 ml (3 tablespoons) oil
3 onions, chopped
1 red pepper, deseeded and
  chopped
225 g (½ lb) (2½ cups) sliced button
  mushrooms
2 cloves garlic, crushed
1 kg (2 lb) (4½ cups) cooked
  long-grain rice
2.5 ml (½ teaspoon) turmeric
salt and pepper
15 ml (1 tablespoon) tomato
  paste
30 ml (2 tablespoons) tomato
  ketchup (catsup)
2.5 ml (½ teaspoon) curry powder
225 g (½ lb) (1½ cups) peeled cooked
  shrimps
225 g (½ lb) (1⅓ cups) cooked
  chicken meat, diced
100 g (¼ lb) (1 cup) cooked peas
450 g (1 lb) canned bean sprouts
15 ml (1 tablespoon) chopped
  chives

For the Omelette:
2 eggs, beaten

15 ml (1 tablespoon) water
10 ml (2 teaspoons) butter

1 Heat the oil in a fry-pan set at 150°C, 300°F and sauté the onion until soft and transparent. Add the pepper, mushrooms and garlic and fry until tender.

2 Add the rice and fry for a few minutes, turning frequently, until the rice is golden. Mix in the turmeric, season and add the tomato paste, ketchup (catsup) and curry powder. Mix in the shrimps and chicken, cover and reduce the heat to the lowest setting.

3 Stir in the peas and arrange the drained bean sprouts on top. Replace the cover.

4 Make the omelette: whisk the eggs but do not overbeat them. Season and add the water. Heat the butter in a small frying pan (skillet) and pour in the egg mixture. Stir gently as it sets. When it is golden underneath, turn it over and cook on the other side. Remove the omelette and cut into strips.

5 Serve the rice topped with a lattice of criss-crossing omelette strips and sprinkled with the chopped chives.

Serves 6

Spanish Seafood Paella

one 1½ kg (3 lb) boiling chicken,
  cooked
50 ml (2 fl oz) (¼ cup) olive oil
1 onion, chopped
2 cloves garlic, crushed
1 red pepper, deseeded and sliced
350 g (¾ lb) (1½ cups) long-grain
  rice
225 g (½ lb) shelled peas
550 ml (1 pint) mussels
175 g (6 oz) (1 cup) peeled, cooked
  prawns (shrimps)
chicken stock
juice ½ lemon
1 bay leaf
salt and pepper
pinch powdered saffron
6 king prawns (large shrimps)
  uncooked
15 ml (1 tablespoon) butter,
  melted
15 ml (1 tablespoon) lemon juice
8 stuffed olives, sliced

1 Remove the chicken flesh from the carcass and cut into chunks or strips. Heat the oil in the fry-pan set at 170°C, 325°F and fry the onion and garlic until transparent. Add the red pepper and sauté until soft.

2 Stir in the rice and fry until it is a pale golden colour. Add the shelled peas, mussels, prawns (shrimps) and the chicken meat. Pour in enough chicken stock to completely cover the ingredients in the pan. Add the lemon juice and bay leaf, cover with the lid and reduce the temperature to 110°C, 225°F. Cook until the rice is tender and all of the liquid has been absorbed. Season to taste and stir in the saffron, mixing it well throughout the rice mixture so that it is evenly coloured.

3 While the rice is cooking, grill (broil) the king prawns (large shrimps), brushing them occasionally with melted butter and lemon juice.

4 Transfer the paella to a serving dish and garnish with the grilled (broiled) prawns (shrimps) and sliced stuffed olives.

Serves 6

Italian-style Pork Chops

25 g (1 oz) (2 tablespoons) butter
15 ml (1 tablespoon) oil
450 g (1 lb) onions, thinly sliced
4 pork chops or steaks
a little gravy browning
100 ml (4 fl oz) (½ cup) Marsala
  (or port)
salt and pepper

For the Velouté Sauce:
30 ml (2 tablespoons) flour
15 g (½ oz) (1 tablespoon) butter
300 ml (½ pint) (1¼ cups) chicken
  stock
squeeze lemon juice
15 ml (1 tablespoon) cream

1 Heat the butter and oil in the fry-pan at 180°C, 350°F and fry the

*Spanish Seafood Paella is a
complete meal in
itself and can all be prepared in
the same electric fry-pan*

onions until soft and golden. Remove and keep warm.

2 Fry the chops until well-browned on both sides (about 15-20 minutes). Remove from the pan and keep warm.

3 Meanwhile, while the chops are cooking, make the velouté sauce. Make a roux with the flour and butter. Cook for 3 minutes, then add the stock and bring to the boil, stirring until it is thick and smooth. Simmer gently and stir in the lemon juice and cream.

4 Add the velouté sauce, gravy browning and Marsala to the pan juices and boil up, stirring well, until thick and smooth and reduced by one-third.

5 Return the onions and chops to the pan. Heat through in the sauce, season and serve with new potatoes and green vegetables.

Serves 4

See also page 338 for Microwave version of Paella.

Slow Cookers

The slow cooker is a modern version of an ancient cooking method – leaving food to cook very slowly in a stoneware pot inside a warm oven. A slow cooker, however, uses very much less electricity than an oven, and the food is sealed in so that none of the juices, flavour or nourishment is lost. It's ideal for cooks who are out of the house all day and want to be able to serve up a hearty meal as soon as they return; or for cooking a stew or soup overnight. Slow cookers vary slightly in method so the manufacturer's instructions should be followed.

Lamb Azinna

5 ml (1 teaspoon) Indian tea
  leaves
225 g (½ lb) (1½ cups) dried peaches
1 kg (2 lb) shoulder of lamb
50 g (2 oz) (½ cup) flour
5 ml (1 teaspoon) curry powder
50 ml (2 fl oz) (¼ cup) oil
1 large onion, chopped
225 g (½ lb) carrots, peeled and
  sliced or diced
2 courgettes (zucchini), sliced
3 large sticks celery, cut in
  chunks
150 ml (¼ pint) (⅝ cup) orange juice
juice 1 lemon
100g (¼ lb) canned red peppers
  (pimentoes)
2 tomatoes, peeled and chopped
15 ml (1 tablespoon) tomato
  paste
550 ml (1 pint) (2½ cups) chicken
  stock
salt and pepper
2 mint leaves, finely chopped

1 Infuse the tea for 5 minutes in 900 ml (1½ pints) (3¾ cups) boiling water. Strain out the tea leaves and pour the tea over the dried peaches in a bowl. Leave for 2 hours to soak.

2 Meanwhile, bone the shoulder of lamb. Remove any excess fat and cut the meat into 2 cm (¾ in) cubes. Mix the flour and curry powder and dust the meat with it.

3 Set the slow cooker to HIGH or follow the manufacturer's instructions. Heat the oil in a large saucepan and fry the meat for about 3 minutes until browned on all sides. Strain the meat from the pan and place it in the slow cooker.

4 Fry the onion and carrot in the oil for 5 minutes to soften. Strain and place them in the cooker. Drain the excess oil from the saucepan and place the peaches and tea, and the rest of the ingredients in it, mixing with a wooden spoon. Bring them to the boil.

5 Remove the saucepan from the heat and transfer the contents to the slow cooker. Cover and cook for 30 minutes. Change the setting to LOW and continue to cook for 6-7 hours. Serve with boiled rice or baked potatoes.

Serves 6-8

Devonshire Rabbit

1 large rabbit
225 g (½ lb) cooking (green)
  apples, peeled, cored and sliced
2 onions, peeled and chopped
salt and pepper
sprig each fresh rosemary,
  parsley and thyme
juice 1 lemon
5 ml (1 teaspoon) tomato paste
550 ml (1 pint) (2½ cups) medium
  cider

1 Set the slow cooker to HIGH or follow the manufacturer's instructions.

2 Cut the rabbit into joints and place them in a pan. Cover with cold water and bring to the boil. Cook for 2 minutes, then discard the water.

3 Place the rabbit joints in the slow cooker and cover them with

the slices of apple and chopped onion. Sprinkle with salt and pepper. Tie the fresh herbs together to make a bouquet garni and add it to the slow cooker.

4 Mix together the lemon juice, tomato paste and cider and pour over the rabbit. Seal and cook on HIGH for about ½ hour. Turn the setting to LOW and continue to cook for about 7 hours. Serve hot.

Serves 4-6

Chicken Mogador

1 chicken, jointed
50 ml (2 fl oz) (¼ cup) oil
2 onions, sliced
2.5 ml (½ teaspoon) powdered
  cumin
2.5 ml (½ teaspoon) turmeric
pinch cayenne pepper
salt
juice and finely grated zest
  1 lemon
300 ml (½ pint) (1¼ cups) chicken
  stock
50 g (2 oz) (½ cup) green olives

1 Set the slow cooker to HIGH or follow the manufacturer's instructions.

2 Cook the chicken joints in the oil until golden-brown on each side. Drain them from the pan and place in the slow cooker.

3 Fry the onion slices in the oil for 3 minutes until soft. Stir in the cumin, turmeric and cayenne and cook for 1 minute. Place the onion on top of the chicken.

4 Add a pinch of salt, the lemon zest and juice, and the chicken stock. Seal and cook for ½ hour. Turn the setting to LOW and continue to cook for about 7 hours.

5 Add the olives and cook for ½ hour on HIGH. Serve at once.

Serves 4-6

Lamb Azinna can be prepared in the evening and cooked through the next day to stay deliciously succulent and tender

All About Microwave Cooking

Using your microwave

Safety First

Microwave ovens are among the safest of household appliances if used in accordance with the manufacturers' instructions. They are manufactured to meet stringent safety standards and manufacturers have gone to great lengths to make sure that microwaves stay inside the ovens. Safety devices, such as the door seal, are built-in to prevent any energy leakage. As soon as the door is opened the microwave energy stops. The following simple precautions are important.

- Do not try to operate the oven with the door open.
- Do not place any object between the front face of the oven and the door or allow any build up of dirt or cleanser residue.
- Never try to operate the oven if it does not seem to be working properly.

Which Dish?

There's no need to rush out and buy special cookware for your microwave oven. The kitchen cupboard is probably full of bowls and casserole dishes which are ideal — Pyrex, Corning-ware, china bowls and plates and casseroles for example. Even ordinary items such as paper or plastic plates, wooden or wicker baskets can be used if you just want to warm food. For cooking, utensils need to be tough enough, however, to withstand extremely hot food or boiling water: with microwave, the food heats the dish. If food cooks or reheats in less than 5 minutes, however, the cookware may keep quite cool.

Microwave-safe materials include heatproof glass, glass ceramic, earthenware, stoneware, china (without a metal trim) and even porcelain (but don't use your finest). If you have a browning element, utensils must be non-flammable.

Plastic food storage containers or supermarket packages are fine just for defrosting but tend to melt or distort once cooking temperatures are reached. Do not use plastic containers, like ice cream buckets and take-away food and butter tubs, in the microwave.

Basic Equipment

Paper plates are useful for heating dry foods and paper napkins or kitchen paper for absorbing moisture.

Special microwave containers are available for freezer-to-table meals. You can mix, cook, freeze, defrost, reheat and serve all in the one dish.

Item	Use
20 × 20 cm (8 × 8 in) square dish	Cakes, slices, whole corn cobs, confectionery, vegetables, lasagna.
Roasting dish and rack	Pork, beef, lamb, chicken, duck, turkey and all roasts.
Browning casserole dish	Broiling chops and steaks, stews and curries, baking scones, frying seafood, crumbed foods, eggs and small quantities of chips.
3 litre (5 pint) casserole with lid	Soups, pasta, rice, casseroles, corned beef, vegetables, chowders.
Casserole lid	Pies, quiches, vegetables, omelettes, cheese cakes and for cooking small quantities of food.

Item	Use
Ring dish	Baked custards, breads, scone rings, cakes, whole potatoes.
Flan ring	Cheese cake, fruit flans, quiches, vegetables.
Loaf dish	Meat loaves, loaf cakes, breads.
Flat round platter	Fruit or savoury pizzas, vegetable platters, sweet and savoury cookies, fruit flambe.
Various sized basins 1 or 2 litre (2 or 3½ pint) jugs	Melting, blanching, sauteeing. Savoury sauces, custards, reheating.
Souffle dish	Cakes, souffles, reheating soups, casseroles.

Wooden or wicker baskets can be popped into the oven to heat up a bread roll, but crack if left in too long.

To find out whether or not a favourite dish is microwave safe, try this simple test. Place the dish in the oven on high with 150 ml (5 fl oz) (¼ pint) of water for 2 minutes (china, pottery) or 20 seconds (glass, plastic). If the water heats but not the dish, then it is safe to use.

Shape is important in microwave cookery. Round dishes or ring dishes with straight (not bowl-shaped) sides give best results. If a recipe states a specific size or shape, use it. Cooking times can change when you use square or rectangular dishes and food can overcook at the corners with microwaves penetrating from both sides. Shallow dishes are best for foods like vegetables or portions of fish or meat. High-sided dishes are preferable for cooking rice, pasta, soups, stews and casseroles. Do not cook using a container with a restricted opening, such as a cordial or salad oil bottle.

Cover Story

Covering food with a lid or plastic wrap holds in steam keeping the food moist, tender and full of flavour. Loose coverings will also prevent splatters and small pieces of aluminium foil can be used to shield protruding angles or edges of roasts or poultry to prevent overcooking. You can also shield foods with a sauce to keep them moist.

Plastic wrap and plastic bags:
Use recognised brand names for covering seafood, sauces and vegetables when no casserole lid is available.
Lids are better if you need to turn or stir food during cooking.
Plastic oven bags are microwave-safe so long as they are pierced. Tie bags with strong — not metal ties.

Plastic storage bags should be removed if you are heating food.
Do not use plastic wrap and bags when cooking roasts or broiling as the plastic can melt. Do not completely seal cake and bread dishes with plastic wrap as condensation can result.

White kitchen paper:
Reheating dry foods such as cakes and breads.
Lining dishes and covering food to prevent splatters.
Absorbent paper allows steam to escape stops fat splattering and absorbs excess moisture.
Greaseproof paper is less absorbent, provides a loose cover for preventing splatters and is useful as a lining.

Aluminium foil:
When baking cakes.
As long as the density of the food is greater than the amount of aluminium foil, it can be used on the edges of roasts, cakes and drumsticks.
During standing time partially cover roasts so that heat is retained.
Aluminium foil liners can also

Chocolate Sauce

be used to prevent the sides of a fruit cake from drying out. Use aluminium foil to cover the cooked portion of a cake when the centre is still moist.

Even Cooking

The following simple techniques for microwave cooking make sure that the food cooks evenly in the oven.

Arranging and spacing Place individual portions such as potatoes or chops, an equal distance apart in the dish and in a single layer. Never stack foods for microwave cooking. With drumsticks, chops or similar portions, make sure that the thicker part faces the outside of the dish where it will receive most microwave energy.

Stirring Stir food to spread and redistribute heat during cooking. As the outside will heat first, stir from the outside towards the centre. Rotate foods which can't be stirred — cakes and breads, for example — to prevent one side or corner overcooking.

Turning Many recipes tell you to turn foods — usually about half way through the cooking time. This makes sure that top and bottom cook evenly.

Testing for 'Doneness'

When testing for 'doneness', always allow for the recommended standing time.

Cakes leave the sides of the dish when cooked and any moist spots on the surface will dry during standing time.

Egg mixtures Test quiche fillings and baked custard by inserting a knife one-third in from the edge. The knife should be clean when withdrawn. Stand cooked custard in cold water when cooking is complete to cool and to stop further cooking.

Seafood Green scampi, lobster and crabs turn pink when cooked. Cooked fish will flake easily when tested with a fork. Scallops, oysters and mussels become firmer when cooked.

Meats are fork tender when done. Always allow standing time. A final test for doneness can be carried out with a meat thermometer.

Drumsticks will move freely and juices will run clear when poultry is cooked.

Vegetables are brightly coloured when cooked. Overcooking discolours and dulls vegetables. Large vegetables like whole potatoes and beetroot and quartered pumpkin should be turned during cooking.

Jacket potatoes, which still feel firm when removed from the oven, will keep cooking during standing time, so don't overcook them. They will also keep hot if wrapped in aluminium foil for 30–40 minutes after cooking.

Roast Orange Duck

Microwave Browning Tricks

If you don't have a browning dish, a browner or a combination oven, there are still a number of ways you can enhance microwaved food. If you use a little imagination, there are any number of things you can do to help brown food in microwave cooking. See what delicious and attractive ideas you can invent.

Meat and poultry: Meat and poultry due to longer cooking times will brown in their own fat, but not to the same extent as in a conventional or combination oven. However, if you brush with melted unsalted butter and sprinkle with paprika before cooking, this will help. Food can be coated with butter or Parisian essence, Worcestershire, barbecue or soy sauce, which not only add to the appearance but provide added flavour.

Chicken brushed with honey, brown sugar and soy sauce is delicious — and looks good too.

Dry poultry and meat with kitchen paper towels before cooking as this will aid browning.

Ham and poultry can be brushed with jellies, preserves,

glazes or marmalades after half the cooking time has elapsed.

Soy, teriyaki and barbecue sauce are excellent brushed over hamburgers and other meats and poultry. Onion soup and gravy mix are also very good for colour.

Cakes, Bread and Pastry: To colour cake tops sprinkle a mixture of cinnamon and sugar or cinnamon and coconut over the surface before serving.

Cake recipes which contain colouring agents like chocolate, coffee, carrot, dates, or banana are always best in a microwave.

Grease your cake or loaf container and sprinkle it with chopped nuts and brown sugar, toasted coconut or biscuit crumbs before pouring in the cake mixture.

Before cooking savoury pastry brush it with a mixture of 1 egg yolk and 1 tablespoon soy sauce; for sweet pastry use molasses, maple syrup or a mixture of vanilla essence and beaten egg.

Bread and bread rolls respond well to being brushed with beaten egg or milk and sprinkled with poppy seeds or toasted sesame seeds before cooking.

Sausage, Bacon and Eggs ▷

316

Breakfast

Cooking Hints

Many recipe books suggest that eggs cannot be cooked in their shells in a microwave oven, but this is not true. Just follow the directions given and the eggs will not explode. Eggs require careful handling when cooked in a microwave oven. Egg yolks and whites cook at different speeds, so both the whites and the yolks must be pierced with a toothpick before frying.

Overcooking will give you a rubbery, tough egg, so remove your eggs or egg dishes from the oven just before they are fully cooked and allow them to stand outside the oven for a few minutes and they will finish cooking on their own.

When a particular dish calls for a cheese topping, remember to add it at the end of the cooking period as cheese quickly becomes tough and rubbery.

Oatmeal for One

¼ cup quick cooking oats
pinch of salt
100 ml (4 fl oz) (½ cup) water, at room temperature

Place oatmeal, water and salt into a serving bowl. Cook 1 minute 30 seconds on high, stir, cover and let stand for a few minutes before serving. **Note:** May be cooked in advance and reheated.

Time: 1½ minutes.

Grilled Grapefruit for Two

1 grapefruit
2 teaspoons brown sugar
2 teaspoons sherry

Cut grapefruit in half and segment. Place onto a plate and sprinkle with brown sugar and sherry. Cook 1½–2 minutes on high for 2 halves.

Time: 2 minutes.

Boiled Egg

1 egg at room temperature
1 teaspoon salt
water to cover egg

Boil water in a small jug or bowl. Add salt, then the egg. Cook on *Defrost Cycle* for 3½–4 minutes.

Time: 3½ minutes.

Scrambled Eggs for Two

4 eggs at room temperature
50 ml (2 fl oz) (¼ cup) milk or cream
pinch of salt
1½ tablespoons butter

Combine eggs, milk, salt in a bowl. Melt butter, on high, in a glass bowl for 30 seconds. Pour in egg mixture and cover with plastic food wrap. Cook on high 2 minutes, stir well and cook another 1½ minutes on high stirring 2 or 3 times.

Remove eggs when softer than required and let stand for 1 minute.

Time: 4 minutes.

Fried Egg

1 egg at room temperature
½ teaspoon butter

Melt butter on a plate for 25 seconds. Add egg, prick yolk 2–3 times with a toothpick. Cook 30 seconds on high. **Note:** 2 eggs — 1 minute 5 seconds; 3 eggs — 1 minute 35 seconds; 4 eggs — 2 minutes.

Time: 55 seconds

Savoury Scone Ring

2 tablespoons butter
2 tablespoons sugar
1 cup cooked pumpkin, mashed
1 small onion, finely cut
2 tablespoons parsley, chopped
1 egg
100 ml (4 fl oz) (½ cup) milk
2½ cups self-raising (rising) flour
½ teaspoon salt

Cream butter and sugar. Add pumpkin, onion and parsley, add well-beaten egg, add milk slowly. Cut in sifted flour and salt.

Place into a well-greased microwave baking ring and cook 7–8 minutes on high, remove and let stand for 4 minutes.

Time: 7 minutes.

Poached Eggs

2 eggs at room temperature
500 ml (16 fl oz) (2 cups) water

Boil water in a bowl. Add eggs and cook, covered, on the Defrost Cycle 3½–4 minutes.

Time: 3½ minutes.

Sliced Mushrooms

225 g (½ lb) mushrooms, thinly
  sliced
1 tablespoon lemon juice
1 tablespoon parsley, chopped
50 g (2 oz) (¼ cup) butter

Arrange mushrooms in a shallow dish. Sprinkle with lemon juice and parsley. Dot with butter and cook covered for 2 minutes on high.

Time: 2 minutes.

Stuffed Mushrooms

6 medium mushrooms, whole
2 slices ham
125 g (4 oz) (½ cup) cream
  cheese
1 tablespoon chives

Remove stalks from mushrooms. Chop ham finely and combine with cheese and chives. Spread mixture into cavity of mushrooms and cook, covered, 3 minutes on high.

Time: 3 minutes.

Whole Mushrooms with French Dressing

6 medium mushrooms
French dressing or other
  dressing

Arrange mushrooms in a circle on a plate and sprinkle each with your favourite dressing. Cook covered for 2 minutes on high.

Time: 2 minutes.

Tea, Coffee or Cups of Soup

Fill cups or coffee mugs with cold water. Heat uncovered in the oven on high.
1 cup — approx 2½ minutes, depending on size of cup.
2 cups — approx 4½ minutes

Then add instant coffee, tea bag, or single serve of instant soup mix. *Note:* Milk may be heated for coffee or tea, also for oatmeal.

Poached Eggs

2 eggs at room temperature
500 ml (16 fl oz) (2 cups) water

Boil water in a bowl. Add eggs and cook, covered, on the Defrost Cycle 3½–4 minutes.

Time: 3½ minutes.

Golden Corn Bread

25 g (1 oz) (2 tablespoons) butter
  or vegetable oil
25 g (1 oz) (2 tablespoons) sugar
150 g (60 oz) (1½ cups) plain
  flour
20 ml (4 teaspoons) baking
  powder
100 g (4 oz) (1 cup) cornmeal
1.25 ml (¼ teaspoon) salt
1.25 ml (¼ teaspoon) chilli
  powder
2 eggs, beaten
150 ml (6 fl oz) (¾ cup) milk
125 g (4 oz) (1 cup) cream style
  corn
15 g (½ oz) (¼ cup) red
  capsicum, diced

Cream butter and sugar. Add sifted flour and baking powder. Add cornmeal, salt and chilli powder. Stir in eggs, milk and beat until smooth. Fold in corn and capsicum.

Place into a well-greased microwave baking ring and cook 7–8 minutes on high. Remove and let stand 4 minutes.

Time: 7 minutes.

Grills

Sausages

Heat browning dish for 8 minutes on high. Lightly grease dish. Place up to 6 sausages in the dish and cook 3 minutes on each side on high. **Note:** Prick sausages well before grilling and allow 2–3 minutes standing time.

Bacon

Place bacon on several layers of white absorbent kitchen paper on a flat dish with one layer of paper covering the bacon. Cook bacon for about 1 minute per slice on high.

Sliced Tomatoes

Heat browning dish for 6 minutes on high. Grease lightly with butter. Add 9 thick slices of tomato and coat with seasoning of buttered herbed crumbs. Cook 1 minute, turn slices and cook another 1–1½ minutes on high. **Note:** Use 3 tomatoes cut into 3 thick slices each, cutting off top and bottom so that slices lie flat.

Stuffed Mushrooms

Soups & Snacks

Bread Cases

6 thin slices of brown or white
  bread
butter
1 micromuffin pan

Filling Suggestions:
225 ml (8 fl oz) (1 cup) cheese
  sauce and add either:
150 g (5 oz) (1 cup) of cream
  style corn
150 g (5 oz) (1 cup) flaked salmon
150 g (5 oz) (1 cup) assorted
  seafood (prawns (shrimp),
  crabmeat, oysters)
1 cup chopped green asparagus

Remove crusts from bread.
Place bread in oven and cook 1
minute to refresh. Butter
bread. Place butter side down
in muffin pan, so that the corners form four peaks. Place into
oven and cook on high 2–3 minutes. Remove cases, which
should be firm and crisp.

Time: 4 minutes.

Macaroni and Cheese

150 g (5 oz) (1 cup) macaroni,
  uncooked
1 litre (2 pt) hot water
½ teaspoon salt
500 ml (16 fl oz) (2 cups) cheese,
  grated
2 eggs
225 ml (8 fl oz) (1 cup) milk
½ teaspoon prepared mustard
dash of salt
dash of Worcestershire sauce
dash of paprika

Place macaroni into 2 litre
(3½ pt) casserole with water
and salt. Cook in oven 10 minutes on high or until macaroni
is tender. Stir after 5 minutes.
Drain, rinse in hot water.

Place a layer of macaroni in a
baking dish and sprinkle with
grated cheese. Repeat, alternat-
ing macaroni and cheese, ending with cheese. Beat eggs
lightly in a bowl. Add milk,
mustard, salt and Worcestershire sauce. Stir well. Drizzle
mixture on macaroni. Sprinkle
with paprika. Cook, covered, on
high 8 minutes, stirring after 4
minutes.

Time: 18 minutes. Serves 4

Tuna-stuffed Capsicums

4–6 large capsicums
500 g (1 lb) canned tuna
150 g (5 oz) (1 cup) soft
  breadcrumbs
40 g (1½ oz) (½ cup) finely diced
  celery
75 ml (2½ fl oz) (⅓ cup)
  mayonnaise
1 egg
2 tablespoons lemon juice
2 tablespoons prepared
  mustard
2 tablespoons soft butter
1 tablespoon finely chopped
  onion
¼ teaspoon salt
⅛ teaspoon tabasco sauce
2 slices cheese

Cut a slice from the upper third
of each capsicum. Dice strips
that have been cut off. Remove
seeds and membrane from inside of capsicum. Parboil capsicum in oven for 5 minutes on
high. Drain. Mix diced capsicum with remaining ingredients. Fill capsicums and stand
them in a casserole dish. Cook
covered on high 12 minutes.

Top with cheese strips in
form of cross. Cook 1 minute on
high.

Time: 18 minutes. Serves 4

Quiche Lorraine

Pastry:
200 g (7 oz) (1¼ cups) plain (all-
  purpose) flour
¼ teaspoon baking powder
pinch of salt
20 g (¾ oz) (⅓ cup) margarine
2 tablespoons water
squeeze of lemon juice
1 egg yolk

Filling:
3 eggs
225 ml (8 fl oz) (1 cup) cream
225 ml (8 fl oz) (1 cup) milk
pinch of nutmeg, sugar,
  cayenne pepper and white
  pepper
4 rashers (slices) bacon,
  chopped
125 g (4 oz) (1 cup) grated tasty
  cheese
parsley for garnish

Sift dry ingredients for pastry
into bowl. Rub in margarine
using fingertips until mixture
resembles fine breadcrumbs.
Combine remaining pastry ingredients. Make a well in the
centre of dry ingredients,
gradually add liquid, mixing to
form a dry dough. Turn onto a
lightly floured surface, roll out
to fit a deep 23 cm (9 in) glass
pie plate. Cook 6 minutes on
high.

For filling, whisk eggs,
cream, milk, and spices in mixing bowl. Lightly fry bacon.
Sprinkle bacon and cheese over
cooked pastry shell. Pour liquid
mixture carefully into pastry
shell. Cook, uncovered in microwave oven for 12 minutes on
medium. Allow to stand 5 minutes before serving. Garnish
with parsley and serve.

Time: 18 minutes. Serves 4–6

Tuna Stuffed Capsicums

Crab and Sweet Corn Soup

1½ litre (3 pt) (6 cups) chicken
  stock
150 g (5 oz) (1 cup) crabmeat
150 g (5 oz) (1 cup) cream style
  corn
1 tablespoon cornflour, water
1 tablespoon sherry (dry)
½ teaspoon salt
½ teaspoon oil
½ teaspoon sesame oil
2 eggs, beaten
40 g (1½ oz) (½ cup) shallots
  (scallions), finely chopped

Place stock into a large casserole dish and cook 15 minutes or until boiling on high. Add crabmeat and corn and cook a further 2 minutes. Add blended cornflour, sherry, salt and oils and bring to the boil, approximately 3 minutes. Remove from oven and add egg slowly to form egg flower. Add shallots (scallions). Serve hot.

Time: 20 minutes. Serves 6

Moussaka

3 eggplants
4 tablespoons olive oil
500 g (1 lb) minced beef (ground
  beef)
1 small tin tomato paste
salt, cayenne and oregano
2 medium onions, sliced
1 egg
225 ml (8 fl oz) (1 cup) sour
  cream
325 ml (12 fl oz) (1½ cups)
  buttered breadcrumbs
tomato for garnish
parsley for garnish

Cut unpeeled eggplant into 1 cm (½ in) slices. Sprinkle with salt and leave to stand for 30 minutes. Drain off liquid. Heat browning skillet 8 minutes, add oil and heat a further 3 minutes. Cook eggplant on each side 2 minutes on high. Combine meat, tomato paste and seasonings.

Place layers of eggplant, meat mixture and sliced onion in a greased casserole. Combine beaten egg with sour cream. Spread over mixture. Sprinkle thickly with buttered crumbs and cook 15 minutes on high. Serve hot garnished with tomato and parsley.

Time: 30 minutes. Serves 6

Seafood Crepes

Crepes:
60 g (2 oz) plain (all-purpose)
  flour
150 ml (5 fl oz) milk
salt and pepper
parsley, finely chopped
1 egg
15 g (½ oz) butter, melted
30 g (1 oz) lard (shortening) to
  grease crepe pan

Filling:
125 g (4 oz) cooked crabmeat,
  frozen or canned
125 g (4 oz) cooked prawns
  (shrimp)
125 g (4 oz) cooked scallops
500 ml (16 fl oz) (2 cups) cheese
  sauce (see recipe)
2 tablespoons finely cut chives
1–2 tablespoons finely chopped
  parsley
lemon wedges for garnish

Mix all crepe ingredients except lard to make a batter. Grease crepe pan with lard. Heat on range top. Add 1½–2 tablespoons of mixture. Cook until mixture bubbles, turn over and cook a further minute until lightly brown.

Combine all filling ingredients. Place 2 tablespoons mixture onto each crepe. Roll up and place side by side into a casserole dish and cook for 5 minutes on medium. Serve with lemon wedges.

Time: 5 minutes. Serves 6

Cream of Mushroom Soup

125 g (4 oz) mushrooms
4 tablespoons butter
4 tablespoons plain (all-
purpose) flour
325 ml (12 fl oz) (1½ cups) milk
325 ml (12 fl oz) (1½ cups)
  chicken stock
225 ml (8 fl oz) (1 cup) cream
salt and pepper
chopped chives

Slice and dice mushrooms. Place butter into a 2 litre (3½ pt) casserole dish and cook 1 minute to melt. Add mushrooms, and cook on high covered 3 minutes. Stir in flour, cook a further 2 minutes. Blend in milk and stock. Cook 9 minutes on high. Add cream and cook 2 minutes to reheat. Season with salt and pepper. Add a few chopped chives before serving.

Time: 17 minutes. Serves 4

Clam Chowder

3 rashers bacon, rind removed,
  (1 cm) (½ in) dice
50 g (2 oz) onion, finely chopped
50 g (2 oz) celery, finely chopped
50 g (2 oz) carrot, finely chopped
50 g (2 oz) potato, peeled &
  diced (1 cm) (½ in)
25 g (1 oz) (3 tablespoons) plain
  flour
200 ml (8 fl oz) (1 cup) clam juice
600 ml (1 pt) (2¾ cups) milk
1 (250 g) (½ lb) can clams
2.5 ml (½ teaspoon) thyme
1 bay leaf
5 ml (1 teaspoon) salt
2.5 ml (½ teaspoon) pepper
60 ml (2 fl oz) (¼ cup) cream
15 ml (1 tablespoon) parsley,
  finely chopped

Sprinkle bacon into 2 litre (3 pt) casserole dish, cook 2 minutes on high. Add vegetables and cook 1 minute. Blend in flour, add clam juice and milk, stir to blend. Add clams and cook 5 minutes on high. Add thyme, bay leaf, salt and pepper and cook 12 minutes on high, stirring after every 3 minutes.

Let stand covered for 5 minutes. Remove bay leaf, stir in cream, correct seasoning, sprinkle with parsley and serve.

Time: 20 minutes.

Lasagne with Topside Mince (Ground Beef)

250 g (8 oz) lasagne noodles
880 ml (4 pints) (8 cups) boiling
  water
1 tablespoon salt
1 tablespoon oil
1 tablespoon butter, softened
150 g (5 oz) (1 cup) sliced onion
15 g (½ oz) (¼ cup) sliced
  mushrooms
500 g (1 lb) topside mince
  (ground beef)
1 clove chopped garlic
1 x 250 g (8 oz) can tomato
  puree
1 x 180 g (6 oz) can tomato paste
325 ml (12 fl oz) (1½ cups) beef
  stock
½ teaspoon sugar
½ teaspoon salt
dash of pepper
1 teaspoon basil
500 g (1 lb) (3 cups) cottage
  cheese
250 g (8 oz) mozzarella cheese
  slices
40 g (1½ oz) (½ cup) grated
  Parmesan cheese

Place lasagne noodles in a casserole. Pour over boiling water. Add salt. Cook 16 minutes on high until tender. Drain and mix with a little oil. Set aside.

Melt butter in casserole 30 seconds. Saute onion in butter 3 minutes. Add mushrooms. Cook 3 minutes. Remove from casserole. Cook topside mince and garlic in casserole 6 minutes, stirring every 2 minutes. Add onion and mushroom mixture, tomato puree, tomato sauce, stock, sugar, salt, pepper and basil. Stir well. Cook, covered, 10 minutes, stirring every 3 minutes to make meat sauce.

Layer meat sauce, noodles, cottage cheese and mozzarella cheese in a deep casserole dish. Repeat layers 3 times, ending with meat sauce. Sprinkle Parmesan cheese on top. Cook on high 10 minutes.

Time: 48 minutes. Serves 6

Cabbage Rolls

12 cabbage leaves, medium size
500 g (1 lb) topside, minced
  (ground beef)
250 g (½ lb) pork, minced
  (ground)
125 g (4 oz) chopped onion
75 g (3 oz) (¾ cup) cooked rice
½ teaspoon cumin powder
1 egg
1 teaspoon thyme
1 tablespoon chopped parsley
1 clove garlic, chopped
1 tablespoon salt
¾ teaspoon pepper
550 ml (1 pint) (2½ cups) fresh
  tomato sauce (ketchup) (see
  recipe)
15 g (½ oz) (¼ cup) butter

Place cabbage leaves in 2 tablespoons water in a casserole dish. Cook covered on high for 8 minutes or until soft. Combine mince, pork, onion, rice, cumin, egg, thyme, parsley, garlic, salt, pepper, and ½ cup of tomato sauce.

Place two tablespoons stuffing on each cabbage leaf and wrap leaves around mixture firmly. Place cabbage rolls in a casserole dish. Spread butter on top of rolls and remaining tomato sauce. Cook, covered, 20 minutes on high, or until meat is cooked and rolls are tender. Let stand, covered, 10 minutes.

Time: 28 minutes. Serves 6

Cabbage Rolls

Lasagne with Topside Mince

Party Pizzas

Lebanese bread

Sauce:
250 g (8 oz) can tomato paste
1 teaspoon sugar
½ teaspoon oregano
½ teaspoon freshly ground
 black pepper
½ teaspoon basil

Topping Suggestions:
fresh mushrooms, sliced
onion rings
mozzarella cheese slices
capsicum rings
rolled or flat anchovies
ham, cut in strips
sliced continental salami
black or green stuffed olives
Parmesan cheese, cayenne,
 paprika
grated tasty cheese
parsley

Have sauce prepared and the toppings arranged on a serving platter for guests to make their own selection.
Method:
Spread Sauce over bread round, add toppings and cook 4 minutes on high. Cut into wedges.

Time: 6 minutes.

Chilli con Carne

½ tablespoon butter
500 g (1 lb) topside, minced
 (ground beef)
1 small onion, diced
½ teaspoon garlic salt
1 tablespoon chilli powder
½ teaspoon dry mustard
salt and pepper
250 g (4 oz) can tomatoes
250 g (8 oz) can kidney beans
250 g (8 oz) can baked beans
250 g (8 oz) can sliced
 mushrooms
2 stalks celery, diced
2 tablespoons tomato paste
1 teaspoon paprika
½ teaspoon oregano

Place butter, beef, diced onions and garlic salt into a 2 litre (3½ pt) casserole dish. Cook on high 3 minutes until brown. Add chilli powder, mustard, salt, pepper and remaining ingredients. Cook for 10 minutes stirring after the first 5 minutes. Serve with rice or buttered toast.

Time: 13 minutes. Serves 6

Anchovy Bread

1 loaf French bread
1 small can anchovy fillets
finely chopped parsley
90 g (3 oz) butter

Drain anchovies, soak in a small amount of milk for 15 minutes. Drain and dry on kitchen paper. Mash anchovies with butter and parsley.

Cut bread into slices ¾ through the loaf. Spread slices with butter. As the loaf will be too long for the microwave oven, cut into four sections.

Wrap in plastic food wrap and cook for 1½ minutes on high. Serve hot.

Time: 1½ minutes.

Bacon and Oyster Rolls

6 narrow strips bacon
12 fresh oysters
toothpicks

Remove rind from bacon. Cut rashers in half. Cook between white kitchen paper for 3 minutes on high until partly cooked. Drain oysters. Wrap each bacon rasher around an oyster and fasten with a toothpick. Cook between layers of kitchen paper 2–3 minutes on high until bacon becomes crisp.
Note: Smoked oysters may also be used.

Time: 6 minutes.

COOKING CHART FOR FRESH VEGETABLES

Item	Quantity	Directions	Suggested Cooking Time in Minutes
Asparagus	500 g (1 lb)	¼ cup water, ⅓ teaspoon salt in covered casserole	5–6
Beans	750 g (1½ lb)	⅔ cup water, ¼ teaspoon salt in covered casserole	17–20
Beetroot	4 whole medium	cover with water, ⅓ teaspoon salt in covered casserole	16–18
Broccoli	1 small bunch	cut away stalks, ½ cup water, 1 teaspoon salt in covered casserole	8–11
Cabbage	1 medium head chopped	3 tablespoons water, ⅓ teaspoon salt in covered casserole	11–15
Carrots	4 medium sliced	¼ cup water, ⅓ teaspoon salt in covered casserole	8–10
Cauliflower	1 medium head	½ cup water, 1/5 teaspoon salt in covered casserole	12–14
Celery	6 cups	¼ cup water, ⅓ teaspoon salt in covered casserole	12–14
Corn	3 ears	remove silk, leave husk on and tie with elastic band	7–8
Corn kernels	3 cups	⅓ cup water, ⅓ teaspoon salt in covered casserole	6–7
Eggplant	1 medium	¼ cup water, ⅓ teaspoon salt in covered casserole	7–8
Onion	2 large (cut in quarters)	½ cup water, ⅓ teaspoon salt in covered casserole	11–13
Parsnips	8 medium (cut in quarters)	½ cup water, ⅓ teaspoon salt in covered casserole	11–13
Green Peas	1 kg (2.2 lb)	⅓ cup water, ⅓ teaspoon salt in covered casserole	11–12
Spinach	500 g (1 lb)	Put in casserole with water to cling to leaves, ⅓ teaspoon salt and cover	6–7
Potatoes	1 medium 2 medium 3 medium 4 medium 5 medium 6 medium 7 medium 8 medium	Scrub potatoes, and place on paper towel leaving at 2.5 cm space between potatoes. Note: Prick potatoes before placing in oven	5 7 9 12 14 16 20 22
Potatoes	4 medium (thinly sliced)	2 tablespoons butter in casserole, sprinkle with salt and dot with butter. Cover	11
Sweet Potatoes	2 medium	Place on paper towel, leaving 2.5 cm space between potatoes	7–8

Beetroot (Beets) with Orange Sauce

4 precooked beetroots (beets)
  (see Cooking Chart)
2 tablespoons brown sugar
225 ml (8 fl oz) (1 cup) orange
  juice
2 tablespoons tarragon vinegar
1 tablespoon butter
1 tablespoon cornflour

Use a melon baller and scoop
out balls of beetroot from
cooked beets. Combine sugar,
juice, vinegar, butter and
cornflour in a bowl. Cook 3 minutes on high, stir and cook until
boiling. Add beets, cook further
2 minutes and serve.

Time: 17 minutes. Serves 4

Cabbage

500 g (1 lb) shredded cabbage,
  washed and drained
2 cloves garlic, chopped finely
1 tablespoon butter
2 large peeled tomatoes,
  roughly chopped
salt to taste

Place all ingredients in a small
casserole dish or an oven bag
lightly tied with string or an
elastic band. Prick bag once or
twice near opening. Cook 7 minutes on high, turning once during cooking.

Time: 7 minutes. Serves 4-6

Parsley Potato Balls

750 g (1½ lb) potatoes
water
2 tablespoons butter
2 tablespoons finely chopped
  parsley
salt to taste

Cut potatoes into balls using a
melon baller. Place into casser-

Beets with Orange Sauce

ole with water. Cook covered on
high for 12 minutes, stirring
twice during cooking. Cook butter 20 seconds to melt. Add
parsley and salt. Pour over
drained potatoes. Stir to coat.

  Note: Chopped mint may be
used in place of parsley.

Time: 12 minutes. Serves 4-6

Cauliflower au Gratin

2 tablespoons butter
500 g (1 lb) cauliflower florets
¼ teaspoon garlic salt
pepper
2 large peeled tomatoes, sliced
1 cup cheese sauce (see Sauces
  and Jams)
chopped parsley
paprika

Cook butter in casserole 20
seconds to melt. Add cauliflower, garlic salt, pepper and

cook covered for 6 minutes. Top
with sliced tomatoes, cheese
sauce and parsley. Cook 3 minutes on high. Dust lightly with
paprika before serving.

Time: 9 minutes. Serves 4-6

Leaf Spinach

500 g (1 lb) spinach leaves, no
  stalks, washed and drained
1 tablespoon butter
1 small onion, finely chopped
¼ teaspoon nutmeg
60 g (2 oz) peanuts, roughly
  chopped

Place spinach, butter, onion,
and nutmeg into an oven bag.
Fasten with an elastic band.
Prick twice near opening. Cook
7 minutes on high, turning once
during cooking. Top with
roughly chopped peanuts.

Time: 7 minutes. Serves 4

Parsley Potato Balls

Zucchini Special

500 g (1 lb) unpeeled zucchini, sliced
1 tablespoon butter
onion or garlic salt
1 teaspoon fresh chopped dill
1 large peeled tomato, seeds removed, roughly chopped

Place all ingredients into a small casserole. Cover and cook 8 minutes on high.

Time: 8 minutes. Serves 4

Vegetable Kebabs

Spear a variety of vegetables onto bamboo sate sticks: cherry tomatoes, mushroom caps, chunks of red and green capsicums, canned mini corn, small onions, and zucchini. Layer in dish and cook 6 minutes on high, turning every minute and basting with a mixture of melted butter and lemon juice.

Time: 6 minutes. Serves 4

Fresh Broccoli Hollandaise

500 g (1 lb) fresh broccoli
1 tablespoon water
2 tablespoons butter
onion salt

Cut broccoli into even lengths, remove skin from stalk and split ends with a knife. Place into a covered casserole dish or oven bag, with water, butter and onion salt. Cook 8 minutes on high. Arrange onto serving dish and mask with Hollandaise Sauce (see recipe).

Time: 8 minutes. Serves 4

Scalloped Sweet Potatoes

750 g (1½ lb) orange sweet potatoes, sliced thinly
2 rashers (slices) of bacon, diced and precooked
2 tablespoons plain (all-purpose) flour
1 teaspoon salt
100 ml (4 fl oz) (½ cup) finely cut shallots (scallions)
500 ml (16 fl oz) (2 cups) milk
225 ml (8 fl oz) (1 cup) tasty cheese, grated nutmeg and paprika
chopped parsley

Combine all ingredients in a greased casserole dish. Cover and cook 15 minutes on high, stirring every 4 minutes. Sprinkle with extra nutmeg, paprika and chopped parsley.

Time: 15 minutes. Serves 6

Carrots with Marsala

500 g (1 lb) carrots, sliced crosswise
1 onion, finely chopped
1 tablespoon brown sugar
75 ml (2½ fl oz) (⅓ cup) Marsala
1 tablespoon butter

Combine all ingredients and place in casserole dish just large enough to hold all ingredients. Cook 7–8 minutes on high, stirring twice during cooking.

Time: 8 minutes. Serves 4–6

Vegetable Medley

250 g (8 oz) (1½ cups) cauliflower florets
125 g (4 oz) carrots, sliced crosswise
250 g (8 oz) (1½ cups) Chinese cabbage, sliced

125 g (4 oz) sliced mushrooms
1 small can asparagus spears
2 slices ham, diced
chopped parsley

Sauce:
2 tablespoons butter
2 tablespoons plain (all-purpose) flour
225 ml (8 fl oz) (1 cup) chicken stock
500 ml (16 fl oz) (2 cups) milk

Place cauliflower and carrots into a casserole dish. Add 2 tablespoons water and cook covered 6 minutes on high. Place carrots and cauliflower into a larger casserole, cover with cabbage, mushrooms and asparagus spears. Spoon sauce over, top with ham and parsley. Cook covered 6 minutes.

Cook butter for sauce to melt 20 seconds. Stir in flour and cook 2 minutes on high. Stir in stock and milk. Cook 6 minutes until thick and boiling. Stir during cooking.

Time: 20 minutes. Serves 4–6

Braised Red Cabbage

½ head sliced red cabbage
2 tablespoons butter
2 green apples, peeled and sliced
1 small onion, chopped
½ teaspoon salt
¼ teaspoon pepper
2 cloves
1 bay leaf
2 tablespoons tarragon vinegar
225 ml (8 fl oz) (1 cup) dry red wine
1–2 tablespoons brown sugar

Combine all ingredients in casserole. Cook covered 12 minutes on high, stirring every 4 minutes.

Time: 12 minutes. Serves 6

Scalloped Sweet Potatoes

Rice

Cooking Rice

- Rice can be cooked in a microwave oven in eight minutes, two-thirds of the normal cooking time. Brown rice takes only 15 minutes to cook in a microwave oven — a considerable time saving.
- Always wash rice before cooking it. The best way to do that is to place it in a colander and let cold water run over it.
- When cooking rice remember that rice triples in bulk during cooking time. Allow 50 g or ¼ cup of uncooked rice per person, and let it cook in 500 ml or 2½ cups of water.
- Always cook rice covered with a fitted glass lid or a plastic wrap, and allow rice to stand covered before serving. The rice will finish cooking while covered. It is best to use a large casserole dish, to prevent spills during cooking.
- The method of cooking rice in the following recipes is the absorption method. Should you prefer the grains to be separate, the rice may be washed in hot water after cooking and allowed to drain.
- If you cook more rice than needed at the one time, remember that rice can be stored in an airtight container in a refrigerator for one week, or it can be frozen

Ginger Saffron Rice

for longer periods. You can then serve it cold, covered in a vinaigrette dressing, or coated with a thinned down mayonnaise.
- To defrost frozen rice, allow 2 minutes in the microwave oven using the *Defrost Cycle.*

Rice

1 cup washed rice
2 cups boiling water
nob of butter
pinch of onion salt

Place rice into 1 litre (2 pint) casserole dish, add salt, butter and pour over boiling water. Cover. Cook 8 minutes on high. Allow to stand 10 minutes before serving or using in other recipes.

Time: 8 minutes. Serves 4

Vegetarian Rice

2 tablespoons butter
1 carrot, diced
2 large mushrooms, finely crushed
1 onion
½ red capsicum
½ green capsicum
150 g (5 oz) (1 cup) corn kernels
150 g (5 oz) (1 cup) peas
400 g (14 oz) (3 cups) cooked rice
salt and pepper
1 clove garlic, finely crushed
1 slice ginger, finely crushed
2 tablespoons chopped parsley
hard-boiled eggs

Dice all vegetables to the size of the corn. Wash and drain. Place butter into a 2 litre (3½ pt) casserole. Cook 15 seconds. Add all the vegetables and cook on high covered 4 minutes. Fold in rice and add salt, pepper, garlic, ginger and parsley. Cook 5 minutes, covered. Garnish with diced, hard-boiled eggs.

Time: 9 minutes. Serves 4–6

Tomato Rice

150 g (5 oz) (1 cup) washed rice
½ teaspoon sugar
pinch oregano
pinch onion salt
nob of butter
225 ml (8 fl oz) (1 cup) tomato juice
225 ml (8 fl oz) (1 cup) chicken stock
chopped parsley

Bring tomato juice and chicken stock to the boil on hotplate. Place rice into a 1 litre (2 pt) casserole dish, add sugar, spices, butter and tomato juice and stock. Cook covered on high 8 minutes. Allow to stand 10 minutes. Sprinkle with chopped parsley. Serve with chicken dishes or casseroles.

Time: 8 minutes. Serves 4

Ginger Saffron Rice

150 g (5 oz) (1 cup) washed rice
pinch of salt
2 tablespoons diced red capsicum or crystallised ginger
½ teaspoon powdered saffron
nob of butter
500 ml (16 fl oz) (2 cups) boiling water

Place rice into a 1 litre (2 pt) casserole, add salt, capsicum or ginger, saffron, butter and boiling water. Cook on high 8 minutes. Allow to stand 10 minutes before serving. Can be moulded and turned out on serving plate.

Time: 8 minutes. Serves 4

Paella

3 tablespoons oil
150 g (5 oz) (1 cup) sliced onion
1 clove garlic, crushed
150 g (5 oz) (1 cup) uncooked
  rice, washed
500 ml (16 fl oz) (2 cups) boiling
  chicken stock
1½ teaspoons salt
¼ teaspoon saffron
⅛ teaspoon pepper
1 can 125 g (4 oz) prawns
  (shrimp), drained
190 g (6½ oz) (1½ cups) cooked
  chicken, 2 cm (¾ in) cubes
6 mussels, in the shell
150 g (5 oz) (1 cup) peas
40 g (1½ oz) (½ cup) sliced
  stuffed olives

Heat oil in a 2 litre (3½ pt) casserole for 3 minutes. Add onion, garlic and heat a further 2 minutes. Add rice, chicken stock, salt, saffron, pepper and cook for 3 minutes. Stir. Fold in prawns, chicken, mussels and peas and cook a further 5 minutes, stirring after 2½ minutes. Add olives. Remove from oven and allow to stand 10 minutes before serving.

Note: Keep casserole covered while cooking.

Time: 13 minutes. Serves 4-6

See also page 310 for Spanish Seafood Paella.

Rice Pilaf

60 g (2 oz) butter
1 small onion, chopped finely
150 g (5 oz) (1 cup) long grain
  rice, washed
500 ml (16 fl oz) (2 cups) boiling
  chicken stock
salt and pepper

Place 30 g (1 oz) butter and the onion into a casserole dish. Cook 3 minutes on high, stir in rice. Cook a further 3 minutes on high. Add stock, seasonings, cover with a lid and cook 8 minutes. Mix in remaining butter,

allow to stand 5 minutes before serving.

Time: 8 minutes. Serves 4

Vegetable Pilaf

30 g (1 oz) cooked peas
30 g (1 oz) diced capsicum
30 g (1 oz) diced tomato
60 g (2 oz) grated cheese

Prepare Rice Pilaf as above. After cooking, fold all Vegetable Pilaf ingredients into rice with remaining butter and allow to stand 5 minutes before serving to heat through.

Time: 14 minutes. Serves 4

Mushroom Pilaf

125 g (4 oz) sliced fresh mushrooms can be added to the rice and cooked as above.

Fried Rice

3 rashers (slices) bacon
30 g (1 oz) fresh mushrooms
1 small onion
2 shallots (scallions)
30 g (1 oz) shelled prawns
  (shrimp)
2 eggs
400 g (14 oz) (3 cups) cold cooked
  rice, cooked with 1 chicken
  cube
1 tablespoon dark soy sauce

Dice bacon, mushrooms, onions, shallots and prawns. Place bacon on glass dish, cover with white kitchen paper and cook 3 minutes on high. Remove from dish, add onion, mushrooms and cook 2 minutes.

Fold lightly beaten eggs into rice, and add to dish. Cook on high 2 minutes, then stir, add bacon, soy sauce and stir mixture again. Cook 2 minutes. Stir in shallots and prawns. Cook 2 minutes to reheat. Season.

Time: 11 minutes. Serves 4

Saffron Rice

15 g (½ oz) butter
1 small onion, chopped
¼ teaspoon powdered saffron or
  turmeric
150 g (5 oz) (1 cup) washed rice
30 g (1 oz) currants or sultanas
  (golden raisins)
500 ml (16 fl oz) (2 cups) boiling
  chicken stock (can use stock
  cube)
30 g (1 oz) almond slivers,
  toasted

Place butter into 1 litre (2 pt) casserole dish and cook 15 seconds. Add onion, saffron and cook on high 3 minutes. Add rice, currants and boiling stock. Cook covered 8 minutes. Allow to stand 10 minutes. Sprinkle with almonds before serving.

Time: 11 minutes. Serves 4

Paella

Meat

- Meat should be roasted on a roasting rack in a shallow glass baking dish and always cover the meat with white kitchen paper to prevent splattering. Never use salt before roasting as this dehydrates the meat.
- Large roasts will brown in a microwave oven but smaller portions will not brown. To give the surface a browned appearance apply a sauce or a baste: try soy sauce, teriyaki, or Worcestershire sauce. These add colour and flavour.
- For steaks and chops, use your browning skillet as suggested in the recipes.
- The internal temperature of the meat can be checked by inserting a meat thermometer into the thickest part, away from bone and fat. However, you must use a meat thermometer specially designed for use in a microwave oven. When the meat has finished cooking, take it out of the oven and cover it with foil. Then allow it to stand for 15–20 minutes to equalise the heat.

Seasoned Shoulder of Lamb

1 boned shoulder of lamb —
  2 kg (4 lb)

Seasoning:
150 g (5 oz) (1 cup) fresh
  breadcrumbs
1 tablespoon butter
¼ teaspoon nutmeg
¼ teaspoon salt
¼ teaspoon pepper
1 tablespoon chopped mint
pinch mixed herbs

2 tablespoons milk
2 shallots (scallions), finely cut
40 g (1½ oz) (½ cup) sliced fresh
  mushrooms

Peach Sauce:
150 g (5 oz) (1 cup) cranberry
  sauce
40 g (1½ oz) (½ cup) diced
  peaches
2 tablespoons sweet vermouth
or sherry

Combine all ingredients for seasoning. Place seasoning on boned lamb. Roll up. Tie firmly with string or fasten with bamboo sate sticks. Place onto roasting rack, fat side down. Cook 36 minutes on high, turning halfway through cooking time. Wrap in aluminium foil and stand for 15 minutes before carving.

Combine ingredients for Peach Sauce and cook 3 minutes on high to heat.

Time: 39 minutes. Serves 4–6

Beef Olives

500 g (1 lb) very thinly sliced
  rump steak
1 rasher (slice) bacon, diced
1 small onion, chopped
15 g (½ oz) (¼ cup)
  breadcrumbs
1 tablespoon chopped parsley
1 teaspoon grated lemon rind
1 small carrot, grated
black pepper
¼ teaspoon salt
1 egg
seasoned plain (all-purpose)
  flour
30 g (1 oz) butter
150 ml (5 fl oz) brown stock
150 ml (5 fl oz) red wine
3 teaspoons arrowroot
1 tablespoon cold water
parsley for garnish

Cut steak into 10 cm (4 in) squares. Pound with meat mallet. Place bacon and onion into bowl, cook 3 minutes. Add breadcrumbs, parsley, lemon

rind, carrot, pepper, salt, and egg. Blend together. Spread filling over meat slices. Roll up and tie with string. Coat meat with seasoned flour. Preheat browning skillet 6 minutes. Add butter to melt. Add beef rolls, cook 3 minutes on high on each side. Add stock, wine and cook covered 12 minutes medium.

Remove string from rolls, transfer to serving plate. Reserve juices and add 3 teaspoons arrowroot blended with 1 tablespoon cold water to skillet juices. Cook on high 2–3 minutes to form sauce. Mask rolls with sauce. Sprinkle with cut parsley.

Time: 30 minutes. Serves 3–4

Roast Pork

2.5 kg (5 lb) leg or loin of pork
  in one piece
3 tablespoons oil
1 teaspoon salt
1 teaspoon five spice powder
juice of half a lemon
apple and pineapple slices for
  garnish
apricot jam for glaze

Score rind of pork. Brush with oil. Rub salt and five spice powder into the skin and allow to stand for 15 minutes. Pour lemon juice over. Place on roasting rack in casserole dish and cook 40–45 minutes on high. (It is not necessary to turn pork over during cooking.) Wrap in aluminium foil and allow to stand 20 minutes before carving. During last 4 minutes of cooking, place slices of apple and pineapple around pork. Glaze slices with apricot jam.

Time: 45 minutes. Serves 6

Roast Pork

Roast Leg of Lamb

1 x 2.5 kg (5 lb) leg of lamb
3 cloves garlic, peeled
lemon-flavoured black pepper
1 teaspoon powdered ginger
variety of vegetables
1 can drained pears
1 jar mint jelly

Trim excess fat from lamb. Cut garlic in slivers and stud lamb. Sprinkle with lemon-flavoured black pepper and rub lightly with ginger. Place lamb, fat side down, on a roasting rack in an oblong casserole dish or just place into casserole dish. Cover with a sheet of white kitchen paper and cook 25 minutes on high. Turn leg over and baste with pan drippings. Cook a further 15 minutes. Wrap in aluminium foil, allow to stand for 15 minutes before carving.

During this time vegetables can be cooked in the baking dish. Suggested vegetables: whole onions, sweet potato, pumpkin, potatoes. Place vegetables into pan and baste with drippings. Cook 5 minutes on high. Turn over to cook a further 5 minutes or until tender. Fill pears with mint jelly and heat 3 minutes.

Time: 53 minutes. Serves 8

Guard of Honour

2 racks of lamb, each with 8
  cutlets

Stuffing:
60 g (2 oz) butter
1 small onion, finely chopped
275 g (10 oz) (2 cups) fresh
  breadcrumbs
1 tablespoon chopped parsley
pinch dry mixed herbs
1 egg, beaten
1 teaspoon grated lemon or
  orange rind
garlic slivers

Place butter into bowl for 15–20 seconds to melt. Add onion and cook 2–3 minutes on high. Combine with remaining ingredients.

Interlace cutlet bones to form an arch. Stud with garlic slivers and season lightly. Place seasoning in centre of cutlet racks, and fasten with bamboo sate sticks to retain shape. Cook 20 minutes on high. Cover with aluminium foil and allow to stand 10–15 minutes. Top cutlet bones with frills. Serve with minted Potato Balls, Glazed Carrots and a green vegetable (see Vegetables).

Time: 23 minutes. Serves 4-6

Vienna Schnitzel

500 g (1 lb) fillets of veal
50 ml (2 fl oz) (¼ cup) lemon
  juice
seasoned plain (all-purpose)
  flour
1 egg, beaten
2 tablespoons milk
1 teaspoon soy sauce
150 g (5 oz) (1 cup) breadcrumbs
225 ml (8 fl oz) (1 cup) oil
lemon wedges

Pound veal fillets with meat mallet until thin. Marinate in lemon juice for 20 minutes. Dust with seasoned flour. Combine egg, milk and soy sauce. Dip veal fillets into egg mixture, and coat with breadcrumbs. Preheat browning skillet for 8 minutes on high. Add oil and heat for 3 minutes. Add schnitzels, cook 2 minutes on each side. Serve with lemon wedges.

Time: 15 minutes. Serves 2-3

Potato Pie

2 tablespoons butter
1 small onion, finely chopped
500 g (1 lb) cold roast lamb,
  minced (ground)
2 tablespoons chopped parsley
250 g (9 oz) (1½ cups) peas,
  cooked
250 g (9 oz) (1½ cups) cooked
  carrots, sliced
250 g (9 oz) (1½ cups) fresh
  mushrooms, sliced
1 teaspoon curry powder
1 x 165 g (5 oz) can mushroom
  soup
salt and pepper
2 cups hot mashed potato
nutmeg and paprika

Melt butter in casserole dish for 15 seconds. Add onion and cook 3 minutes on high. Fold in lamb, parsley, peas, carrots, mushrooms, curry powder, soup, salt and pepper. Pipe potatoes over top of mixture. Sprinkle with nutmeg and paprika. Cook 9 minutes.

Time: 12 minutes. Serves 4-6

Roast Pork Ribs

750 g (1½ lb) pork spareribs

Marinade:
1 medium onion, chopped
2 tablespoons dark soy sauce
3 tablespoons honey
2 tablespoons lemon juice
1 clove garlic, crushed
¼ teaspoon salt
pinch pepper
½ teaspoon curry powder
¼ teaspoon chilli powder
½ teaspoon ground ginger
50 ml (2 fl oz) (¼ cup) oil

Combine marinade ingredients. Remove rind and excess fat from ribs. Prick with skewer and place in marinade for 2 hours. Place ribs onto a roasting rack and cook 20 minutes on high, turning after 10 minutes. Spare ribs may also be cooked in an oven bag.

Note: Chicken wings can be cooked in this method.

Time: 20 minutes. Serves 4

Roast Pork Ribs

Beef Stroganoff

2 tablespoons oil
500 g (1 lb) rump steak
½ teaspoon salt
½ teaspoon pepper
2 tablespoons plain (all-
  purpose) flour
2 onions, sliced
1 clove garlic, cut finely
250 g (9 oz) (1½ cups) fresh
  mushrooms, sliced
150 ml (5 fl oz) red wine
150 ml (5 fl oz) beef stock
1 tablespoon tomato paste
1 carton sour cream

Preheat browning skillet for 8 minutes on high. Add oil and heat for 2 minutes. Combine salt, pepper and flour. Cut meat into very thin slices, across grain. Roll in seasoned flour. Add to pan and cook 3–4 minutes, stirring frequently to brown meat. Add onions, garlic and cook 3 minutes. Add mushrooms, wine, stock, tomato paste and cook 6 minutes on medium. Blend in sour cream, cook to reheat 2 minutes. Serve with rice or buttered noodles.

Time: 25 minutes. Serves 4–6

Lamb Casserole

500 g (1 lb) lean lamb shoulder,
  cut into 2 cm (¾ in) cubes
2 tablespoons plain (all-
  purpose) flour
½ teaspoon salt
¼ teaspoon lemon pepper
1 x 500 g (1 lb) can tomato
  pieces
200 ml (6 fl oz) (¾ cup)
  consomme or stock
250 g (8 oz) sliced mushrooms
1 medium-sized onion,
  quartered
½ teaspoon oregano
1 sprig fresh rosemary
1 x 300 g (10 oz) packet frozen
  chunk-style beans, thawed

In a 2 litre (3½ pt) casserole place lamb, flour, salt and pepper and stir to coat lamb. Add tomatoes, consomme, mushrooms, onion, oregano and rosemary.

Cover and cook on high 5 minutes. Reduce to medium and cook 20 minutes. Stir, recover and cook on medium 30 minutes. Add beans and cook on medium 10 minutes until beans are cooked.

Time: 65 minutes. Serves 6

Braised Pork Chops

4 shoulder pork chops
seasoned plain (all-purpose)
  flour
2 tablespoons oil
1 onion, sliced
3 large mushrooms, sliced
2 tomatoes, peeled and sliced
100 ml (4 fl oz) (½ cup) chicken
  stock
100 ml (4 fl oz) (½ cup) port wine
2 cloves
salt and pepper

Coat chops with seasoned flour. Heat browning skillet 6 minutes on high. Add oil and heat for 3 minutes. Press chops into skillet and cook 3 minutes on each side to brown. Add onion, mushrooms, tomato, stock, port, cloves, salt and pepper. Cover and cook for 8 minutes. Allow to stand 5 minutes before serving. Sauce may be thickened lightly with cornflour.

Time: 23 minutes. Serves 4

Pepper Steak

4 thin slices fillet steak
2 tablespoons ground black
  pepper
2 tablespoons oil
2 cloves garlic, finely chopped
2 tablespoons brandy
50 ml (2 fl oz) (¼ cup) white wine

Cover steaks with ground pepper and pound with mallet. Heat browning skillet 6 minutes on high. Add oil and garlic. Heat for 3 minutes. Press steak into pan, cook 3 minutes on each side. Add brandy and wine, cook 2 minutes.

Time: 17 minutes. Serves 4

Corned Silverside

1 litre (2 pts) (4 cups) boiling
  water
1.5 kg (3 lb) corned silverside
3 cloves
1 small onion, chopped
1 cinnamon stick
¼ teaspoon nutmeg
1 tablespoon brown sugar
1 bay leaf
1 tablespoon vinegar

Defrost Cooking Cycle Method:
Place water, meat and remaining ingredients into a covered casserole dish and cook on defrost cycle 1¾–2 hours, or until tender when pierced with a fork. Allow to stand 10 minutes before carving.

Oven Bag Method:
Soak beef in 2 changes of cold water for 2 hours. Place meat into an oven bag with remaining ingredients and 1½ cups of cold water. Tie bag. Place in large pyrex bowl. Pierce bag once or twice. Cook 30 minutes on high, turn meat over and cook 30 minutes on medium. Allow to stand 10 minutes before carving.

Time: 1–2 hours (see instructions). Serves 6–8

Lamb Curry

750 g (1½ lb) boneless leg of
  lamb
30 g (1 oz) butter
250 g (8 oz) (1⅜ cup) onions,
  chopped
1 clove garlic, chopped
2 tablespoons curry powder
1 tablespoon plain (all-purpose)
  flour
1 tablespoon chutney
2 teaspoons coconut
1 tablespoon sultanas (golden
  raisins)
60 g (2 oz) chopped apple
2 tablespoons tomato paste
225 ml (8 fl oz) (1 cup) beef stock
salt

Trim lamb and cut into even
sized pieces. Preheat browning
skillet 6 minutes on high. Add
butter and heat for 2 minutes.
Cook lamb pieces 3 minutes on
each side with onion and garlic.
Drain off any fat, add curry
powder and flour. Mix well and
cook 2 minutes. Add chutney,
coconut, sultanas, apples, tomato paste and stock. Cook
covered 20 minutes on high,
stirring occasionally. Serve
with plain boiled rice and
cucumber sambal.

Time: 36 minutes. Serves 4-6

Veal Marsala

500 g (1 lb) veal steak
seasoned plain (all-purpose)
  flour
3 tablespoons butter
½ cup Marsala

Pound veal with mallet to
flatten. Dust with seasoned
flour. Heat browning skillet 6
minutes on high. Add butter to
melt. Add veal and cook 2 minutes on each side. Add Marsala
and cook 3-4 minutes to form a
sauce with pan drippings.

Time: 14 minutes. Serves 4

Veal Mozzarella

500 g (1 lb) veal escalopes
75 g (3 oz) (¾ cup) grated
  mozzarella cheese
1 tablespoon finely chopped
  parsley

Sauce:
250 g (8 oz) (1½ cups) tomato
  paste
¼ teaspoon oregano
½ teaspoon basil
¼ teaspoon garlic salt
½ teaspoon sugar
⅛ teaspoon white pepper

Combine all sauce ingredients
in a medium-sized bowl and
cook on high 2 minutes. Reduce
power to medium and cook 6
minutes. Set aside.

Place veal escalopes in a
single layer in baking dish and
cook on medium 8-9 minutes.
Drain.

Spoon sauce over veal.
Sprinkle with cheese and
parsley and cook on medium
6-7 minutes until cheese melts.

Time: 22 minutes. Serves 4

Meat Loaf

2 bread slices, 1 cm (½ in) thick
500 g (1 lb) minced topside
  (ground beef)
60 g (2 oz) onion, chopped finely
60 g (2 oz) green capsicum,
  chopped finely
60 g (2 oz) celery, chopped finely
40 g (1½ oz) (½ cup) grated
  tasty cheese
1 tablespoon chopped parsley
125 ml (4 fl oz) (½ cup) tomato
  juice
2 eggs
¾ teaspoon salt
dash of pepper and nutmeg
2 tablespoons Worcestershire
  sauce
60 g (2 oz) tomato sauce
  (ketchup)

Soak bread slices in water until soft. Squeeze out water
thoroughly. Mix mince, bread,
onion, green capsicum, celery,
cheese, parsley and tomato
juice in a bowl. Stir well. Add
eggs, salt, pepper and nutmeg.
Stir well again. Shape meat into
a loaf and place in dish. Cook 20
minutes on high. Blend Worcestershire sauce and ketchup.
Drizzle liquid over top of loaf.
Cook 5 minutes.

Note: Fruit chutney and extra grated cheese can be spread
on top of meat loaf during last
5 minutes of cooking.

Time: 25 minutes. Serves 4-6

Veal Cordon Bleu

4 x 125 g (4 oz) slices veal
2 slices Gruyere cheese
2 slices lean ham
seasoned plain (all-purpose)
  flour
1 beaten egg
1 tablespoon milk
1 teaspoon soy sauce
1 cup seasoned breadcrumbs

Pound veal slices with mallet
until thin. Place 1 slice each of
cheese and ham on 2 veal slices.
Top with remaining veal. Seal
outer edges of veal by tapping
with meat mallet.

Combine egg, milk and soy
sauce. Dust veal with seasoned
flour, dip into egg mixture and
coat with breadcrumbs. Preheat browning skillet 8 minutes
on high. Add oil and heat for 3
minutes. Cook veal for 4 minutes on each side.

Time: 19 minutes. Serves 2

Veal Cordon Bleu

Poultry

- Poultry cooked in a microwave oven has a delicate flavour and is very tender and juicy. Whole or large pieces of poultry will brown easily in a microwave oven, but smaller portions can be browned by searing either in a fry pan, under the grill, or in the microwave browning skillet.
- Never season poultry with salt before roasting as this tends to dehydrate the flesh and make it tough. Other herbs and spices may, however, be used.
- Place poultry portions in a shallow dish wide enough to lay them flat in a single layer for even heat penetration. Always arrange the portions having the most flesh near the edge of the dish and place bones, such as drumstick ends, wings and backs, in the centre of the dish.
- When cooking, always cover kitchen pieces with white kitchen paper to prevent splattering.

Braised Lemon Chicken

Braised Lemon Chicken

30 ml (2 tablespoons) dark soy sauce
15 ml (1 tablespoon) dry sherry
200 ml (1 cup) lemon juice
1 kg (2¼ lb) chicken breasts, cut into serving pieces
45 ml (3 tablespoons) oil
2 thin slices of green ginger
1 clove garlic, peeled and crushed
180 ml (¾ cup) water
7 g (1 tablespoon) cornflour
salt
30–45 ml (2–3 tablespoons) water

Mix soy sauce, sherry, lemon juice, sugar in a bowl. Add chicken pieces and marinate for 20 minutes. Preheat browning skillet for 6 minutes. Add oil and heat for 2 minutes. Add ginger, garlic, chicken pieces and cook 3 minutes on each side. Place chicken, garlic and ginger into a casserole dish. Add remaining marinade and water. Cook covered 15–18 minutes, stirring twice during cooking. Add blended cornflour, cook 2 minutes. Season. Serve with plain boiled rice.

Time: 52 minutes (high).
Serves 4–6

Spanish Chicken

1 kg (2 lb) chicken breasts, cut into pieces
seasoned plain (all-purpose) flour, salt and pepper
4 tablespoons oil
2 onions, chopped
1 clove garlic, crushed
2 tablespoons chopped parsley
2 tablespoons chopped shallots (scallions)
4 tomatoes, sliced
1 green capsicum, chopped
125 g (4 oz) button mushrooms
300 ml (10 fl oz) (1¼ cups) red wine
1 teaspoon red chilli, finely chopped
salt
pepper
150 g (5 oz) (1 cup) frozen lima beans, cooked

Toss chicken pieces in seasoned flour. Preheat browning skillet for 6 minutes on high. Add 2 tablespoons oil and heat a further 2 minutes. Place the chicken pieces in skillet and cook 3 minutes on each side. Place chicken pieces into a 2 litre (3½ pt) casserole dish.

Reheat browning skillet for 2 minutes, add onions, garlic, remaining oil and cook for 2 minutes. Remove and add to chicken. Add parsley, shallots, tomatoes, capsicum, mushrooms, wine, chilli, salt and pepper. Cover casserole and cook 15 minutes. Add cooked beans and cook a further 3 minutes. Serve with boiled rice.

Time: 36 minutes. Serves 4–6

Chicken in Red Wine

1 chicken, cut in serving pieces
60 g (2 oz) seasoned plain (all-purpose) flour
3 tablespoons oil
120 g (4 oz) bacon, diced
1 clove garlic, chopped
6 small onions
500 ml (16 fl oz) (2 cups) red wine
120 g (4 oz) button mushrooms
salt and pepper

Coat chicken pieces lightly with seasoned flour. Preheat browning skillet for 6 minutes. Add oil and heat for 2 minutes. Place in chicken pieces pressing down on all sides to seal and colour. Cook 3 minutes on high on each side.

Remove chicken from pan and place in 2 litre (3½ pt) casserole dish. Reheat browning skillet for 4 minutes, add bacon, garlic and onions, cover with kitchen paper and cook for 3 minutes. Add this mixture to chicken. Gradually blend in wine with remaining flour to form a smooth paste. Add mushrooms and cook covered 15–18 minutes on high, stirring twice during cooking.

Time: 39 minutes. Serves 4–6

Mexican Chicken

1 large chicken, jointed, or
  chicken pieces
seasoned plain (all-purpose)
  flour
4 tablespoons oil
3 large onions, sliced
2 cloves garlic, crushed
1 red capsicum, diced
1 tablespoon sesame seeds
½ teaspoon oregano
200 ml (6 fl oz) (¾ cup) dry red
  wine
150 g (5 oz) (1 cup) blanched
  almonds
150 g (5 oz) (1 cup) sliced stuffed
  olives
½–1 teaspoon chilli powder (to
  taste)
225 ml (8 fl oz) (1 cup) chicken
  stock
225 ml (8 fl oz) (1 cup) whole
  kernel corn

Dust chicken pieces lightly
with seasoned flour. Preheat
browning skillet for 6 minutes
on high. Add oil, heat for 2 minutes. Add chicken pieces and
cook for 3 minutes on each side.
Remove chicken and place into
a 2 litre (3½ pt) casserole dish.

Place onions, garlic, capsicum, into browning skillet and
cook 3 minutes, stirring after 2
minutes. Add sesame seeds,
oregano, wine and pour over
chicken pieces. Add almonds,
olives, chilli powder, stock, and
cook covered 15 minutes. Fold
in corn kernels and cook 3 minutes longer.

Time: 35 minutes. Serves 4-6

Gourmet Chicken

2 whole chicken breasts
seasoned plain (all-purpose)
  flour
3 tablespoons oil
15 g (½ oz) (¼ cup) blanched
  slivered almonds
1 small onion, diced

1 clove garlic, crushed
1 cup celery, diced
2 tablespoons parsley, chopped
75 g (3 oz) (¾ cup) dry sherry
150 g (5 oz) (1 cup) button
  mushrooms
1 tablespoon cornflour
  (optional)
parsley sprigs and almonds for
  garnish

Cut chicken breasts into serving pieces and dust lightly with
seasoned flour. Preheat browning skillet for 6 minutes on
high. Add oil and heat for 2
minutes. Add almonds, brown
slightly, set aside for garnish.
Reheat skillet for 2 minutes,
add chicken pieces and cook 3
minutes on each side on high.
Remove chicken and place into
a 2 litre (3½ pt) casserole dish.

Place onion, garlic, celery,
parsley into browning skillet
and cook 2 minutes. Add
sherry, mushrooms and stir
well. Pour mixture over chicken
pieces and cook covered 15-18
minutes. Thicken slightly with
cornflour if necessary and cook
2 minutes longer. Serve garnished with almonds and
parsley sprigs.

Time: 38 minutes. Serves 4

Chilli Chicken

2 whole chicken breasts, cut
  into serving pieces
4 red chillies, seeds removed
  and chopped finely
2 slices green ginger, chopped
  finely
2 cloves garlic, chopped finely
1 medium onion, chopped finely
2 teaspoons lemon or lime juice
1 teaspoon turmeric
1 teaspoon sugar
salt

Salt chicken pieces lightly.
Combine all other ingredients
in a bowl. Add chicken pieces
and allow to stand 15-20 min-

utes. Place chicken and marinade in an oven bag. Tie bag
loosely with string or elastic
band. Cook 10 minutes on high,
then turn bag over and continue cooking a further 10
minutes.

Note: The chicken in the oven
bag must be in one layer, not
bunched up.

Time: 20 minutes. Serves 4

Roast Chicken

1 large chicken, size 16 (3 lb),
  washed and dried

Stuffing:
1 small onion, chopped finely
150 g (5 oz) (1 cup) white
  breadcrumbs
pinch of mixed herbs
1 tablespoon butter
¼ teaspoon salt
pinch pepper
1 tablespoon chopped parsley

Basting Sauce:
1-2 tablespoons melted butter
1 teaspoon soy sauce

Saute onion in butter, 3 minutes on high. Add remaining ingredients. Place stuffing into
cavity. Truss chicken to a neat
shape. Baste with 2 tablespoons melted butter mixed
with 1 teaspoon soy sauce.
Place into an oven bag. Tie
loosely with string and prick
bag once or twice. Cook 15 minutes on high, breast side down.
Turn over and cook a further 15
minutes. Let stand in bag for
10 minutes before carving.

Note: Baked rabbit can also
be cooked in this way.

Time: 33 minutes. Serves 4-6

Mexican Chicken

Crumbed Chicken Drumsticks

8 drumsticks
500 ml (16 fl oz) (2 cups) cooking
  oil
1 clove garlic, peeled and
  crushed
4 tablespoons plain (all-
  purpose) flour
salt and pepper to taste
pinch oregano
½ level teaspoon five spice
  powder
1 egg
50 ml (2 fl oz) (¼ cup) milk
250 g (9 oz) (1½ cups) dry
  breadcrumbs
50 ml (2 fl oz) (¼ cup) sesame
  seeds

Combine flour, salt, pepper, oregano and five spice powder. Beat egg and milk together. Combine breadcrumbs and sesame seeds.

Heat oil in pan on top of range. Add garlic, brown and remove. Roll drumsticks in seasoned flour. Coat with egg mixture, then with breadcrumb mixture. Fry drumsticks until a rich golden colour. Remove and drain.

Arrange on a glass platter with the thickest part of the drumstick to the outside edge. Cover with white kitchen paper. Cook for 8 minutes on high, turn over after 5 minutes of cooking. Serve with fried rice *(see recipe)*.

Note: This method combines the crispness of pan frying with the moist cooking of the micro-wave oven.

Time: 8 minutes. Serves 4

Crumbed Chicken Drumsticks

Apricot Chicken Casserole

3 tablespoons oil
1 kg (2 lb) chicken breasts, cut into serving pieces
2 tablespoons butter
1 large onion, diced
1 green capsicum, diced
2 tablespoons plain (all-purpose) flour
250 g (9 oz) (1½ cups) apricot nectar
salt and pepper
pinch oregano
2 teaspoons chopped parsley
3 large tomatoes, peeled and sliced

Preheat browning skillet for 6 minutes. Add oil and heat for 2 minutes. Add chicken pieces and cook for 3 minutes on high on each side. Melt butter in a 2 litre (3½ pt) casserole for 15 seconds. Add onion, capsicum and cook for 3 minutes. Stir in flour and cook for 2 minutes. Stir in apricot nectar to form a sauce. Add browned chicken pieces and remaining seasonings. Cover with tomato slices. Cook covered 18 minutes. Serve with buttered, boiled macaroni, which has been sprinkled with toasted sesame seeds.

Time: 37 minutes. Serves 4-6

Sweet and Sour Chicken

750 g (1½ lb) fresh chicken breasts
3 tablespoons oil
1 clove garlic, chopped finely
1 thin slice ginger, chopped finely

Sauce:
40 g (1½ oz) (½ cup) sugar
100 ml (4 fl oz) (½ cup) vinegar
200 ml (6 fl oz) (¾ cup) pineapple juice or water
1-2 tablespoons dark soy sauce
2 tablespoons oil
1 clove garlic, chopped finely
½ red capsicum, diced

½ green capsicum, diced
15 g (½ oz) (¼ cup) Chinese pickles, diced
15 g (½ oz) (¼ cup) mushrooms, sliced
15 g (½ oz) (¼ cup) bamboo shoots, sliced
3 shallots (scallions), cut into 2 cm (¾ in) lengths
2 tablespoons cornflour blended with 100 ml (4 fl oz) (½ cup) water

Remove flesh from bone and cut into 2 cm (¾ in) dice. Preheat browning skillet for 8 minutes. Add oil and heat for 3 minutes. Add garlic, ginger and cook 1 minute. Add chicken pieces and stir to coat with oil. Cook on high 5 minutes, stir and cook a further 5 minutes.

Combine sugar, vinegar, pineapple juice, and soy sauce. Heat oil in casserole dish for 2 minutes. Add garlic, vegetables and cook for 3 minutes uncovered on high. Add vinegar mixture. Cook for 3 minutes. Blend cornflour and water to a paste. Add to other ingredients and cook for 2 minutes. Add chicken pieces. Reheat for 2 minutes. Serve with plain or fried rice *(see recipe)*.

Time: 34 minutes. Serves 4-6

Red Roast Chicken

1 whole chicken
1 slice ginger
1 clove garlic, crushed

Marinade:
200 ml (6 fl oz) (¾ cup) Chinese barbecue sauce
pinch red food colouring powder
100 ml (4 fl oz) (½ cup) dry sherry

Place ginger and crushed garlic into cavity of chicken. Combine marinade ingredients. Coat chicken with marinade and allow to stand for 2 hours. Place

chicken into an oven bag. Tie loosely with string. Prick bag once or twice. Place in casserole dish and cook on high 15 minutes. Turn over and cook a further 10 minutes. Allow to stand 10 minutes before carving. Serve hot or cold with salads.

Time: 25 minutes. Serves 4-6

Chicken Sate

500 g (1 lb) chicken breasts
150 g (5 oz) (1 cup) pineapple pieces
150 g (5 oz) (1 cup) buttom mushrooms
150 g (5 oz) (1 cup) red capsicum diced same size as pineapple

Marinade:
3 tablespoons soy sauce
1 tablespoon dry sherry
1 tablespoon brown sugar
½ teaspoon powdered ginger
2 teaspoons grated onion

Sauce:
225 ml (8 fl oz) (1 cup) pineapple juice
1 tablespoon cornflour

Debone chicken. Cut into 2 cm (¾ in) cubes. Combine marinade ingredients, add chicken pieces and marinate for 1 hour. Arrange chicken pieces, pineapple and vegetables on bamboo skewers. Preheat browning skillet for 8 minutes. Add 2 tablespoons oil and heat for 2 minutes. Arrange skewers in oil and cook 3 minutes on high, turn and cook a further 3 minutes. Place on serving platter. Heat pineapple juice and cornflour to form a sauce. Spoon over chicken sate and serve.

Time: 16 minutes. Serves 4-6

Roast Orange Duck

1 x 2 kg (4 lb) duck
1 clove garlic
2 tablespoons butter, melted
  and mixed with 2 teaspoons
  soy sauce
1 onion, peeled and cut into
  quarters
1 orange, unpeeled, cut into
  quarters
50 ml (2 fl oz) (¼ cup) dry sherry
100 ml (4 fl oz) (½ cup) orange
  juice
½ teaspoon ground ginger
1 teaspoon salt
parsley
1 tablespoon cornflour
2 tablespoons water

Wipe duck inside and out with
a damp cloth. Cut garlic in half
and rub skin with it. Brush
with butter and soy mixture.
Place onion and orange into
cavity and fasten with a bamboo skewer. Place duck in shallow glass baking dish. Cover
loosely with plastic food wrap
and cook 15 minutes on high.
Pour sherry, orange juice, ginger and salt over duck. Recover and cook a further 15
minutes. Allow to stand 10 minutes. Remove orange and onion.

Blend 1 tablespoon cornflour
with a little water and add to
pan drippings. Cook a further 3
minutes. Carve duck and garnish with orange segments and
parsley. Mask with thickened
orange sauce.

Note: The duck can also be
cooked in an oven bag.

Time: 33 minutes. Serves 4

Alternative Stuffing for Turkey

Stuffing for Cavity:
125 g (¼ lb) butter
60 g (2 oz) onion, finely chopped
125 g (5 oz) (2½ cups) fresh
  white breadcrumbs
fresh or dry mixed herbs
1 tablespoon parsley, chopped
turkey liver, chopped
salt and pepper

Place butter and onion into casserole dish or bowl. Cook 4 minutes on high, add remaining
ingredients, mix well and
place into cavity. Truss turkey
firmly. A small amount of foil
may be placed on the wings and
drumsticks for half the cooking
time to prevent drying out.
Cover the whole turkey with
plastic wrap to retain natural
juices.

Stuffing for Neck Cavity:

500 g (1 lb) sausage mince

125 g (5 oz) (2½ cups) water
  chestnuts, diced

salt and pepper

Combine ingredients and place
into neck cavity. Fasten with
bamboo sate stick.

Roast Turkey

1 turkey, approximately 5 kg
  (10 lb)

Cooking Times:
16 minutes per kg (2 lb) (high)
24 minutes per kg (2 lb)
  (medium)

Clean and prepare turkey for
cooking. Place turkey, breast
side down in a glass baking
dish. Put apple dressing inside
cavity of turkey. Cover bottom
half of wings and legs with
small pieces of aluminium foil.
Secure legs and wings close to
body with string. Cover turkey
lightly with plastic food wrap
— this keeps the inside tender
and juicy. Cook turkey for 40
minutes then remove foil, turn
turkey over, cover and cook a
further 40 minutes. When cooking time is up, rest turkey
15–20 minutes before carving.
Note: If turkey is filled with
apple dressing, add 2 minutes
per kg (2 lb) to cooking time.

Time: 80 minutes.

Apple Dressing

250 g (½ lb) butter
225 g (½ lb) (1½ cups) celery,
  finely chopped
150 g (6 oz) (¾ cup) onion, finely
  chopped
5 ml (1 teaspoon) salt
5 ml (1 teaspoon) sage
150 ml (½–¾ cup) water
250 g (10 oz) dry breadcrumbs,
  more if needed
350 g (¾ lb) pared and chopped
  apple

Melt butter in a large casserole,
saute celery and onion 2–3 minutes on high, stirring after
every minute. Mix salt, sage
and water together. Pour over
breadcrumbs and toss lightly.
Add breadcrumbs to vegetables
and stir in apples. Stuff turkey
just before roasting.

Time: 3 minutes.

Seafood

Cooking fish or shellfish in a microwave oven is very rewarding. As it takes only minutes to be cooked to perfection, fish must be watched carefully during the cooking period. Overcooking toughens the fish and destroys its delicate flavour. Fish should only be cooked until it can be easily flaked with a fork.

To ensure even cooking, arrange the fish with the thickest portions near to the edge of the dish. Turn each portion over about halfway through the cooking period.

Oysters Mornay

12 oysters on the shell. Pierce oysters with toothpick before cooking.

Sauce:
**2 tablespoons butter
2 tablespoons plain (all-purpose) flour
300 ml (10½ fl oz) (1⅓ cups) milk
50 ml (2 fl oz) (¼ cup) Parmesan grated cheese
50 ml (2 fl oz) (¼ cup) Swiss grated cheese**

Put butter into small ovenproof dish and cook 15 seconds to melt. Stir in flour, then milk. Cook 3 minutes on high or until mixture boils. Stir sauce after 1 minute. Stir in cheese. Cover and cook until cheese melts. Spoon sauce over each oyster on the shell. Dust lightly with paprika, or a little extra grated cheese. Cook 1–2 minutes and serve with lemon wedges.

Time: 6 minutes. Serves 1–2

Oysters Kilpatrick

Oysters Kilpatrick

**12 oysters on the shell
4 rashers (slices) bacon, diced without rind
2–3 tablespoons Worcestershire sauce
salt and pepper to taste**

Wash oysters and shell to remove any grit. Dry with a clean cloth. Place diced bacon on white kitchen paper. Cover with a second piece of paper. Cook 3 minutes on high. Pierce oysters with toothpick. Top with bacon. Sprinkle with sauce. Season to taste. Cook 1–2 minutes.

Time: 5 minutes. Serves 1–2

Smoked Salmon Quiche

180 g (6 oz) smoked salmon, thinly sliced

Pastry (Pie Dough):
**2 cups plain (all-purpose) flour
200 g (7 oz) (1¼ cups) butter
½ teaspoon salt
¼ cup cold water**

Custard:
**225 ml (8 fl oz) (1 cup) cream
4 egg yolks
2 shallots (scallions), finely chopped
salt, cayenne pepper, and nutmeg to taste**

Sift dry ingredients in bowl. Rub in butter and mix to a firm dough with water. Knead lightly and roll out to fit a 21 cm (8 in) pie plate. Chill for 15 minutes. Cook for 6 minutes on high.

Blend together custard ingredients, pour into cool pastry shell and carefully float salmon slices on the surface. With a teaspoon, carefully lift some of the custard over the top of the salmon. Bake on the defrost cycle for 25 minutes until centre is set. Stand 3 minutes before serving.

Time: 31 minutes. Serves 6

Fillets of Flounder with Pernod Sauce

**20 g (¾ oz) (½ cup) butter
6 fillets of flounder
fish seasoning
juice of half a lemon
2 tablespoons Pernod
75 ml (2½ fl oz) (⅓ cup) cream
sprinkling of dry basil
chopped chives for garnish**

Melt butter in an oblong dish for 15 seconds. Sprinkle fillets lightly with seasoning and place in butter. Pour over lemon juice and Pernod. Cook covered 6–7 minutes on high. Remove to plate, reheat liquids, add cream, basil and cook 1½ minutes. Spoon over fillets. Sprinkle with chopped chives and serve.

Time: 9 minutes. Serves 4–6

Garlic Prawns (Shrimp)

**4–6 tablespoons peanut oil
4 cloves garlic, finely cut
2 shallots (scallions), finely cut
1 fresh hot red chilli, sliced without seeds, or ½ teaspoon chilli powder
500 g (1 lb) shelled green prawns (uncooked shrimp)**

Combine oil, garlic, shallots and chilli in microwave oven dish. Add prawns and toss to coat with oil. Allow to stand 10 minutes. Cook 2 minutes on high. Stir and cook until they turn pink, another 2 minutes.

Time: 4 minutes. Serves 4

Salmon Stuffed Mushrooms

12 medium to large mushrooms
6 tablespoons flaked red salmon
6 tablespoons soft breadcrumbs
2 teaspoons finely chopped
  shallots (scallions)
2 teaspoons finely chopped
  parsley
2 teaspoons lemon juice
2 tablespoons butter, melted
grated Parmesan cheese

Remove stems from mushrooms. Chop stems finely. Combine salmon, breadcrumbs, stems, shallots, parsley, lemon juice and butter. Fill caps with mixture. Sprinkle with cheese. Arrange mushrooms in a circle on the outer edge of a glass platter. Cook 5 minutes on high.

Time: 5 minutes. Serves 6

Scallops in Oyster Sauce

1½ tablespoons oil
1 slice green ginger, cut finely
1 clove garlic, cut finely
500 g (1 lb) scallops
1 tablespoon dry sherry
2 teaspoons soy sauce
100 ml (4 fl oz) (½ cup) fish stock
2 tablespoons oyster sauce
1 teaspoon sugar
3 teaspoons cornflour
2 shallots (scallions), cut into
  2 cm (¾ in) lengths
½ teaspoon salt

Heat oil in an ovenproof dish for 1 minute. Add ginger, garlic and scallops. Cook for 3 minutes on high. Add sherry, soy sauce and cook 1 minute. Blend the stock, oyster sauce, sugar and cornflour. Add to dish, stir to blend and cook 2 minutes until boiling. Fold in shallots, salt and serve with plain boiled rice.

Time: 7 minutes. Serves 4

Whole Fish with Black Bean Sauce

1 whole fish, approximately
  750 g (1½ lb), or fish fillets
fish seasoning (optional)

Sauce:
1 tablespoon oil
1 slice green ginger, cut finely
1 clove garlic, cut finely
1 tablespoon black beans
½ teaspoon dry sherry
½ teaspoon sugar
2 teaspoons soy sauce
225 ml (8 fl oz) (1 cup) fish stock
  or water
1 tablespoon cornflour
water
3 shallots (scallions), cut finely
red capsicum for garnish

Trim off fins and tail with a pair of scissors. Remove the eyes. Check that all scales have been removed. Wash well and dry with kitchen paper. A small amount of fish seasoning may be sprinkled into cavity. Place fish onto a plate and cover with plastic food wrap. Cook approximately 6–8 minutes on high or until flesh flakes easily.

Heat oil in a bowl for 2 minutes. Add ginger, garlic, beans, and stir. Cook for 1 minute on high. Add sherry, sugar, soy sauce and stock. Cook 1 minute. Blend cornflour and water, stir into mixture. Cook a further 2 minutes. Stir in shallots. Spoon over fish. Serve garnished with shredded red capsicum.

Time: 11 minutes. Serves 4–6

Salmon Ring

1 x 500 g (1 lb) can red salmon
40 g (1½ oz) (½ cup) chopped
  onion
50 ml (2 fl oz) (¼ cup) salad oil
20 g (¾ oz) (⅓ cup) dry
  breadcrumbs
2 eggs, beaten

1 teaspoon dry mustard
½ teaspoon salt

Drain salmon, reserving ⅓ cup liquid. Cook onion in oil for 2½ minutes. Combine onion, dry breadcrumbs, salmon liquid, eggs, mustard, salt and flaked salmon in a basin and mix well. Place into a microwave ring pan and cook for 6 minutes on high. Give pan a quarter of a turn after 3 minutes. Let stand for 5 minutes before serving.

Note: Tuna may be used instead of salmon.

Time: 9 minutes. Serves 6

Whole Fish with Chinese Pickle Sauce

1 whole fish, approximately
  750 g (1½ lb)

Chinese Pickle Sauce:
2 teaspoons tomato sauce
  (ketchup)
½ teaspoon salt
2 teaspoons soy sauce
500 ml (16 fl oz) (2 cups)
  pineapple juice
40 g (1½ oz) (½ cup) diced
  Chinese mixed pickle
1 slice pineapple, diced
2 tablespoons vinegar
3 tablespoons brown sugar
small piece capsicum, diced
1–2 tablespoons cornflour

Prepare and cook the fish in the same way as Whole Fish with Black Bean Sauce *(see recipe)*.

Combine all ingredients in a bowl except cornflour. Cook 4–5 minutes on high until boiling. Stir after 3 minutes. Thicken with blended cornflour. Cook 2 minutes, serve over fish.

Note: Allow 5 minutes per 500 g (1 lb) cooking time.

Time: 15 minutes. Serves 4–6

Baked Orange Fish

1 large orange
1 small clove garlic
1 tablespoon butter
1 small onion, finely cut
1 tablespoon finely chopped
  parsley
salt and pepper
150 g (5 oz) (1 cup) fresh bean
  sprouts, roots removed
200 ml (6 fl oz) (¾ cup) orange
  juice
1 whole fish 750 g–1 kg
  (1½–2 lb)

Peel orange and cut into segments. Cut garlic into small pieces and half the orange segments into dice. Place butter, onion, garlic, orange segments, parsley, salt and pepper into a microwave oven dish and cook covered on high for 2 minutes. Add bean sprouts.

After trimming fins and tail, place fish on a baking dish, removing eyes and checking for any scales which may have been missed. If the fish is large it may be scored 2 or 3 times on each side to ensure even cooking. Season cavity with salt and pepper. Stuff cavity with onion and orange mixture. Cover fish with plastic wrap and cook 5 minutes on high. Pour juice over fish and arrange remaining segments over fish neatly. Continue cooking 2½ minutes until flesh flakes easily.

Note: Allow 5 minutes per 500 g (1 lb) cooking time.

Time: 9½ minutes. Serves 4

Baked Orange Fish

Coquilles St. Jacques

4 tablespoons butter
1 small onion, finely chopped
250 g (9 oz) scallops
2 teaspoons lemon juice
½ teaspoon salt
marjoram
dash paprika
6 tablespoons white wine
2 tablespoons plain (all-
  purpose) flour
10 ml (4 fl oz) (½ cup) cream
60 g (2 oz) mushrooms, sliced
  thinly
fresh white breadcrumbs
1 teaspoon chopped parsley

Combine 1 tablespoon butter and onion in a medium sized casserole dish. Cook uncovered 1 minute. Stir in scallops, lemon juice, seasoning and wine. Cook, covered 3 minutes on high. Drain liquid and reserve. Melt 3 tablespoons butter for 30 seconds. Blend in flour then stir in reserved liquid and cream. Heat, uncovered, 2 minutes or until sauce thickens. Add scallop mixture, mushrooms and spoon into 4 individual ramekins, or scallop shells. Sprinkle with breadcrumbs and parsley and heat uncovered 3 minutes.

Time: 9½ minutes. Serves 4

Fresh Trout with Asparagus Sauce

2 whole trout, approximately
  250 g (9 oz) each
2 small branches of fresh dill
fish seasoning
1 shallot (scallion), cut finely
1 tablespoon dry vermouth
4 tablespoons fish stock or
  white wine
1 lemon, peeled and sliced
butter

Wash and dry trout, remove eyes. Place fresh dill into cavities and season. Place in a glass dish, sprinkle with shallots, vermouth, fish stock and cover with slices of lemon. Dot lightly with butter. Cover with plastic food wrap and cook 6–7 minutes on high.

Time: 7 minutes. Serves 2

Asparagus Sauce

1 340 g (11 oz) can green
  asparagus spears
125 ml (½ cup) chicken stock
salt and pepper
20 ml (1 tablespoon) fresh
  cream

Combine asparagus with stock, salt, pepper and cream. Puree in blender until smooth. Correct seasonings.

Pour into glass jug and cook on high 2 minutes. Mask trout with sauce.

Time: 2 minutes.

Curried Prawns

25 g (1 oz) butter
15 g (½ oz) fresh ginger, grated
60 g (2 oz) minced onion
60 g (2 oz) plain flour
15 g (½ oz) curry powder
250 ml (1 cup) milk
250 ml (1 cup) coconut milk
10 ml (2 teaspoons) lemon juice
500 g (1 lb) green prawns

Place butter, ginger and onion in a 2½ quart casserole and cook 2 minutes on high. Sift in flour and curry powder and stir to a smooth paste. Add both milks and cook 5 minutes on high, stirring every minute. Blend in remaining ingredients. Mix well and cook 6 minutes on high, stirring after 2 minutes.

Serve with plain boiled rice and toasted coconut. (Mango chutney optional.)

Time: 13 minutes.

Desserts & Cakes

- Cakes baked in a microwave oven require careful watching because of the rapid cooking process.
- White or yellow cakes do not brown but, as most cakes are frosted, this should present no problem.
- Use greaseproof paper to line the bottom of your baking dish if the cake is to be removed before serving. Do not use waxed paper under cakes as the wax may melt. For best results, grease the baking dish first, then line it with greaseproof paper and grease again.
- Remember that overcooking toughens a cake. Cook cakes until a wooden skewer inserted into the centre of the cake comes out clean.
- When the cake is cold wrap it in plastic food wrap and it will remain fresh for one week.

Grasshopper Torte

60 g (2 oz) butter
1 package chocolate flavoured plain biscuits, crumbed
450 g (4 cups) white marshmallows, diced
200 ml (6 fl oz) (¾ cup) milk
60 ml (2 fl oz) (¼ cup) green creme de menthe
30 ml (2 tablespoons) white creme de cacao
10 ml (2 teaspoons) gelatine
30 ml (2 tablespoons) cold water
250 ml (8 fl oz) stiffly beaten cream

Place butter in glass bowl and cook for 45 seconds on high. Stir in biscuit crumbs. Put half the mixture into a 23 cm (9 in) round glass dish and chill.

Place marshmallows and milk into a large bowl. Cook 1½–2 minutes to melt marshmallows. Stir in creme de menthe and creme de cacao. Blend gelatine and water in small bowl. Heat 15 seconds on high. Blend into mixture and cool.

Fold in whipped cream, pour into crumb-lined dish and top with remaining crumbs. Chill until firm. Cut into wedges and pipe with whipped cream.

Time: 3 minutes.

Baba au Rhum

Fruit:
1 tablespoon raisins
1 tablespoon currants
1 tablespoon sultanas (golden raisins)
1 tablespoon rum

Baba Batter:
60 g (2 oz) butter
105 g (3½ oz) caster (superfine) sugar
3 eggs
125 g (4 oz) self-raising (rising) flour
2 tablespoons milk

Syrup:
40 g (1½ oz) (½ cup) sugar
1 cinnamon stick
225 ml (8 fl oz) (1 cup) syrup from tinned apricots
2 tablespoons lemon juice
4 tablespoons rum

Combine fruit and rum and set aside. Cream butter and sugar. Add eggs, one at a time. Add flour all at once and fold in milk and fruit. Place batter in greased and lined glass Baba mould. Cook 5–6 minutes on high. Turn out on a serving platter.

Combine sugar, cinnamon stick and syrup together and cook 5 minutes on high. Add lemon juice and rum. Cool.

Spoon syrup over Baba. Serve decorated with whipped cream, apricots and glace cherries.

Time: 11 minutes. Serves 8

Apple Crumble

6 cooking apples, peeled and sliced
100 ml (4 fl oz) (½ cup) water
40 g (1½ oz) (½ cup) sugar
½ teaspoon cinnamon
60 g (2 oz) soft butter
15 g (½ oz) (¼ cup) plain (all-purpose) flour
40 g (1½ oz) (½ cup) coconut
40 g (1½ oz) (½ cup) brown sugar

Place apples, water, sugar and cinnamon into a 1 litre (2 pt) casserole dish, cover and cook 5 minutes on high. Rub butter into flour, coconut, brown sugar and sprinkle over apples. Top with extra cinnamon and cook 3–4 minutes. Serve with Custard Sauce *(see recipe)*.

Time: 9 minutes. Serves 6–8

Queen Pudding

4 slices of buttered, stale, plain cake
5 eggs
2 tablespoons sugar
500 ml (16 fl oz) (2 cups) warm milk
vanilla extract
strawberry jam

Cut cake into cubes. Place into well-buttered baking ring. Beat eggs, sugar and vanilla, add warm milk. Pour over cake cubes and cook 60 minutes on defrost.

Spread top of custard with strawberry jam. Top with piped meringue *(see recipe Pineapple Meringue Pie)* and cook 2–3 minutes on high. Sprinkle with sugar lightly coloured with a few drops of pink food colouring.

Time: 63 minutes. Serves 6

Grasshopper Torte

Savarin

60 g (2 oz) butter
105 g (3½ oz) caster (superfine)
 sugar
3 eggs
125 g (4 oz) self-raising (rising)
 flour
2 tablespoons milk or cream

Syrup:
225 ml (6½ fl oz) water
250 g (9 oz) (1½ cups) sugar
5 tablespoons Grand Marnier

Beat softened butter and sugar
to a cream. Add eggs, one at a
time. Add flour, all at once.
Fold in milk or cream. Grease
and line base of micro-ring dish.
Grease again. Pour in mixture
and cook 5–6 minutes on high.
Turn out on a cooking rack.

Boil water and sugar to form
a syrup. Add Grand Marnier.
Spoon warm syrup over cake
until all is absorbed. Place on
serving platter. Fill centre with
fresh fruit salad. Decorate with
whipped cream and extra fruit.

Time: 6 minutes. Serves 8

Caramel Tart

1 precooked pastry case (see
 recipe Pineapple Meringue Pie)
2 tablespoons butter
150 g (5 oz) (1 cup) brown sugar
4 egg yolks
3 drops vanilla extract
pinch salt
2 tablespoons plain (all-
 purpose) flour
500 ml (16 fl oz) (2 cups) milk
1 quantity meringue (see recipe
 Pineapple Meringue Pie)

Beat butter and sugar until
fluffy. Beat in egg yolks. Add
vanilla, salt, fold in sifted flour,
stir in milk. Cook 4–5 minutes
on high, stirring every minute
until mixture thickens. Spoon
into pastry case. Top with
meringue and cook 2–3 minutes
on high.

Time: 8 minutes. Serves 8

Baked Bread and Butter Custard

30 g (1 oz) butter
500 ml (16 fl oz) (2 cups) milk
5 eggs
15 g (½ oz) (¼ cup) raw sugar
1 teaspoon vanilla extract
4 slices white bread, crusts
 removed, then buttered
nutmeg
2 tablespoons sultanas (golden
 raisins)

Place butter into milk and heat
for 2 minutes. Beat eggs, sugar
and vanilla, add milk and butter mixture. Sprinkle buttered
bread lightly with nutmeg, cut
into cubes, and place into a
greased baking ring with sultanas. Pour custard over bread
and cook uncovered 60 minutes
on defrost.

Time: 62 minutes. Serves 6

Rice Custard

Note: 150 g (5 oz) (1 cup) of
precooked rice can be used in
place of the buttered bread.

Time: 22 minutes.

Peaches Flambe

30 g (1 oz) butter
1 can drained peach halves
5 tablespoons Grand Marnier
30 g (1 oz) sugar

Heat butter in glass serving
dish for 1–2 minutes. Add
peach halves and 2 tablespoons
Grand Marnier. Sprinkle with
sugar and cook 3 minutes on
high. Heat 3 tablespoons Grand
Marnier in glass jug for 25
seconds, flame and pour over
peaches. Serve with vanilla ice
cream.

Time: 5½ minutes. Serves 4

Pineapple Meringue Pie

Pastry:
125 g (4 oz) butter
20 g (¾ oz) (⅓ cup) sugar
275 g (10 oz) (2 cups) plain (all-
 purpose) flour, sifted
3 drops vanilla extract
2 teaspoons water
1 egg yolk

Filling:
1 x 500 g (1 lb) can crushed
 pineapple
1 egg yolk
2 tablespoons custard powder
1 tablespoon arrowroot
50 ml (2 fl oz) (¼ cup) orange
 juice

Meringue:
3 egg whites
40 g (1½ oz) (½ cup) caster
 (superfine) sugar

Rub butter into sugar and flour.
Add vanilla, water and egg
yolk. Knead lightly and let rest
15 minutes. Roll out pastry and
line a 23 cm (9 in) pie plate.
Prick well and cook for 4 minutes on high. Allow to cool.

Place pineapple into a casserole dish and cook 4 minutes until boiling. Beat egg yolk, add
custard powder, arrowroot and
orange juice. Mix into hot pineapple and cook for 2 minutes on
high. Cool and spoon into
pastry case.

Beat egg whites, adding
sugar, 1 tablespoon at a time,
until soft peaks form. Pipe or
spread over pineapple filling
and cook to set for 2–3 minutes.
Place under grill for a few minutes if a light golden colour is
required.

Time: 13 minutes. Serves 8

Savarin

Pineapple Ginger Cake

60 g (2 oz) butter
20 g (¾ oz) (⅓ cup) brown sugar
6 small slices of canned
   pineapple
6 maraschino cherries

Cake:
80 g (3 oz) (¾ cup) butter
40 g (1½ oz) (½ cup) white
   (superfine) sugar
1 egg
100 ml (4 fl oz) (½ cup) golden
   (corn) syrup
75 ml (2½ fl oz) (⅓ cup) milk
250 g (9 oz) (1½ cups) plain (all-
   purpose) flour
1 teaspoon bicarbonate of soda
1 teaspoon ground ginger
1 teaspoon ground cinnamon
pinch salt

Cream 60 g (2 oz) butter and
brown sugar together and
spread into the bottom of a baking dish. Place pineapple rings
into mixture with a cherry in
the centre of each ring.

Cream together 80 g (3 oz)
butter and white sugar, add
egg, golden syrup and milk. Sift
dry ingredients together. Blend
all into a creamy mixture.
Spread over pineapple slices.
Cook uncovered 10 minutes on
high.

Note: Other fruits may be
used: sliced mangoes, peaches
or apricots.

Time: 10 minutes. Serves 8

Chocolate Souffle

6 teaspoons gelatine
75 g (3 oz) (¾ cup) sugar
3 eggs, separated
225 ml (8 fl oz) (1 cup) milk
60 g (2 oz) melted cooking
   chocolate (chop or grate
   chocolate, and cook ¾–1
   minute to melt)
1 cup whipped cream

Pineapple Coconut Cake

Chocolate Souffle

In a large bowl combine gelatine with ½ cup sugar. Stir in egg yolks and beat in the milk. Heat on defrost for 6½–7½ minutes or until gelatine dissolves, stirring occasionally. Stir in chocolate and chill, stirring occasionally until mixture mounds slightly.

Beat egg whites until soft peaks form, gradually add remaining sugar and beat until stiff. Fold in the chocolate mixture with whipped cream. Pour into souffle dish with a collar. Chill. To serve, garnish with extra whipped cream and almond slivers.

Time: 7½ minutes. Serves 6

Apple Tea Cake

60 g (2 oz) butter
75 g (3 oz) (¾ cup) sugar
vanilla extract
1 egg
200 ml (6 fl oz) (¾ cup) milk
250 g (9 oz) (1½ cups) plain (all-purpose) flour
2 teaspoons baking powder
½ teaspoon salt
1 green apple, peeled, cored and sliced thinly
2 teaspoons brown sugar
2 teaspoons cinnamon

Cream butter, sugar and vanilla until light and fluffy. Beat in egg and fold in milk and sifted dry ingredients except the apple, brown sugar and cinnamon. Prepare the micro-baking dish, grease it first, then line it with greaseproof paper and grease it again. Arrange thinly sliced apples and lightly dust with mixture of brown sugar and cinnamon. Pour batter on top of apples. Cook 6 minutes on high or 9 minutes on medium.

Time: 6–9 minutes.

Lemon Meringue Pie

1 precooked pastry case (see recipe Pineapple Meringue Pie)
1 quantity meringue (see recipe Pineapple Meringue Pie)

Filling:
40 g (1½ oz) (½ cup) cornflour
40 g (1½ oz) (½ cup) sugar
200 ml (6 fl oz) (¾ cup) water
75 ml (2½ fl oz) (⅓ cup) lemon juice
20 g (¾ oz) (⅓ cup) butter
3 egg yolks
grated rind of 1 lemon

Combine cornflour, sugar, water, juice of lemon and butter in a casserole dish and cook 2 minutes on high, stir and cook a further 2 minutes. Cool. Beat in yolks and lemon rind. Place in pastry case. Top with meringue, cook 2–3 minutes. Cool.

Time: 7 minutes. Serves 8

Ginger Puff Sponge

2 eggs
60 g (2 oz) sugar
1 teaspoon golden (corn) syrup
30 g (1 oz) cornflour
30 g (1 oz) plain (all-purpose) flour
2 level teaspoons ground ginger
1 level teaspoon cinnamon
1 level teaspoon cocoa
¼ level teaspoon bicarbonate of soda
½ level teaspoon cream of tartar

Beat eggs until thick and creamy, gradually adding sugar, beating until dissolved. Add golden syrup and beat until well mixed. Fold in sifted dry ingredients. Place into a well-greased micro-baking ring and cook for 2½ minutes on high, turning every minute. When cold, split and fill with cream.

Time: 2½ minutes.

Baked Honey Pears

4 firm pears
Combine
50 g (2 oz) (4 tablespoons) chopped dates
25 g (1 oz) (2 tablespoons) chopped walnuts
60 ml (¼ cup) (3 tablespoons) honey
1.25 ml (¼ teaspoon) cinnamon

Peel pears, cut off caps 2.5 cm (1 in) from top. Core each pear without cutting right through. Remove seeds. Fill centres with date mixture, replace caps. Arrange in a circle on a glass plate and cook on high 6–8 minutes. Pears can be served whole; remove cap and top with whipped cream, or cut in half, served with a rosette of whipped cream.

Time: 8 minutes.

Baked Honey Pears

Marble Cake

60 g (2 oz) butter
75 g (3 oz) (¾ cup) sugar
vanilla extract
1 egg
200 ml (6 fl oz) (¾ cup) milk
250 g (9 oz) (1½ cups) plain (all-purpose) flour
2 teaspoons baking powder
½ teaspoon salt

Cream butter, sugar and vanilla until light and fluffy. Beat in egg, fold in milk and sifted dry ingredients alternately. Divide the mixture into 3 separate bowls:

Leave one plain.

Add a few drops of red food colouring to the second one.

Add 2 tablespoons cocoa, pinch of bicarbonate and 1 tablespoon milk to the third.

Drop into greased, lined and greased micro-baking ring in alternate colours. Lightly mix with a metal skewer to blend colours. Cook 6 minutes on high or 9 minutes medium.

Time: 6–9 minutes.

Strawberry Cream Dessert

2 punnets ripe red strawberries
4 eggs, separated
1 tablespoon gelatine
8 tablespoons sugar
1 carton whipped cream

Wash and hull strawberries. Place 1½ punnets into a blender and puree. Blend puree, egg yolks, gelatine and sugar. Place into a glass bowl and cook on defrost 7 minutes until gelatine dissolves, stirring constantly. Chill until slightly set.

Beat cream to form stiff peaks. Fold into strawberry puree and beaten egg whites.

Marble Cake

Pour into individual glass sweet dishes to set. Decorate with whipped cream and remaining strawberries.

Time: 7 minutes. Serves 6–8

Pineapple Coconut Cake

60 g (2 oz) butter
75 g (3 oz) (¾ cup) sugar
vanilla extract
1 egg
100 ml (4 fl oz) (½ cup) milk
150 g (5 oz) (1 cup) well-drained crushed pineapple
40 g (1½ oz) (½ cup) coconut
250 g (9 oz) (1½ cups) plain (all-purpose) flour
1 teaspoon baking powder
½ teaspoon salt

Cream butter, sugar and vanilla until light and fluffy. Beat in egg and fold in milk, crushed pineapple, coconut and sifted dry ingredients. Grease and line micro-baking dish. Pour mixture into dish and cook 6 minutes on high or 9 minutes on medium.

Time: 6–9 minutes.

Date Loaf

2 tablespoons butter or margarine
40 g (1½ oz) (½ cup) raw sugar
1 egg
150 ml (5 fl oz) (⅔ cup) milk
40 g (1½ oz) (½ cup) dates
40 g (1½ oz) (½ cup) chopped walnuts
250 g (9 oz) (1½ cups) self-raising (rising) flour
pinch salt
½ teaspoon cinnamon
½ teaspoon ginger
1 teaspoon mixed spice

Beat butter and sugar to a cream. Add well-beaten egg. Add milk gradually. Add chopped dates and nuts. Stir in

lightly the sifted flour, salt, and spices. Spoon mixture into prepared micro-baking dish. Cook 6 minutes on high or 9 minutes on medium.

Time: 6–9 minutes.

Meringue-topped Chocolate Cheese Cake

Base:
150 g (5 oz) (1 cup) biscuit crumbs
40 g (1½ oz) (½ cup) melted margarine (to melt margarine put in oven ¾–1 minute)

Filling:
375 g (13 oz) cream cheese (to soften cheese, cut up and place in oven on defrost 1 minute)
2 eggs
40 g (1½ oz) (½ cup) caster (superfine) sugar
1 teaspoon vanilla extract
60 g (2 oz) melted chocolate (to melt chocolate, cut up and place in oven and cook 1 minute)

Topping:
2 egg whites
5 tablespoons caster (superfine) sugar
20 g (¾ oz) (⅓ cup) coconut
2 teaspoons cornflour

Combine base ingredients and press evenly into a 20 cm (8 in) pyrex pie plate. Chill until firm.

To make filling, beat cream cheese using an electric mixer until smooth. Add eggs one at a time. Add sugar, vanilla, and beat until creamy smooth. Pour into crumb crust. Swirl in melted chocolate to give a marble effect. Cook 3 minutes.

Whip egg whites until stiff, using an electric beater, gradually adding sugar, beating to dissolve. Fold in coconut (can be lightly toasted if desired) and cornflour. Pipe onto cheese cake and cook 3 minutes. Serve cold.

Time: 9 minutes.

Orange Tea Ring

60 g (2 oz) butter
75 g (3 oz) (¾ cup) sugar
vanilla extract
1 egg
3 tablespoons orange juice
3 tablespoons milk
2 teaspoons grated orange rind
250 g (9 oz) (1½ cups) plain (all-purpose) flour
2 teaspoons baking powder
½ teaspoon salt

Cream butter, sugar and vanilla until light and fluffy. Beat in egg and fold in orange juice, milk, orange rind and dry ingredients alternately. Drop into a greased, lined and greased micro-baking ring. Cook for 6 minutes on high or 9 minutes on medium. Cool and top with orange frosting.

Time: 6–9 minutes.

Banana Cake

60 g (2 oz) butter, melted
50 ml (2 fl oz) (¼ cup) milk
1 egg, beaten
40 g (1½ oz) (½ cup) mashed banana
40 g (1½ oz) (½ cup) brown sugar
150 g (5 oz) (1 cup) self-raising (rising) flour
40 g (1½ oz) (½ cup) chopped nuts

Topping:
15 g (½ oz) (¼ cup) brown sugar
15 g (½ oz) (¼ cup) chopped nuts
1 tablespoon plain (all-purpose) flour
2 tablespoons coconut
pinch cinnamon
15 g (½ oz) softened butter

Combine butter, milk, egg, banana, and brown sugar in a basin. Mix well. Fold in flour and nuts. Pour into a greased and lined round 21 cm (8 in) pyrex souffle dish. Combine topping ingredients and sprinkle in souffle dish. Cook on medium 10½–11½ minutes. Let stand 5 minutes before turning out.

Time: 10½ minutes.

Popcorn Crunch

300 g (1½ cups) sugar
250 ml (8 fl oz) (1 cup) golden syrup
100 g (4 oz) butter
250 g (8 cups) popcorn, already popped
60 g (2 oz) (2 cups) puffed wheat cereal
30 g (1 oz) (1 cup) flaked almonds, toasted
3.75 ml (¾ teaspoon) cinnamon
5 ml (1 teaspoon) vanilla

Place sugar and golden syrup in a heatproof dish, stir and cook until sugar is dissolved, approximately 4 minutes on high. Add butter and cook for 6 minutes on high.

Meanwhile, place popcorn, cereal and almonds into a separate bowl. Add cinnamon and vanilla to golden syrup mixture. Combine syrup with popcorn, cereal and almonds and spread over base of lightly greased 25 cm (10 in) × 30 cm (12 in) baking tray.

Allow to cool, break into pieces and store in an airtight container. *Note:* Can be piled into ice cream cones for children's parties.

Time: 10 minutes.

Carrot Cake

40 g (1½ oz) (½ cup) butter or margarine
40 g (1½ oz) (½ cup) firmly packed brown sugar
1 egg
150 g (5 oz) (1 cup) firmly packed fresh grated carrot
1 dessertspoon crystallised ginger
40 g (1½ oz) (½ cup) seeded raisins
40 g (1½ oz) (½ cup) sultanas (golden raisins)
250 g (9 oz) (1½ cups) double sifted plain (all-purpose) flour
1 teaspoon baking powder
½ teaspoon soda
½ teaspoon cinnamon
½ teaspoon nutmeg
200 ml (6 fl oz) (¾ cup) milk

Frosting:
250 g (9 oz) (1½ cups) icing sugar (confectioner's sugar) mixture
90 g (3½ oz) cream cheese
3 tablespoons butter
1 teaspoon vanilla extract
1 teaspoon sherry

Cream butter or margarine and brown sugar. Beat in egg until well blended. Stir in carrots, ginger, raisins and sultanas. Sift together flour, baking powder, soda, cinnamon and nutmeg. Stir into the mixture with milk. Blend well. Turn into a well greased micro-ring dish and cook in oven 6 minutes high then 3 minutes medium. Serve cold with lemon frosting or hot with lemon sauce.

Beat all frosting ingredients until fluffy — spread over cake. Decorate with mandarin quarters or small marzipan carrots.

Time: 9 minutes.

Orange Tea Ring

Black Forest Cherry Cake

Black Forest Cherry Cake

1 packet chocolate cake mix

Filling:
1 can stoned black cherries
75 ml (2½ fl oz) (⅓ cup) Kirsch
2 tablespoons arrowroot
3 tablespoons cherry syrup
300 ml (10 fl oz) (1¼ cups) cream
grated dark chocolate
red cherries

Make cake as directed on packet. Grease and line a microwave baking ring. Pour cake mix into prepared dish. Cook in oven 5½–6 minutes on high. Turn onto a cake cooler and cover before cake is cold.

Place cherries, 2 tablespoons of Kirsch and syrup from cherries into a bowl to cover. Cook 4 minutes on high or until boiling. Blend arrowroot with 3 tablespoons syrup. Stir into cherry mixture, cook 2 minutes and allow to cool.

Split cake into 3 layers. Spread cherry mixture over base, top with second layer.

Whip cream with remaining Kirsch. Spread half over second layer, top with third piece of cake. Spread top and outside edges lightly with cream. Mark top into serves. Dust top and sides with grated chocolate. Pipe a rosette of cream on edge of each marked portion and top with a whole red cherry.

Time: 12 minutes.

Sauces

Sauces are very quick and easy to make in a microwave oven. Be sure to stir frequently when making sauces. You can leave the wooden spoon in the bowl in the oven to make this a simple operation. Always use a large glass container for sauce preparation to prevent boiling over.

When thickening sauces remember that arrowroot makes a more transparent sauce than one thickened with cornflour.

Basic White Sauce I

1 small onion, peeled
6 whole cloves
600 ml (1 pint) (2½ cups) milk
1 bay leaf
60 g (2 oz) butter
60 g (2 oz) plain (all-purpose) flour
salt and pepper

Stud onion with cloves. Pour milk into a glass jug, add onion and bay leaf. Cook on high for 4½ minutes to heat and infuse flavours.

Place butter into a glass jug or casserole and cook 1 minute to melt. Add flour and stir with wooden spoon. Cook 1 minute.

Stir in milk to blend. Cook for 4 minutes, stirring after 2 minutes. Remove onion and bay leaf. Season with salt and pepper.

Time: 10½ minutes. Makes about 2 cups

Parsley Sauce

Onion Sauce

Basic White Sauce I ingredients
60 g (2 oz) onion, diced

Melt butter in Basic White Sauce I recipe. Add onion and cook 3–4 minutes before adding the flour.

Add milk and cook as above.

Serve with roast mutton, corned beef, or corned ox tongue.

Parsley Sauce

2 tablespoons chopped parsley
1 quantity Basic White Sauce I

Serve with seafood, vegetables, or corned meats.

Fold 2 tablespoons of parsley into Basic White Sauce I.

Egg Sauce

2 hard-boiled eggs
1 quantity Basic White Sauce I

Dice eggs finely. Fold in Basic White Sauce I. A little finely cut parsley may also be added.

Cheese Sauce I

1 quantity Basic White Sauce I
60 g (2 oz) grated tasty cheese
1 egg yolk, beaten

Add 2 tablespoons of Basic White Sauce I to egg yolk and beat quickly. Return to remainder of sauce, along with cheese. Reheat for 2 minutes if necessary. Do not allow to boil.

Serve with seafood or vegetables.

Veloute Sauce

60 g (2 oz) butter
60 g (2 oz) flour
600 ml (1 pt) (2½ cups) stock, suitable for sauce required
salt and pepper

Place stock into a glass jug and cook on high 4 minutes.

Place butter into a jug or casserole dish and cook on high 1 minute to melt. Stir in flour with wooden spoon. (A wooden spoon may be left in sauce during cooking for ease of stirring.) Cook 2 minutes on high. Blend in stock and continue cooking 4 minutes, stirring well after 2 minutes. Add seasonings.

Time: 11 minutes.

Mushroom Sauce

125 g (4 oz) sliced button mushrooms (canned mushrooms can be sliced and used if a mild flavour is required)
1 egg yolk, beaten
60 ml (2¼ fl oz) (4 tablespoons) fresh cream

Melt butter in a jug or casserole. Add mushrooms and cook for 1 minute on high. Blend in flour and cook a further minute. Blend in warm stock (veal or chicken) and cook 4 minutes on high to thicken.

Stir after 2 minutes. Combine egg yolk and cream. Add 2 tablespoons sauce, blend well and fold into remaining sauce. Season with salt and pepper.

Use with steak, veal or chicken.

Demi Glace Sauce

300 ml (10 fl oz) (1¼ cups) Brown Sauce (see recipe)
250 ml (8 fl oz) (1 cup) brown stock
50 ml (1½ fl oz) (¼ cup) Madeira

Combine ingredients in a jug. Cook 4–6 minutes on high, stirring twice during cooking time.

Time: 6 minutes.

Cheese Sauce II

Ingredients are the same as Basic White Sauce II except that you add ¼ teaspoon dry mustard with the flour. After sauce has cooked, stir in ½ to 1 cup shredded cheese until melted.

Time: 4 minutes. Makes about 1 cup

Chasseur Sauce

30 g (1 oz) butter
1 shallot (scallion), cut finely
60 g (2 oz) mushrooms, sliced
50 ml (1½ fl oz) (¼ cup) dry white wine
125 g (4 oz) tomatoes, chopped, deseeded
300 ml (10 fl oz) (1¼ cups) Demi Glace Sauce (see recipe)
parsley, chopped
salt and pepper to taste

Cook butter in a casserole for 1 minute. Add shallots and cook 2 minutes on high. Add mushrooms and cook covered 2 minutes. Drain off butter. Add wine and cook 2–3 minutes until boiling and reduced to half. Add tomatoes, Demi Glace Sauce and cook 5 minutes. Add parsley, salt and pepper.

Serve with steaks, chicken, barbecued food or lamb.

Time: 13 minutes.

Basic Brown Sauce

30 g (1 oz) butter
60 g (2 oz) carrot, diced
60 g (2 oz) onion, diced
30 g (1 oz) celery, diced
45 g (1½ oz) (½ cup) pre-browned flour
1 tablespoon tomato paste
1 bay leaf
600 ml (1 pint) (2½ cups) brown stock

Place butter into a casserole, cook 1 minute to melt. Add carrots, onion and celery, cook 4 minutes on high. Blend in flour and cook 1 minute. Add tomato paste, bay leaf, blend in stock and cook 3 minutes, stir well and cook another 3 minutes. If slower cooking is required, cook sauce on defrost 15–20 minutes, stirring from time to time. Strain.

Serve with roast meats or as a base for other sauces.

Time: 12 minutes.

Basic White Sauce II

2 tablespoons butter
2 tablespoons plain (all-purpose) flour
½ teaspoon salt
little white pepper
250 ml (9 fl oz) (1½ cups) milk

Place butter in a glass bowl. Cook for 45 seconds or until melted. Stir in flour, salt and pepper. Add milk and cook on high approximately 3 minutes until boiling, stirring from time to time.

Note: Use a wooden spoon when stirring.

Time: 4 minutes. Makes about 1 cup

Hollandaise Sauce

20 g (¾ oz) (⅓ cup) butter
2 tablespoons lemon juice
2 egg yolks
¼ teaspoon salt

Place butter into a small bowl, heat for 45 seconds on high. Stir in lemon juice and egg yolks, beat with whisk until well mixed. Cook 60 seconds, whisking every 15 seconds. Stir in salt halfway through.

Time: 1 minute 45 seconds

Curry Sauce

30 g (1 oz) butter
1 clove garlic, chopped
60 g (2 oz) chopped onion
1 tablespoon curry powder
30 g (1 oz) plain (all-purpose) flour
2 teaspoons tomato paste
450 ml (15 fl oz) (nearly 2 cups) chicken stock or fish stock for seafood
60 g (2 oz) apple, chopped
1 tablespoon fruit chutney
1 tablespoon sultanas (golden raisins)
1 tablespoon chopped almonds
salt and pepper

Cook butter in casserole 1 minute to melt. Add garlic, onion and curry powder. Cook 3 minutes on high, blend in flour and cook 1 minute. Add tomato paste and stock, blend with wooden spoon. Add remaining ingredients and cook 4–6 minutes, stirring after 2 minutes.

Serve with seafood, poultry, hard-boiled eggs or vegetables.

Time: 11 minutes.

Mint Sauce

250 g (9 oz) (1½ cups) sugar
60 g (2 oz) arrowroot
dash salt
500 ml (16 fl oz) (2 cups) warm water
2–3 drops green food colouring
1 teaspoon finely chopped mint
2 drops peppermint essence (extract)

Combine sugar, arrowroot and salt in a 4 cup glass measure. Stir well, add water. Cook for 6 minutes on high, stirring after first 2 minutes and then after every minute. Bring to boil. Add food colouring, chopped mint, and essence. Heat for 30 seconds.

Time: 9 minutes.

Apple Sauce

500 g (1 lb) cooking apples
3 tablespoons water
30 g (1 oz) butter
30 g (1 oz) sugar
¼ teaspoon cinnamon or nutmeg

Peel, core and slice apples. Place into a casserole with sugar, butter and water. Cook covered for 12 minutes on high or until a puree is formed. Stir twice during cooking. Strain, stir in nutmeg or cinnamon.

Serve with roast pork or poultry

Time: 12 minutes.

Port Wine Sauce

300 ml (10 fl oz) (1¼ cups) Demi Glace Sauce (see recipe)
3 tablespoons port wine
30 g (1 oz) butter

Cook Demi Glace Sauce in jug for 3–4 minutes on high. Add port wine and cook 2 minutes. Blend in the butter.

Serve with roast or barbecued meats.

Time: 6 minutes.

Custard Sauce

375 ml (12 fl oz) (1½ cups) milk
45 ml (3 tablespoons) sugar
30 ml (2 tablespoons) custard powder
2 egg yolks
5 ml (1 teaspoon) vanilla

Combine custard powder and sugar with milk.

Heat 4 minutes on high, until sauce thickens, stirring twice. With a wire whisk quickly beat in the egg yolks, heat for 1–2 minutes on the *Defrost Cycle*, then flavour with vanilla.

Time: 6 minutes.

Chocolate Sauce

300 ml (½ pt) milk
75 g (3 oz) (1½ cups) sugar
5 ml (1 teaspoon) butter
15 g (½ oz) (¼ cup) cocoa
15 g (½ oz) (¼ cup) cornflour

Blend cornflour and cocoa with 3 tablespoons milk. Place remaining milk into a jug and cook 3 minutes on high to boil. Blend in cornflour mixture and cook 2 minutes on high. Blend in sugar and butter.

Time: 5 minutes.

Index